100 YEARS OF THE ISLE OF MAN TT

A Century of Motorcycle Racing

100 YEARS OF THE ISLE OF MAN TT

A Century of Motorcycle Racing

David Wright

THE CROWOOD PRESS

First published in 2007 by
The Crowood Press Ltd
Ramsbury, Marlborough
Wiltshire SN8 2HR

www.crowood.com

Revised edition 2013

British Library Cataloguing-in-Publication Data
A catalogue record for this book is available from the British Library.

ISBN 978 1 84797 552 2

Photograph previous page: Rem Fowler. (Courtesy Vic Bates)

Typeset by Servis Filmsetting Ltd, Stockport, Cheshire

Printed and bound in India by Replika Press Pvt. Ltd.

Contents

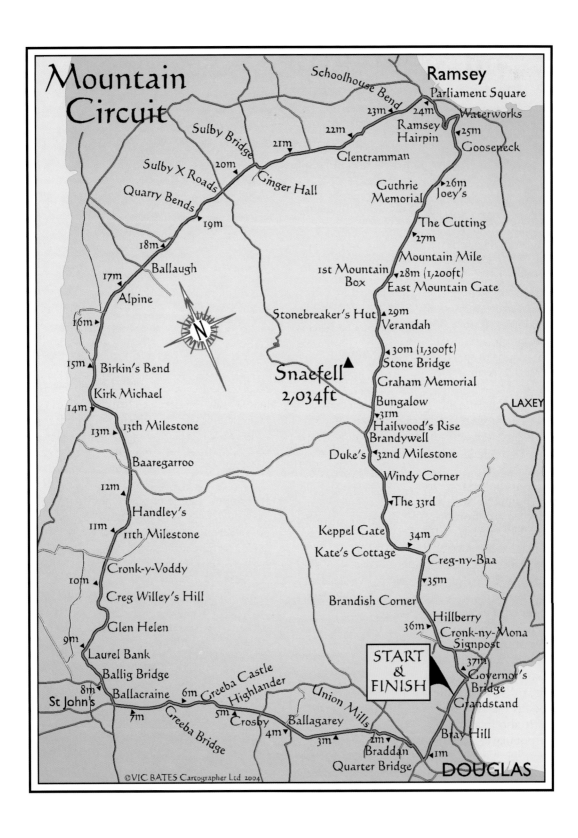

Introduction

The Isle of Man Tourist Trophy race meeting for motorcycles comprises a sporting event without parallel. For over 100 years, in early summer the island's principal roads have been dedicated to the pursuit of speed on two wheels over the world-famous 37¾-mile (60.75km) Mountain Course, where riders and machines are tested to their limits in front of thousands of spectators.

The TT is an important part of motorcycling history, having contributed widely to the development of almost every mechanical aspect of the motorcycles we have today, and having been contested by manufacturers from many parts of the world. British companies such as Norton, Triumph, Matchless, Rudge, AJS, Cotton, HRD, New Imperial and Excelsior competed with success, together with foreign entries from the likes of Indian, Moto Guzzi, Husqvarna, BMW, Gilera, MV Agusta, Honda, Yamaha, Suzuki, Kawasaki and Ducati. All sought the prestige associated with winning a Tourist Trophy, for an Isle of Man victory – then and now – says more than any amount of commercial advertising and is guaranteed to promote sales, not only for the maker of the winning machine but also for the associated suppliers of tyres, fuel, oil, brakes and so on.

For riders who achieve a TT win, it usually comes as the realization of a lifetime's ambition. It also guarantees a boost to an individual's popularity, career progress and earning power. However, competing for a Tourist Trophy has always been about meeting the challenge of pure road racing, where the nature of the course requires competitors to put aside thoughts of personal safety if they are seriously riding to win. Not all motorcycle racers are prepared to take on the challenge of the TT and some thirty-five years ago racing began the process of polarization that now sees it divided into two widely differing disciplines. On the one hand there is road racing, with its acceptance of natural hazards such as walls and kerbs, and, on the other, circuit racing that incorporates maximum run-off areas and gravel traps. Although there are still riders who happily contest both disciplines, increased specialization means that they usually choose one or the other.

The TT has developed into more than a race meeting and now advertises itself as a 'TT Festival'. However, racing remains at the core of a fortnight's two-wheeled activities, and as it reaches its centenary the customary questions will be asked about the event's future. But that has been the way throughout its existence, for the TT has rarely been free from criticism and change. As always, its strength lies in the fact that riders still seek to race, organizers are still prepared to run this unique event, and the Isle of Man continues to welcome its annual presence. Whatever the outcome of today's questions and answers, nothing can erase the Tourist Trophy meeting's 100 glorious years of motorcycle racing history, the highs and lows of which are captured within these pages.

Acknowledgements

The first acknowledgement should be to recognize the splendid vision of the pioneer motorcyclists who created the Tourist Trophy meeting in 1907, both as an outlet for their competitive activities and as a means of developing the early motorcycle from its primitive single-speed, belt-driven format to the sophisticated racers of today.

Amongst present-day enthusiasts for the TT who have helped with information for this book are Geoff Cannell, Bill Snelling and Paul Wright. The archives of the Manx Museum Library have also been a source of information, and the words are much enhanced by photographs supplied by Vic Bates, Ed Cawley, Ron Clarke of Manx Racing Photography, FoTTofinders, Pat East, Wolfgang Gruber, Alan Kelly of Mannin Collections, Richard Radcliffe, Ken Smith, the Vintage Motor Cycle Club and John Watterson. I am grateful to all for their assistance.

David Wright
Isle of Man

1 How It All Began

The Isle of Man was relatively slow to adopt the use of motor vehicles and fewer than fifty were registered for use on its roads in the first few years of the twentieth century. As its principal commercial activities at the time were fishing, agriculture and tourism, not even the most ardent enthusiast of the early internal combustion engine could have predicted that this largely horse-powered Crown Dependency in the middle of the Irish Sea would develop over the next century into the 'Road Racing Capital of the World'. Rather more predictable was that, among the early users of cars and motorcycles in other parts of Britain, there were some who wished to compete against each other to see who was the fastest driver and who had the fastest machine. With an overall speed limit of 14mph (22.5km/h) on British roads in the early 1900s (rising to 20mph/32km/h in 1904), there were few opportunities for them to do so in legal fashion.

Four Wheels First

Early in 1904 the Automobile Club of Great Britain and Ireland was looking for somewhere to run eliminating trials to choose a team of drivers to contest the Gordon Bennett Cup, a prestigious car race to be held in Germany. As legislation prevented it from organizing such competition over British roads, Club Secretary Julian Orde paid a visit to his cousin Lord Raglan on the Isle of Man in February 1904, with a view to running trials for the four-wheelers over the Island's roads. Orde borrowed

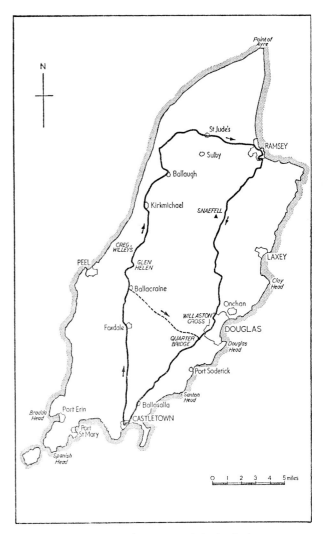

The 52-mile course used in eliminating trials for the Gordon Bennett Cup held on the Isle of Man in May 1904. Competitors covered six laps and the trials also included separate hill-climb and sprint events.

his cousin's Daimler and set out in search of a circuit that would test machine reliability and driver skill, rather than out-and-out speed. In this he was successful, choosing some 50 miles of the principal roads linking Douglas, Castletown and Ramsey, including the particularly testing Mountain section that climbed from Ramsey to skirt the slopes of Snaefell *en route* to Douglas.

Amendments to Manx laws were needed before the roads could be used for racing, and Lord Raglan used his influence to speed through the required legislation in spring 1904. Haste was necessary because time was short, but not everyone agreed with the cutting of legislative corners on behalf of motorists and one member of Government expressed the view that 'it was undignified to hurry the measure through in such fashion'.

After the considerable time and effort spent on preparations, only eleven cars came to the line in May 1904, but a large number of people turned out to watch the associated flurry of motoring activity and the event was rated a success.

Two-Wheelers' Turn

Motorcyclists gained their equivalent of the four-wheelers' Gordon Bennett races when they were able to compete in the International Cup race in France in September 1904. As a result, when the cars returned to the Isle of Man in May 1905, the two-wheelers joined them and held a race to decide who would represent Britain in the next International Cup. The race, which was also referred to as an 'eliminating trial', was run by the Auto Cycle Club who intended to use the 52-mile course chosen for the cars, but a last-minute decision saw the motorcycles running over a shorter distance of some 25 miles. Their route took the same roads south to Castletown and north to Ballacraine, but then turned east and returned to Douglas (shown by the dotted line on the map) instead of continuing north to Ramsey. Drawing eighteen entries, eleven 'weighed in'

but subsequent problems saw four scratch before the start. The result was that only seven came to the line and were despatched for five laps of what *Motor Cycle* described at the time as 'the first legalized road races for motorcycles ever held in these islands'. Regrettably, only two motorcycles finished their five laps before the roads were reopened to the public at 8am; the three-man team sent to race for the International Cup in France fared even worse, for none finished the event. British motorcycle manufacturers clearly had much to learn about speed and reliability over distance in those early days.

The next International Cup race for motorcycles was to be held in Austria in July of 1906, but as the cars were not due to return to the Isle of Man until September, the Auto Cycle Club, which could not afford to arrange independent trials on the Isle of Man, used a short course in the grounds of Knowsley Hall in Lancashire to select a British team comprised of Charles Franklin, Harry Collier and Charlie Collier.

Austria won the International Cup in 1906, with Harry Collier being the only British finisher. However, growing problems on the international motorcycle racing scene brought accusations of cheating against the organizing countries, and Charlie Collier later claimed that 'due to the most glaring breaches of the rules on the part of the Austrian riders and officials alike, the results of the 1906 race were declared null and void'. There was also growing discontent in Britain as to how continental riders were fitting ever larger and more powerful engines into spindly machines that had to comply with an overall weight limit of a mere 110lb (50kg), and there were many who considered that such moves were taking the development of motorcycles in the wrong direction.

The Tourist Trophy

As early as February 1906 Walter Staner, editor of *Autocar* (the parent journal of *Motor Cycle*),

Britain's representatives in the International Cup race of 1906 held in Austria: Charles Franklin (left), Harry Collier (middle) and Charlie Collier (right). The machines they rode were stripped and lightened versions of the ones shown here.

proposed at a dinner of the Auto Cycle Club that an international race should be organized to encourage the development of efficient and reliable touring motorcycles, as opposed to out-and-out racers. A few months later a major step in that direction was taken by Henry Collier, Freddie Straight and the Marquis de Mouzilly St Mars. Henry was founder of the Matchless concern and father of two of the British team in the 1906 International Cup: Harry and Charlie Collier. Freddie Straight was the energetic secretary of the Auto Cycle Club, and the Marquis was a French noble with strong British interests, fluent in several languages and a member of the Auto Cycle Club's organizing committee. Returning by train from Austria after the International Cup in 1906, they fell to discussing their ideas for an event for ordinary touring motorcycles. Envisaging limits on engine size, an easing of machine weights and the setting of petrol consumption limits as a means of controlling speeds, they realized that they were going down the same road that the cars had taken in 1905 when they raced for a Tourist Trophy over the roads of the Isle of Man. Feeling that was the way forward for powered two-wheelers, the Marquis offered to provide a Tourist Trophy for – in words of the time – 'a race for the development of the ideal touring motorcycle'. Receiving a favourable response, he commissioned the magnificent figure of Mercury mounted on a winged wheel that is now renowned throughout the racing world and is still competed for. It was thus that the Tourist Trophy for motorcycles

came into being and was gratefully accepted for competition by the Auto Cycle Club in 1907.

An early photograph of the Tourist Trophy.

Preliminary proposals for the first motorcycle Tourist Trophy (TT) race were made public in the specialist press in December 1906 and much discussion followed as to the regulations that should apply. The first formal set of rules for the race were published in February 1907 and specified that machines should be 'of touring type', have a soundly constructed frame, be fitted with saddle, brakes, mudguards, efficient silencer, tyres of at least 2-inch size, a 2 gallon fuel tank and carry a minimum of 5lb of tools in a toolbox. No weight limit was imposed and the only restriction on engine size was that individual cylinders should not exceed 500cc. Pedalling gear was optional. In addition to the above constructional matters, a rule of particular importance related to fuel allowances, wherein it was proposed that competitors would receive an allocation of petrol at the rate of 1gal for 90 miles of race distance. Following pressure from potential entrants of multi-cylinder machines, the rule was changed so that they received 1gal for 75 miles, single-cylinder machines getting the original 1 gallon for 90 miles. The unintentional effect of this rule was to create two races, one for singles and one for multis – but that raised the question of who was to receive the Tourist Trophy. It was decided that it would go to the winner of the single-cylinder race and Dr H.S. Hele-Shaw offered a trophy for the best performance on a multi-cylinder machine (although it never materialized), while Maurice Schulte of Triumph Motorcycles paid for gold and silver medals as lesser awards. Entry fees were set at 5 guineas (£5.25) for trade entries and 3 guineas (£3.15) for private runners. Each winner was to receive £25, with £15 and £10 going to the placemen. Most competitors were official factory entries since, quoting *Motor Cycle*'s respected commentator 'Ixion', 'The trade was at last convinced that nothing but race work could bring our machines up to the continental standard'.

The organizing committee specified a minimum entry number of twenty, but with riders slow to respond there was a risk in early April that the event would be called off. The closing date for entries was set for the middle of May, by when a total of twenty-eight had been received, comprising twenty single-cylinder machines and eight twin-cylinder. Marques such as Triumph, Matchless, Rex, Roc and NSU were represented among the single-cylinder entries, with Norton, Kerry, Bat, Vindec and Rex in the multi-cylinder class. All were single-speed, clutchless, belt-driven models with minimal brakes and virtually no suspension. Very few had been subject to racing over long distances and the event was undoubtedly a great adventure for all involved.

The faded cover of the Programme for the first TT of 1907.

Those pioneers rode motorcycles fitted with an array of controls that would be quite unfamiliar to riders of today's race machines. It was before the common use of Bowden cables and some had to contend with levers and rods to control ignition settings, air/fuel mixtures, throttle and brakes. Additionally, a decompressor was used when push-starting and a plunger oil-pump had to be depressed at intervals to provide lubrication to the engine on the total loss principle. Riders were required to make dead-engine starts of their clutchless machines: the basic starting technique was to pull on the decompression lever (which lifted the exhaust valve off its seat, thus reducing the compression to push against), heave the machine into motion and, after some momentum had been gained, let go of the decompression lever and hope the simple ignition system would fire the engine into life. Some machines were still fitted with bicycle-type pedalling gear, which could be used to assist starting. Not only were riders required to start with dead-engines, but they also had to be cold engines, no warming-up being allowed.

The Course

It was no surprise that the Isle of Man was chosen as the location of the first motorcycle TT and a course to suit the capabilities of the machines was plotted in the west of the island. It measured just over 15½ miles (25km) in length and competitors were required to cover ten laps, giving a claimed total distance of 158½ miles (255km). Known as the St John's Course, and later as the Short Course, the start and finish were located opposite the historic Tynwald Hill at St John's. From there riders travelled in an anti-clockwise direction to Ballacraine, where they turned left and headed north over country roads to Kirk Michael. At Douglas Road corner in Kirk Michael they turned left and followed the coast road south to Peel, threading their way through its narrow streets before turning east and returning to St John's.

When riders tackled that first race they found none of the smooth, wide, well-drained, tar/bitumen-surfaced roads that we know today. Instead they were faced with narrow, twisting lanes overhung by hedges and surfaced with a rolled macadam that was very loose and dusty when dry, and slippery and rutted when wet. Yet the bravest of those

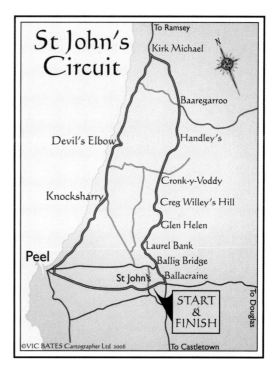

The St John's Course used for the TT from 1907 to 1910. The stretch from Ballacraine to Kirk Michael is used to this day.

pioneer racers still rode at speeds of up to 60mph (96km/h) on their narrow puncture-prone tyres, occasionally being forced to take a hand off the handlebars to deliver a few strokes to the oil pump or attend to one of the other controls, most of which were fitted to the side of the petrol tank. Attempts to lessen the dusty road conditions by spraying an acid solution called Akonia were ineffective, although an unexpected result was that the solution got onto riders' clothes and ate holes in riding jackets and trousers.

In the two weeks prior to race day there were loosely organized practice sessions over the course. They were restricted to early morning, but some riders indulged in unofficial sessions, speeding through the narrow streets of Peel at all hours of the day and bringing threats of prosecution if they were caught doing so outside official times. It was not felt necessary to close the roads to other traffic during official practice periods and, to make things even more interesting, a change in the route taken by the cars (who were also racing), meant that the four-wheelers were practising over some of the same roads as the bikes, but travelling in the opposite direction!

Weights and Measures

Although there was no rule restricting the weight of rider or machine, the organizers insisted on weighing both on the day before the race. Using facilities at St John's railway station, they discovered that machines weighed between 140 and 196lb (63–89kg), and riders tipped the scales at 134 to 166lb (61–75kg).

Among the several modifications made to the originally published rules was the one that required all machines to be fitted with a fuel tank of at least 2gal (9ltr) capacity. Few met the original requirement, so the minimum capacity was dropped to 1¼gal (5.7ltr). The result of the change was to create the need for mid-race refuelling, something that has been a feature of most TT races ever since. At the first running it was decreed that riders had to refuel during a compulsory ten-minute stop at St John's at the half-way point, when they could also take a rest and refreshment. They were handed their race allowance of fuel in sealed cans

before the start and were expected to arrive at the mid-race stop with the wire seals on their fuel tank caps intact. The serious riders among the entry experimented with gearing and carburettor settings during practice to obtain a level of fuel consumption that would allow them to complete the race on the petrol allowed. Rumours spread that some would have to ride at less than full throttle. How much of that was true and how much was gamesmanship designed to mislead the opposition varied from make to make, but there is no doubt that there were riders who had to tune for economy at the expense of speed.

The First Race for the Tourist Trophy

Race day was set for Tuesday, 28 May 1907, with the roads of the course being closed to all other traffic from 10am to 4pm by means of the official Road Closing Orders issued under the provisions of The Highways (Motor Car) Act 1905. On an unseasonably cool morning, race officials, riders and spectators gathered at Tynwald Hill in dry, cloudy, but breezy conditions, for the 10 o'clock start. The principal officials had a small tent and table at the edge of the course near the start-line, and blackboards were erected to display riders' race

Pushing away from the Start.

positions as the race progressed. Wearing their designated armbands, other officials busied themselves in the supervision of the fuelling of machines and in general preparations for the race. Some perhaps felt overly important, for a local newspaper reported that 'at times the officials in the less responsible positions became somewhat officious'.

The variety of machines gathered to race was matched by the variety of the riders' clothing, for there was no standard race-wear as there is today. Most wore stout tweed jackets and trousers, although leather jerkins and breeches were also to be seen. Heads were covered with cloth hats, balaclavas or leather helmets held in place with a pair of goggles, and feet were clad in lace-up leather boots of varying lengths. Leather gloves or gauntlets completed the riding kit and the majority of riders carried spare butt-ended inner tubes tied around shoulders or waists, for most expected to have to deal with a puncture at some stage of the race.

Riders ranged themselves in pairs behind the start-line, for the regulations required them to be despatched two at a time at one-minute intervals, with single-cylinder machines preceding the multis. The first pair to the line was Frank Hulbert and Jack Marshall on Triumphs, followed by Matchless-mounted Charlie and Harry Collier, with the remainder of the twenty-five starters behind them. At 10 o'clock timekeeper 'Ebbie' Ebblewhite gave the nod, the starting flag twitched and the first two riders heaved their machines into life, or attempted to, for Marshall's Triumph was reluctant to fire. Indeed, with cold engines tuned for economy, others were similarly troubled, moving one newspaper to tell its readers that 'the starting of a motorcycle is a very awkward and uncertain business'.

Eventually they all got away. Some ten minutes after the last competitor departed in the direction of Ballacraine, those at the start heard the steady beat of a single-cylinder engine approaching from Peel to complete the first lap. Despite his original starting difficulty it was Jack Marshall (Triumph) who led the field, followed by Charlie Collier (Matchless), both being on singles. Rem Fowler (Norton) was the first to complete a lap on a twin-cylinder bike, with Billy Wells (Vindec) his closest challenger. Less fortunate were W.A. Jacobs (Rex), who retired on the first lap, Oliver Godfrey, who lost time through a puncture, and joint first rider away, Frank Hulbert, who had to stop and change a plug.

The interval method of starting was one that was destined to become a TT tradition, but it required timekeepers and spectators to do a little mental calculation when trying to establish who was leading the race, for it was not necessarily the first man on the road. That was the case in 1907, when at the end of the first lap Charlie Collier led the race on corrected time, even though he was in second place on the road. Charlie continued to pull away from his challengers (soon taking the lead on the road) and by the compulsory ten-minute refuelling break he had a lead of several minutes. T.H. Tessier (BAT) and G. Horner (Royal Cavendish) both ran out of fuel before the break and Oliver Godfrey's bike burst into flames while being refuelled. A Manx policeman tried to smother the flames with his overcoat but Godfrey's bike was too badly damaged to continue. Sixteen of the original twenty-five machines were fit to start the second part of the race and all got away. Charlie Collier appeared to have a relatively trouble-free ride at the head of the single-cylinder race, but his nearest rival, Jack Marshall, suffered a time-consuming fall and puncture. Rem Fowler lost the lead in the twin-cylinder machine race on his Peugeot-engined Norton, and both he and his closest rival, Billy Wells, suffered a host of problems. Rem fell off twice, repaired a front-wheel puncture, changed sparking-plugs several times, tightened his drive belt twice and fixed a loose mudguard. But at the end of the ten punishing laps, which had taken more than four hours to complete, it was Charlie Collier

Singles

1 C.R. Collier (Matchless)	4 hours 8 mins 8 secs	average speed 38.22mph
2 J. Marshall (Triumph)	4 hours 19 mins 47 secs	average speed 37.11mph
3 F. Hulbert (Triumph)	4 hours 27 mins 50 secs	average speed 35.89mph

Fastest lap: H.A. Collier (Matchless) 41.81mph

Twins/Multis

1 H.R. Fowler (Norton)	4 hours 21 mins 53 secs	average speed 36.22mph
2 W.H. Wells (Vindec)	4 hours 53 mins 4 secs	average speed 32.21mph
3 W.M. Heaton (Rex)	5 hours 11 mins 4 secs	average speed 28.50mph

Fastest lap: H.R. Fowler (Norton) 42.91mph

and Rem Fowler who finished at the head of their respective fields. There were eleven finishers and last man 'Pa' Applebee (Rex) took 5¾ hours, getting to the end just before the roads were reopened to normal traffic. Final results are shown in the table (*above*).

Reported to have 'had a great reception as he rode up the victor' on his family-produced Matchless, Charlie Collier's ride to victory meant that his name became the first to be inscribed upon the Tourist Trophy. As the promised award for the first multi-cylinder machine did not materialize, Rem Fowler's efforts went unrewarded in that respect. It was

not until fifty years later, at the Golden Jubilee TT of 1957, that the aged winner from 1907 was presented with a specially commissioned trophy in recognition of his efforts of half a century earlier.

Post-mortem

Looking back on the first TT meeting, Charlie Collier's win was not unexpected, for he was an experienced competitor and, with Jack Marshall, had started as favourite. Charlie clearly got the balance between tuning for speed and economy just right with his single-cylinder JAP

Seventy-five years after the first race, the Isle of Man postal authorities issued this commemorative stamp showing Charlie Collier winning the 1907 TT.

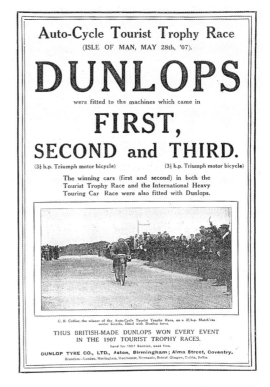

Rem Fowler poses with his Norton at the back of the Tynwald Inn after the 1907 TT.

engine, as he averaged 94.5mpg (3ltr/100km) for the race (the allocation for singles being based on a consumption limit of 90mpg), while Jack Marshall returned 114mpg (2.48ltr/100km), which suggested that he could have gone faster if his machine would have allowed. 'Privateer' Rem Fowler's win in the multi-cylinder race surprised a few people but, although entered as a private runner, he received the considerable support and attention of James Norton, owner of the Norton concern, before and during the race. Rem's Norton was fitted with a 671cc V-twin Peugeot engine that delivered a comfortable 87mpg (3.25ltr/100km), but the second man on a twin, Billy Wells, had very little petrol left in the tank of his Vindec at the finish, having consumed it at a rate of 77mpg (3.67ltr/100km), which was very close to the twin's 75mpg allocation.

Racing generates many 'what if' situations and in their post-race advertising in 1907 Triumph hinted at the result that might have been in that first race for the Tourist Trophy by claiming in respect of Marshall's performance: 'The Triumph made faster time than any machine in the race after deducting time lost for repairing punctures'. Racing can also lead to tensions between competitors and Norton took advertising space to contest Triumph's claim, stating: 'The fastest machine in the Tourist Trophy was the Norton twin, in spite of misleading statements to the contrary'. Speed was clearly an important factor in the sales appeal of early motorcycles, just as it is today.

The Dunlop Tyre Company was present at the first TT and advertised the success of its products in Motor Cycle.

Light Pedal Assistance

The St John's Course was chosen to be taxing – but not too taxing – for the single-speed machines competing in the first TT and it was free from any really severe hills. However, the climb out of Glen Helen by way of Creg Willey's was steep enough to force some riders to jump off and run alongside and caused others to make use of the pedals with which some machines were fitted. The latter action, known in old bike circles as LPA (Light Pedal Assistance), proved contentious and brought complaints from competitors who had not thought to fit them. The race regulations stated: 'Pedalling will only be allowed for the purpose of starting or restarting in traffic, or at sharp bends or on steep gradients. Excessive pedalling will disqualify'. Among the pedallers was Charlie Collier on his race-winning 3½hp Matchless and, since reports at the time made the claim that sturdy pedalling could add the equivalent of 1hp to a machine's output for brief periods, it was an increase that was well worth having. Some of the pedallers were even said to have had their legs massaged during the half-way stop, rather like racing cyclists.

The press reported favourably on the running of the first TT, with *Motor Cycle* describing the course as well calculated to test the machines and find their weak points. However, knowing that not all its readers supported the racing of motorcycles, it wrote: 'It is useless to say that fast speeds are not to be encouraged, human nature being what it is', and then went on to explain that the testing of motorcycles to their limits in braking, road-holding, engine revolutions and speed during a race could prove beneficial in eliminating problems from ordinary road-going motorcycles that were asked to perform at much lower levels. The *Isle of Man Times and General Advertiser* gave a quite detailed report of the meeting, claiming that 'thousands of visitors and residents gathered at various points of vantage' and going on to say that 'the event passed off most successfully from various points of view'.

What those many spectators at the first TT did not realize was that, in the words of motorcycle historian James Sheldon:

> It was this race which was to provide, in future years, a ready proving ground for every new idea in motorcycling, every development, every angle of design. However right in theory a new idea might be, it was not until it was proved in the Isle of Man that it was accepted.

Racers Return

Motorcycles and cars returned to the Isle of Man in 1908 to compete for their respective Tourist Trophies, arriving in September. Local business-people were happy for them to come in either May or September, since the presence of riders, officials and spectators at those times helped to extend the Island's tourist season, which was normally concentrated into a few summer months.

The organizing Auto Cycle Club spent the early part of 1908 successfully fighting off challenges to its position as the controlling body of British motorcycle sport and, on the way, renamed itself the Auto Cycle Union (ACU). Its mission also to encourage development of touring motorcycles was confirmed when the regulations for the 1908 TT races were published. Prospective entrants found that pedalling gear had been banned and the petrol allocation reduced, so that single-cylinder machines received 1 gallon for 100 miles of race distance and multi-cylinder runners 1 gallon for 80 miles. Although prize money for the previous year's event had been raised by benefactors within the trade and sport, for 1908 the organizers widened their funding appeal to include the general public, issuing a notice that read:

> Motorcyclists who feel disposed to assist the ACU in awarding some cash prizes to the successful competitors in the Tourist Trophy Race, should forward a postal-order for one

shilling or twelve stamps to the secretary of the Auto Cycle Union.

Part of the pre-race procedures involved the testing of machines for exhaust noise and brake efficiency. For those tests everyone moved from the general 'weighing-in' area at St John's to a nearby short but steep hill that led away towards Peel. Machines were required to be ridden up the hill with throttle wide open, and officials stationed themselves on the hill and 'judged' if silencers were effective. Returning down the hill, riders had to apply their brakes at a given point and stopping distances were measured to assess efficiency.

A total of thirty-seven entries were received for the 1908 TT and they included two genuine multi-cylinder machines in the form of 4-cylinder models made by the Belgian F.N. marque. Other foreign-made machines in the entry were two Indians and two NSUs, the latter being the first TT machines to be fitted with two-speed engine pulleys, thus giving a choice of gearing. Although single-cylinder machines had dominated the entry in 1907, in 1908 they were just outnumbered by twins/multis when the thirty-three starters came to the line in front of 2,000 spectators at St John's. The weather was fair, the roads had been 'scraped and swept to a good state of order' and, with rider safety in mind,

> a body of trained ambulancemen from Douglas, well supplied with stretchers and appliances for the succour of any rider who should be unfortunate to suffer mishap attended with bodily injury, were conveniently disposed around the course.

The only hitch came when the start was delayed for a quarter of an hour to allow the passage of a train across the course at the St Germain level crossing outside Peel.

When the race got under way Jack Marshall (Triumph) moved into the lead, but by half-distance he had lost the position to Charlie Collier (Matchless). Both were on singles and the leader of the multi-cylinder class was Harry Reed on a DOT of his own manufacture. Jack Marshall rode well and recovered the lead in the latter part of the race. He had good reason to do so, for a newspaper report claimed 'there was a whisper of romance about him that a very nice girl had promised to be his bride if he won the race'. Win he did, bringing his Triumph home ahead of Charlie Collier, thus reversing the finishing positions in the single-cylinder race of 1907. Triumph made much of their victory and the publicity earned by Marshall's winning ride was known to have boosted the sales of Triumph motorcycles in what was a flat market in 1908.

Harry Reed held on to his lead to win the multi-cylinder class from Bill Bashall (BAT), but 1907 multi-cylinder class winner Rem Fowler was forced to retire early in the race. The reason for Rem's retirement offers a glimpse of the basic nature of those early

This was the Triumph machine logo at the time of Jack Marshall's win in 1908.

machines. He used a twin-cylinder engine of Norton's own design (modelled on the previous year's Peugeot engine) and it featured non-adjustable tappets. The basic steels in use at the time allowed the valves to stretch in use and, with non-adjustable tappets, all clearance could sometimes vanish after 20 miles (32km) of racing. To cope with the problem, Rem planned to carry a 6-inch file, so that he could stop during the race, file down the valve tops, recover some clearance (and compression) and continue at speed. Unfortunately, he forgot to carry his file and, in his words, 'it soon overheated, lost its compression and ran to a standstill'. Not only did valves stretch but they sometimes broke. Riders in those early races usually carried a spare valve that, at the risk of burnt fingers, they could change at the side of the road in about ten minutes.

The engines of the early TT racers were 'all-iron' and had poor heat-shedding qualities. Hard riding increased the chance of overheating, which could result in loss of power, failure of components and seizures. The climb out of Glen Helen needed every scrap of power available if riders were to avoid having to jump off and run alongside – something that could be

A twin-cylinder Norton engine similar to the one used by Rem Fowler in 1908.

very wearing if done on each of the ten laps. The 1908 winner, Jack Marshall, told how he eased the throttle on the stretch from Ballacraine to Glen Helen so that his Triumph would deliver maximum power for the ascent of Creg Willey's. The Rex concern even came to an arrangement with a lady who lived in a cottage at Laurel Bank (just prior to Glen Helen), whereby she left buckets of cold water outside her cottage. This allowed the Rex riders to stop and ladle cooling water over their engines before rejoining the race and building up speed to tackle the subsequent hill.

Rules are Rules

Every TT generates points of contention. These are usually between riders and organizers, and sometimes between individual riders, with the organizers called in to act as arbiters. In 1907 the big issue had been that of excessive pedalling and in 1908 it was that the organizers had used very brittle wire to seal competitors' fuel caps. At least that was the claim made by several competitors who arrived at the finish with their seals broken. Unable to find proof of illicit refuelling the organizers could do nothing, even though some of those who arrived with their seals intact clamoured for the disqualification of the rule breakers. Another indication of how the rules were pushed to the limit and beyond, from the earliest days of TT racing, comes in the words of Noel Drury who finished 4th in the multi-cylinder race in 1908 on what he described as his 'genuine touring' machine. Noel later expressed surprise that some of the leading machines featured 'cycle racing saddles, 2-inch mudguards made of aluminium sheeting, no lamp brackets or tool holders, short handlebars, etc'.

Press comments

The motorcycle press had a vested interest in praising the machines of the day but the Manx press could afford to be more critical. As well

Noel Drury on his JAP-powered machine for the 1909 TT: 'I was put out of the race by hitting a large boulder which fell out of a loose wall around a bend in Glen Helen and I came a purler, bending the forks and other damage'.

as supporting the principle of racing motorcycles over Manx roads, however, a local newspaper also recognized the attraction of the motorcycle as a means of transport: 'A self-contained vehicle capable of travelling nearly 160 miles in 4 hours, with one brief halt for fuelling, is bound to attract the favour of a numerous class of travellers'.

Despite support from some elements of the press and the much-increased numbers in use, powered vehicles were still not particularly welcomed on British roads, where four-legged horsepower still held sway. Prior to the 1908 TT, *The Times*, *Daily Mail* and other national newspapers ran articles criticizing the racing of cars and motorcycles over the public roads of the Isle of Man.

Before the running of the first TT, competitive events for motorcycles in Britain had largely been confined to hill climbs of dubious legality, run, as one magazine of the day put it, 'whenever the goodwill of the police permits'. There were also speed events on boarded cycle race-tracks, but only those who ventured

This is the sort of emporium that early riders would patronize. Motorcycles were even manufactured in such small garages. Note the cans of fuel stacked outside in those pre-petrol pump days.

abroad could legally participate in races on the road. In early 1908 Brooklands held the first race for motorcycles on its new, purpose-built race track in Surrey, and it was to become a centre for competition and the development of motorcycles for the express purpose of racing and record breaking. As a result of the competitive climate created, there were factions in the ACU who sought to reduce the touring emphasis of machines used at the TT. These were largely resisted for 1909, but there were three important changes to the rules of the TT run that September. Most significant was the abolition of restrictions on petrol allocation. This meant that machines could now be tuned for maximum speed, a process that was also helped by the removal of the need for engines to race with silencers fitted. Finally, instead of running races for single and multi-cylinder machines, the event now became one race, with single-cylinder machines restricted to a maximum capacity of 500cc and multis to 750cc.

Which Way?

In *Motor Cycle*, the principal voice of motor-cycling in its early years, 'Ixion' later wrote of 1909:

> Nobody felt sure what form motorcycles would ultimately assume. The multi-cylinders offered smoother running and easier starting; the singles were cheaper and lighter. Hill-climbing, the main bogey of the hobby, was as yet unsolved. Some people advocated gears, others opposed them.

The uncertainty shown by early manufacturers is understandable, for a glance at the vast range of motorcycles available on today's market shows that the all-purpose machine that will suit every user has yet to be designed.

Prior to the 1909 TT, practising was allowed on fourteen weekday mornings (when silencers had to be used). Among the fifty-seven race starters were James L. Norton,

the forty-year-old proprietor of the firm carrying his name, and Walter O. Bentley (Rex), who was later to manufacture motor cars bearing his name. The famous continental rider Giuppone (Peugeot) was riding for the first time and the winner's prize money was increased to £40. There were no longer any restrictions upon the amount of petrol that a competitor could use, but refuelling was restricted to a prescribed point at the start/finish area and another located some 200 yards from Douglas Road corner on the outskirts of Kirk Michael.

The appearance of a Scott in the race heralded the first TT racing two-stroke and, although it did not particularly impress with its performance, spectators liked the novelty of its rider starting his engine by way of a kick-starter and the sound of its distinctive exhaust note.

With the change in rules that created just one race for 1909, multi-cylinder machines became eligible to win the Tourist Trophy for the first time and two riders of V-twins seized the opportunity to head the rest of the field. G. Lee Evans took his 5hp Indian into the lead and held it for five laps before Harry Collier took over on his 5hp Matchless and rode to victory by almost four minutes, recording an average speed for the race of 49.01mph (79km/h) and setting the fastest lap at 52.27mph (84.1km/h). Harry Collier's fastest lap was a substantial 10mph faster than the previous year's winning speed. Just how much of that increase was down to machine development and how much due to the abolition of petrol restrictions and ability to run without silencers will never be known, but it was significant that out of fifty-seven starters, only nineteen finished the race. Some observers put the reason for this down to the fact that, with fuel economy no longer a factor, bikes had been tuned for out-and-out speed, thus increasing the stress on engines and reducing reliability.

Harry Collier at speed on his Matchless.

Here to Stay

By 1910 the demand for motorcycles was booming, with Triumph reported to be making a hundred machines a week. However, it was a competitive market and manufacturers were aware that one way in which they could demonstrate the reliability and competitiveness of their products to potential customers was in organized sporting competitions. Long-distance trials were popular, as were hill climbs, but as there were still only limited opportunities for racing their products on the roads the Tourist Trophy event on the Isle of Man quickly established itself as a very effective showcase for sporting motorcycles. Well supported by riders, manufacturers and spectators, a Manx newspaper greeted the end of the May event in 1910 with 'Magnificent Contest of Athletes – Great Test of Human

Endurance', and the motorcycle press already recognized that 'Nothing brings forward the weak points in an engine and its construction better than a race like the TT'.

Other writings in the local press told that practice would take place 'from daybreak to seven am' and that 'anyone riding the wrong way around the course will be disqualified from the race itself'. Those early-morning sessions were full of incidents, with reports that:

Groves on the Ariel buckled a wheel; A.E. Woodman, all the way from New Zealand, had a nasty smash near Kirk Michael when a puncture threw him into a wall; Alexander on the Rex had a narrow shave when the rear wheel punctured at speed and he had extreme difficulty in staying on his machine – to get home he stuffed the tyre with grass.

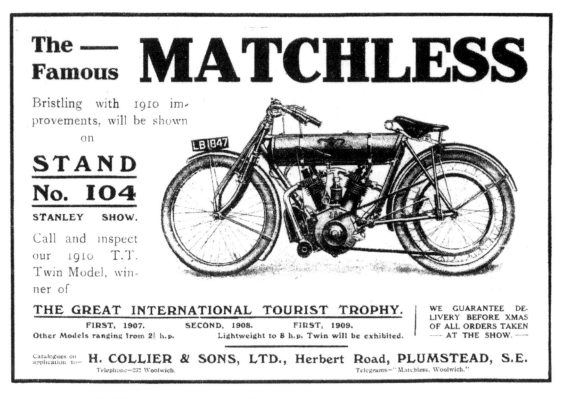

An advertisement for H. Collier & Sons Ltd and its Matchless machines.

Godfrey on the Indian seized when his piston broke and he was tossed from his mount; Bert Yates of the Humber team also departed from his machine when the rear brake came adrift and jammed the rear wheel; Brewster drove his machine straight into a brick wall at Ballacraine – his machine is a total wreck.

Despite general awareness that TT racing took a heavy toll on men and machines, entries surged to eighty-three for 1910 and the organizers considered limiting acceptances to seventy. They decided to allow everyone in, calculating that there would be some non-starters, and that proved to be the case with seventy-three competitors eventually coming to the line. Among these were thirty-nine riders on twins who, in another rule change, were now limited to a maximum engine capacity of 670cc. There were also an encouraging thirty private entrants.

Mechanical advances saw chain drive featured on Indian, Scott and a Rex, while Zenith used their patent Gradua variable gear. Some of the Humbers had overhead valves and there were experiments with dry-sump lubrication. Despite the organizers' attempts to reduce the performance differential between singles and twins by reducing the latter's permitted engine size to 670cc, twin-cylinder machines showed that they still had the edge over the singles. It was the Collier brothers who again moved to the front of the race at about half-distance on their Matchless twins, and they finished with the major honours – Charlie was first and Harry second – being followed home by a batch of Triumph singles among the twenty-nine finishers.

Charlie Collier (left) and Harry Collier (right) were the most successful of the TT pioneers.

In the first four years of its running, the Tourist Trophy event had gripped the imagination of the motorcycling world. Entries increased year-on-year as more competitors took up the challenge, but results showed that the winning formula at the TT was not one that relied simply on out-and-out speed. It was the successful Collier brothers who showed that all-round riding skills, speed allied to reliability, plus experience, organization and racecraft, made a combination that was difficult to beat. Other riders had led races, but it was the Colliers who, by successfully pacing themselves to several well-deserved victories, were the star performers in those early Island races.

2   A Mountain to Climb

The ACU, the organizing body for the TT meeting, had seen the number of entries for the races grow each year from their first running in 1907, and by 1911 it was confident that it operated from a position of strength and could shape the event in the manner of its choice. Showing considerable vision, despite opposition from manufacturers and riders, it moved the races from the relatively flat St John's Course to a distinctly more testing one that gave a lap distance of just over 37 miles (60km) and incorporated a 1,400ft (425m) climb from sea level to skirt the northern flank of Snaefell. The adoption of what quickly became known as the Mountain Course was a move that, according to *Motor Cycle* some years later, 'drove the whole motorcycle industry to develop engines of greater flexibility and to equip them with reliable and efficient variable gears'.

On the approach to the 1911 TT, manufacturers worried about how their existing big single- and multi-cylinder machines would cope with the demanding new Mountain Course, but the ACU had no such concerns and showed it by creating an additional race for singles up to 300cc and multis up to 340cc (resisting manufacturers' calls for these smaller machines to be allowed pedalling gear). Thus two separate races were run in 1911 on different days and they were given the titles of 'Junior' (run over four laps) and 'Senior' (five laps). They attracted 104 entries, with the split between the classes showing thirty-seven Junior and sixty-seven Senior runners. Entry fees were double those of the first TT in 1907,

being a substantial 10 guineas for trade and 7 guineas for private runners. In a further attempt to even out the performance differential between singles and multis in the Senior race, the capacity limit of multis (generally twins) was reduced from 670 to 585cc.

Manufacturers had received a foretaste of the demands that the climb of Snaefell would make on their machines when, just after the 1909 and 1910 TTs, the ACU ran a 6-mile (9.6km) hill climb from the sea-level outskirts of Ramsey to almost the highest point on the Mountain Road at the Bungalow Hotel. Several firms experimented thereafter with variable gears, and on machines that adopted them for use in the 1911 TT there could be seen examples of epicyclic hubs, epicyclic engine-shaft gears, sliding countershaft gears and expanding pulley gears. Such ability to vary the gearing, if only modestly by later standards, helped overcome the previous situation where the single gear fitted had to be a compromise between being high enough to offer the best possible speed on level going, without robbing the machine of reasonable hill-climbing ability.

Riders knew there was another transmission problem to cope with when tackling gradients, for the belt drives fitted to most early machines to convey engine power to the back wheel tended to stretch in use, thus allowing the belt to slip under load. Some makes used a jockey-wheel to help maintain tension, but problems of belt grip/slip could be aggravated by wet conditions, or by the belt getting coated in oil from the usually less than oil-tight

P. Owen is ready to race his belt-driven Forward in the Junior race of 1912. The Forward Company's venture into motorcycle manufacture was short lived, for it found it more profitable to specialize in the making of drive belts and their associated fasteners.

engines of the day. It was not unknown for a belt to break in use and most competitors carried a spare (pre-stretched) belt during a race, plus the means to repair a broken one.

With a lap of the new Mountain Course for 1911 extending to more than 37 miles, riders were keen to get in as much practice as possible and a pre-race report of the time said: 'Once again between the hours of three and seven in the morning, when most people are wasting these good hours in bed, scenes of excitement will take place, and the roars of the engines will be heard.' Those were clearly the words of a motorcyclist and it is doubtful if people living adjacent to the course spoke of the early morning practice sessions with such enthusiasm. Before practice riders were told: 'All dangerous parts of the course will be marked by banners some distance from the point of danger'.

Machine reliability was a necessity for those seeking TT success and New Hudson was said 'to have everything brazed on and every nut is split-pinned'. Despite the striving for reliability, most companies experimented with some

new aspect of design during practice. In attempts to lighten and improve lubrication of pistons, Norton fitted one with thirteen circular grooves (excluding ring grooves) in their single-cylinder models, while Zenith lightened their pistons with holes in the walls. Brown and Barlow appeared with a new variable-jet carburettor that was chosen for use by several riders, and former winners Harry and Charlie Collier were back seeking further glory on Matchless machines fitted with a variable pulley gear offering belt-driven ratios between 3:1 and 5:1.

A problem with some variable pulley systems with a normal fixed-length drive belt was that as the size of the pulley was changed to alter the gearing, the belt could lose tension and slip. Various methods were used to deal with this problem. Zenith overcame it with their 'Gradua' arrangement, which moved the rear wheel to shorten or increase wheelbase as pulley diameter changed. The Rudge concern was uncertain what form of gearing to use in 1911 and a pre-race report said, 'The Rudge TT models will be of the ordinary standard

Several Rudge-Multis being prepared on the Island for the TT.

pattern as far as outward appearance goes, but it is not yet decided whether a direct drive, clutch or two-speed gear will be used. Probably one of each type will ultimately be adopted.' In the final run-up to the TT, Rudge designed an improved form of variable pulley system that allowed constant belt tension to be maintained: although it allowed only a variation in gearing of 5¾ to 3¼ to 1, they named it the 'Multi'.

The American Indian Company was another manufacturer with variable gearing, and its system was advanced for the time, comprising a two-speed countershaft gearbox, clutch, and all-chain drive. It was a system that greatly reduced the problems associated with the climbing of hills and one that paid rich dividends in the Isle of Man in 1911, for their twin-cylinder machines (with engines scaled down to the 585cc TT limit and featuring overhead inlet and side exhaust valves) came home a triumphant 1-2-3 in the Senior TT. Englishman Oliver Godfrey was the man to get his name inscribed upon the Tourist Trophy by taking first place from his teammates Charles Franklin and Arthur Moorhouse, and their red Indians finished ahead of machines from Ariel, Bradbury, Zenith-Gradua, NSU, Rex and others.

A copy of the original Tourist Trophy was made to award to the winner of the newly created Junior race, and Percy Evans was the first recipient after riding his V-twin (Humber) into first place, nine minutes ahead of Harry Collier (Matchless).

The start and finish point of the 1911 races in Douglas was located on a flat section of road between the bottom of Bray Hill and the descent to Quarter Bridge, where the latter's downward slope was very welcome to those who had difficulty bump-starting their machines. Clerk of the Course Mr J.R. Nisbet controlled affairs at the start with the aid of a megaphone, scoreboards were erected at the side of the road, the timekeepers had a small

Charles Franklin sits astride his Indian before the start of the 1911 TT, in which he finished in second place. Note the spare butt-ended inner tubes tied around his waist in case he needed to repair a puncture.

wooden shed to work in, and the press occupied a room in an unfinished cottage close to the finishing line. However, there was no room for a riders' 'replenishment area', so official refuelling points were created at Braddan and Ramsey.

Although it is not possible to make a direct comparison between the old and new TT courses, it is worth mentioning that Oliver Godfrey's average race speed over the Mountain Course in 1911 was 47.63mph (76.65km/h), while Charlie Collier's winning speed on the easier St John's Course in 1910 had been 50.63mph (81.48km/h).

Outside Assistance

In what had become the customary post-race squabble over non-compliance with race regulations, Charlie Collier (Matchless), who was initially awarded second place in the 1911 Senior race, was disqualified for taking on petrol at other than the officially permitted refuelling points, and Jake De Rosier (Indian) received the same treatment for borrowing tools to adjust his valve-gear out on the course. Their actions came under the heading of receiving 'outside assistance', an expression that has become enshrined in TT lore as a forbidden activity. A rider was only permitted to carry out repairs on the course using the tools that he carried with him, but in the quest for lightness and speed some riders carried fewer tools than they had previously been obliged to do by the race regulations. TT history shows that the receipt of 'outside assistance' has resulted in the disqualification of many other riders down the years, several of whom lost race wins as a result.

Commercial Pressures

Even from the earliest days there was a strong commercial aspect to the TT races. While manufacturers entered knowing that racing yielded useful practical lessons in design and construction, they soon became aware that mere participation in a TT race raised the status of their products and increased their appeal to many potential buyers in what was a crowded but, by 1911, a profitable market. The esteem earned by TT participation was also sought by associated suppliers such as petrol and tyre companies (known as 'The Trade'), and they were prepared to pay to have their names linked to TT success. The recipients of such payments were usually the successful riders and a report in *Motor Cycle* in 1911 opined that 'it is worth nearly £200 to a trade rider to win the Tourist Trophy. Apart from the £40 cash offered by the ACU, a windfall from the makers of the tyres, belt, magneto, carburettor, petrol and the oil employed by the winning machine usually follows'. With such rewards available, it is little wonder that riders sometimes attempted to bend the rules by accepting 'outside assistance' to get to the finish.

The 1911 TT performance of Indian and other machines fitted with variable gears provided a convincing demonstration of the way forward for the motorcycle industry, and entries for the 1912 Senior TT featured only one single-geared machine. In yet another change of rule regarding engine sizes, the upper engine capacity limit for the Senior class was set at 500cc for all entries, singles or multis, and a similar ruling applied in the Junior, where the upper limit was set at 350cc. But all was not well on the organizing side, for there were differences of opinion between the ACU and British manufacturers over the running of the TT. Some of the latter boycotted the 1912 event at the end of June, and entries fell to twenty-five Juniors and forty-nine Seniors.

In an overview of the motorcycling scene in 1912, the British press considered that 'The industry has settled down into a comfortable state of energetic prosperity'. On the run-up to the TT, however, it stressed the importance to the British motorcycle industry of recovering the Tourist Trophy from the foreign victor of the previous year.

The American Invasion

—of distinctly American motor cycles—of distinctly American design—built for distinctly American conditions, should prove a warning to the wideawake Britisher. Machines manufactured abroad of foreign material, and designed for service under different conditions, never **can** be as reliable and efficient as a British Built

"THE UNAPPROACHABLE"
NORTON

—made in England—of British Material by British workmen —designed for British service. Have a "Norton" with every up-to-date refinement.

Machines on show at Olympia.

THE NORTON MFG. CO., LTD., Deritend Bridge, Floodgate Street, Birmingham.

HARDY'S

Not everyone took Indian's fine win in the 1911 TT in true sporting spirit, as this advertisement from Norton shows. Despite the disparaging tone that Norton adopted towards the American product, neither of its single-cylinder entries actually finished the race. It was the first year that Norton used a new 79 × 100mm bore and stroke for its engine, but one with those 'longstroke' dimensions then remained a feature of the Norton range until 1963.

Approaching May Hill on the outskirts of Ramsey in 1912, this rider takes a wide line to maintain momentum. Standing water can be seen in the road and riders sometimes used the left-hand footpath to avoid the worst conditions here.

A Two-Stroke Win

The Scott marque's TT debut in 1909 had not met with particular success, but in the 1911 Senior race Frank Phillipp gave a hint of things to come by setting the fastest lap at 50.11mph (80.64km/h). He also anticipated future fashion by riding in leathers that were dyed Scott purple. Unconventional in many respects, the Scotts entered for the 1912 TT were powered by 486cc twin-cylinder, two-stroke engines fitted with water-cooled barrels, gear-driven rotary valve, and with the engine cradled in an open frame that had an early form of telescopic front suspension. With two-speed gearboxes and all-chain drive, they were light, nimble, fast and, as the race showed, sturdy enough to last for five laps of racing over the Mountain Course and bring Frank Applebee home to victory six minutes ahead of the opposition. Applebee's race average speed was 48.69mph (78.36km/h) and it would have been a Scott 1-2 had the rear tyre of his team-mate Frank Phillipp not burst on the last lap when he was holding a secure second place.

Scott motorcycles were initially built in Bradford and were technically ahead of the opposition almost from Alfred Angus Scott's first experiments with a powered two-wheeler in 1901. An exponent of two-strokes from the outset, such was his sweeping success when he entered them in major competition that other manufacturers persuaded the ACU to handicap his product, and for several years an 'equalizing factor' was applied whereby his two-stroke engine's actual capacity had to be multiplied by 1.32 for competition purposes. Scott used this point to advantage by stressing it in the company's catalogue (even after the ruling was rescinded). It was respected racer, journalist and author Vic Willoughby who later wrote:

> Scott had an uncanny flair for combining highly original ideas with sound, practical engineering. Such was the range of his vision that not only were the basic features of his design practically unchanged throughout the marque's production, but he anticipated technical trends by up to half a century.

Another slightly unconventional machine took victory in the Junior race of 1912. This was the Bristol-built Douglas fitted with a horizontally opposed, twin-cylinder side-valve engine mounted longitudinally in the frame, thus giving it an overall low build. The 1912 Junior event was the first TT to be held in wet conditions and they proved a severe challenge to the smaller machines. Bill Bashall's winning Douglas was belt-driven and he is said to have stopped eight times to adjust the belt that slipped badly in the wet and muddy conditions. Only eleven riders finished the race because, apart from belt troubles, many were forced out with electrical problems due to ineffective shielding of magnetos and sparking plugs. Among the lessons learnt from this wet event were that the business of weight-saving for racing by reducing the shielding to belts and electrics could be taken too far. Bashall's average speed of 39.65mph (63.81km/h) in 1912 is the lowest ever race-winning speed recorded over the Mountain Course by a 'Junior' machine.

The roads faced by TT competitors were still surfaced with rolled macadam. They were narrow, bumpy, with a loose, stony and often

This photograph is from 1913 when a Scott ridden by Tim Wood was again victorious in the Senior TT. Using an early form of 'dump-can', the rider adds fuel whilst his attendant tops up the radiator.

Quarter Bridge during the very wet 1912 Junior TT, showing the conditions riders had to cope with for the 150-mile race distance.

pot-holed surface containing many horseshoe nails, while most of the stretch over the Mountain comprised just two stone-filled wheel ruts with a grassy rut down the middle. Not only did riders have to be exceptionally brave to race over them at speed, but the physical challenge of racing for five laps and 187½ miles over those primitive roads was such that competitor 'Pa' Applebee (father of 1912 Senior winner, Frank) was quoted as saying: 'a rider was considered amazingly fresh if he could stand at the end of a race'.

To further emphasize the basic conditions under which the races were run, marshals were few and far between, particularly during early-morning practice. There were just three official telephone points on the Course: at the grandstand, Ballacraine and Creg ny Baa, and medical support was very scarce. If a rider fell and needed medical assistance he might receive it from one of the few policemen or volunteer ambulancemen on duty, but if it was a serious injury a message would have to be taken to the nearest doctor (a major task, for there were no radio communications or mobile phones) and the doctor would have to make his way to the scene of the accident. Depending upon where the rider was located it might then be possible to get him off the Course and to hospital by back roads, or he

might have to remain where he fell until the race finished. A race win in those days took nearly four hours and by the time all the stragglers were in it could well be over five hours from the starting time.

A TT victory became much coveted by manufacturers and the supporting trade concerns, for it virtually guaranteed a boost to their profits. Victorious riders would also benefit, for apart from the prize and bonus money to be earned, their names would be publicized and become familiar to motorcyclists of the time. Taking advantage of the associated glory that ensued, it became common practice for them to go into business and profit from their names: the winners of the 1911 and 1912 TTs, Oliver Godfrey and Frank Applebee did just that, and in later years they were followed by many others, thus establishing the 'Rider Agent' category of dealer that many were proud to advertise.

Two-Day TT

Pursuing its theme of increasing the TT's challenge to riders and machines, in 1913 the ACU extended the race distances to seven laps for the Senior and six laps for the Junior and, with full manufacturer support restored, received a combined total of 148 entries.

However, mindful of the demands that the course made upon riders, a report of the time noted that:

> It was supposed that even the toughest athlete, in the pink of condition, could never stand six or seven successive TT laps on the same day, so two laps of the Junior were run off on the Wednesday morning, after which the machines were locked up and the Senior men did three laps. Everybody recuperated during Thursday, and on Friday the survivors in both races covered four laps together.

So, after their day's rest, Senior and Junior riders were set off alternately, and to further differentiate between the classes they wore coloured waistcoats: red for Seniors and blue for Juniors. Although the two-day TT was an interesting experiment, it was not repeated.

In the Junior race, where thirty-two of the forty-four entries were mounted on twins, Hugh Mason left his hospital bed to ride a NUT-JAP V-twin to a brave win, having crashed in practice earlier in the week. In the Senior, where only twenty-four of the 104 entries were on twins, victory went to a Scott for the second year running. It produced the closest finish since the races began, with Tim Wood (Scott) snatching victory from the relatively unknown Ray Abbott (Rudge) who, when leading on the last lap, overshot a corner and lost the race by a mere five seconds.

A busy start-line scene in 1913 when riders were despatched from a point on the flat between the bottom of Bray Hill and Quarter Bridge.

The man who came second in the 1913 Senior TT, Ray Abbott, poses with his Rudge Multi.

The winning Rover team of 1913.

Prize money was increased to £50 to the winner of the Senior race in 1913 and £40 to the Junior winner. To encourage support from the motorcycle trade, a Manufacturers' Team Award was presented for the first time and, with its members Brown, Lindsay and Newsome being the only team to finish intact, the award went to the Rover concern.

Spreading the Word

At the time of the first TT in 1907 there were 35,000 motorcycles registered for use on the roads of Britain and by 1914 there were 124,000. Although many were bought and used for utility purposes, the majority were acquired by 'enthusiasts' who were prepared to put up with the anti-motoring attitude of the police and public, the relative unreliability of machines, poor roads, restrictive speed limits, and so on, all so that they could pursue their passion for travel by powered two-wheelers. Most of them bought the two principal specialist magazines of the time, *Motor Cycle* and *Motor Cycling*, to keep up with affairs, and this gave the magazines enormous influence over the thinking of their readers. Fortunately the magazines were very pro-TT, printing much news before and after the races, and raising the profile of the event and of the successful machines and riders. As early as 1911 *Motor Cycle* described the Isle of Man as 'The motorcyclist's Mecca', although relatively few riders were able to make the TT pilgrimage before

the First World War. Recognizing this, *Motor Cycle* sought to satisfy the tremendous demand for race information from those who could not attend by telegraphing progress reports and results to motorcycle dealers across Britain. The dealers would then post them in their showroom windows for information-hungry enthusiasts to read. Not to be outdone in catering for its TT-minded readership, *Motor Cycling* arranged day trips to watch the Senior race, involving travel by train to Liverpool and then by Steam Packet boat to Douglas. It tempted its readers with the words 'Men who have watched every kind of sporting event have often said that nothing in the world is so thrilling to watch as this hotly-contested struggle for the blue ribbon of the motorcycling world'.

The many news reports, the advertising and the increasing numbers of visitors saw the names and places on the Isle of Man TT Mountain Course become part of the language of the average motorcyclist, just as they are today. Places like Bray Hill, Ballacraine, Ballaugh Bridge, Parliament Square in Ramsey, and spots on the Mountain like the Bungalow and Creg ny Baa were spoken about with authority by many who, although they may never have visited the Island, carried mental pictures of the locations, the lines that riders should take and the danger involved, with the majority of that information having come from the detailed reports carried in the motorcycle press.

Maps of the 37¾-mile Mountain Course show many of the names that it has acquired over the past hundred years. When first used the Course was slightly shorter, because riders turned right at Cronk ny Mona on the outskirts of Douglas and headed across to the top of Bray Hill.

By 1912 the TT's high profile saw manufacturers trying to increase the number of machines they sold by developing more sporting versions of their touring motorcycles. Indeed, many included a 'TT Model' in their catalogues (whether they contested the event or not) and this became a generally accepted name for any machine without pedals, but fitted with flat or slightly downturned handlebars, tuned engine and sporting pretensions.

The TT's growing popularity with motorcyclists was generally shared by the Manx people, although there were dissenting voices from a small but vocal element of locals who spoke of the motorcycles and races 'desecrating the peace of Mona with these dangerous nuisances'. A newspaper report from the early days, however, confirms the high level of local support that existed, claiming that 'The Island indulged itself in a National Holiday' on race days. So frequent did this indulgence become that the authorities eventually declared the day of the Senior TT race to be a Bank Holiday – as it is on the Island today.

A New Start

It was in 1914 that the start of the race was moved to the top of Bray Hill, just south of St Ninian's crossroads. This allowed the creation of a grandstand for 1,000 people and pits for riders to refuel, although the latter were very cramped. The organizers still referred to the pits as the Replenishment Depot. While it was a place where a rider could have the services of one assistant, he was limited to helping with topping up petrol, oil and water, as only the rider was allowed to do any work or repairs to his machine. Basic information on the progress of a race was still conveyed to those at the start area by the marking of information on large scoreboards; this was augmented by a man with a megaphone, for public address systems and radio commentaries were still to be invented.

Both the Junior and Senior TT races had entries from approximately twenty different makes of machine. They were examined for compliance with the regulations on the day before each race and usually left overnight in a tent under the control of the ACU and a policeman. However, at about 9pm on the evening prior to the Junior race a squad of soldiers with fixed bayonets surrounded the tent and remained on guard all night, for there had been rumours in the Island about a possible disturbance by suffragettes.

A machine going through the weighing-in process prior to the 1914 TT.

Safety

Organizers, riders and spectators had been aware from the very first TT that the racing of motorcycles was a dangerous business – indeed, that was the attraction for many. It was in 1911 that Victor Surridge earned the sad distinction of becoming the first TT fatality when he crashed his Rudge at Glen Helen during practice.

Concerned to ensure a reasonable level of competence among those who entered the races, from 1914 race regulations stipulated that riders were required to complete a minimum of six laps of practice in order to qualify to race, an additional rule being that one of those laps had to be completed within a maximum time of seventy minutes for Junior and sixty minutes for Senior runners. Not all of that year's total entry of 160 reached the qualifying standard and thus some were not permitted to start.

To further improve safety, the organizers introduced an ambulance sidecar outfit at Ballacraine in 1913. For 1914 they increased the number of marshals and rigged more warning banners on the approach to danger points. Their early-morning arrangements for opening the gates across the Mountain Road prior to practice, however, were not totally effective, and early in the 1914 meeting there were alarming reports in relation to the gates,

admitting that 'already several smashes have occurred'.

When the races switched to the Mountain Course in 1911 much was made of the demands that would be imposed on machinery by the arduous climb from Ramsey to Snaefell, but riders soon found that – even discounting the common hazard of wandering sheep – there were considerable dangers to both man and machine from the flat-out descent towards Douglas and the finish. F. Bateman was contesting the lead of the 1913 Senior when a tyre came off the rim and burst while he was riding down the Mountain at speed. Bateman was killed and there were several other serious accidents in 1913, some of which were attributed to racers with mainly 'track' experience trying too hard on the TT's 'road' course. The history of the organization of the TT shows that lessons are usually learnt from the mistakes, incidents and accidents that occur, and that measures are subsequently introduced to counter the problems revealed. In a safety-oriented move for 1914, security bolts were made compulsory to help keep the beaded-edge tyres on their rims. Then, although riding gear had progressed to the stage where most riders wore leather jackets, trousers, boots and gloves, there was no recognized form of headgear that offered protection to such a vital area. Tom Loughborough, who

Norman Norris (Dunkeley Precision), dressed to race in 1914. Note the obligatory cut-outs around the ears so that the rider could hear those overtaking.

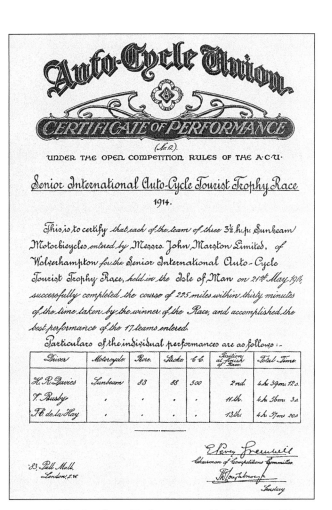

The Certificate of Performance issued by the ACU to John Marston Ltd, maker of Sunbeam motorcycles, in 1914. Notice that Tommy de la Hay, in thirteenth place, was racing for almost 5 hours.

was Secretary of the ACU, 'Ebby' Ebblewhite, the TT Timekeeper, and Dr Gardner, the Medical Officer at Brooklands, got together and produced an ACU-approved design of crash-helmet that was made compulsory wear for TT competitors in 1914.

Although rider safety was at the forefront of the organizers' minds in 1914, they could do little to prevent the fatal crash of third-placed Freddie Walker at the finish of the Junior race when, dazed after earlier falls, he failed to turn right at the top of Bray Hill and crashed into a barrier that had been placed across the road to define and safeguard the course.

Victory went to single-cylinder machines in both Junior and Senior races in 1914, thus reversing the trend of the previous few years that had seen twins to the fore. Speeds had increased relatively slowly despite four years of intense competition over the Mountain Course between top makes such as Indian, Matchless, Triumph, Rudge and Scott, but the number of finishers had gradually grown as manufacturers achieved greater reliability in the stern test of racing for six laps and some 225 miles. Winner of the Junior race of 1914 was Eric Williams on an AJS that the factory had put much effort into preparing for the TT. Despite experiencing many troubles during practice, AJS riders also took second, fourth and fifth places in the race. The result boosted sales overnight and brought about the need for the four Stevens brothers (who comprised AJS) to take larger premises in Wolverhampton. The Senior race saw a spirited battle for race honours, with a new rider and new make of machine challenging for the lead in the form of Howard Davies (Sunbeam), but victory eventually went to Cyril Pullin who averaged 49.49mph (79.64km/h) on a belt-driven Rudge. Howard Davies had to share second place with Oliver Godfrey (Indian) – an unusual occurrence – for both finished thirty-six seconds behind the winning Rudge. It proved to be the last TT victory by a belt-driven machine and, with the onset of the First World War just two months away, the last TT race for six years.

3   From Tourers to Racers

When the TT races returned to the Isle of Man in 1920 after their enforced six-year break, the machines raced were still recognizably derived from the road-going models illustrated in the manufacturers' catalogues. The decade ahead, however, brought major changes in appearance and specifications, with bikes developed strictly for the purpose of racing gradually taking the place of touring-derived models, particularly among the firms that were serious about winning.

In the first year of the TT's return there was little to see in the way of newly developed machinery, for despite wartime advances made with engines for aviation purposes, the attributes of large capacity, continuous running and low revving required for powered flight were not ones that were overly relevant to motorcycle use. But although new engines were scarce, there were plenty of new faces among the competitors. Some pre-First World War riders, such as the Collier brothers, chose not to resume their racing careers, while other former riders had been lost in battle: third-placed man in the singles race of 1908, Captain Sir R.K. Arbuthnot, Bt, went down with his ship at the Battle of Jutland (by then he was a Rear-Admiral), and 1911 Senior winner Oliver Godfrey was killed in aerial combat against the Red Baron's squadron. Howard Davies was the young man who, at just eighteen years old in his first TT in 1914, tied for second place with Oliver Godfrey. Going on to wartime service in the Royal Flying Corps, Davies was also shot down and reported as killed. His obituary

appeared in the motorcycle magazines, but fortunately the magazines were wrong and Howard Davies returned to the Isle of Man to resume his racing career in 1920. The twenty-four starters in the Senior TT were split equally between newcomers and former contestants. Among the newcomers was Graham Walker, who would have much influence on British motorcycling for the next forty years as TT competitor, TT winner, race-team manager, editor of *Motor Cycling*, TT commentator for BBC radio, and finally as Curator of the motorcycle section of the National Motor Museum at Beaulieu.

Change to the Course

A small change to the Course in 1920 saw it altered in its last few miles. Instead of riders turning right at Cronk ny Mona and heading across to the finish at the top of Bray Hill, they continued to Signpost Corner, dropped down through the Nook to Governor's Bridge, and rode along the Glencrutchery Road to pass a new start and finish line just before the top of Bray Hill, where pits and grandstand were provided in the comparatively spacious surroundings of Nobles Park Playing Fields. With the exception of a small stretch of road in Ramsey, the use of which was subject to dispute, the roads of the Mountain Course ridden in 1920 were the same 37¾ miles that are ridden today. Unfortunately for the returning riders of 1920, the condition of those roads was little better than when they were first used in 1911.

James 'Pa' Norton (right) takes refreshment after early morning practice, standing on the Glencrutchery Road with the Scoreboard in the background and opposite the new Pits, which were slightly nearer to the top of Bray Hill than today's pits and scoreboards.

Organization

Organization was still in the hands of the ACU who, after thoughts of dropping the Senior 500cc race owing to worries over speed, decided to retain it and also introduce a class for 250cc machines to run alongside the 350s during the Junior race. Organization was still very basic, although approximately twenty-five white-coated flag marshals were on duty to warn riders of incidents. Their coats were provided by Dunlop tyres and came with a sash bearing the company's name, thus earning them the nickname of 'Dunlops'.

A policeman was stationed at every major corner; these members of the constabulary were regarded as the first line of medical support for injured riders, for all were first-aid trained. It was part of a policeman's duties to

Four gentlemen of Ramsey in attendance at a TT of the early 1920s, including a 'Dunlop'.

examine any competitor who fell at his spot and decide if it was necessary to call out the official doctor based at the start. Apart from the obvious perils caused by falling from a motorcycle at speed, the very basic level of medical support available certainly added to the risk that riders took by competing in the TT races. AJS-mounted Bert Haddock fell at Keppel Gate during practice in 1920 and was injured. There was no policeman present but a message was conveyed to the marshals half a mile away at Creg ny Baa and they used their telephone to summon the doctor from the start. After he had made his own way to Keppel Gate and examined the rider, the doctor then requisitioned the horse-ambulance from Douglas Hospital (presumably via the telephone at Creg ny Baa); according to a contemporary report: 'The ambulance was sent with two horses at breakneck speed, and succeeded in reaching there in what must have constituted a record time for this old ambulance'. No doubt the gallant horses did their best, but faced with a constant uphill gradient from Douglas, their efforts would hardly have stood comparison with the response times demanded of today's high-speed medical rescue services. In another incident during practice involving two fallen riders, it was reported how 'the Clincher Tyre Company's fine big van (which had been used during the war as a hospital ambulance), was again requisitioned for its original purpose'. The irony of the above is that by the time race week arrived, the hospital at Douglas had received a long sought-after motor-ambulance, paid for by public fund-raising efforts.

Races of the Early 1920s

AJS had won the 1914 Junior TT with their light and speedy side-valve racers, and in 1920 the company brought one of the few newly designed engines to the Island. It was of an innovative overhead valve layout featuring inclined valves operated by long push-rods, and had a hemispherical combustion chamber formed in a cast iron head. Fitted with a three-speed countershaft gearbox, a double primary drive arrangement meant riders had a choice of six gears. Powerful, light in weight and with good handling, the new 350 proved to be a winner on its first appearance, easily outpacing the opposition. However, although AJS expected to sweep the board with the six 'works' machines entered, lack of team discipline saw its riders fighting for the lead among themselves, leading to mechanical breakdowns and failures. In consequence, Cyril Williams was the only AJS finisher – fortunately in first place – but even he broke down on the last lap and had to push in from Keppel Gate to claim the win. Although the fastest lap of the race was a healthy 10 per cent faster than in 1914 at 51.36mph (82.65km/h), the race average was much slower at 40.74 mph (65.56km/h), due to the winner's long push to the finishing line. In the concurrent Lightweight race, R.O. Clark, Gus Kuhn and Frank 'Pa' Applebee took the first three places on two-stroke Levis machines, with the winner averaging 38.30 mph (61.64km/h) over the same five-lap race distance.

The Senior race, in which race and lap speeds were just a couple of mph faster than 1914, saw a win for Tommy de la Hay (Sunbeam). Tommy's race average speed was 51.48mph (82.85km/h), but credit for the fastest lap went to George Dance (Sunbeam) at 55.62mph (89.51km/h), with Dougie Brown (Norton) taking second place and Reg Brown (Sunbeam) finishing third.

In his book *Britain's Racing Motor Cycles*,

former TT racer Les Higgins wrote of the Sunbeams in the 1920 Senior TT: 'There was nothing very exceptional about these side-valve racers: they owed their success to a basically good design and almost unfailing reliability. The engines were standard sports models, carefully built and tuned to give their very best.' While it is true that the Sunbeam 'works' machines for the 1920 TT were based on standard models, the extra work that went into preparing them for such a gruelling race was enormous. Only the most skilled members of the company's staff were allowed to work on the TT bikes and, as with other small factories who competed, output of normal road-going motorcycles dropped in the weeks running up to the event as effort was concentrated on the race bikes.

One company that was large enough to mount a TT campaign without severe disruption to normal output was Britain's biggest motorcycle producer, BSA. It designed and built a bike specifically for the Senior TT in 1921, utilizing a new inclined, 4-valve engine fitted into a cradle frame that allowed for a steeply downward sloping petrol tank. Much was expected of the new design and six machines were entered. Despite successful pre-TT running at Brooklands, however, the supremely testing Isle of Man Mountain Course proved the new BSA to be underdeveloped and

all six 'works' entries retired from the race. This was a bitter blow to such a large concern and BSA turned its back on road-racing for many years, seeking publicity for its products in other fields of competition.

Sunbeam brought a redesigned 500cc engine to the 1921 TT hoping to repeat their success of 1920. It featured a long-stroke of 105.5mm and a completely new lubrication system but, like everyone else, it was a year in which Sunbeam had to give best to AJS. Having already taken the first three places in the Junior race with Eric Williams, Howard Davies and Manxman Tom Sheard, AJS then stunned the opposition by winning the Senior TT with a 350cc machine that came home ahead of such accomplished performers as Indian-mounted Freddie Dixon and Bert Le Vack, who had to settle for second and third. (Theirs were the only non-British machines among the sixty-five race starters.) In a feat that has never been repeated, it was Howard Davies who rode the 350cc AJS machine to Senior victory, and in so doing he set a new average speed of 54.50mph (87.71km/h) for the 226½-mile race.

Mile-a-Minute

Three men destined for future TT glory made their debuts at the 1922 TT meeting: Walter

Tommy de la Hay on his Sunbeam for the 1921 Senior TT. As winner of the 1920 Senior he carried number 1.

AJS team men in 1921: Harry Harris (left), Howard Davies (centre) and Eric Williams (right).

Handley, Jimmy Simpson and Stanley Woods. Before commencing their winning ways, however, they first had to serve racing apprenticeships on the Mountain Course. The long and difficult-to-learn circuit still relied almost totally on rolled macadam for its surfacing, so creating conditions that favoured riders who could cope with loose surfaces and had the physical strength to fight their machines over the rougher sections of its 37¾-mile lap. In the same year the 250cc machines were given their own separate race and thirty-eight riders competed for the new Lightweight Tourist Trophy.

That Lightweight race was run prior to the Junior TT on the Tuesday of race week and victory went to Geoff Davison (Levis), whose little two-stroke had a top speed of only 60mph (96.5km/h) but averaged 49.89mph (80.29km/h) for the race. The Junior race saw the first TT victory by a Manxman when Tom Sheard was fastest over the five laps on an AJS, and it also saw the first appearance at the TT of an overhead camshaft unit in Bert Le Vack's 350cc JAP-engined New Imperial, which led the race for several laps. Alec Bennett (Sunbeam) took what turned out to be the last-ever TT win by a side-valve machine when he completed the Senior at record-breaking pace and became the first man to complete a six-lap race in under four hours (3 hours 53mins 2secs). Alec only just missed setting a mile-a-minute average when recording the fastest lap at 59.99mph (96.54km/h).

Druid achieved excellent publicity for their forks with TT successes.

Alec Bennett's Senior TT-winning Sunbeam of 1922 still relied on basic rim and block front and rear brakes, while other manufacturers were fitting internal expanding brakes.

The 1922 TT races were contested by a wide variety of machines and it is interesting to see that the total of nine podium places offered by the three races were occupied by eight different makes (Sunbeam, Triumph, Scott, AJS, Sheffield-Henderson, Levis, Rex-Acme, Velocette), with two additional makes involved in setting fastest laps (New Imperial and O.K.).

In his book *Racing Round the Island*, Bob Holliday sees the 1922 event as a turning-point in TT history with Bennett's near-60mph lap having such an impact that: 'Dramatically, from being a happy-go-lucky, free-for-all sporting adventure, the TT had become serious, professional business'. This was regarded as seriously fast in 1922 and its near achievement as an average lap speed registered so strongly with racegoers and the general public that the huge publicity generated made every motorcycle manufacturer and associated trade supplier want to share in it. Manufacturers, of which there were many in the early 1920s, realized that if they were to gain the maximum publicity of a TT win, they would have to put more effort into racing than their competitors. More effort meant the development of faster and specialized racing machines by staff who were allocated full-time

to the task of working on race bikes, rather than the previous custom of selecting several sports models from the production line a couple of months before the TT, then using existing staff to tune and prepare them for the event. All the extra effort being put into racing meant more expense, and manufacturers looked to their trade suppliers of petrol, oil, tyres, carburettors, sparking-plugs and so on for help towards the cost. Anxious to obtain their share of publicity, the trade increased their financial and technical contributions, with the result that racing became ever more commercial. Seeing the considerable extra effort and money that was being pumped into racing, the best riders, who quickly realized the worth of their contributions, looked for and received a share of those extra monies, making the 1920s a particularly rewarding time for the select few men capable of winning a TT.

The early 1920s also offered large potential profits for successful manufacturers, as the motorcycle market was booming. The post-war motorcycle industry struggled back into production with 115,000 machines registered in 1919. The following year's figure was 278,000 and in 1921 it climbed to 373,000. Publicity was well worth seeking in that sort

A start-line scene from the early 1920s. The rider stands poised with his machine in what was called the 'Island Square', waiting for the signal to go from the timekeepers. The scoreboard in front of the pits stretches off to the right and a similar one went off to the left. In the centre is the Continuous Leader Board, which was maintained with painted figures and times on a rolling basis throughout the race. Surrounding the clock are the actual Tourist trophies.

of market, particularly as strong demand for new motorcycles allowed high selling prices to be maintained. But so many small makers, who were really no more than assemblers of bought-in proprietary parts, joined the market that the industry then entered a period of over-production that caused prices to fall.

Not all motorcycle manufacturers with racing pretensions could afford to set up dedicated race departments, but they still found it worthwhile to compete in the TT, for there were few better forms of publicity than this unique event, which generated wide public interest allied to great respect, and even awe, for those who took part – both men and machines.

But it was not just manufacturers who incurred increasing costs in racing at the TT, for expenditure by the ACU in running the meeting became a source of concern to the sport's governing body in the early 1920s. The Manx Government was reluctant to contribute towards the ACU's expenses and this brought rumbles of discontent and mutterings about taking the races elsewhere. Fortunately, they remained on the island.

TT Replicas

The dream of anyone contesting the Isle of Man races was to come home victorious and 'win' one of the coveted Tourist Trophies. For most it remained just a dream and, anyway, they were perpetual trophies, which meant that the race winners only kept them for one year. Prior to 1922 the winner (and those who finished within half an hour of his total time) received a gold medal to retain. At the 1922 event, winners and those who finished within a nominated percentage of the winners' overall race times, received miniature silver replicas of the main Tourist Trophies. These, plus bronze replicas, are awarded to this day, and are recognized and coveted throughout the racing world as a reward for high achievement.

Sidecars

A three-lap race for sidecars was introduced at the 1923 TT, attracting just fourteen entries. The event received little support from the manufacturers of sidecars, who felt that the antics of race passengers in climbing all over these naturally unwieldy devices to maintain balance was not conducive to selling them to the family men that they were produced for. Makers of the motorcycles to which they were attached were also less than enthusiastic. The Mountain Course was demanding enough for solos and the addition of a sidecar only added to the risk of mechanical breakdown and possible tarnishing of a maker's name. Such breakdowns could

Harry Reed, who rode solo in the 1908 TT, here takes a DOT sidecar outfit around Ramsey hairpin on his way to fifth place.

be caused by more than just engine failure, for the stresses of sidecar racing frequently resulted in the fracture of frames and forks. So real was this problem that heavy bracing was added to those components to cope with the extra loads imposed at the TT.

The addition of the sidecar race required the TT meeting to be run over three days instead of two, but it only remained in the race programme for three years and, with few recognized specialist sidecar racers, victories went to top solo men: Freddie Dixon (1923), George Tucker (1924) and Len Parker (1925).

The year of 1923 brought a popular victory in the Senior TT for Manxman Tom Sheard on a flat-twin Douglas fitted with experimental disc brakes. Graeme Black (Norton) was second some two minutes behind, and Freddie Dixon brought a single-cylinder Indian into third place, in what was the last-ever appearance of the American marque at the TT.

Ultra-Lightweights

With the Lightweight (250cc) TT well established and showing respectable lap times over 50mph, the organizers introduced a race for

---

Why so Named?

Brandish Corner
Located between Creg ny Baa and Hillberry, the fast left-hand sweep of Brandish Corner left little room for mistakes in the early days of racing over the Mountain Course, for it was enclosed by banks on both sides. Walter Brandish did not get it quite right during practice on his Triumph Ricardo in 1923. While attempting to pass a slower rider, he hit the outside bank and broke his leg. He is remembered more for that episode than for his fine riding performances, which included second place in the Senior TT of 1922.

Although much widened down the years, Brandish Corner still merits great care from riders as it is approached at maximum speed on a down-grade from Creg ny Baa.

Walter Brandish was the first to have a place on the TT Course named after him. This photograph is from 1921, when he made his TT debut on a Rover and finished thirteenth in the Senior race. He is seated in front of the pits, with St Ninian's church in the background.

Ultra-Lightweights in 1924 with the capacity limit set at 175cc. For the first time they also prescribed a massed-start for the seventeen entries. Although there were predictions of multiple pile-ups at the bottom of Bray Hill, the race got away smoothly and provided a victory for Jock Porter on a New Gerrard at a race average speed of 51.20mph (82.40km/h). It was a race in which four-strokes completely outclassed the two-stroke entries. Like the sidecars, the Ultra-Lightweight race only remained in the TT race programme until 1925. After that the meeting settled into just three races, each of seven laps: Senior, Junior, Lightweight. That was the way things remained for many years.

Joe Craig rode a Norton in the 1924 Senior TT and finished in twelfth place. Here at his mid-race pit-stop, his attendant adds petrol while Joe checks the oil and a Boy Scout cleans his number plate.

Time to relax for competitor Harry Brockbank (front left) and friends outside their hotel, which was the headquarters of the Speedwell oil concern for the 1924 TT period.

Return to Victory

With wins in the Senior and Sidecar races in 1924, Norton Motors Ltd achieved its first TT victories since Rem Fowler won the multi-cylinder race in 1907. It was the speedy Alec Bennett who brought a new ohv Model 18 home first at a record-breaking race average speed of 61.64mph (99.20km/h) in the Senior, despite having to ride in misty conditions over the Mountain section of the course. Alec's win added to that of George Tucker, who had brought another of Bracebridge

Street's products home first in the Sidecar race a couple of days earlier.

Scott was a firm with a successful TT history and had hopes of repeating earlier successes in 1924, but they – with rider Harry Langman – had to be content with second place in the Senior, some 1½ minutes behind the winning Norton.

It was a time when TT wins were big news and were reported on in detail in the national press. As a result of such publicity, the winning rider and manufacturer could usually expect to be feted when they returned home: a report of 1924 tells how 'There were post-race civic junketings in Birmingham that year, for as well as Norton's two trophies, another of the city's factories had had a dual success, the brothers Kenneth and Eric Twemlow having won the Junior and Lightweight events for New Imperial.' The winning Birmingham-built machines of 1924 were carried on the backs of lorries, while riders and dignitaries followed in cars, passing through welcoming crowds *en route* from New Street Station to the Town Hall, where they were greeted by the Lord Mayor.

It was the turn of a former TT-winning rider to taste victory again the following year,

1925. Since his sensational win in the 1921 Senior on a 350cc AJS (and second place in the same year's Junior race), Howard Davies had failed to impress at the TT. Frustrated by his lack of racing success, in mid-1924 he set up as a motorcycle manufacturer in Wolverhampton and exhibited several JAP-engined models at the 1924 Motor Cycle Show under the name HRD (his initials). Few were surprised when he appeared at the 1925 TT with machines of his own make. However, what did surprise the TT world was the way in which he took his new and virtually untried 350cc HRD into second place in the Junior TT, and then went on to ride the 500cc version to victory in the Senior race. It was a quite stunning performance that saw Howard Davies not only return to TT-winning form but, in doing so, leave fifty of the best British sporting motorcycles from almost twenty other manufacturers to either fall by the wayside or trail home behind him. The HRD was not the product of a specialized race department like some of the other top runners, but was made by a firm that had only been in production for a few months and whose proprietor had ridden his own product to first place. It was a fairy-tale victory that moved *Motor Cycle and Cycle Trader* to write: 'In the annals of the trade there has probably been nothing so romantic nor any achievement so outstanding as that which may be placed to the credit of HRD'.

Speeds Increase

Major improvements to the roads of the TT course in the mid-1920s saw increased use of tarred surfaces, particularly over the Mountain section. This made a significant contribution to the setting of new race and lap records in all classes in 1925. Howard Davies pushed the race average speed in the Senior TT up by almost 5mph to 66.13mph (106.42km/h), with Jimmy Simpson achieving the fastest lap at 68.97mph (110.99km/h). Wal Handley raced his Rex-Acme to win the Junior at 65.02mph (104.64km/h) and set the fastest lap at 65.89mph (106.04km/h). Eric Twemlow won the Lightweight race on a New Imperial increasing his previous year's race-winning speed from 55.44mph to 57.74mph (92.92 km/h); Wal Handley set the fastest lap of 60.22mph (96.91km/h). Handley also recorded the first double race win in a week by adding the Ultra-Lightweight victory at 53.45 mph (86.02km/h) to his Junior success, again on a Rex-Acme.

Howard Davies (HRD) receives congratulations after winning the 1925 Senior TT. Leaning over his left shoulder is Bert Le Vack of JAP, who tuned the winning engine.

Formed in the early 1920s by the amalgamation of the Rex and Acme concerns, the new Rex-Acme company achieved three TT victories in the 1920s with Wal Handley riding.

Among the three-wheelers at the 1925 TT, Len Parker wrestled a Douglas to side-car victory at 55.22mph (88.86km/h), with Freddie Dixon (Douglas) setting the fastest lap at 57.18mph (92.02km/h). Jimmy Simpson's fastest lap in the Senior race of 68.97mph (110.99km/h) took 32 minutes 50 seconds to complete. The organizers still required competitors to achieve prescribed qualifying times in practice before being permitted to race and in 1925 they were: Senior forty-five minutes, Junior fifty minutes, Lightweight fifty-five minutes.

Getting to the Island

The growth in speeds and the exciting racing at the TT brought spectators flocking to the Island, even though for 1926 the organizers reverted to just three races. Each, however, was over seven laps, a distance of 264 miles (425km), and this meant that the Senior winner was racing for just under four hours, whilst many lesser lights were racing for considerably more. This was particularly so in the Lightweight race, where even third-placed W. Colgan on a Cotton took almost five hours to complete the distance.

Wherever visiting TT spectators came from

they faced a boat crossing to reach the mecca of racing in the middle of the Irish Sea. One persuasive advertisement of the time encouraged them with the words:

> there is no difficulty whatsoever in getting the motorcycle aboard at Liverpool, and plenty of porters are available should no pals be present to assist up the gangway at high tide. It is less easy to get it ashore at Douglas, but here again there are porters in plenty, though it is wise to fix a fee with them before giving the order.

The first-class return passenger fare was £1 and third-class 12/6 (62½p). An accompanied motorcycle was charged at 4/6 (22½p) each way.

Britain's rail and parcel services were much more in tune with the needs of their customers than today and visiting motorcyclists would often send their luggage in advance, confident that it would be at their hotel or boarding house when they arrived. Full board could be obtained for between £2 and £3 a week. Spectators who sailed from ports like Liverpool or Belfast, but chose not to take their motorcycles to the Island, could find garages where they could be stored for a few pence a day. Many competitors used the train services

Visitors pushing their machines aboard an Isle of Man Steam Packet Company boat in the mid-1920s.

Pietro Ghersi came all the way from Italy to race Moto Guzzis in the Lightweight and Senior classes. Excluded from the results of the Lightweight race owing to a rule infringement after coming home in second position, he was out of luck in the Senior and retired with mechanical trouble.

to get them and their race machines to the port of departure, for few had vans or trailers.

Alcohol Banned

A change in race regulations for 1926 resulted in the banning of alcohol-based fuels at the TT. These had made a distinct contribution to the increase in race speeds in previous years but, hereafter, competitors were restricted to using commercially available petrol-benzole mixtures. The new ruling affected some makes of engine more than others and the bigger JAP power units seemed to particularly miss the cooling effects of alcohol fuel. The change did not seem to slow AJS machinery, for Jimmy Simpson recorded the first 70mph (112.65 km/h) lap in the Senior race. Jimmy explained that his race philosophy was always 'set a cracking pace to begin with and burn up as many of your competitors as possible'. However, as in many other instances, Jimmy's ultra-rapid progress proved too much for his bike in the 1926 Senior; his AJS put a con-rod through the crankcase and he failed to complete the race, as did a further thirty-four of the fifty-seven starters. This left Stanley Woods to ride his Norton to victory at an average speed of 67.54mph (108.69km/h). It was Stanley's second TT win (his first being on a Cotton in the 1923 Junior) and was achieved on a machine fitted with Webb girder forks, to achieve better handling than with the Druids

previously used, and capable of a top speed of about 90mph.

Although the organizers banned the use of alcohol in engines at the 1926 TT, the regulation did not apply to riders and they commonly 'refuelled' with a swig of something alcoholic at pit stops.

Norton sought to increase sales with this advertisement following their 1926 Senior TT success.

Mechanical Developments

By the mid-1920s the motorcycles raced at the TT had very little in common with the pioneer machines that had first tackled Island racing twenty years earlier. Gone were single-speeds and belt drive, being replaced by three- and four-speed countershaft gearboxes with primary and secondary drive by chain. Gone were the primitive brakes acting via tank-mounted levers and rods on the wheel rims, to be replaced by internal expanding brakes front and rear, with one controlled by a handlebar-mounted lever and Bowden cable, while the other was operated by a foot pedal (although AJS used two foot-operated pedals). After the last victory of a side-valve engine in 1922, overhead valve engines became commonplace until 1926 when Alec Bennett convincingly won the Junior on an overhead camshaft Velocette, so setting a trend for many other manufacturers to follow. Advances in metallurgy allowed greater use of aluminium and aluminium-bronze in components like cylinder heads, while a switch to dry-sump lubrication with mechanical oil pumps also helped reliability and cooling. Much was being learnt about engine breathing, valve angles and such, and engines were operating at up to 7,000rpm, although higher revving brought problems with reliability. Top speed of a 'works' 500 was about 90mph (145km/h).

The development process saw manufacturers constantly modifying and improving their machines to keep up with the opposition, with factories copying each other's advances, and even, on occasion, copying others' failures, where they recognized that a good idea needed improving to make it work. Making use of such developments as 4-valve heads, hairpin valve springs, twin exhaust ports, enclosed push rods, positive-stop foot gearchange and twist-grip throttles, manufacturers improved the performance and reliability of both race and road-going motorcycles. Component suppliers also improved essential items like sparking-plugs, carburettors and magnetos, while advances made by the petrol

and oil companies allowed race machines to run on compression ratios of about 6.5:1. Tyre manufacturers did their bit, improving reliability and safety by moving from beaded-edge construction to a more secure wired-on form, fitted to well-base wheel rims.

Despite substantial progress in design, racing engines of the 1920s would not accept seven laps of the TT course at full throttle as today's machines will do (over six laps). According to Stanley Woods:

> When I started racing in the early 1920s it was an accepted fact that whoever led in the early stages of a race did not win, or finish for that matter. Usually it was engine trouble that put an end to a meteoric start, but not one component part of machines of those days could be described as above suspicion.

There were few riders able to stand the physical strain of 264 miles flat-out, and both men and machines had to race at a pace designed to get them to the finish, a task in which some were more skilled than others.

The general adoption of ohv engines for racing and fast roadsters by the mid-1920s resulted in taller engines having to be accommodated within the motorcycle frame. This had repercussions for the frame top tube and the petrol tank, often meaning that the tube

Stanley Woods looks pleased with his win after the 1926 Senior TT on a Norton, but he has a large adjustable spanner tucked in the top of his right boot, and probably carried a plug spanner in the top of the left one.

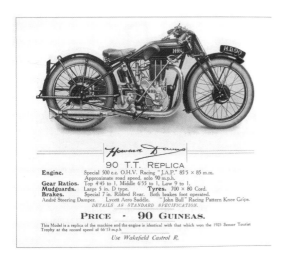

90 T.T. REPLICA

Engine.	Special 500 c.c. O.H.V. Racing "J.A.P." 85·5 × 85 m.m.
	Approximate road speed, solo 90 m.p.h.
Gear Ratios.	Top 4·45 to 1, Middle 6·55 to 1, Low 9 to 1.
Mudguards.	Large 5 in. D type. **Tyres.** 700 × 80 Cord.
Brakes.	Special 7 in. Ribbed Rear. Both brakes foot operated.
André Steering Damper.	Lycett Aero Saddle. "John Bull" Racing Pattern Knee Grips.

DETAILS AS STANDARD SPECIFICATION.

PRICE - 90 GUINEAS.

This Model is a replica of the machine and the engine is identical with that which won the 1925 Senior Tourist Trophy at the record speed of 66/13 m.p.h.

Use Wakefield Castrol R.

HRD was among the pioneers in using a saddle-tank. The young company also sought to build on its victory in the 1925 Senior TT by marketing a 'TT Replica' model.

had to be bent upwards and/or tank capacity reduced. To counter this, the saddle-tank gradually came into general use, whereby part of the petrol tank went over the frame tube instead of being suspended underneath. It brought about a major change in appearance, particularly when combined with a general move towards the use of a shorter wheelbase and lower saddle height, which, in turn, contributed to improved handling.

It was a time when the advances in design made in racing quickly filtered down to be used on road machines. Indeed, many makers boasted that one year's TT machine would be the next year's sports roadster, and several reinforced this claim by calling their fastest model 'TT Replica'. But not every motorcyclist wanted to look like a TT star on the road and manufacturers developed a vast range of models to suit all tastes. However, the motorcycle market began to shrink in the second half of the 1920s as the effects of financial depression were increasingly felt in the motorcycle industry. Prices of road machines were reduced in attempts to maintain sales, model ranges were trimmed and some makers went out of production, including Howard Davies's

HRD concern, which folded at the end of 1927.

Norton had improved the handling of its racers at the 1926 TT with a change of front fork and the company achieved further improvements in 1927 with a new cradle frame. Handling was an area of machine performance that could yield reductions in lap times by allowing faster cornering and reducing rider fatigue, and was one for which Norton became well known. However, the feature that attracted most attention on the 500cc factory-entered Nortons at the 1927 TT was a new Walter Moore-designed ohc engine fitted to at least two of the four 'works' entries. Fast in practice – they were timed at 93.7mph (150.79km/h) on the Sulby Straight – the new ohc models dominated the Senior race. Stanley Woods led for four laps and set the fastest lap speed before his clutch failed, then Alec Bennett took over the lead, held it to the end and finished with a record race average speed of 68.41mph (110.09km/h). In only his second year at the TT, the relatively unknown Jimmy Guthrie took second place in the Senior on a New Hudson, giving notice that he was a man to watch for the future.

Bert Le Vack joined New Hudson from JAP in early 1926 and applied his skills as a trained engineer and experienced tuner to its engines, for use in competition at Brooklands and the TT. Guthrie's second place in the 1927 Senior was to be the high-point of the company's sporting success and, like many others, it sought racing success to promote sales of its road-going machines in a market where buyers were becoming fewer.

There had been a smattering of TT entries from Italian factories like Bianchi, Garelli and Moto Guzzi from the mid-1920s and in 1927 the latter was rewarded with second place in the Lightweight race, with rider Luigi Arcangeli finishing eight minutes behind winner Wal Handley on his Rex-Acme fitted with a Blackburne engine.

One innovation at the 1927 TT that was to run for almost sixty years was the introduction

Freddie Dixon

It was just before its demise in 1927 that HRD Motors Ltd employed the services of the renowned Freddie Dixon to ride its machines in the Senior and Junior classes of that year's TT. A vastly experienced rider, it had been fifteen years earlier, in 1912, that Dixon made his TT debut, riding a Cleveland in the Senior race but failing to finish. He returned to the event after the First World War and used 500cc Indians from 1920 to 1923, taking second place in 1921 and third in 1923.

In addition to his Indian ride in the Senior TT, in 1923 he also rode a Douglas in the first Sidecar TT and, with the aid of a banking sidecar, showed his versatility by bringing it home in first place. Dixon stayed with Douglas for four years riding two- and three-wheelers, but despite top six finishes, a solo win eluded him on the Island.

Freddie Dixon poses on his single-cylinder Indian at a TT of the early 1920s.

The JAP-engined bikes provided by HRD for Dixon to ride at the 1927 TT were expected to be outpaced by more highly developed race machinery from other factories, but if anyone could get the best out of the HRDs it would be Freddie, for he had excellent tuning skills as well as riding ability and, as he was working for J.A. Prestwich (JAP) at the time, it was anticipated that he would allocate himself a 'quick' motor.

Freddie was a hard man and an individualist who tailored the bikes he rode to his own specification. Perhaps showing the influence of his Indian days, he fitted his HRD with footboards and a left-hand throttle twist grip. He also had a backrest to the saddle, a flyscreen and one or two other gimmicky items that were said to have been fitted more with an eye to the possible 'bonus' payments they might earn than for any practical purpose. He frequently rode without goggles and sometimes without gloves.

After performing well during practising in 1927, his long-held wish for a solo TT win came true when he brought his HRD home in first place in the Junior TT. *Motor Cycle* summarized his performance with the words: 'Freddie has never before had a bike that would stand his thrashing; and yet he has never once taken a toss in a TT. A most popular victory, and long overdue.' Although holding a job with JAP at the time, Freddie was professional in his approach to his racing, for he knew that the rewards of a TT win were high. Writing more than twenty years later, *Motor Cycle* claimed that 'in the middle of the 1920s a rider who played his cards could net £3–5,000 in bonuses' for a TT win. As well as his contractual arrangements with HRD, Freddie Dixon used a Burman gearbox, Webb forks and brakes, Coventry chains, Lycett saddle, Binks carburettor, Bosch magneto, KLG plug, Hutchinson tyres, Andre steering damper, Fibrax brake linings and Pilgrim oil pump. Fuel and lubricants were BP Spirit, Wakefield Castrol oil and Tecalemit grease. No doubt all of the above concerns sought publicity from his win and were invited to contribute towards recognizing it with appropriate 'bonus' payments. And, because he liked to celebrate, some of those winnings were probably spent on post-race partying, a pastime for which he gained a degree of notoriety.

There were even thoughts of a double win for HRD at the 1927 TT (and dreams of double bonuses by Freddie!), because he held second place for much of the Senior race. A loose gear-change quadrant, however, slowed him in the later stages of the race and he finished fifth. Although he returned to the TT on Douglas machinery in 1928, it was not a successful event and turned out to be his last TT appearance on two wheels. A local newspaper reported of the 1929 TT: 'Somehow the TT atmosphere is not the same without his cheery face'.

Spending more of his time racing cars, Freddie Dixon actually achieved a TT win in a car (though not on the Isle of Man) and so, as further proof of his versatility, became the only man to have won a TT on two, three and four wheels.

Jimmy Guthrie poses with his New Hudson and tuner Bert Le Vack, after taking second place in the 1927 Senior TT.

of the *TT Special* by former Lightweight winner Geoff Davison. A tabloid newspaper that initially appeared as an eight-page issue at the end of race week, it gradually grew into three editions (covering each race) and then expanded with additional editions to cover each practice. This was before the days of Manx Radio and round-the-course commentaries, which meant that spectators watching in remote spots had little idea of what went on at other points on the course. For them, and for people who could not get to the races, the *TT Special* provided in-depth information of what had occurred.

Triumph and Tragedy

As with so many TT races, the triumph enjoyed in 1927 by winning factories like Norton, HRD, Rex-Acme, and by their riders Alec Bennett, Stanley Woods and Wal Handley, was overshadowed by tragic events on the track.

The TT meeting was spread over a full three weeks in the 1920s, with two weeks allocated for practice and racing taking place on three days of the third week. Practising was restricted to defined early-morning hours (starting at about 4.30am), but the roads remained open to ordinary traffic during those rider training sessions. Local traffic was

thin and attempts were made to discourage the Manx from using their roads at such times, but carters needed to get goods to the boats in Douglas from all parts of the island and farmers were reluctant to change their ways of working, so riders had to be on the look-out for traffic heading in both directions, as they tried to ride at speed and learn the course well enough to race over it. (There were occasions when riders unofficially broke the lap record while practising on open roads!) In a tragic incident involving a fish-van on the outskirts of Kirk Michael, 'Archie' Birkin swerved to avoid it and was killed. Many other riders had experienced near-misses down the years, and it was to the riders' relief that the Manx authorities extended the Road Closing Orders to include practice periods at the 1928 event.

Although closing the roads for practice removed other traffic from the course, it did allow riders to try harder, set higher speeds and, inevitably, fall off more often. Slightly worryingly, a report in a local newspaper on the run-up to the TT mentioned that, while the local hospital had room for seventy-two patients, seventy-one beds were already taken!

Sunbeams Shine

Bucking the trend for ohc engines, saddle-tanks and ever larger brakes, the Sunbeam concern brought slightly old-fashioned looking models to the 1928 TT, which retained pushrod-operated overhead valves, 'flat tanks' and relatively small brakes. Maybe the weather conditions for the 1928 Senior TT (said to be the wettest on record) put a premium on rider skill rather than out-and-out machine performance, but it was Charlie Dodson who brought his Sunbeam home to victory by seven minutes over George Rowley's AJS. Charlie had ridden Sunbeams each year since 1925, finishing no higher than eighth and having several retirements. He suffered a heavy fall at Keppel Gate during the 1928 Senior, damaged his machine, split his crash helmet and lost the

AJS reverted to using its chain-driven ohc models at the 1929 TT, where rider Wal Handley came second in the Junior, but had to retire in the Senior.

lead to Graham Walker (Rudge). Walker's machine, however, failed 10 miles from the finish and Dodson, renowned as an exceptional rider in the wet, rode on to record Sunbeam's first victory since 1922.

Velocettes took first and second places in the 1928 Junior race through riders Alec Bennett and Harold Willis, the latter having introduced the first positive-stop foot gear-change mechanism into the Velo' gearbox. It was a design feature quickly adopted by other makers, who recognized that a rider not having to take a hand from the handlebar meant improved machine control.

Proving that the development of machines for racing was sometimes of the 'two steps forward and one step back' variety, AJS dropped the chain-driven ohc engines they used in 1927 and reverted to improved pushrod engines for 1928. They also reverted to three-speed gearboxes (from four), but did bring back a previously tried (but dropped) form of dry-sump lubrication. However, their race problems sprang from a different area. Given the company's long experience of TT racing, it was surprising that they allowed themselves to be talked into using a form of valve-spring for the Junior race that differed from the one they used in practice: five of their six Junior entries retired from the race

with broken valve-springs. With the sixth machine suffering from big-end failure, the race was a disaster for AJS and provided an expensive lesson about the use of untried components.

The make of O.K. had contested earlier TTs when produced by the partnership of Humphrey and Dawes. Following the firm's break-up in 1927, Ernie Humphreys established O.K.-Supreme and in 1928 the marque took its only TT victory. It was achieved when Frank Longman came home first in the Lightweight event after a spirited race with Wal Handley that saw Handley forced to retire his Rex-Acme towards the end of the race.

Claiming to race only modified production machines, Sunbeam returned to the TT in 1929 and Charlie Dodson again took victory for them in the Senior event, at record speed. Emphasizing their reliability, Sunbeam also took the team prize for the third year in succession. Fitted with saddle-tanks for 1929, the 'works' Sunbeams had the outward appearance of Model 9 production machines, but there were many visible and invisible departures from standard. Even the new petrol tank was of larger capacity than the roadsters, although retention of the same outline shape disguised the fact.

Charlie Dodson waits with his Sunbeam on the 'Island Square', before riding to victory in the 1929 Senior TT.

The Senior TT always attracted the most publicity, but new race records were set in the Junior, where Freddie Hicks rode his Velocette to victory, and in the Lightweight where Syd Crabtree (Excelsior) came home first. Already a five times TT winner, Alec Bennett was relegated to second place in the Senior and third in the Junior. Alec was not used to being outridden at the TT and decided it was time to retire to a motor business in Southampton.

A local newspaper reported at the time of the 1929 TT: 'Although the motorcycle of today is as near perfection as human brains can make it at the moment, the day is yet far distant when designers will have nothing to learn from the TT races'. Indeed, designers still had much to learn, for while the 1920s had proved a fascinating era for TT racing, with many manufacturers fighting for victory, no single concern achieved real supremacy and success seemed to go in short-lived cycles. After their two Senior victories in 1926 and 1927, it was surprising that Norton machines did not feature in the top three in either the Junior (for which they had developed a camshaft engine) or Senior races in 1928 and 1929. And, although the fact was unknown to them at the time, Sunbeam's period of TT supremacy was over.

Status of the TT

Motorcycle racing was popular all over Europe in the 1920s and many teams who contested the TT races also competed in major events like the French, Swiss, Dutch and Belgium Grand Prix, using out-and-out racing machinery that by now owed less and less to the touring motorcycle. Manufacturers were pleased to advertise their successes in Continental events, but such wins did not have the status of an Isle of Man TT win, as a contemporary report explained: 'The Tourist Trophy races have a glamour about them which is not to be found in any similar event in the whole world, and the value of these races to designers and manufacturers of the modern motorcycle can scarcely be measured in terms of pounds, shillings and pence'. The TT had developed into the world's premier road race meeting, with the thirty-five races held between 1920 and 1929 providing victories for thirteen different makes and twenty-two riders. In the weeks following the event the motorcycle press was full of advertisements from firms such as Castrol, Pratt's, Dunlop and Fibrax advertising their successes and contributions to the races, so gaining publicity and increased sales of their products.

The popularity of the TT races owed much to the thrills to be obtained through both participating and spectating, but there was a price to pay for such high-speed activity and there were several rider fatalities during the 1920s.

The Future of the TT

Given the many favourable comments made about the Tourist Trophy races in the late 1920s, it is surprising to find editorial opinion in *Motor Cycle* after the 1929 event questioning the future of the races:

> Have we witnessed the last of those great sporting events, the TT motor cycle races? . . . As a sporting event the TT is magnificent, but – as we said last year, and as many others are now saying – the Tourist Trophy is not fulfilling its avowed purpose. The word 'Tourist' in its application to the Tourist Trophy Races is a misnomer, since the event is merely fostering the super-sporting motor cycle of the semi-racing type and endowing it with speed capabilities far in excess of ordinary requirements, and, more important still, to the exclusion of other desirable qualities. On reflection, it must be agreed that the time has come to call a halt. Actually, we have more speed than is necessary or desirable, so the question arises as to whether the TT be continued as a great sporting event, whether it be so modified that it is a true aid to development, or whether it be abandoned.

The piece concluded with the view that the races should be remodelled 'on lines which will sustain the enthusiasm of the public and at the same time advance motor cycle design'. It was a view that was no doubt heard by the organizers, but it was not one that they acted upon.

A New Decade

For the first time on record the overall number of motorcycles registered for use on the roads of Britain fell in 1930, being some 7,000

below that of the previous year. It reflected a depressed economy and a much reduced market for new machines, with makers cutting prices just to stay in business. However, the TT races continued to receive support from manufacturers, and approximately 140 entries were submitted for the 1930 event, spread over the now customary Senior (500cc), Junior (350cc) and Lightweight (250cc) classes. One change to previous arrangements was a reduction in the time allowed for practice. Instead of two complete weeks, riders now had nine early-morning sessions starting on a Thursday and continuing through the following week to finish on Saturday. Increases in speed meant reductions in lap times and the fastest riders could sometimes put in four laps in a session if they chose to. During practice each machine carried its rider's competition number on an oval plate at the front, with side-plates added for the race. Seniors had white numbers on a red background, Juniors had white on blue and Lightweight white on green. Riders also wore tie-on waistcoats bearing their riding numbers.

The roads comprising the TT course were much improved over those of the early 1920s, but they were still very ordinary roads that had to withstand the wear and tear of a growing amount of everyday local traffic and the effects of wet Manx winters that sometimes washed out sections of the Mountain road. The Manx highway authorities did their best to restore the surfaces before TT time, but one of the first questions asked by riders arriving for another year's racing was, 'how are the roads – better or worse than last year?', for they knew that their condition would affect both performance and safety. Surfacing and binding materials were not up to today's standards, and the edges of the roads accumulated lots of loose chippings. This was well before the advent of mechanical roadsweepers, and as the loose material was too much to sweep by hand over 37¾ miles, it was a major hazard that caused the downfall of many a rider who strayed off line. Race speeds had grown year-on-year through the 1920s (except when affected by bad weather), but with the roads still very bumpy and machines having virtually no suspension, most riders were forced to wear a supportive body-belt of the type now seen only in Motocross.

Finance and Foreigners

From the outset of the TT races the Manx Government incurred much indirect expenditure in support of the event, but it refused requests from the organizing ACU for direct financial support towards the costs of running the meeting in the 1920s. In 1930, however, it did provide a direct grant of £5,000, some £3,500 of which was allocated to attract more foreign competitors to the meeting. Nineteen nations were represented at the races, with entries from countries such as Austria, Belgium, Egypt, Hungary, Iraq, Jamaica, South Africa, Sweden, Australia and Japan. Despite the healthy number of foreign riders, virtually the whole entry was mounted on British single-cylinder machinery.

First prize in the Senior TT was increased to £200, although few of the foreign riders stood a chance of taking it as TT wins were still the preserve of experienced British racers, usually on 'works' machinery. Technically the winning rider did not receive the prize money, for the race regulations specified that it was paid to the entrant – usually a factory or dealer. The rider would have a contract with the entrant that, in the case of factory riders, guaranteed them a sum considerably greater than the race prize money if they came home first. Meanwhile, a few factories continued to invest money in the development of racing machinery as a means of capturing sales in a declining market, while others folded when unable to cope with the difficult trading conditions encountered in the early 1930s.

A Big Year for Rudge

Rudge had contested the TT races for many years, narrowly losing out on a win in the 1913 Senior, but being successful the following year when Cyril Pullin achieved the last win on a belt-drive machine. It was not until

Kenzo Tada came from Japan to race a Velocette in the 1930 TT and finish in a creditable thirteenth place. He later helped organize motorcycle sport in Japan.

1929 that the Coventry firm's name reappeared among the first three in a race, when Henry Tyrell-Smith took third place behind Dodson and Bennett in the 1929 Senior.

That podium finish by a Rudge in 1929 was the prelude to much greater achievements in 1930, when the company returned to the TT with 500cc machines similar to those used the previous year, but with 350s that were much improved and fitted with fully radial 4-valve heads operated by pushrods and complex transverse rockers. It was Tyrell-Smith who revealed the new Junior Rudge's TT potential when he broke the lap record in practice by half a minute – and that was from a standing start. Practice was not without problems, however, for the pistons on the Junior bikes kept cracking around the gudgeon pin. George Hack, the Rudge designer, calculated that the pistons would last eight laps at the TT before they failed, but as each rider had to do one steady pre-race running-in lap of a new piston and the race itself was over seven laps, confidence was not over-high in the Rudge camp before the Junior event, for everyone was aware that speed counted for nothing without reliability in such a long race.

On Junior day George Hack's calculations proved slightly pessimistic, for Rudge took the first three places at record race and lap speeds. Henry Tyrell-Smith was first man home, followed closely by Ernie Nott and Graham Walker, with Nott setting the new record lap speed of 72.20mph (116.19km/h).

Having swept the board in the Junior TT, it must have been a dream come true for Rudge when two days later they also took first and second places in the Senior with Wal Handley and Graham Walker. Handley, a last-minute addition to the team, broke both the race and lap records and became the first man to lap in less than thirty minutes – his best being 29 minutes 41 seconds, representing 76.28mph (122.76km/h). It was a victory that made him the only rider at that time to have won all four TT solo classes: Senior, Junior, Lightweight and Ultra-Lightweight.

While Rudge swept all before them at the 1930 TT, what became of the efforts of other recognized top runners like Velocette, AJS, Sunbeam and Norton? Velocette tried a longer stroke engine, which did not finish in the top six. AJS persisted with virtually unchanged chain-driven ohc engines in their 350cc (R7) and 500cc (R10) models but failed to shine, while Sunbeam relied on further tuning of their previous winning ohv engines. The latter were still quick, but not quick enough for victory, and Sunbeam had to settle for fourth and fifth places in the Senior, their machines ridden by Charlie Dodson and Tommy Bullus. Norton ran modified ohc engines designed by Joe Craig and Arthur Carroll, but could not match the Rudge machines for speed and their riders were handicapped by having only three-speed gearboxes. The best Norton placings were sixth in the Junior with Stanley Woods and third place in the Senior for Jimmy Simpson. It was not the start to a new decade that Norton had hoped for, but the fact that Jimmy Simpson had finished the race gave them grounds for encouragement, for Jimmy had a reputation for being notoriously hard on engines. As will be seen, Norton Motors' optimism was well founded.

Wal Handley sweeps round Creg ny Baa on his way to victory for Rudge in the 1930 Senior TT.

4   Norton Dominate

Joe Craig had been a successful racer and employee of Norton in the latter half of the 1920s, but he left them in 1928 when the Walter Moore-designed ohc racing engine went backwards in performance. Returning after Moore left for NSU in 1929, Craig took charge of the practical side of design and set about producing a new race engine with Arthur Carroll providing the engineering theory. Results achieved with the new engine in 1930 showed they were on the right track and by the time of the 1931 TT the Junior and Senior Norton race machines had, as well as the new engines, four-speed gearboxes with fully enclosed positive-stop gear change mechanism, forks and brakes of Norton manufacture (previous items were bought in) and other minor changes.

Whatever advances Norton had made, Rudge, the double TT winners, had not been idle and its several victories early in the 1931 season indicated that it was still the team to beat. But Craig knew that his Nortons were now very competitive, and to enhance Norton Motors' chances of success some of the best riders were engaged, arriving at the 1931 TT with a team comprising Jimmy Guthrie, Stanley Woods, Tim Hunt and Jimmy Simpson. Managed by Craig, the machines and men representing the Bracebridge Street factory were formidable opponents for the twenty other makes and 150 other riders entered for the meeting. Eight of those other makes were foreign, including NSU, Moto Guzzi and Husqvarna.

Factory teams and trade representatives usually tried to get settled into their garages and hotels a day or two before practice opened, which in 1931 was on Thursday 4 June. Former rider Reuben Harveyson represented Perry Chains and Lycett saddles, and advertised that he would be based at the Castle Mona Hotel. Mr Hill of Tecalemit (grease) was reported to have been busy with grease nipples and guns in many of the team garages, while Castrol reminded people of earlier TT successes by advertising in advance of the races that the Senior had been won fifteen times in succession on their oils.

Mixed Weather

In what some might say was a typical week of Manx weather, competitors had to cope with heavy mist, rain and strong winds in some practice sessions, while others were dry and sunny. Such sessions were still restricted to early mornings and that of Saturday 6 June was reported as 'The Worst Morning Ever' for weather. Despite the deplorable wet and foggy conditions, sixteen riders braved the elements, with several of them putting in two laps. In contrast, Monday morning offered almost perfect conditions and Jack Williams (Raleigh) was clocked at an average speed of 101.2mph (162.86km/h) over a measured mile at Sulby, while Tim Hunt (Norton) averaged 100.6mph (161.85km/h) at the same location.

The Norton team showed well in practice, with Tim Hunt setting the fastest lap in the Senior class on two occasions, while Jimmy Simpson and Stanley Woods vied for the

Tim Hunt (Norton) was both fast and successful at the 1931 TT.

fastest Junior lap, and Stanley bettered the lap record during the week. Encouraging as those practice performances were, after the permitted nine sessions Ernie Nott (Rudge) and Freddie Hicks (AJS) were also seen to be very fast in the Senior class and, although of no great concern to Nortons, Nott and Graham Walker were the fastest Lightweights on their 250cc Rudge machines. But performances in practice are difficult to evaluate, for riders and teams sometimes seek to conceal their true capabilities from the opposition. Norton's racing effort received the full support of its senior management, and Director Dennis Mansell, who was with the team on the island, later told how he secretly timed Norton riders and the opposition over the stretch from Kate's Cottage to Hillberry. Discovering that the Nortons were consistently fastest over this stretch was valuable information that the team was able to use in its race strategy. But although the Norton and Rudge factories were clear favourites to carry off the race wins in 1931, at the conclusion of practice press pundits found it difficult to forecast which individual rider would come home first in each of the three races (Lightweight, Junior, Senior).

The early 1930s saw much spectator interest in the TT with record crowds and vehicles coming to the island. One unusual item of concern was that with the growth in use of light aircraft, their pilots might try to fly the course at low altitude to view and obtain pho-tographs of the action. Just prior to race week the Air Ministry issued a notice to fliers requesting them not to overfly the course at less than 2,000ft.

The 1931 Races

The Monday of race week was blessed with good weather for what was expected to be a hotly contested Junior race. Jimmy Simpson (Norton) held the lead for the first four laps. After a slow start due to plug trouble, Tim Hunt (Norton) worked his way through the field to lie second. Hunt then took the lead on lap five and went on to win from Jimmie Guthrie (Norton), with Ernie Nott (Rudge) third. To Hunt went race and lap records, his best lap of 75.27mph (121.13km/h) being an impressive 3mph faster than the record set in 1930 by the then all-conquering Junior Rudges.

Rudge did achieve a popular victory in Wednesday's Lightweight race when 'heavy-weight' Graham Walker came home at the head of the field on his 250, after the leader for most of the race, Ernie Nott, experienced tappet troubles with his Rudge, which dropped him to fourth. Graham's first TT had been in 1920 and now, aged thirty-four, his win was watched from the Grandstand by his wife and young son Murray.

The Senior TT had been known as the 'Blue Riband' event for many years and it gave Norton the chance to make an emphatic

Rudge riders Graham Walker and Ernie Nott (seated) at the end of the 1931 Lightweight race.

The successful Norton team after their 1-2-3 victory in the 1931 Senior TT: winner Tim Hunt (30), second Jimmie Guthrie (20) and third Stanley Woods (16). Norton team-manager Joe Craig stands between Hunt and Woods.

statement of its superiority over other manufacturers by taking the first three places at record speeds with Tim Hunt, Jimmie Guthrie and Stanley Woods. The Nortons led home the Rudges of Nott and Walker. After becoming the first man to lap at over 80mph, Simpson was forced to retire the fourth 'works' Norton after a fall at Ballaugh Bridge due to a grabbing front brake. It was a race that earned the headline 'England Defeats All-Comers', for, apart from Ted Mellors (NSU) in sixth place, the remainder of the foreign challenge faded during the race. Indeed, by the end of the week it was clear that TT supremacy lay with British men and machines in all classes. Ordinary motorcyclists who were inspired to emulate the members of the winning Norton race team could, for 1932, buy road-going replicas of the race machines, which the factory called the Model 30 International (490cc) and the Model 40 International (348cc), while the cheaper CJ and CS camshaft sports models remained available.

Reduced Entries

Although no-one could come up with a valid reason why, entries for the 1932 meeting were down by slightly over one-third (to ninety-five) on the 1931 figures. The quality was still there with 'works' entries, trade support and

This photograph of Stanley Woods gives a side view of Norton's successful racer.

top riders; although there was reduced foreign interest, Jawa brought four-stroke machines to contest the Senior under the guidance of celebrated Brooklands star George Patchett.

It was inevitable that the reduction in entries had pessimists questioning the future of the TT, but a long article in *Motor Cycle and Cycle Trader* offered a careful analysis of the many factors that combined to make up the TT meeting. It recognized that the nature of the races could change significantly if manufacturers and the trade withdrew support, but it did not think they would, and so concluded

61

with the encouraging words: 'We think, therefore, that those who feel anxious for the future of the races can safely rid themselves of their apprehensions'.

While the Island prepared itself with enthusiasm for a royal visit from Prince George, who would watch the Senior race, riders got on with the business of practising and bringing their machines to race pitch. They could have done without what a local newspaper described as 'the biggest adventure' of the second morning's practice, which involved 'the appearance on the Course of 5 or 6 horses'. The beasts had been found loose between Union Mills and Glen Vine before the first rider came through and were herded into a field beside the course. Freeing themselves after practice started, they regained the course and went clattering through Crosby, increasing speed with every rider that passed them. Making it to the top of the hill before The Highlander, they were eventually rounded up by two young spectators.

Stanley's Double

Although pushed hard in the Junior race by the Rudges of Ernie Nott and Henry Tyrell-Smith, it was the Norton-mounted Irish rider Stanley Woods who came home first in that opening race of the 1932 TT meeting, adding 3mph to the average race speed and the same amount to the lap record. Stanley led from start to finish, and while his three Norton team-mates all occupied top-three placings at some stage of the race, it was left to the Dubliner to keep the Rudges at bay. After its sweeping successes of 1930 the Rudge concern was finding it difficult to record another win and, although there were no Nortons in the Lightweight event to worry about, they even had to accept second and third positions in the mid-week race for 250s, where Leo Davenport set record speeds to win on his New Imperial ahead of Graham Walker and Wal Handley.

An unusual view of Ballaugh Bridge in 1932, as it is tackled by Ernie Knott (Rudge).

The four-man Norton team started as clear favourites for the Senior event and did not disappoint its followers. On machinery that was lighter than the previous year, but otherwise subject to only minor improvements, the team matched its 1931 performance by taking the first three places to record another hat trick with Stanley Woods, Jimmy Guthrie and Jimmy Simpson finishing 1-2-3, at record-breaking speeds. The only disappointment for Norton was that the previous year's winner, Tim Hunt, was forced to retire after falling at Quarter Bridge on the first lap. When the race got under way at 10am on the Friday morning, Jimmy Simpson held the lead for the first two laps and no doubt had thoughts of a possible win. Despite setting the fastest lap of the race at 81.50mph (131.16km/h), however, Jimmy was overtaken first by Woods and then by Guthrie after his front brake cable snapped. In his ten-year TT racing career to that point, Simpson had started in more than twenty races, leading many of them, set new speeds (first man to lap at 60, 70 and 80mph), taken lap records, but suffered many breakdowns. It really seemed as though he was destined not to win on the Island.

Why so Named?

Handley's Corner
Previously a spot with no particular name, the tricky left-right bend soon after the 11th Milestone, now known as Handley's, earned its name when Wal Handley crashed there during the Senior race of 1932. Geoff Davison tells in *The Story of the TT* how in the crash Handley 'damaged his spine and lay for some seconds in the road, unable to move and at the mercy of any approaching machine; and furthermore his Rudge was alongside of him, with the engine roaring away and petrol flowing all over the place, so that Walter himself was soaked in it'. Disaster was avoided when help quickly arrived. When Davison visited Wal in hospital a few hours later 'he was as cheerful as ever and in his own inimitable style was describing it as a humorous incident'!

Wal Handley made his TT debut in the 1922 Lightweight race on a 250cc O.K. Between 1922 and 1934 he rode in twenty-eight TT races, taking four victories.

Almost Another Sidecar Race

The organizers included a race for sidecars in the 1933 TT programme, but although the press were supportive – for there was talk of some of the top solo riders adding a third

wheel and competing – a report of the time said: 'The Trade were against the Sidecar race and set their faces against it'. With only eight entries from three-wheeled competitors, the proposed race was scrapped and the report concluded: 'It is unlikely that this once popular feature of TT week will ever be revived'.

The decision was not well received by those who had prepared outfits to race. One of them was Tommy Hatch, who agreed to ride a Scott Special outfit built by large Liverpool dealers A.E. Reynolds. Hatch reported that he had 'selected a champion gymnast as my passenger'. Another contender was Alan Bruce, who had a JAP-engined Vincent HRD fitted with a banking sidecar ready to go. Thwarted by the decision to cancel, Bruce told 'Kirkstone', the motor cycling correspondent of the British daily *News Chronicle*, that he would claim the right to attempt to break the sidecar speed record over the course before one of the races. The record stood at 57mph (91.7km/h) and Bruce confidently expected to average 67mph (107.8km/h). Unfortunately, the organizers did not consider that Bruce had any right to make a record-breaking attempt, so the record remained intact.

Questions?

The TT races attracted attention and comment from all over the world, and the well-informed Manx press also had views on the races that ran on its doorstep. The *Isle of Man Weekly Times* made a couple of pertinent points in its pages on the run-up to the 1933 TT. Foreign entries totalled twenty-three and most TT fans felt that the presence of men and machines from abroad added interest to the races. However, the paper asked if the Island was getting value-for-money from the monies it paid towards the expenses of foreigners, saying that 'none of them had the remotest chance of winning'. Having questioned the worth of the foreign entry, it then pointed an accusing finger at the successful Norton team with: 'While we admire the Nortons, we doubt if their repeated successes are in the best interest of the races'. Such provocative comments hardly seemed likely to benefit the island or the TT but, right or wrong, the Manx press has never been afraid to speak its mind on the topic of the races, for it is a subject that, in one form or another, affects every resident.

A Double Treble

The question of whether domination of the major TT classes by Norton served to discourage other manufacturers from entering was aired in other publications, but with the entry for 1933 matching that of 1932 there did not seem to be too strong a case. It was certainly not a topic that the Bracebridge Street manufacturer troubled itself with, as it proved by taking the first three places in both the Junior and Senior events. It was Stanley Woods, at the peak of his form, who came home first in both races, setting new race and lap records in the process. While there were other Nortons competing, it was the 'works' riders who accompanied Stanley onto the rostrum, with Tim Hunt and Jimmie Guthrie taking second and third in the Junior. In the Senior, Jimmy Simpson was second, Tim Hunt third and Jimmy Guthrie fourth, putting all four 'works' Nortons firmly at the head of the field. Since before the time that the TT moved to the Mountain Course Norton's advertising had described its motorcycles as 'Unapproachable'; in 1933 no one could deny the truth of the slogan, for its dominance also extended to Continental Grand Prix, where, often riding to orders as to who should come home first, its four-man team won most of the events.

Rudge was unable to commit the finance or technical input to its racing effort of previous years and there was no Rudge in the top ten in the Junior of 1933, while Ernie Nott's fifth place was their best result in the Senior. Although not a serious challenge to the

'works' Nortons at that stage, Velocette machines put in some excellent performances, giving a hint of what was to come from the Hall Green manufacturer in future years.

Although TT success had eluded them for a few years, Velocette was proud to include this transfer on the tanks of its road-going machines in the 1930s.

The Lightweight race offered a far more open contest with Excelsiors, New Imperials, Cottons and Rudges all considered capable of winning. On the almost straight from the drawing board Excelsior 'Mechanical Marvel' models, Wal Handley and Sid Gleave set the pace during the race, and at the finish it was Gleave in first place, followed by Charlie Dodson (New Imperial) and Charlie Manders (Rudge). The winner's average speed was slightly up on 1932 at 71.59mph (115.21km/h) but the lap record was not broken.

At Last!

Having raced every year since 1922 in Senior, Junior and one Sidecar race, the speedy Jimmy Simpson finally achieved his sought-after TT win in 1934. It was gained under slightly unusual circumstances, for not only did his win come in the Lightweight class – at the first time of racing a 250 on the Island – but he did not rush off flat-out from the start in his customary manner. Indeed, mounted on a Rudge, it was the third lap before he moved into first place, a position he held to come home more than three minutes ahead of similarly mounted 250 runners Ernie Nott and Graham Walker in wet and misty conditions, recording one of the most popular of TT victories. In a fitting tribute to a man who set the fastest lap in eight TT races, today's award to the overall fastest solo rider at the TT is named the Jimmy Simpson Trophy.

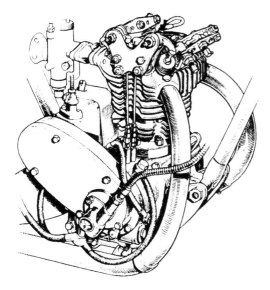

The 250cc Rudge engine that gained first, second and third place in the 1934 Lightweight TT.

The races of 1934 were good ones for Jimmy, because he also took second place in the Junior and Senior events on his Nortons. However, having taken an appointment in Shell's competition department at the end of 1933, he decided, at the age of thirty-five, to retire from racing after the TT. The two big classes in 1934 were won by Jimmie Guthrie for Norton, so leaving the name of Stanley Woods missing from the winners for the first time in several years. Stanley had been unhappy with some of the riding-to-order requirements of Norton (setting up his own signalling system on the Island to be better informed) and, after receiving a good financial offer to ride Husqvarnas, he decided towards the end of 1933 that he would switch to the Swedish marque in 1934.

Husqvarna's 1934 TT effort suffered a setback even before it left Sweden prior to the event, for as a lorry loaded with 350 and 500cc V-twin racers was being loaded onto a ship at Gothenburg, a cable failed and the lorry fell to the dockside, finishing upside down. The bikes went back to the factory for quick repairs and the three Husqvarna riders – Stanley Woods, Ernie Nott and Gunnar Kalen – were late receiving their race bikes. Nott was the only one with Senior and Junior Husqvarnas; although forced to retire in the Senior, he took a fine third place in the Junior, some six minutes behind the winner.

Those who wondered if Stanley Woods had done the right thing in leaving Norton to ride for Husqvarna had their question answered when Stanley showed his machine's quality by holding second place for much of the Senior race. Setting the fastest lap at 80.49mph (129.53km/h) in damp conditions, his threat to leader Jimmie Guthrie ended on the last lap when he ran out of fuel less than 10 miles from the finish. It was the nearest that Norton had been to defeat for several years, and it created a sense of expectation among TT fans and a feeling that the all-conquering Nortons could be challenged in future events, particularly as Walter Rusk had taken a Velocette into a fine third place in the Senior.

A Year to Remember

The 1935 TT meeting did not get off to the best of starts due to a general strike on the Island, but luckily it was called off just as most of the racers and officials, as well as tyre, petrol, oil and other trade representatives, arrived for practice. A few of the earliest arrivals had to carry their own bags to their hotels and eat cold meals by the light of candles, but most were spared such inconvenience.

The total entry of 107 comprised forty-one Senior, thirty-seven Junior and twenty-nine Lightweights, with a strong foreign challenge coming from Moto Guzzi (5), NSU (6), Jawa (5), DKW (4) and Terrot (2). The Norton team was based at the Castle Mona and was much changed, its members being Jimmie Guthrie, Walter Rusk and Johnny Duncan. Apart from those works entries there were

only three other Nortons in the Senior race: 'Crasher' White on a factory-supported machine, plus privateers Bill Beevers and Chris Tattersall. Norton entries were also outnumbered by the small Vincent-HRD company, which had made its TT debut only the previous year, for this Stevenage concern had four works entries using engines of its own design and manufacture and also entered three JAP-engined machines on behalf of their engine maker, J.A. Prestwich. For its second year on the Island, Vincent-HRD based itself in garages at the Falcon Cliff Hotel, along with the New Imperial and NSU camps.

Over half of the Junior entry were Velocette-mounted, which showed the worth of the company's policy of marketing their over-the-counter KTT racer for purchase by the ordinary rider. There were also Velocette 'works' entries for Wal Handley, Ernie Nott, Harold Newman and Les Archer in the Junior and for the first three of those in the Senior. The magazine *Motor Cycling* described the Velocettes as beautifully prepared, adding 'a black and gold finish takes a lot of beating'. Experienced TT riders George Rowley and Henry Tyrell-Smith had 'works' AJS entries in both Junior and Senior classes, as did up-and-coming former Manx Grand Prix (MGP)

runner Harold Daniell. The eight makes represented in the Lightweight race saw entries on Excelsior, New Imperial, Rudge, Cotton, Terrot, Moto Guzzi, DKW and CTS.

Stanley Woods's hopes of bettering his performance of 1934 with a Husqvarna were foiled by lack of entries from the Swedish concern, but he turned to the manufacturer of another V-twin, the Italian Moto Guzzi, with which to mount his Senior TT challenge in 1935. Stanley had ridden a 250cc single-cylinder Guzzi to fourth place in the 1934 Lightweight race and in 1935 he had entries on the red machines in both the Lightweight and the Senior, as did his team-mate Omobono Tenni. Based at the Majestic Hotel in Onchan, the Moto Guzzis, together with the Vincent-HRDs, were among the few machines of the day fitted with rear suspension.

After more than a week of cold early-morning practice sessions, honours were divided in all classes among the top runners from Norton, Moto Guzzi, Velocette and New Imperial. While no clear favourites emerged, only the teams themselves really knew if they were showing their best performances, or if they were holding something back. While the experienced top runners headed the practice leaderboards, those who were new to the Mountain Course put in many extra road-learning miles over open roads outside of the official practice periods. A report in *Motor Cycle* noted that 'The DKW riders are out all day on their touring machines . . . Tenni takes a Guzzi out every day . . . Steinbach on the NSU does six laps in the morning and six in the afternoon every day'. Such application was very necessary if they were to be able to ride the course at racing speeds. Inevitably some newcomers tried too hard too soon and there were accidents in practice, including one to the experienced Wal Handley, and they reduced the eventual number of race starters.

Travelling Marshals

New to the TT organization in 1935 were motorcycle-mounted Travelling Marshals, whose job was to provide pre-race information to the Clerk of the Course on weather and road conditions, and to speed to race incidents and assist the static marshals at any point on the 37¾ miles of the Mountain Course. In their first year of operation they were on duty only on race-days, but this was later extended to include practice sessions. Former TT riders Vic Brittain and Arthur Simcock were the first two Travelling Marshals. They, and those who followed, became an indispensable part of the organization, being described by several of those who carried out Clerk of the Course duties in the control tower at the grandstand as acting as their 'eyes and ears' out on the course.

Another new arrangement for 1935 was that riders were permitted to warm their engines before the start. Most did this by riding up and down a defined section of the Glencrutchery Road near the grandstand. The consequent aromas of Castrol 'R' that wafted over the crowds no doubt added to the pre-race atmosphere, as did the newly introduced parade of riders to the grid behind Boy Scouts carrying the flags of the competing nations.

Trying to catch some of that atmosphere was a film crew shooting crowd scenes for the George Formby film *No Limit*, based loosely around the TT, but the finished product must have given a somewhat distorted view to those not familiar with the races.

Familiar and Unfamiliar Results

For all the talk of a serious foreign challenge in 1935, the first race of the week – the Junior – saw a familiar Norton 1-2-3, with Jimmie Guthrie leading home Walter Rusk and John 'Crasher' White in damp conditions. The Lightweight TT, however, run on the Wednesday in poor weather, provided emphatic proof that there was strength in the foreign challenge, for Stanley Woods on his small Moto Guzzi rode to a comfortable win, almost three minutes ahead of Henry Tyrell-Smith (Rudge), with Ernie Nott (Rudge) another four minutes behind. It was the first TT victory by a foreign machine since the Indian 1-2-3 of 1911. Although the Lightweight race was not as highly regarded as the Junior and Senior classes, Stanley's 500cc Moto Guzzi had been right up with the fastest runners in Senior practice and racegoers looked forward to Friday's 'Blue Riband' event with eager anticipation.

Postponed

Previously every TT had gone ahead, whatever the weather, but for the first time ever the organizers decided to postpone the Senior race due to adverse weather conditions. With the growth in speeds, the occurrence of several serious accidents in poor conditions, and the round-the-course information coming in from the new Travelling Marshals – Vic Brittain reported on the Friday morning that 'at no point on the Mountain was visibility more than 20 yards' – the sensible decision was taken to postpone the race until Saturday.

The decision caused a degree of chaos on the crowded Island, for there were no contingency arrangements in place to cope with the

A Sensational Race

Based on past performances, practice times and informed comment, most people expected the Senior race to be a contest between Norton team-leader Jimmie Guthrie (starting at number 1) on his finely honed single-cylinder racer, and the impressive but less well-known Italian twin-cylinder Moto Guzzi of multiple former winner Stanley Woods (starting 14½ minutes later at number 30). Guthrie was backed by a strong Norton team, but Woods was the lone Moto Guzzi runner, since his team-mate Omobono Tenni, described as 'the most brilliant debutant the Island has ever welcomed', was out of the race after a fall in the Lightweight.

In what was to be one of the most dramatic of TT races, Jimmie Guthrie went flat-out from the start, seemingly confident in his own ability and the reliability of his Norton to withstand such punishment for seven laps and 264½ gruelling miles. In contrast, Woods, who experienced major mechanical failure with the Guzzi in several pre-TT races, went off at a slower pace (although they both broke the lap record from a standing start!) The deficit at the end of the first lap was 28 seconds between Guthrie and Woods, with Walter Rusk (Norton) actually holding second place just one second ahead of Woods. Guthrie increased his lead to fifty-two seconds by the end of the third lap. Although Woods moved into second and was aware of the growing gap (he later told how his private telephone stations and timing staff worked perfectly to supply him with race information), he concentrated on working harder on the bends rather than risk overworking the engine, restricting himself to Carlo Guzzi's prescribed 7,400rpm for the first two laps, increasing to 7,700rpm on lap three.

Seldom, if ever, does a rider achieve a perfect racing lap on the Mountain Course, for mistakes are made, slower riders prove difficult to pass, and so time is lost. Woods became slightly discouraged by several major hold-ups to his race progress and by the way that Guthrie, who by starting at number 1 had a clear road, extended his lead. However, vastly experienced at the TT, he kept his head. As he left his pit after refuelling at the end of the third lap, Woods weighed up his strategy for the remaining four laps.

With his signalling stations telling him that he was slowly eating into Guthrie's lead on laps five and six, Woods's mind was busy with mental arithmetic calculating the number of seconds that he had gained and the number that he needed to catch the flying Scotsman. Although growing in confidence, he saw that half-way around the sixth lap he was still twenty-nine seconds down on Guthrie, with a threatening Rusk (Norton) and Duncan (Norton) lying third and fourth.

Woods had told his pit attendant to be prepared for him stopping at the end of the sixth lap for a possible 'splash and dash' top-up of fuel. His attendant duly set about his preparations in good time, even before Guthrie came through to start his last lap. This was something that the Norton people must have noticed. Whether it lulled them into signalling Guthrie to hold his pace is not known – and whether Guthrie could have increased his already record-breaking pace is doubtful. Woods made his decision not to stop at the end of the sixth lap just after he rounded Governor's Bridge, saying: 'Glencrutchery Road, and a quick glance into my petrol tank to make sure that all is well'. All was well and he roared past the pits without stopping. For the first time in the race he allowed his Guzzi to achieve maximum revs in third, before changing into top beyond the pits where he got the message from his private signalling station that Guthrie's lead was down to twenty-one seconds. That figure had been measured at his previous signalling point at Sulby, and his mental calculations as he plunged down Bray Hill at the start of his last lap suggested that it should now be less.

Would Guthrie have received a last-lap message to speed up? Woods did not know, but he did know that his last lap had to be an all-out effort and he let the revs climb to just under 8,000. Giving it everything, it was with massive disappointment that he discovered from his signalling board at Sulby that he had actually been twenty-six seconds behind Guthrie at the start of the last lap, not the thirteen or so that he had calculated. Not a man to give up, Woods let the Guzzi rev to 8,000 (118mph) on the Sulby Straight and thereafter revved it to its maximum on the stretch to Ramsey and up the Mountain climb. Coming down the Mountain he did not pay too much attention to the ever-climbing engine revolutions, for he was flat on the tank and seeking to take every corner at the fastest possible speed. Barely conscious of the massed spectators waving him on, Woods knew that, for all his efforts, he had to exercise an element of caution on the tricky bends that ran from the foot of the Mountain, through Hillberry, Cronk ny Mona, Signpost, Bedstead, The Nook and Governor's Bridge to the finish, but he was desperate to gain time.

Flashing over the finishing line, applying the brakes hard and turning back into the Paddock, Woods was smothered by jubilant Italians. The starting interval between him and Guthrie had been 14 minutes 30 seconds and the gap at the finish was 14 minutes 26 seconds. Woods had won by four seconds with an incredible last lap of 26 minutes 10 seconds, a record-breaking speed of 86.53mph (139.35km/h).

Most post-race pictures show riders smiling for the camera, but in this one Stanley Woods shows the strain of racing to victory in 1935 on his 500cc Moto Guzzi.

effects of a postponement. Cafés and pubs filled with damp spectators seeking to dry out and consider their transport and accommodation arrangements, which had been thrown into confusion. As well as the thousands of spectators who were over for the entire race week, the Isle of Man Steam Packet Company landed an additional 11,000 race fans on the Island before 7.30am on Senior race day. As there were only four telephone lines from the Island to the mainland they were swamped with people trying to make new arrangements. Not all could, and many disappointed fans had to leave without seeing the big race.

Special approvals had to be obtained to close the roads for running the race on Saturday and, at a time when most people worked at least half the day, local marshals found it difficult to get time off work to man the course. Early inspections on Saturday morning had Travelling Marshal Arthur Simcock reporting poor visibility at the Bungalow. Aware of the considerable responsibility attached to his weather assessment, he later reported that, although visibility was still restricted, he did not consider that it would affect rider safety. The decision was taken for the Senior to go ahead, although injuries sustained by some riders in practice and the need for other competitors to honour commitments elsewhere meant that the number of starters was reduced, and only twenty-eight of the forty-one entries came to the line.

Whoops!

Few people had thought that Stanley Woods could pull back twenty-six seconds on Jimmie Guthrie on the last lap of that 1935 Senior TT. Remember, they were almost fifteen minutes apart on the road, and when Jimmy crossed the finishing line, impatient radio commentators, organizers, photographers and the Norton team were all keen to get on with the victory celebrations. It was only after much congratulatory shaking of hands, the broadcast of eulogies to Guthrie and Norton over the public-address system and the taking of celebratory photographs, that news came through of Stanley's win. It was one that caused an all-round reddening of faces of those involved in the premature celebrations of a Norton victory.

While it is only natural for spectators and the press to concentrate their attentions on the winner (or supposed winner!), there were other fine performances in the Senior. Taking just under 3 hours 10 minutes for his race, Walter Rusk (Norton) finished third and John Duncan (Norton) was fourth. The first all-foreign combination was Otto Steinbach (NSU) in fifth, followed in sixth by Ted Mellors (NSU); the latter pair of entries show that other manufacturers as well as Moto Guzzi were seeking to challenge Britain's domination of the TT races.

Although no real threat to the leaders, the Vincent-HRD concern must have been pleased to get five of its seven entries to the finish in only its second year at the TT, boosting the company's reputation and sales.

Lessons Learnt

One year before the momentous 1935 Senior race, several experienced TT men had been asked by one of the weekly magazines to forecast the future of racing machinery. Graham Walker saw multi-cylinders, unit-construction and enclosure as ideals, Stanley Woods spoke of multis and supercharging, Charlie Dodson multis and spring frames, while Tyrell-Smith also thought the future lay with multis. In those days, the term multi was used for any machine of more than one cylinder. Of course, not every company could, or wanted to meet all such ideals, but the winning Moto Guzzi met several of them – twin-cylinders, unit-construction of engine and gearbox, rear springing – leaving the British motorcycle industry to contemplate if they were the reasons for its defeat by the Italian invader.

Technical Progress

It would be wrong to suggest that the British motorcycle industry had not improved its products during the first half of the 1930s. The TT was still regarded by manufacturers as a proving-ground for new developments, a fact appreciated by the buying public, who recognized the worth of strong (not necessarily winning) performances over the demanding Mountain Course, even though there were a few who claimed that the TT no longer had a major influence on the design of road-going machines. The early 1930s had seen advances in metallurgy that saw growing use of alloys for improved heat-shedding, lightness and durability. They were sometimes used to produce

items like aluminium-bronze heads, or to give aluminium finning around a steel barrel, but were also used as direct replacements, as with elektron crankcases, hubs and alloy wheel-rims, with engine internals occasionally utilizing aluminium components.

All aspects of racing machinery were subject to experimentation and improvement. It became common for previously exposed valve-gear to be enclosed, the steels in use for frame tubing and such were improved and pressed steel frames were tried. Megaphone exhausts came into use, twin carburettors were used in experiments on single-cylinder machines, supercharging was tried, rear suspension proved its worth but was slow to be accepted, and the Cross concern utilized its own form of rotary-valve and oil/water cooling.

Riders had customarily supplemented the standard road-going saddle with a 'bum-pad' on the rear mudguard, which better allowed them to adopt a race posture. In the mid-1930s many adopted an elongated seat instead of the two separate fittings, and manufacturers slowly began to adopt rear suspension.

Beyond technical developments, an important topic that came to the fore in 1935 was the susceptibility of the Mountain Course to bad weather (the proverbial 'Mist on the Mountain'), which meant that even if the poor conditions extended for only a few miles over the high ground the whole circuit could be put out of use. The pessimists correctly forecast that the first TT postponement of 1935 was the prelude to others, and *Motor Cycle* asked 'whether it is not time that the ACU gave up the Mountain Circuit?' In his book *TT Thrills*, the respected Laurie Cade mentions that in the mid-1930s:

> The Manx Highways Board did in fact survey and produce an entirely new course, measuring twenty miles; this was claimed to have an enormous advantage in that it did not traverse the mountains, and so was not subject to the Mantle of Mona, that quickly-arising

mist which sometimes enveloped the high roads.

As the 1936 TT approached it became clear that there was to be no immediate change from the Mountain Course, as the TT programme explained: 'Although considerable controversy arose following the 1935 races, the ACU, for various reasons, has decided for this year at least, to utilise again the course that has been used for every post-war race – known throughout the world as the Mountain Course.'

Spectators

Riding on the excitement of the 1935 races, spectators from all over Europe flocked to the Island in 1936, with many foreign visitors keen to see if their riders, such as Tenni, Steinbach and Geiss, could do even better.

Opened the previous year, the Mersey Tunnel gave easier access to the Isle of Man boats to those approaching Liverpool from the south. However, one persistent difficulty for all motorcycle-riding visitors to the TT was the Steam Packet Company's regulation that petrol tanks had to be pumped dry before loading for the unavoidable boat crossing. *Motor Cycle* publicized this requirement and highlighted a service for RAC members with the words:

> Riders who are taking their machines over to the Island for the TT will be pleased to hear that the usual arrangements have been made by the RAC at Liverpool, Douglas and Fleetwood. RAC guides will be in attendance at these ports, equipped with quick-acting suction-pumps for emptying the petrol tanks – tanks must be drained dry of petrol before they are taken on the boats. Riders will be given a voucher which will entitle them on arrival on the other side to a small quantity of petrol, to enable them to ride to the nearest garage under power.

Riders who were not members of the RAC had their tanks pumped dry but were left to fend for themselves on landing. There was also a requirement for every rider to take out temporary registration of his bike before using it on the Island's roads by way of an Exemption Registration Certificate. The cost for this was 2/6 (12½p) and there was a need for a temporary driving licence costing 1/- (5p).

At peak times the Steam Packet boats were completely crammed with bikes and bodies. Most of the bikes made the crossing on the open decks, with road machines often roped to adjacent competition machines that were destined for the races, for it was still the time when few factories used vans to transport bikes to the Island. Unfortunately, despite spectator enthusiasm and the effort made by everyone concerned with the races to get there, total entries for 1936 were only eighty-five, of which a mere twenty-four were for the Senior.

Consistency

Amid signs that British manufacturers were heeding both the 'words of the wise' and the racing lessons of 1935, unit construction New Imperials were entered in the Lightweight TT, while there were 4-cylinder supercharged AJS models for George Rowley and Harold Daniell in the Senior, plus experimental supercharged singles from Vincent-HRD, which promised much but reverted to normal aspiration for the race. Norton's racing efforts were mostly paid for by monies from Castrol oils and for 1936 the company chose to continue with its proven single-cylinder racers, although it did adopt a basic form of plunger rear suspension on the 'works' entries of Jimmie Guthrie, John 'Crasher' White and MGP winner Freddie Frith.

The Norton engines had slight alterations to bore and stroke (the '500' going from 490 to 499cc). They also had increased finning to the engines, and were fitted with larger diameter brakes. Experimental double overhead

Jimmie Guthrie outside the Norton team garage during practice week in 1936 shows the new plunger rear suspension.

camshaft engines were tried in practice but were considered to have had insufficient development time to be used at the 1936 TT.

While Norton honed their race machinery and their experience by contesting the TT every year, such consistency was lacking on the part of some manufacturers. Despite its successes in 1935, Moto Guzzi did not return in 1936 because Italy was busy waging war in Abyssinia. This meant that Stanley Woods was forced to look elsewhere for machinery and in 1936 he was entered on a DKW in the Lightweight and on ever-improving Velocettes in the Junior and Senior events. The German DKW concern claimed to be the biggest motorcycle manufacturer in the world at the time. Its TT machine was a two-stroke with a

Wakefield Patent CASTROL is a better oil — so we use it

Freddy Frith   *Jimmie Guthrie.*

The famous NORTON riders

Norton teamsters Freddie Frith and Jimmie Guthrie appeared on these advertising cards issued by Castrol in the mid-1930s.

piston-pump form of forced induction, while the four-stroke Velocettes came with new pivoted-fork rear suspension aided by oleomatic units providing air springing and oil damping.

Early Risers

In 1936 practice sessions were still restricted to early mornings. For some race officials this meant getting up at 3am to prepare for such tasks as closing roads. For riders, mechanics, factory personnel and keen spectators a slightly later wakening was acceptable, and an unusual service offered in the advertising of the Falcon Cliff Hotel was 'guaranteed practice calls at 3.45am, with refreshments'. A report of an early practice in 1936 told of Jack (C.J.) Williams being first in the queue of starters at 4.15am with his 500cc Vincent-HRD. When the course inspection and road-closing car arrived back at the start he was told 'good visibility, lots of wind and millions of rabbits'. He was first man away, at 4.33am, knowing full well that the bark from his exhaust would awaken many nearby residents and hoping that it would also clear the course of rabbits.

Upon completion of their lap or laps riders would adjourn to a refreshment tent at the rear of the grandstand where they would find hot cocoa or coffee supplied by Cadbury's or Dunlop. In the chill of the early morning, riders, mechanics, factory executives, trade representatives, journalists and sponsors rubbed shoulders in the damp and cigarette smoke-filled air. It was a place where first-hand information could be exchanged, machine performances discussed, sponsorship deals negotiated, plenty of tall tales told and much gossip exchanged. In the words of well-known competitor Phil Heath: 'Practising was great fun. There was nothing to beat the excitement of a couple of laps in good weather with the bike running well and the prospect of a chinwag and hot cup of cocoa at the end'.

Riders take refreshment after early-morning practice.

Lightweight Variety

The 1936 meeting saw the Lightweight TT attract the greatest number of entries with thirty-four riders competing on ten different makes of machine. Having been very influential in this class in the early 1930s, the Rudge concern had managed to weather severe financial difficulties but it could no longer afford to support a race team and only one privately entered 250cc machine carried the Coventry firm's name on its tank. Other entries were mounted on New Imperial, Excelsior, Cotton, O.K.-Supreme and, worryingly for those British makes, there were three 'works' DKWs that proved very quick in practice.

With the race postponed from Wednesday to Thursday owing to poor weather conditions, thirty-one riders presented themselves for the 11am start. All races had moved from a 10 to 11 o'clock start-time in order to allow more time for mist to clear from the Mountain. Also, as an aid to visibility in poor conditions, a yellow line was painted along the middle of the Mountain Road from the Gooseneck to Creg ny Baa, while the flattening and widening of Ballig Bridge was believed to have saved riders between three and five seconds a lap.

Few were surprised when the talented and vastly experienced Stanley Woods (DKW) took an early lead in the Lightweight race, but they were impressed to see newly married Bob Foster (New Imperial) holding second place, for Bob had much less experience over the Mountain Course. Woods was well ahead of the other DKW riders, but Foster had Jack Williams (New Imperial) and Henry Tyrell-Smith (Excelsior) chasing him for second place. Foster moved ahead of Woods on the third lap when the DKW rider stopped out on the course to replace a plug. Both men refuelled at the end of the third lap and, catching spectators by surprise, the surviving DKW riders, Woods and Geiss, stopped again at the end of the fourth lap to top up their thirsty two-strokes for the three-lap run through to the finish. Quite the noisiest machines to have been heard at the TT, *Motor Cycling* mentioned the DKW of Geiss 'going like a scalded cat – and making quite as much noise!' Although Woods regained the lead for the fourth and fifth laps he had further plug trouble and that allowed Foster back into the lead. Passing his pit at the start of his seventh and last lap, Stanley gave a brief thumbs-down to his crew. Foster, still believing that the speedy Stanley might catch him, rode to the limit of his own and his machine's performance to take a very popular, record-breaking victory, so recovering the Lightweight Tourist Trophy for Britain. With Woods forced to retire on the Mountain during the last lap, Foster had five minutes in hand over second-place Tyrell-Smith (Excelsior), but

73

the latter was only three seconds ahead of Geiss (DKW).

With unit-construction and gear-driven primary drive (as on the company's light-weight roadsters), Bob Foster's machine broke fresh ground for a British racing machine, moving New Imperial Motors Ltd to advertise its TT success with the statement: 'Unit-Construction is the most up-to-date feature in modern motorcycle design'. Unfortunately, the company was not able to advertise similar success with its V-twin in the Senior, where 'Ginger' Wood was forced to retire on the last lap when lying in fifth place, and the New Imperial racing team folded later in 1936.

In both big classes at the 1936 TT Norton headed the practice leader-board, but some experienced observers felt that Veloce Ltd stood a chance of victory in the Junior, where riders of its Velocette models were Stanley Woods and Ernie Thomas. But on race-day it

was Norton machinery that led the way home, with former MGP winner (but first-timer at the TT) Freddie Frith winning at record speed from his team-mate 'Crasher' White, and with Ted Mellors (Velocette) third. Although Jimmie Guthrie led the race for the first four laps and looked set to win, a stop near Hill-berry to refit a drive chain cost him time and created a clash with the organizers over whether he did or did not receive outside assistance in restarting. It led to the submission of an official protest from the Norton camp that was somewhat unsatisfactorily resolved by allowing Guthrie to retain his fifth finishing place but being paid the same prize money as White in second place.

Guthrie made no mistakes *en route* to winning the Senior, which he led throughout despite being closely pursued by Stanley Woods (Velocette). In what was the Velocette company's best Senior TT performance to date, Stanley failed by just eighteen seconds to catch the flying Scotsman, although in doing so he set the fastest lap of the race and beat his own record of the previous year. He was also left wondering what might have been, had his Velo' not developed an intermittent misfire on the last lap that knocked the edge off his speed. So, in 1936 single-cylinder machines again dominated the Senior; AJS's attempt at 'progress' with its supercharged 4-cylinder racers was unsuccessful, for the mounts of Rowley and Daniell were heavy, did not handle well and were plagued with carburation troubles.

WINS

THE

Lightweight

T. T.

1st

A. R. FOSTER

SPEED: 74.28 m.p.h.

New Imperial Motors Ltd., Spring Road, Hall Green
Birmingham, 11

New Imperial's celebrations of their victory in the 1936 Lightweight TT included this advertisement and the transfer they added to the petrol tanks of their road bikes.

Truly an island of speed, just before the TT a 'round-the-houses' car race in Douglas attracted many of the top names of the day. The Island was also part of a major air race that started from London and finished at Ronaldsway. Immediately following the motorcycle TT came the 'Bicycle TT' run over the same Mountain Course. Proving rather more dangerous than motorized racing, ten of the eighty push-bike competitors finished up in hospital.

Rumbles

Despite its high standing with the majority of road race supporters, the TT has always been a target for criticism – often from those who were not winning or had personal axes to grind. Right in the middle of the 1936 TT, the influential magazine *Motor Cycling* floated the proposal that it should be the last year of the races in their present form, that a shorter British Grand Prix should be held in England (could it have been speaking on behalf of Donington?), and that the TT should revert more to a long-distance reliability Trial format, for production-based machines.

It was common knowledge that an ACU sub-committee was already considering the topic of the TT Mountain Course, spurred by the problems caused by poor weather and postponements. Manx newspapers joined in the discussion, with the *Isle of Man Weekly Times* rating a move of the TT from the island 'nothing short of a calamity'. It put forward proposals for a new 8-mile course to be covered thirty times, which it believed could be learnt in two practice sessions. In doing this it recognized that the Mountain Course with interval starts was 'too long to hold the interest of a sensation-seeking public'.

Norton's dominance of the TT (and foreign Grand Prix) continued to rankle with some. There were even suggestions that the company should abstain from competing at the TT to give other manufacturers a chance. The Manx press had a view on this too, saying 'the supremacy of the Norton machines has been, to some extent at least, responsible for the decline in entries'. Norton had achieved sixteen TT wins, but what a hollow victory it would have been for another manufacturer if Norton had withdrawn from the TT in order to give others a chance. On the other hand, what wonderful publicity it would have generated for the Bracebridge Street manufacturer and its 'Unapproachable' machines!

In truth, the performance gap between Norton and other makes had closed, but Joe Craig was very aware of this and worked hard during the winter to extract more from the Norton single-cylinder powerplant. The biggest change for the 1937 TT was the use of double overhead camshaft engines, with a train of five gears in the head replacing rockers. Craig claimed measurable extra power from the 500cc race engine with the dohc arrangement (less benefit from the 350), which had been well tested during the latter part of 1936. He had become a well-seasoned race manager, making haste slowly with new developments and used to juggling highly tuned race machinery and riders to get the best results. Of the latter he said: 'in some cases and in certain circumstances, the riders can be as temperamental as the machines usually are'.

Nicknamed 'The Wizard of Tune', this was how Sallon saw Norton's Joe Craig.

Back to Normal?

When entries closed for the 1937 TT they were up to 103 (from 85) and talk of moving the event from the Mountain Course or changing the nature of the races had seemingly subsided. What the Isle of Man did not know, however, was that during the period of the 1937 races the organizing ACU was actually 'negotiating with an English municipality with a view to having the races run in another area'. Ignorant of these behind-the-scenes manoeuvrings, riders from thirteen countries looked forward to competing in the traditional TT races, with all that meant in terms of getting to learn (or relearn) the 37¾-mile course during the extensive period allowed for practice.

One change to the practice arrangements was the introduction of the first evening session. This took place on the second Thursday between 6.30 and 9pm and was introduced to let competitors see how their engines performed in conditions nearer to those that they could expect in a race, for the customary early morning sessions often did not allow for optimum carburation tuning. Evening practice proved more accessible to the local population and the Manx turned out in large numbers to watch in excellent weather, with Jimmie Guthrie (Norton) unofficially breaking Stanley Woods's 1936 record lap by fifteen seconds. With Freddie Frith also beating his own Junior lap record in practice, spectators looked forward to fast racing in all classes, particularly as the Lightweight Moto Guzzis of Stanley Woods and Omobono Tenni, plus the DKWs of Ewald Kluge and Ernie Thomas, were reported to be capable of over 100mph (160km/h).

Race week started with the customary Junior event on Monday, and Stanley Woods's race had barely got under way when he had a frightening near-miss with a stray dog at the foot of Bray Hill. But it was the Norton team that quickly established its superiority over the opposition: the final result was Guthrie, White and Frith (Nortons), with Woods (Velocette) taking fourth place. The high speeds promised by practice week were realized in the race when Guthrie and Frith both broke the Junior lap record with identical times of 26 minutes 35 seconds, a speed of 85.18mph (137.08

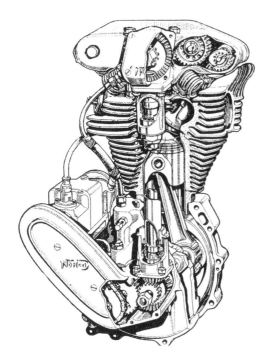

An example of the all-conquering Norton single-cylinder engine of 1937 with double ohc.

km/h), comfortably beating Frith's 1936 record lap of 81.94mph (131.87km/h).

Wednesday's Lightweight race also saw the establishment of new race and lap records. It was one that had three different leaders, the first being Ewald Kluge (DKW), but he soon lost first place to Stanley Woods (Moto Guzzi) before retiring his two-stroke with a broken throttle cable. Woods eventually lost the lead on the sixth lap to Guzzi team-mate Omobono Tenni. Both Woods and Tenni gave a thumbs-down signal to the Moto Guzzi pits as they went through to start their last laps. Stanley's problem proved terminal at Sulby but Tenni, although he stopped to change a plug, continued his race and took victory from 'Ginger' Wood (Excelsior), Ernie Thomas (DKW) and Les Archer (New Imperial). There was much jubilation in the Moto Guzzi camp at the first victory by an Italian rider on an Italian machine, and Signor Parodi, a director of the company, wired the news to Mussolini.

Friday, Senior race day, dawned with fine weather for what turned into a titanic contest between Norton and Velocette. It was team leaders Jimmie Guthrie (Norton) and Stanley Woods (Velocette) who contested the lead for the first four laps, with Freddie Frith (Norton) pulling through the field to threaten them. Guthrie retired on the fifth lap, but Woods and Frith continued at a tremendous pace and started the seventh and last lap tying on time for first place. Woods rode at number 4 and Frith at 24, so the race was a classic TT battle on time, with the contestants miles apart on the road. Pushing his Norton harder than one had ever previously been ridden at the TT, Frith reached the finish fifteen seconds earlier than Woods on corrected time. Such was the race pace that he became the first man to lap at more than 90mph (90.27mph/145.27km/h), he broke Jimmie Guthrie's 1936 Senior lap record by almost a minute, and he completed the 264½ miles in five minutes less than the previous fastest race time. It was a contest, however, in which the Velocette machines from Hall Green pressed their Birmingham counterparts from Bracebridge Street harder than ever before. Though overall victory still eluded Veloce Ltd, through Woods, Mellors and Archer it took the team prize from Norton Motors.

Stanley Woods shows the heavily finned engine of his Velocette at the 1937 TT.

A lone 'works' rider in the Senior was Jock West. He was mounted on a horizontally opposed, twin-cylinder, supercharged, shaft-driven BMW with telescopic front suspension and plunger at the rear. After a steady race that showed the bike's handling needed developing to cope with the bumps of the Mountain Course, Jock came home in sixth place in what was the BMW company's first TT.

One firm that had an exceptionally successful TT in 1937 was Dunlop Tyres, a great supporter of the races. Best known for supplying tyres and providing a fitting service, they also supplied rims and wheel-building, saddles, copious supplies of rubber bands, French chalk, rider hospitality and publicity banners. At the end of the meeting the company was pleased to advertise that its products had been used by the first three place-men in Senior, Junior and Lightweight races.

Political Overtones

The TT races have always offered the opportunity for participants to escape the wider problems of the world by spending a fortnight in a high-octane atmosphere aimed solely with getting men and motorcycles to circulate the Isle of Man Mountain Course at maximum velocity. Indeed, prior to a mid-1930s TT meeting *Motor Cycle* captured the prevailing attitude with: 'Who cares what Hitler says, or whether there has been another coup in the Balkans? This week we don't read the national papers – we live, dream and read motorcycles.' At the 1938 event, however, it was impossible to avoid the overtones of impending war and there was a strangely unreal feel about going motorcycle racing at a time of such tension. As the island gave a sporting welcome to BMW and DKW TT teams (just as it had to German pilots in the preceding week's international air race), Britain was openly preparing for war. A local newspaper identified the anomalous position between racing and real-life activities, posing the question 'Why are we in England working day and night in our armament fac-

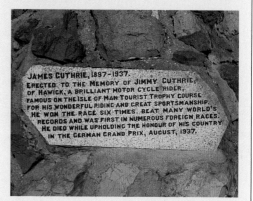
tories, arranging to evacuate women and children from London at a moment's notice, adopting all sorts of methods for saving our population from being bombed to pieces. . . ?'

Manx Influence

Almost 50 per cent of the 109 entries in the 1938 TT were from competitors who had formerly competed in the Manx Grand Prix (MGP), a race for up-and-coming racers held over the Mountain Course in September of each year. It is an event that still breeds TT winners and it was just nine months after his double win in the 1937 MGP that Maurice Cann was entered for his first TT. He was on a Velocette in the Junior and an Excelsior in the Lightweight; through no fault of his own, however, it was to be more than a decade before Maurice achieved the TT win of which his earlier MGP wins had hinted he was capable.

There was only one true Manxman entered in the 1938 TT – Harry Craine – but there were several other competitors riding with 'Manxman' after their names, for they were mounted on Excelsior models that the factory had christened 'Manxman'.

While Manx-born competitors were rare in the TT at that time, some 300 locals turned out to marshal and help run the races which, while organized in the name of the ACU, relied very heavily on local input in all areas.

An increase in the number of evening practice sessions to two received the support of riders and Manx people, particularly as the organizers decided that there would be no practice on the morning following an evening one, thus giving everybody a lie-in. This was particularly welcome in 1938 when many early-morning sessions suffered atrocious weather, seriously hampering riders' efforts to prepare for racing. It generated some lobbying for daytime practice, which, if granted, would clearly impact on the everyday lives of local people even more than morning and evening sessions.

The 1938 Races

Good weather greeted riders and spectators for the opening Junior race, although there was some low cloud on the Mountain. Only two foreign makes had been entered, but since they did not come to the start the thirty-nine machines that went through the warming-up process on the Glencrutchery Road were all British, comprising nineteen Nortons, fifteen Velocettes and five AJS. Warming-up should have been a straightforward activity, for the organizers placed a line of metal dustbins down the centre of the road and competitors rode down one side, turned at the end and returned up the other side. Unfortunately – and not for the first time – there was a collision between two riders during the warm-up and C.B. Sutherland's bike sustained damage to the frame that forced him to withdraw from the race.

Riders were required to cut their engines fifteen minutes before the 11 o'clock start time. They then went through the procedure of changing to harder sparking-plugs and parading to the line behind Scouts carrying their national flag. After that they sat fiddling with goggles, gloves, petrol taps and so on, while nervously awaiting to be started at half-minute intervals. When the starting maroon sounded and the flag dropped at 11am it was the Velocette pairing of Stanley Woods and Ted Mellors who soon moved into the lead. Freddie Frith (Norton) was their nearest challenger during the race, but at the finish he had to settle for third place, ahead of his teammates Harold Daniell and 'Crasher' White. All three were on substantially 'improved' machines that, despite having been lightened and fitted with telescopic front forks, recorded slower race speeds than the previous year. The winner, Stanley Woods, reported a trouble-free run in which he broke the lap record but left the race record intact. It was the first TT win by a Velocette since 1929 and was just reward for the company's sustained race efforts through the 1930s.

Having earned the reputation of being fast but temperamental, the DKW team managed to get one machine to the finish of the Lightweight race – in the all-important first place. Ewald Kluge battered the record book and the opposition on his way to recording the

German company's first TT win, setting a race average speed of 78.48mph (126.30km/h) and a fastest lap of 80.35mph (129.31km/h), both figures being some 5 per cent faster than the existing records. Excelsiors proved their reliability by finishing in the next six places, but second-placed 'Ginger' Wood was over eleven minutes behind Kluge in a race time that was slightly slower than his second-place finish in 1937. DKW had clearly leap-frogged the Lightweight opposition in the performance stakes, while Excelsior had stood still.

Despite the general apprehension about impending war, there was little reservation in the Manx press or the national motorcycle magazines about entertaining German men and machines at the TT. Their practice efforts were fairly reported and the thoroughness they showed in all aspects of preparation was openly admired. What was of serious concern was that the 'Blue Riband' Senior TT might well be won by the flat-twin BMWs from Germany. Its team of Georg Meier, Karl Gall and Jock West was a formidable one on paper, particularly with the exceptional speeds recorded on the Sulby Straight from their supercharged engines rated at more than 60bhp. Unfortunately, for all their apparent thoroughness, Gall put himself out of contention with an out-of-hours crash in practice week, and Meier went out on the first lap of the race with engine trouble, leaving just Jock West to participate on the fringes of the epic battle between single-cylinder runners from Norton and Velocette that occurred at the head of the Senior race.

At the end of the first lap just thirty-three seconds covered Freddie Frith (Norton), Stanley Woods (Velocette), 'Crasher' White (Norton) and Harold Daniell (Norton). Woods took the lead on the third lap from Frith and Daniell, with the latter then equalling the lap record on the fifth lap and tying with Frith for second place, the two Norton runners being just three seconds behind Velocette-mounted Woods. With a reputation for getting faster as a race progressed, Daniell broke the 25-minute barrier on his sixth lap to take the lead and leave Woods and Frith, both previous Senior winners, tying for second place five seconds behind him. Neither could match the pace of the bespectacled Daniell, who, knowing he had only a slender lead, went even faster on the last lap, setting a new absolute lap record of 91.00mph (146.45 km/h) and finishing fifteen seconds ahead of Woods, who was a mere 1½ seconds ahead of Frith. 'Crasher' White's fourth place ensured the team prize went to Norton and by coming home fifth, Jock West salvaged some pride on behalf of BMW.

Bill Beevers flies his Norton over the St Ninian's crossroads, prior to wrestling it down the bumpy Bray Hill and another TT lap in 1938.

Stanley Woods

Born in Dublin in 1903, Stanley Woods was probably the greatest TT rider of his era. Making his first visit to the Island in 1921, he returned to compete in 1922 and then took his first win in the 1923 Junior on a Cotton. Thereafter he was a consistently highly placed finisher, riding Royal Enfield, New Imperial, Norton, Husqvarna, Moto Guzzi, DKW and Velocette machines, with which he took TT wins against such high-calibre opposition as Charlie Dodson, Jimmy Simpson, Ernie Knott, Jimmy Guthrie and Freddie Frith.

Stanley was a thinking rider who devised his own signalling system at the TT to augment the single signal that riders received at the end of a lap, and which was already a lap out of date. His racing career included many wins in premier Continental races, and the ten TT victories he had achieved by the time he finished racing in 1939 put him at the head of the winners' list for nearly thirty years.

A regular post-war visitor to the TT, Stanley took part in several Laps of Honour, his last ride being in 1982 when he was seventy-nine.

Stanley Woods portrayed by 'Sallon'.

A Bumper Entry

The TT race regulations published in February 1939 were little changed from the previous year's. The entry fee for individual events was £10, prize money totalled £1,800, and evening practice sessions had grown to three. There were still six early morning sessions.

Dunlop Tyres hoped to add to its impressive score of TT successes. This advertisement is from the 1939 TT Programme, which also contained an advertisement offering travel by air for visitors, while Motor Cycling *announced that it was still running its combined rail and sea excursions to the Senior.*

It may have been that competitors sensed this was to be the last TT for some years, for they flocked to pay their entry fees to this historic competition. Finally closing at 147, the total number of race entries was almost 40 per cent up on the previous year. Containing fifty-one Senior, sixty-five Junior and thirty-one Lightweights, the entry list saw an even

81

stronger German contingent than in previous years, with BMW and NSU entries in the Senior, DKW and NSU in the Junior, and DKW in the Lightweight; many of their machines were supercharged. There was also a 'dark horse' from Italy, with a Benelli entered in the Lightweight along with Moto Guzzi. Although needing the best possible machinery to counter this enhanced foreign challenge, the 'works' Norton riders were handicapped by having to ride 1938 models without factory back up, as the company was concentrating all its production effort on Government contracts. The Velocettes were still sporting girder front forks (although they did bring their supercharged twin-cylinder 'Roarer' to try in practice), and Walter Rusk's portly water-cooled and supercharged AJS V4 weighed in at 100lb (45kg) heavier than the BMWs. The overall strength of entry, however, moved a local newspaper to write: 'The 1939 TT will be an unquestioned success, but we prefer not to speculate on TTs in 1940 and onwards.'

Sadly, the BMW challenge was reduced to two riders when Karl Gall died from injuries sustained in a practice-period crash at Ballaugh. His team-mates decided to race on and their practice performances showed they would be serious contenders for race honours, with Jock West timed at 130mph (209km/h) for a measured mile at Sulby and Meier finishing practice at the head of the Senior leaderboard.

Race week in 1939 started with the customary Junior event, which saw Stanley Woods take a narrow victory for Velocette over the Norton of Harold Daniell at slightly under record pace, with Heiner Fleischmann (DKW) in third place. It was Stanley's tenth win in his seventeenth successive year competing in the TT. Two days later he set the fastest lap at 78.16mph (125.78km/h) on his Moto Guzzi in the Lightweight race before retiring and letting team-mate Omobono Tenni into the lead, only to see him retire on the third lap. Ted Mellors deliberately restrained his pace in the early stages, believing that the Guzzi teamsters would not last the pace, and brought his speedy little Benelli to the front on lap three. He held the position to

How the Isle of Man Weekly Times *saw the opposing forces lined up to contest the 1939 TT.*

This memorial plaque to Karl Gall is located just after Ballaugh Bridge.

the end, so giving the Italian firm a TT victory on its first Island appearance. Unable to match his pace of 1938, Ewald Kluge on his DKW was nearly four minutes behind Mellors at the finish and only two minutes ahead of Henry Tyrell-Smith on an Excelsior, although poor weather contributed to restricting speeds.

With weather and road conditions perfect for Friday's Senior, Britain's worst fears came true when Georg Meier and Jock West headed the field throughout the race and came home in first and second places on their BMWs. Not only did this offer the German government-backed effort a useful propaganda coup, it also earned BMW the right to take the Marquis de Mouzilly St Mars' splendid Senior Tourist Trophy away with them. Three months later all sporting pretensions were put to one side as the principal opposing TT nations – Britain, Germany and Italy – went about the dirty business of war.

Georg Meier and his supercharged BMW in front of the pits in 1939.

5   Foreign Challengers

The Second World War officially ended in the summer of 1945, but although enthusiasm for racing quickly resurfaced, the post-war economic situation did not allow an immediate running of the TT races. Most essentials, including petrol (available only in a lowly 72 octane), were in short supply and rationed. Factories required licences to purchase materials and the government dictated that the majority of motorcycle production should go for export to earn foreign currency and pay off wartime debts. The manufacture of racing bikes was low on the order of official priorities, although Norton listed single ohc 'Manx' models for 1947.

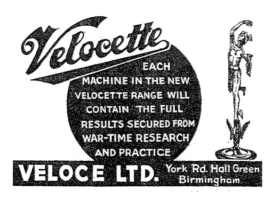

Veloce Ltd looked forward to getting back into normal production, as this advertisement from June 1945, after victory in Europe, shows.

Short-circuit racing, mostly on former airfields – for Donington and Brooklands had been lost to racing – did get under way in England in 1946. After much effort on the Isle of Man in patching up the grandstand and pits,

pulling together the race organization and somehow arranging petrol and other supplies, it was the running of the 1946 MGP that brought motorcycle racing back to the Mountain Course.

It was not until the summer of 1947 that the TT returned. The competitors who arrived for the comeback event's traditional Senior, Junior and Lightweight races were a mixture of experienced Mountain Course riders and newcomers to the circuit. The former had no doubt dug out their pre-war two-piece leathers (and in many cases their pre-war crash helmets), and almost all the riders were mounted on 1930s machinery de-tuned to suit the low-grade fuel provided. Compression ratios, which had been something over 10:1 to utilize the petrol-benzole mixes available pre-war, were dropped to nearer 7.5:1 and power outputs were much reduced. The decision of the international controlling body for motorcycle sport, the FICM (later FIM), to ban supercharging at the end of 1946 meant that a number of actual and planned racers from the pre-war era were ruled out of post-war competition.

AJS was the only concern with a new design at the 1947 TT, bringing two virtually untried low-slung parallel twins for Jock West and Les Graham to ride. The AJS twin, nicknamed 'Porcupine', owing to the copious spiked finning of its cylinder heads, had originally been designed to be supercharged, and the extra finning was an attempt to avoid the weight penalty of water cooling. Seemingly, AJS had learnt lessons from its heavy, water-cooled, supercharged 4-cylinder machines of pre-war years, whose weight was a handicap and whose handling lagged behind engine performance. Although much redesign took place on the post-war AJS twin after the ban on supercharging, it was several years before careful development lifted output from the unit-construction, twin ohc engine to just over 50bhp at 7,600rpm.

The 1947 entry list was missing some famous names, most noticeably ten times former TT winner Stanley Woods, who had retired, but pre-war stars like Freddie Frith, Harold Daniell, Bob Foster, Maurice Cann and Manliff Barrington were back. Given that they had been away from the Isle of Man for eight years, many presumed that these former stars' skills might have been blunted, but when the chequered flag dropped on the last rider at the end of the 1947 week of races it was the established stars who had been victorious. In the Senior it was Harold Daniell home first on a Norton, in the Junior Bob Foster (Velocette) and in the Lightweight Manliff Barrington (Moto Guzzi). In line with pre-race forecasts and lower power outputs, no race or lap records were broken.

Italian Moto Guzzi machines were the only foreign make entered in the 1947 TT, but the Mandello del Lario concern's challenge for the Senior was thwarted by a practice accident to Freddie Frith when the front brake of his 500 locked on the approach to Ballacraine. Thrown from the bike, the resulting shoulder injury put him out of the race. Moto Guzzi, however, was very successful in the Lightweight race, taking first and second places on the two machines entered. Strangely, the Lightweight race had some claiming that there were two winners – both on Guzzis! Although Manliff Barrington was credited with finishing in first place, forty-four seconds ahead of Maurice Cann, there were many who considered that the timekeepers made an error of one minute in Cann's race time of 3 hours 37 minutes 11 seconds and that he actually won the race by sixteen seconds.

Rising Stars

There were plenty of newcomers in 1947 prepared to give their all for a TT win, although few had a realistic chance of doing so. But, as is sometimes the case, one newcomer outshone all the others that year. Although not a young man when he made his TT debut (he was thirty-two), Artie Bell's promising road-race career in Ireland had, like so many others', been halted by the war. Norton team manager Joe Craig recognized Bell's talent and brought him into the 'works' team. In the Senior he finished second to Harold Daniell and tying for the fastest lap at 84.07mph (135.29km/h) with another promising newcomer, Peter

Artie Bell manages a smile after his TT success on a 'works' Norton, with Joe Craig (left) sharing the pleasure.

Goodman, grandson of the founder of the Velocette concern. Maintaining his rapid rise to TT fame, Artie Bell then went one place higher in 1948 and took first position in the Senior.

Artie Bell was followed home in the 1948 Senior by yet another rising star and TT newcomer, Bill Doran, who was riding a privately entered Norton. Doran was another whose TT career had been badly affected by the war. Unable to make his Island debut until the MGP of 1946, Doran was thirty-one at the time and thus had a relatively short racing career ahead of him.

Why so Named?

Doran's Bend
About 8 miles from the start is a sweeping left-hand bend after Ballig Bridge, approached at full-bore, that is today called Doran's Bend. Bill Doran's fall at this point in 1950, when he broke a leg, is established as part of TT history, even though his fine riding performances, including two second places, between 1948 and 1953 on

T.T. & GRAND PRIX MOTOR CYCLE RACING PERSONALITIES
No. 30

W. DORAN

AJS and Norton machinery may have faded from memory.

There is no nameboard on the course identifying Doran's Bend, but in his day he was recognized as a 'Motor Cycle Racing Personality', as the postcard illustrated shows.

With the established stars pressed by up-and-coming newcomers in the first post-war TT meeting, race wins in 1948 and 1949 were evenly distributed between the two categories. Still a relative newcomer, Artie Bell led a Norton 1-2-3 in the 1948 Senior, although

pre-war Italian star Omobono Tenni (Moto Guzzi) actually led the race for the first four laps and set the fastest lap before his 120-degree twin slowed with valve-spring problems and he finished in ninth place. Resuming the pre-war struggle between the two premier British racing companies, Freddie Frith and Bob Foster on Velocettes led home Artie Bell (Norton) in the Junior, while Maurice Cann (Moto Guzzi) achieved his overdue victory in the Lightweight. The following year there was a different mix of riders, with 1938 and 1947 Senior winner Harold Daniell taking his third victory in the 'Blue Riband' race (after Bob Foster had retired his Moto Guzzi from the lead on the sixth lap), Freddie Frith won

Maurice Cann and Mrs Cann after his Moto Guzzi victory in the 1948 Lightweight race. Multi-MGP winner Denis Parkinson holds the left handlebar.

The 350cc AJS 7R made its TT debut in 1948 without great success, although Geoff Murdoch did bring his home in a surprising fourth place in the Senior race. What looked like a first TT victory for the 7R in 1949 was lost when Bill Doran retired on the last lap while in the lead.

the Junior on his Velocette (fitted with an improved dohc engine), and Manliff Barrington gave a third consecutive Lightweight victory to Moto Guzzi.

It was invariably a 'works' bike that took first place in a TT, but by the late 1940s British factories were turning out production versions of some of their racers for sale to private runners, and these filled the entry lists. Among those available to buy were the AJS 7R and Norton 350 and 500cc Manx models. At Hall Green Velocette produced Mk VIII models in 350 and 500 sizes, although some owners of post-war Velo racers complained that they were inferior in workmanship and performance to the pre-war models.

Petrol was still rationed, but there were plenty of fans willing to save their petrol coupons for a visit to the Island. The lengthy queues at Liverpool Docks were regarded as a necessary hardship on the annual TT pilgrimage.

Clubman's TT

Back in 1939 the ACU had given thought to introducing a TT race based upon sports

TT RACES

in the

ISLE of MAN

JUNE 7, 9 & 11th

Make a Note of the dates and DECIDE NOW on the

ISLE ⊕F MAN

FOR HAPPY HOLIDAYS

For descriptive guide book and accommodation list send p.c. to

C. M. CLAGUE, *Publicity Dept.*, ISLE OF MAN

In the late 1940s the Isle of Man did its best to attract visitors to the races with advertisements like this.

machines produced for road use, and in 1947 it introduced three Clubman's TT races for Lightweight, Junior and Seniors, the latter being open to up to 1000cc models. These races were run under a National Licence during the TT period and were aimed at ordinary riders rather than the stars. They also offered spectators the opportunity to see the running in competition of products from firms such as Ariel, BSA, Triumph and Vincent whose machines did not ordinarily contest races over the TT course. The regulations prescribed that all entries should be as per catalogue, although silencers and lighting sets could be removed. Exactly what was catalogue specification was to prove just one of the headaches experienced by the organizers in the running of the Clubman's events, but they proved popular with budding racers and resulted in total entries for the TT meeting reaching almost 300.

While the TT continued to enhance its reputation as the world's premier road race, the FIM created the first racing World Championships in 1949 for 125, 250, 350 and 500cc solos and 500cc sidecars. Hoping to encourage more manufacturers into international racing, the Championships were run over several rounds that included the three classes run at the TT. Among the first men declared World

Geoff Duke

The Clubman's TT ran from 1947 to 1954 and among the winners were riders who went on to success at the MGP, but few had the class required to move swiftly into the top echelon of racers and gain victory on the International TT-racing scene. One who did was Geoff Duke, whose entry for the 1948 Clubman's was turned down due to lack of racing experience. This former Royal Corps of Signals display rider, who was employed at Norton Motors full-time and also rode as a 'works' Trials and Scrambles rider for the company, made his Mountain Course debut in the 1948 Junior MGP but retired with a split oil tank while contesting the lead.

Still relatively inexperienced over the Mountain Course, Geoff nevertheless brought his 500cc 'International' Norton home in first place in the three-lap Clubman's TT of 1949. Just three months later, on 'proper' racing Nortons, he rode superbly in the MGP, taking second place to Cromie McCandless in the Junior and then sweeping to victory over Cromie in the Senior by 43 seconds.

Although continuing to ride Trials and Scrambles, Geoff was made a member of the Norton 'works' race team for 1950 and, incredibly swiftly, rewarded

How 'Sallon' saw Geoff Duke.

them by winning the Senior TT at record race and lap speeds and riding to second in the Junior behind Artie Bell. Geoff's win earned him some £600 from bonuses and an end of year offer to ride for Gilera in 1951, but he chose to stay with Norton. Seemingly improving with every ride, his performances in 1951 could hardly be bettered, bringing him much publicity and earning acclaim from far beyond the realms of motorcycle racing. For Norton he won the Junior and Senior TTs in record times, took the 350 and 500cc World Championships, was voted Britain's 'Sportsman of the Year' and was awarded the RAC's coveted Segrave Trophy. Interestingly, when asked for the high spot of his year, Geoff replied: 'A personal satisfaction for me was that I had scored an Isle of Man TT double'.

Geoff did move to Gilera for 1953 and went on to further TT wins. By the time he finished his career in 1959 he had ridden in eleven International TT races, won five of them, come second on two occasions and had three retirements; his lowest finish had been in fourth place. It was an impressive record.

Champions in 1949 were British solo riders Freddie Frith, who took the 350cc crown on a Velocette, and Les Graham, who was 500cc champion on his AJS, while Eric Oliver and Denis Jenkinson (Norton) took the Sidecar honours.

Norton Developments

Although Norton was still taking TT victories, the company knew that it could not rely on its dated single-cylinder racers to keep the multis at bay for ever. Moto Guzzi had shown this by leading all the 'works' Nortons for four laps in the 1948 Senior and for six laps in 1949, while Les Graham also looked like beating the Nortons with his twin-cylinder AJS in the 1949 Senior until his magneto shaft failed just 2 miles from the finish. An additional worry for Norton was that 4-cylinder Italian Gileras were contesting and winning Continental 500 GPs, and there was the likelihood that other makers would join the fray.

Feeling that it should investigate multi-cylinder machines, in 1949 Norton, in conjunction with the BRM car racing concern, developed a design for a compact 4-cylinder, water-cooled, transversely mounted dohc engine with built-in gearbox. Regrettably, although a 125cc slave engine was built and subjected to bench testing, Norton's proposed counter to the multi-cylinder threat got no further than a few preliminary engine castings.

Even though it did not proceed with a multi-cylinder model, Norton Motors' racing efforts did not stand still in the late 1940s and early 1950s. Always looking for small increases in power, it also worked on refining the front and rear suspension to improve handling. Its existing frame, however, nicknamed the 'Garden Gate', was heavy, prone to occasional breakages when stressed over bumpy circuits and offered no real scope for improvement. In 1949 freelance engineer Rex McCandless offered Norton a new double-loop welded frame with swinging-fork rear suspension, which he claimed would improve the handling of the race bikes.

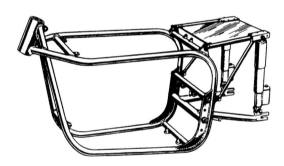

The 'Featherbed' frame as designed by Rex McCandless, although Norton modified the rear end before bringing it into use.

The place that could be guaranteed to reveal if the McCandless claim was correct was the TT Mountain Course. Over the winter of 1949/50 a test was arranged with Geoff Duke and Artie Bell riding examples of the old and new-framed racers over part of the Mountain section of the course – all done on open roads under the benevolent eye of the local constabulary. The test showed Norton that the new McCandless frame was considerably better than the old and it was adopted on the 'works' racers for 1950. The improvement it brought to Norton handling proved vital over the next few years as they fought to resist the multi-cylinder challenge. Nicknamed the 'Featherbed' by Harold Daniell, the new frame contributed to Norton taking a 1-2-3 in both Junior and Senior TTs of 1950, with Artie Bell home first on the three-fifty (followed by Geoff Duke) and Duke victorious on the five-hundred (followed by Bell).

Norton had its own specialized race department, and perhaps this is the place to pause and recognize that a book of this size cannot reveal in detail the vast amount of thought, design, development, testing, financing and production effort devoted to the creation of racing motorcycles by factories and private individuals. That had been the case since the first TT races in 1907, and such effort had to be continuous, for if a manufacturer economized on financial or technical input it risked being left behind by the opposition. Nor can this book show the trials and tribulations experienced by virtually everyone who chose to contest the TT. The nature of the Mountain Course means that it has always been ultra-demanding on race machinery and, when considered alongside the high mileages covered in long practice sessions and races, it is understandable that not only do highly tuned racing machines require constant attention and periodic rebuilds during a TT meeting, but they often suffer major failures. To this day, garage accommodation throughout Douglas sees consistent working late at night by race mechanics to repair and ready bikes for their next 37¾-mile lap, while cooperative small engineering firms throughout the island expect to put some of their normal work aside during the TT period to help weld, turn and fabricate replacement parts for race machines.

Stopped at the end of the full-bore Sulby Straight in 1948 are H. Carter (Excelsior) and L. Martin (Moto Guzzi) from Belgium. Both look to have problems, although sometimes a rider would stop here to take a plug-reading and a representative from a sparking-plug company might arrange to be in attendance at the spot during practice, so that he could do a check for a star rider.

Italian Challenge

Benelli had won the Lightweight TT in 1939 and returned to contest the same race in 1949, but rider Dario Ambrosini retired after falling at Governor's Bridge. Racing on the Island again in 1950, Dario and his Benelli beat Maurice Cann (Moto Guzzi) to the chequered flag by one-fifth of a second in what had been a massed-start race. The Benelli had a tail-fairing housing 2½ gallons of petrol to allow it to make a non-stop run over the seven-lap race distance and at one stage Ambrosini was a minute behind Cann. But the Benelli rider gradually pulled the Guzzi back, and slipped ahead to achieve what was literally a grand-stand finish after 264 racing miles. Following Ambrosini and Cann came a string of British 250s that were really outclassed by the Italian purpose-built racers, for no contemporary British manufacturer made such a model, although Velocette did create a handful of dohc 250s in 1951.

The Italian motorcycle industry was renowned for its lightweight machines from 50cc upwards, although, as will be shown, it was quite capable of producing larger models. Some of its manufacturers like Gilera, Benelli and Moto Guzzi were well established, while others only came into being after the end of the war. They operated in a competitive market and several sought to promote their products in

racing. This they did with expensive and purpose-built four-strokes that often bore little resemblance to their standard road-going products, many of which were utility two-strokes.

Reflecting the new World Championship standing of the Lightweight 125s, the TT

race programme for 1951 was expanded to cater for them with a race over two laps (75½ miles/121.5km), while the Lightweight 250cc race was reduced from seven laps to four (151 miles/243km). In answer to the question on everyone's lips as to how the 'tiddlers' would cope with the Mountain Course, the response was very well, at least from the 'works' machines. It was Mondial who starred in the first Lightweight 125cc TT, taking the first four places with Cromie McCandless, Carlo Ubbiali, Guido Leoni and Nello Pagani riding their high-revving four-strokes, which were capable of 90mph and proved extremely reliable throughout the TT period. Fastest lap went to McCandless at 75.34mph (121.24 km/h), and after the Mondials it was Spanish Montesa two-strokes who occupied fifth and sixth places. Most of the remaining places were occupied by British two-strokes, which, with top speeds on the flat of about 65mph, were totally outclassed.

Maximum speed of the Lightweight 250s was about 105mph and Tommy Wood's Moto Guzzi was first home in 1951, followed by Ambrosini (Benelli) and Lorenzetti (Moto Guzzi). Then in 1952 Fergus Anderson led a Moto Guzzi 1-2-3 in the 250s, while yet another Italian make, MV Agusta, took first

place among the 125s. Ridden by Cecil Sandford, the single-cylinder four-stroke MV put in a fastest lap of 76.07mph (122.42km/h) over an increased race distance of three laps, to beat the Mondials of Carlo Ubbiali and Len Parry.

While Italian machines dominated the Lightweight classes at the TT in the early 1950s, British machinery remained relatively unopposed in the Junior and Senior classes and so swept the board, with Geoff Duke taking a double victory on his Nortons in 1951, setting new race records and leaving the Junior lap record at 91.38mph (147.06km/h) and the Senior at 95.22mph (153.24km/h). Practice speed checks had shown him to be the fastest 500 at 122.48mph (197.11km/h) over the almost flat-out 2-mile stretch through Glen Vine and past The Highlander, while his Norton team-mate, Johnny Lockett, was fastest 350 at 116.13mph (186.89km/h). Geoff was an immaculate stylist who always looked in complete control. Nevertheless, he announced himself as quite happy with premeditated sliding of the rear wheel while cornering, but expressed concern at thoughts of both wheels sliding, despite well-informed sources suggesting that he was actually doing this at fast spots like Hillberry. His race

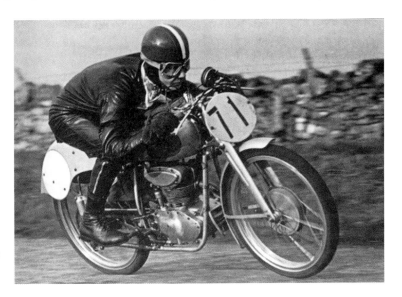

Carlo Ubbiali speeds to second place in the Lightweight 125 TT of 1951 on his Mondial.

performances left fans to wonder whether it was his riding that boosted the Nortons to record-breaking performances and lap times, the still relatively new Featherbed frame, the 80 octane petrol by then in use, or the factory's continuing programme of minor improvements. Geoff believed that his success was 'assisted in no small part by the arrival at Bracebridge Street of a gentleman by the name of Leo Kuzmicki'. Promoted from a menial job on the factory floor to the race department, Leo used his pre-war knowledge as a lecturer on internal combustion engines at Warsaw University to great effect. Indeed, Geoff writes in his autobiography *In Pursuit of Perfection* that, with Leo's input into 'squish' head developments, the power output of the 350 rose from 28bhp @ 7,200rpm to 36bhp @ 8,000rpm.

Leo Kuzmicki undoubtedly made a big contribution at Norton, but the impact of Geoff Duke's race successes went far beyond Bracebridge Street and the world of motorcycling. So widely publicized were his achievements that he became a household name and was voted Britain's 'Sportsman of the Year' in 1951 – a feat unimaginable for a racing motorcyclist today. Looking to build business interests on the back of his racing successes, Geoff established a motorcycle sales company in his home town of St Helens and ceased work at the Norton factory, signing to ride for its team in 1952 only in the 'Classic' races.

The 500cc AJS twin-cylinder 'Porcupine' had been much altered, with cylinders now at 45 degrees and changes to the frame. It seemed to have gained additional reliability and one ridden by Bill Doran finished second to Duke in the 1951 Senior. Cromie McCandless, who, like Geoff Duke, was a former MGP winner elevated to the Norton team, revealed his versatility by backing his ride to first place in the Lightweight 125 race on a Mondial with third in the Senior on a Norton.

The TT results were widely publicized in the motorcycle press, with accompanying advertisements in respect of the Norton wins by Avon, Ferodo, Castrol, Wellworthy, Lodge, Amal and Lucas. Other members of the trade were able to gain credit from supporting the winners of the Lightweight classes, with advertisements being placed by Champion, BTH, Mobiloil, Essolube and Dunlop.

The 'Blue Riband'

The Senior race has always been regarded as the premier event at the TT meeting, being christened the 'Blue Riband' shortly after racing moved to the Mountain Course in 1911. It was the race win that riders coveted, and the one that manufacturers knew attracted the most publicity. A similar situation existed at the Continental Grand Prix and in the status of the individual and manufacturers' World Championships, where success on a 500 (the maximum capacity allowed) was considered the highest achievement. Moto Guzzi knew the value of a 500 win but in the early 1950s its challenge in the big class had faded and Gilera, although winning on fast Continental tracks (and taking the 500cc World Championship of 1950 with Umberto Masetti), had yet to bring its transverse-four to the TT. Fellow Italian company MV Agusta was hungry for race success and, by poaching the services of Gilera chief engineer Piero Remor and one of his senior race mechanics, Arturo Magni, quickly made an impression on the International race scene, particularly with the Lightweight 125 TT win in 1952 referred to above. Remor also turned his hand to the design of a transverse-four for MV and the company from Gallarate near Milan brought an early version to the TT in 1951 for Les Graham to ride in the Senior. Fast, but high, wide, heavy and offering indifferent handling, the MV must have been a difficult ride on the Mountain Course in the early days of its development. While its rating of more than 50bhp would have been welcomed, for speed has always been essential to TT success, its poor handling would have been a major handicap over the seven laps of a Senior TT. In the event it proved unreliable and Graham retired during the race.

Returning in 1952 with his MV Agusta sporting a redesigned engine delivering 56bhp at 10,500rpm, a five-speed gearbox, a new duplex frame and general uprating, Les Graham was clocked at 128.57mph (206.91km/h) at Sulby during practice and was consistently among the fastest lappers. On Friday's race day he trailed Junior winner and early leader of the Senior, Geoff Duke, for four laps, before Duke retired with clutch trouble. Graham then caught Reg Armstrong (Norton) on the road, thus taking the lead on corrected time, but an oil leak and other mechanical troubles slowed him slightly allowing Armstrong to take over the lead, a position the 23-year-old from Dublin held to the end. Eventually finishing in second place some twenty-seven seconds down on the Norton, the MV showed its potential as a still relatively new machine capable of further development, while Norton Motors must have viewed the Italian challenger's efforts with concern, knowing that, despite such improvements as a revised 84 × 90mm engine, new rear-hub and duralumin sprocket, modified carburettor intake and different magneto, its own single-cylinder race bikes were, seemingly, close to their design and performance limits.

As an illustration of the narrow margin between TT glory and failure, the chain on Reg Armstrong's Norton failed just yards before he took the chequered flag to win the 1952 Senior race from the MV Agusta.

Velocette was another British company stuck with an outdated single-cylinder machine and, because it was unable to put as much finance into racing as Norton, it lost its regular leader-board position (and wins with its 350) at the TT in the early 1950s and so withdrew its support for racing. Meanwhile, AJS was still selling plenty of its 350cc racing 7R models. Costing less than a Manx Norton, the 35bhp 7R was popular with ordinary riders and became known as the 'Boys Racer'. Although the 7R was generally regarded as being not quite as good as a Norton, a 3-valve 'works' model was good enough to take Rod Coleman to third place in the 1952 Junior TT. Meanwhile the company persisted with the 'Porcupine' twin-cylinder 500 through the early 1950s. Although the 1952 model was much changed and delivered more power, AJS never bettered Bill Doran's second place to Geoff Duke in the 1951 Senior, which was the pinnacle of its Island success.

While the top riders contested the International TT races in June, the lesser lights were still racing in the Clubman's events. By now down to just two classes, 350 and 500, they were regularly won by riders of the BSA Gold Stars that increasingly dominated the entries.

The chain on Reg Armstrong's Norton snaps just as he takes the chequered flag to win the 1952 Senior TT.

Eric Houseley (22) and Bob McIntyre (76), who finished first and second in the Junior Clubman's TT in 1952 on their BSA Gold Stars. They are photographed with several members of BSA management.

In the early 1950s the popular magazine *Motor Cycling* was edited by former TT winner Graham Walker, who remarked after Geoff Duke's win in the 1952 Junior: 'With consistency which has become almost traditional, Geoff Duke and his 350cc Norton last Monday hoisted the reputation of British motorcycles yet another peg higher in the esteem of the world by winning the International Junior race at an even greater average speed than before'. With the races having a wider public appeal than ever, Graham claimed that 'the man-in-the-street is as keen to know who pulls off the "Senior" as he is to learn the winners of the Derby, the Boat Race and the Cup Final'. Although looked at by some as just a sporting spectacle, Graham Walker pointed out that TT wins made a major contribution to the prestige of the British motorcycle industry and thus helped the drive for exports that were essential to a country still seeking to recover from the war.

Increased Entries

The number of entries for the International TT races of 1953 was up on the previous year. Totalling 265 (excluding Clubman's), they comprised eighty-eight Senior, 107 Junior (including seven reserves), thirty-seven Lightweight 250 and thirty-three Lightweight 125.

The respective number of makes entered in each class was twelve, eight, fifteen and seven. Prize money stood at £200 for Junior and Senior winners, £100 for Lightweight 250 and a mere £50 for Lightweight 125.

Although it had been in existence for more than forty years, the TT meeting was subject to continuous development. In the first two years' running of the Lightweight 125 race, competitors had been set off a few minutes after the Lightweight 250 runners, but in 1953 the 125s had a completely separate race to themselves. This meant that those who wished to could ride in both of the Lightweight races, and eight riders chose to do so. A small change to procedures was that all Junior and Senior runners had to ballot for starting numbers. The custom of offering the previous year's winner the number 1 plate was withdrawn for 1953. Lightweights again had massed starts, so race numbers were not quite so important.

Streamlining

In the quest for ever more speed, racing machines of the early 1950s began to be fitted with streamlining, something in which the Italian factories were well to the fore. There was little in the way of regulations to cover the topic, but the FIM did insist that in the case of a rider falling off he must be able to leave his machine. This ruled out the all-enclosing streamlining used by speed record breakers. It was a highly experimental business: many and varied were the early forms of enclosure. Starting with small fairings and screens to shield the rider, they gradually increased in scale to cover engine, front wheel, rear wheel and seat unit. All the other top runners, including Gilera, MV Agusta, Moto Guzzi, Mondial and NSU, made use of such full enclosures. They were usually made of aluminium and were colloquially called 'dustbins'. Streamlining generally increased a machine's speed, improved fuel consumption and reduced rider fatigue. However, riders found that the customary benefit to be gained from engine braking was reduced, throwing more demands on the brakes and often requiring more use of the gearbox to slow for corners.

Carlo Ubbiali shows the extensive streamlining of his Lightweight Gilera.

The early forms of full streamlining were not always suited to the TT course, particularly in the windy conditions that could often be found on the Mountain. The result was that riders of 350s and 500s sometimes opted for just a small cockpit fairing, so lessening the effect of strong side winds.

In its attempts to stay with the multis, Norton brought an experimental machine to the 1953 TT in which the rider adopted a 'kneeler' riding style behind an extensive fairing. Attracting the name 'Bullet' and 'Eggshell' in press reports of the time, Joe Craig called it the 'Flying Dustbin', but it later became known as the 'Fish'. It was tried in March over the Island's roads and during TT practice by team-leader Ray Amm who lapped at over 90mph, but Ray opted to race a more conventional mount, albeit with bore and stroke changed to 88 × 82mm and 19in wheel rims.

The Norton kneeler of 1953 was later celebrated in this Manx postage stamp.

More Continental Challengers

Eager to gain some of the worldwide prestige being earned by companies who were successful in racing over the Mountain Course, other motorcycle manufacturers with confidence in their engineering abilities sought to participate in the TT races. Already strong challengers in Continental grand prix with Italian riders, in 1953 Gilera gained the services of the disaffected Geoff Duke, who had fallen out with Norton, plus Reg Armstrong and Dickie Dale to ride their 4-cylinder 500s. They all had TT pedigrees and choosing riders with TT experience was an obvious way of lessening one of the biggest handicapping factors in TT racing: detailed course knowledge. NSU took the same approach for their 1953 return in the Lightweight 250 and 125

races, appointing the experienced Bill Lomas to lead their home-grown star rider Werner Haas and help tailor the set-up of the four-strokes to suit the Mountain Course.

BMW also sought a return to past TT glory, but with just one entry from the talented Walter Zeller on a fuel-injected flat-twin. As well as their 250s, Moto-Guzzi brought a 320cc single for Fergus Anderson to ride in the Junior and DKW was back with the pre-war rider Siegfried Wunsche on Lightweight 250 and 3-cylinder Junior versions of their two-stroke machines.

MV Agusta had entries for Les Graham in the Lightweight 125, Junior and Senior classes in 1953. Setting the fastest lap in practice on the Junior 350-4, he had to retire it from the actual race and victory went to Ray Amm (Norton). Things went much better for MV with the 125, where Les brought the little four-stroke home to record his first TT victory. Indeed, 125cc Italian machines dominated the event, occupying ten of the first eleven places, nine of which were taken by MV Agustas. Then, out to make a good showing in the Senior on the big MV, and while holding second place on his second lap, Les lost control at 130mph soon after the bottom of Bray Hill. He was killed in the ensuing crash.

It was Geoff Duke (Gilera) who led that ill-fated 1953 Senior race for the first few laps, some of the time in the company of Ray Amm (Norton), who gave Geoff a close-up view of his sometimes lurid riding style. Geoff, however, slid off at Quarter Bridge on the fourth lap and Amm, fastest man in practice, took over the lead. Despite also sliding off, this time at Sarah's Cottage on the last lap, Amm remounted to win by twelve seconds at record speed from team-mate Jack Brett, with Reg Armstrong bringing his Gilera into third. So, and almost unbelievably for some watchers, it was yet another Junior and Senior double TT win for the trusty single-cylinder Manx Norton that Joe Craig was still coaxing to greater performance, while retaining the reliability essential for winning long-distance races like the TT.

NSU had shown much promise in the Lightweight classes on its TT return, and Bill Lomas set the fastest 125 and 250 laps in practice. However, a spill towards the end of practice sidelined him and it was left to newcomer Werner Haas to take two fine second places, following Les Graham's MV home in the 125 race and Fergus Anderson's Guzzi in the 250.

More winter course-learning by NSU men, this time in 1954. They are stopped at Signpost Corner, where removal of a wall improved the line for riders on the Mountain Course. Signpost was also the point where the new Clypse Course joined the original for the run back to the grandstand and finishing line, although it omitted the Governor's Bridge dip.

Why so Named?

The Graham Memorial

Les Graham's tragic death in the 1953 Senior TT robbed racing of a rider who would, surely, have gone on to more TT victories. Several years after his death a memorial was erected to him at the sweeping left-hand bend prior to The Verandah.

The memorial took the form of a marshals' shelter of striking design, and it was later ridden past many times by Stuart Graham (son of Les), who rode for Honda and Suzuki and, like his father, took one TT victory.

Les Graham was the reigning 500cc World Champion when he wheeled this AJS Porcupine out for practice at the 1950 TT.

Another TT Course

Riders arriving for the 1954 TT found that the Mountain Course had received its customary improvements and stretches of resurfacing. These included road widening at Handleys, Creg ny Baa and Signpost Corner, which was expected to reduce lap times, and, with rider safety in mind, the provision of extra warning signs.

New for the 1954 TT was the use of the 10.8-mile (17.4km) Clypse Course for Lightweight 125s and the reintroduced Sidecar race. Making use of the existing start and finish areas, riders in the massed-start races over the Clypse turned right at the top of Bray Hill and travelled through Willaston to join the Mountain Course at Cronk ny Mona. From there they travelled in the reverse direction to Creg

ny Baa, turned right and made their way over narrow country roads to the built-up area of Onchan, before rejoining the Mountain Course at Signpost Corner to run in the normal direction (but excluding the dip at Governor's Bridge) to finish their ten-lap races at the grandstand.

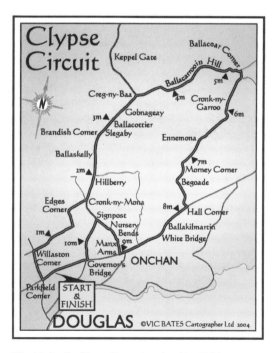

The 10.8-mile Clypse Course introduced in 1954.

Supposedly less likely to be affected by 'mist on the mountain', and causing less disruption to the Island as a whole when closed for racing, use of the new Clypse Course had riders in the bigger Junior and Senior classes concerned as to whether they would be forced to use it. However, a greater threat to those large-capacity classes came from the FIM, which was actively addressing a proposal to eliminate the 500cc class from International racing in 1956, followed by the 350s shortly after.

Other changes at the 1954 TT saw the Junior race reduced to five laps (from seven), the Lightweight 250 reduced to three laps (from four), and the only two remaining Clubman's races (Junior and Senior) being run on the Thursday of practice week. In the latter event Junior victory went to Phil Palmer and Senior to Alastair King, both riding BSA Gold Stars.

Germany's Lightweight Races

The 250 NSU Rennmax returned to the TT in 1954 with a substantially redesigned twin-cylinder engine and six-speed gearbox giving much increased power and speed, the latter being aided by a dolphin fairing at the front. It proved far superior to the opposition and Werner Haas led his team-mates to an NSU 1-2-3-4, lifting the 250 lap record from 84.82mph (136.50km/h) to an incredible 91.22mph (146.80km/h).

Going on to outperform the previously all-conquering MV Agustas in the Lightweight 125 race, Rupert Hollaus brought the smaller NSU home first ahead of Carlo Ubbiali and Cecil Sandford on their MVs.

One man visiting the TT for the first time in 1954 was Soichiro Honda, head of the Japanese company bearing his name. Leaving the island with the intention of returning to

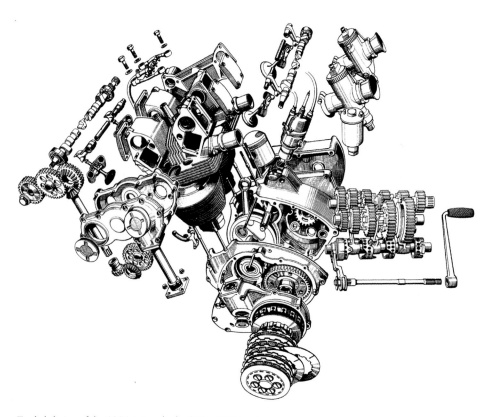

Exploded view of the 1954 twin-cylinder 250cc NSU engine.

Rupert Hollaus brings his 125 NSU through the village of Onchan on his way to TT victory in 1954.

Bob McIntyre raced one of the last versions of the AJS Porcupine (E95, Mk II) in the 1954 Senior TT.

race his products in future Lightweight TTs, he knew that he had much to do to match the successful European manufacturers but, after the success of the 125 and 250 NSUs, he had a clear idea of the design on which he would model his future racers.

However interesting and impressive the performances of the Lightweights, it was the Junior and Senior classes that really gripped racegoers' attention. For 1954 they wanted to know how the Continentals would perform in the big classes after another year of development invested in their multi-cylinder machines. The Italian Gilera and MV Agustas certainly showed they were quick in practice, but in the Junior Rod Coleman gave the 3-valve (one inlet and two exhaust) single-cylinder AJS 7R its first TT win, with Derek Farrant second on another 7R after Ray Amm (Norton) had led until Kirk Michael on the last lap, when an inlet tappet failed.

In the very wet Senior TT Ray Amm rode a Norton with a protruding 'proboscis' fairing and pannier tanks that would have allowed him to go the full race distance without refuelling, while his engine had a squarer bore and stroke necessitating outside fly-wheels. It was also fitted with an oil-cooler and had other minor modifications designed to keep the multis at bay. This Ray managed to do and he

was leading Geoff Duke (Gilera) by more than a minute when the race was stopped at the end of the fourth lap due to the weather. Amm was declared the winner, with team-mate Jack Brett coming home third. Duke, who had stopped to refuel at the end of the third lap and so lost ground to Amm, was rather disgruntled with the way the race was stopped but, whatever his feelings, once again a Norton was at the front of the Senior TT at the chequered flag.

The situation of multis hounding the singles in the Junior and Senior classes at the TT was repeated in the reintroduced Sidecar race on the Clypse Course, where Britain's World Champion Eric Oliver (Norton) managed to keep the faster twin-cylinder BMWs of Fritz Hillebrand and Willi Noll at bay to win by 2 minutes. Riding his Norton outfit fitted with 1952-type 'works' engine and streamlined Watsonian sidecar, which was running on 4.00 × 16 rear and 3.25 × 19 front tyres, with a 3.25 × 10 on the sidecar, Oliver claimed that he could have gone faster if required.

The 1954 Sidecar TT was an event in which the press took an above-average amount of interest, due to the fact that Inge Stoll became the first woman to contest a TT race, when she passengered Jacques Drion to fifth place on a Norton outfit.

'Works' Withdrawals

Norton Motors had become part of Associated Motor Cycles Ltd (AMC), a company that also controlled the AJS and Matchless concerns. For 1955 AMC decided that it would not pursue racing with specialized 'works' machines, but would only race the machines that it produced for sale. In the case of Norton that meant the 30M and 40M Manx models, for AJS the 7R and for Matchless the G45 500cc twin. AMC did intend to provide support to selected riders who would try developments that, if successful, might be incorporated into the following year's production racers. As if its withdrawal were not a big enough bombshell for the racing scene, it then declared itself opposed to the future use of streamlining (despite Norton's extensive experiments with the 'Fish' and the 'Proboscis'), decreeing that its 'over-the-counter' machines would race without streamlining. Ray Amm, who had maintained a valiant and often successful challenge to the multis by riding his Norton to its limits, swiftly left to join MV Agusta. Development of a promising new Norton racer (known as the F-type) with single-cylinder horizontal engine, five-speed gearbox and lowered frame was abandoned. It was a sad day for Britain, for after thirty-two TT wins and several World Championships, Norton had been forced to step back from the cutting-edge of racing. There were few who thought it would ever return to that position.

Motor Cycle's respected journalist 'Ixion' questioned the decision by Norton to enter only over-the-counter racers, calling it 'the quaintest of all imaginable compromises', and adding: 'To give up altogether would be clear-cut and easily defensible. To continue under a self-imposed handicap is – shall we say – illogical?'

As well as its outstanding Lightweight TT wins in 1954, NSU had swept the board in virtually every other meeting it entered. Incredible as it may seem, such sweeping performances had actually attracted criticism in the German press for taking the interest out of racing. Whether this had any effect on its policy is not known, but NSU was another company that decided not to support racing in 1955 with 'works' entries, claiming that it wanted to devote more resources to road machines.

As is so often the case on the racing scene, while some companies were reducing their race efforts, others – mostly Italian firms such as Gilera, MV Agusta and Mondial – were giving it their all, and it was no surprise to see the Senior TT practice leader-board of 1955 headed by Geoff Duke and Reg Armstrong (Gileras) with Ken Kavanagh (Moto Guzzi) the fastest Junior. (Two months earlier, triple TT-winner Ray Amm had been killed at Imola in his very first race for MV Agusta.) The actual results of the 1955 TT made bad reading for British race fans: Senior, Geoff Duke (Gilera); Junior, Bill Lomas (Moto Guzzi); Lightweight 250, Bill Lomas (MV Agusta); Lightweight 125, Carlo Ubbiali (MV Agusta); Sidecar, Fritz Hillebrand (BMW). Their only consolation was that British riders were still doing some of the winning. Bob McIntyre managed to slot a privately entered streamlined Norton into second place in the Junior race, but the runners receiving support from Norton on their unstreamlined production racers did very well to take fourth place in the Senior (Jack Brett riding) and fourth in the Junior (John Surtees), with the latter race reverting from its five laps of 1954 to its previous seven-lap distance. John Hartle also received machinery from the Joe Craig-run Norton effort with development production racers, but both he and John Surtees ran out of fuel before the end of the Senior race. Fortunately, both were close enough to home to push in and secure the team-prize for Norton, but it was difficult to imagine the highly organized Norton team of earlier years allowing two of its riders to run out of fuel. Maybe it was because the rewards were not there: John Surtees revealed that 'Castrol paid us a £500 retainer, but that was the sum total of our financial support as so-called works riders'. At

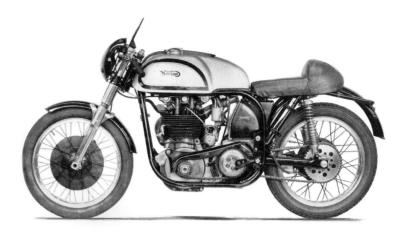

A standard Manx Norton of 1954, when the company ceased making 'works' models.

the end of 1955 Joe Craig announced his retirement, having masterminded the winning of nearly thirty TT races for Norton.

Subsequently, Norton chose to enter only selected events, and their three riders were allowed to race their own machines in other meetings. John Surtees even rode a 'works' BMW at the German Grand Prix.

A 100mph Lap?

Race fans and members of the motorcycle race industry had been talking with some confidence of a rider achieving an average speed of 100mph over the Mountain Course since the early 1950s, and it was during the 1955 Senior TT that the timekeepers announced that Geoff Duke had achieved the 'ton' on his Gilera. Geoff had been generously treated by the Arcore concern on his move to Gilera, doubling his earnings, receiving the gift of a Lancia Gran Turisimo from Commendatore Gilera, and being provided with the use of an apartment close to the factory. In return he had helped the race team with development of the four, particularly its handling, and had given them many race wins and two 500cc World Championships. He would certainly have loved to have given Gilera the publicity arising from the first 100mph TT lap but, some forty minutes after the initial announcement and to boos from the crowds in the grandstand, the timekeepers amended Geoff's lap speed to 99.97mph (160.88km/h).

Any thoughts that Geoff might have had about getting his and Gilera's name in the record books with a 'ton' lap in 1956 were spoilt by a decision of the FIM at the end of 1955 to ban him, Reg Armstrong and some twelve other riders from motorcycle competition for six months. Although this was modified on appeal to a ban only on International events, it ruled the Gilera team out of the TT. The ban was imposed for their nominal support of a riders' protest at the 1955 Dutch TT: in Geoff's words, 'clearly we were set up as an example to deter any other FIM licence holders from contemplating similar protest action in the future'. It was a time when rider power in racing was very weak, and the FIM (and promoters receiving the income from crowds of 100,000 at Continental Grand Prix) intended it should remain that way. The TT organizers were just as mean as their Continental equivalents, still paying only £200 for a Senior TT win and offering nothing towards travel costs.

1956 Races

With Gilera absent in 1956, TT watchers felt that it could be the year that the new MV Agusta team-leader, John Surtees, achieved his first TT win. John's hopes were nearly dashed in practice when, last of a group of three leaving the right-hander of Sarah's Cottage, the two riders in front went left and right leaving John heading straight for a cow that had wandered onto the course. The ensuing collision badly dented the MV, but, as the headline of the next issue of *TT Special* proclaimed, 'Surtees Hits Cow. Both O.K.!' Undaunted by his tangle with Manx livestock, John set the fastest time through the speed trap measured over a mile of the Sulby Straight, averaging 135.38mph (217.87km/h). Walter Zeller (BMW) was next at 130.47mph (209.97km/h), while the fastest rider on a British machine was Mike O'Rourke (Norton) at 128.57mph (206.91km/h). In the Junior class Ken Kavanagh was some 8mph faster than his Moto Guzzi team-mates at a phenomenal 133.33mph (214.57km/h). The three-fifty Guzzis did not put out huge power (some 40bhp) but they were low, well streamlined and light in weight. The last of these was helped by the fact that they were relatively economical on fuel and that their full streamlining was in a light electron alloy rather than aluminium. The streamlining was finished in a drab green rather than Italian red, the reason being that the electron needed the application of a special coating to prevent corrosion and that coating was only available in one colour – drab green. An additional coat of red would have meant more weight to be carried.

The ultra-fast Ken Kavanagh did not lead the initial stages of the 1956 Junior TT, for it was his team-mate Bill Lomas who held John Surtees (MV Agusta) at bay for five laps before Bill's Moto Guzzi engine failed. Surtees then moved into the lead, but some of those who had seen his ultra-quick pit-stop on the fourth lap were not surprised when he retired on the Mountain with an empty petrol tank on the last lap. Seizing his opportunity, Ken Kavanagh brought his Guzzi home for his first TT win 4½ minutes ahead of Derek Ennett (AJS) and John Hartle (Norton), who tied for third place with Cecil Sandford on his 3-cylinder DKW fitted with hydraulic brakes. It had taken tough Australian Kavanagh six years and thir-

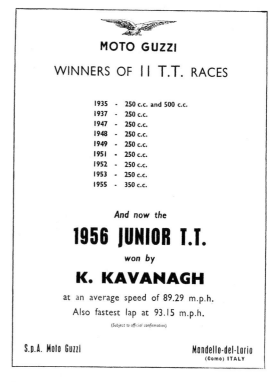

How Moto Guzzi proclaimed its TT successes.

teen Island races to win what he called 'the one race in the world that really mattered'.

It was in Friday's Senior race that John Surtees achieved his first TT victory. Controlling the race from the front (on corrected time), John finished 1½ minutes ahead of John Hartle and Jack Brett (Nortons), with Walter Zeller fourth on his BMW. In the Lightweight races Carlo Ubbiali gave MV Agusta a double win, so giving them a third win of the week (that could have been four if Surtees had not run out of fuel in the Junior), while Fritz Hillebrand (BMW) was first sidecar home ahead of five chasing Norton-mounted drivers.

The Clubman's events moved back to the Mountain Course for what were to be the last races of the series. Held in the week after the International TT events, 350 and 500 wins went to Bernard Codd riding – inevitably –

BSA Goldstars. Although there were mutterings that it was the domination of the entries and wins by Gold Stars that brought about the demise of the Clubman's races, in reality their inclusion in the TT meeting stretched the ACU's organization, and they dropped the National races for up-and-coming riders, perhaps hoping that the Manx MCC would create something similar at the MGP.

Golden Jubilee

The programme of races in 1957 saw the customary running of the Junior TT on Monday, Lightweight 125, Lightweight 250 and Sidecars on Wednesday, and Senior on Friday. But with it being fifty years since the first event there were many celebrations in between. Indeed, even practice week witnessed Stanley Woods come out of retirement to ride demonstration laps on a Moto Guzzi. An unhurried Stanley averaged lap speeds of some 82mph in his comeback ride on an 'A' reserve plate, and also tested the riding skills of some of the Triumph-mounted Travelling Marshals who had been asked to keep an eye on his progress. Showing himself to be as adept with the pen as the twist-grip, Stanley then recounted his ride in the pages of *Motor Cycling*, comparing the machinery and the course of 1957 with those of pre-war years when he was in his prime.

Also back to join in the celebrations in 1957 was the winner of the multi-cylinder class of the first TT, Rem Fowler, who could certainly see the progress in half a century of motorcycle racing over the Island's roads, during which lap speeds had grown from 40 to almost 100mph and the entry list for the Senior was not only sprinkled with 'fours' but also a spectacular water-cooled Moto Guzzi V8 in the hands of Dickie Dale. Rem would also have noticed how far the out and out racing machines of 1957 were divorced from the touring models used in 1907.

With Geoff Duke sidelined through injury and Reg Armstrong retired from racing, the Gilera team for the Junior and Senior races comprised Bob McIntyre and Australian Bob Brown. John Surtees (MV Agusta) lost his team-mate Terry Shepherd to a practice injury, but Moto Guzzi supplied bikes for Dickie Dale, Keith Campbell and John Clark, while Walter Zeller was a lone BMW entry in the Senior. The Lightweight classes were well supported by MV Agusta and Mondial, with 'works' entries also coming from the Czechoslovak CZ factory. With good entries in all events, the majority of riders in the large classes were riding Norton, AJS, Matchless and BSA machinery, many unstreamlined. With the Senior race extended to a celebratory eight laps (302 miles/486km), some riders experimented with additional pannier fuel tanks in the sides of their fairings, with the aim of covering the full race distance without stopping to refuel. Jack Brett, John Hartle and Alan Trow were all mounted on Nortons supplied through the factory and incorporating many small improvements, but which were privately entered in fully streamlined form. Norton's race effort, which was whole-hearted in some directions, but half-hearted and inconsistent in others, left British race fans confused and often in despair. However, for the record crowds (estimated at 80,000, including 14,000 day-trippers over just for the Senior) that made the journey to the Island, a week of dry practice saw lap records unofficially broken in all classes, and everyone looked forward to a feast of Jubilee TT racing.

Making something of a mockery of British efforts, Italian machinery dominated the top three finishing places in all solo classes at new record race and lap speeds, with BMW doing the same for the three-wheelers. It was Bob McIntyre on the relatively new 350cc and 49bhp Gilera-four (as much power as a five-hundred Norton) who opened the week's races with a win in Monday's Junior, and he finished it with a win in the Senior, providing a fitting end to the Golden Jubilee celebrations by setting the first 100mph lap, leaving the lap

This was the four-cylinder Gilera engine used with success at the TT. With a 52 × 58.8mm bore and stroke, it ran a 13:1 compression ratio and delivered nearly 70bhp through a five-speed gearbox.

record at 101.12mph (162.73km/h) and the race record at 98.99mph (159.30km/h). Bob was in tremendous form, breaking the 'ton' four times during the Senior race on his fully streamlined Gilera and delighting the huge crowds. Both races were won on Avon tyres that were a mere 3.5in section on the rear and finished little more than half-worn after 302 racing miles. John Surtees ran with just a handlebar fairing on his MV Agusta and had to settle for second place some two minutes behind the flying Scotsman, with Bob Brown (Gilera) third after Walter Zeller (BMW) dropped out on the fourth lap; Dickie Dale on the V8 Guzzi finished fourth. Mondial were the victors of the eight-lap Lightweight races with Cecil Sandford (250) and Tarquinio Provini (125) heading the MVs that filled the remaining podium places, while BMW took a 1-2-3 in the Sidecar race with Fritz Hillebrand top man.

With the successes they were achieving as a nation in all solo classes at the TT with their fully streamlined machines (mirroring wins in other World Championship races), it seemed strange to read of Italy making strong representations to the FIM in mid-1957 to introduce 'the greatest possible limitation of streamlining and a progressive reduction in the cubic capacity of machines admitted to championship and international races'.

What Might Have Been?

Some British fans no doubt wondered if it might have been Norton gaining the tremendous publicity arising from the Italians' Golden Jubilee wins if only the factory had maintained a fully supported 'works' race effort, while others felt that the single was truly outmoded and had really had its day. The Gilera and MV Agusta concerns had not been idle with their 350 and 500cc fours, because they had worked hard to improve power outputs, handling and other features, and it was increasingly unlikely that even a relatively light, fine-handling 50bhp single could mount a serious challenge to the almost 70bhp @ 10,500rpm output of the Gilera and MV Agusta 500cc racers. Having taken the decision to step back from racing primarily on economic grounds, Norton was unlikely to return with the necessary finance to modernize its singles with measures like fully enclosed valve-gear and enclosed gear-driven primary drive, which were badly needed to prevent oil being thrown over the rear tyre, yet alone to undertake even greater changes to uprate it in power, streamlining and braking.

The Italian companies were not immune to the high cost of top-level racing, and an announcement towards the end of 1957 shook the racing world: three of the principal Italian racing concerns – Gilera, Moto Guzzi and Mondial – were to withdraw from World Championship racing. For Moto Guzzi and Mondial the decision was taken primarily on financial grounds, but for Giuseppe Gilera the spark had gone out of life and racing following the death of his only son, Ferrucio, in October 1956.

MV, MV, MV, MV . . .

In a year when it was unchallenged by its Italian rivals, few were surprised when MV Agusta walked away from the 1958 TT with all four solo Tourist Trophies, the first time it had ever been achieved. John Surtees's Junior and Senior double wins were achieved with 5½ and 4½ minute gaps over the Norton-mounted runners-up, in races in which he had no need to threaten lap records. Tarquinio Provini and Carlo Ubbiali took the Light-weight TTs, in which there was a first appearance for Ernst Degner on the East German MZ two-strokes. With BMW taking first and second places in the Sidecar race, European domination of the TT races was confirmed for all the world to see.

At the end of 1957 the FIM had decreed that, for 1958, streamlining would be restricted to the dolphin-type fairing that left the front wheel exposed, and its adoption

John Surtees on his way to TT victory on his MV Agusta fitted with dolphin stream-lining.

probably knocked a few mph off top speeds. Use of a fairing on the bigger single-cylinder machines left riders wishing for the general availability of five-speeds in the gearbox, because gearing up to take full advantage of the increased top speed allowed by a fairing left them with too high a bottom gear to take Ramsey Hairpin and Governor's Bridge in comfort with a standard four-speed gearbox.

Despite the factory withdrawals, there were new developments to be seen at the 1958 TT. The Lightweight 125 race received interesting entries from new 'works' desmodromic Ducatis (which secured second, third and fourth places) and from East German rotary-valved two-stroke MZs, which finished fifth and sixth. Enforcement of the FIM-imposed minimum weight limit for riders in the 125cc class saw seven of them having to add lead weights to their machines. The diminutive Gary Dickinson was forced to load his MV with 23lb (10.5kg) to bring his weight up to the 132lb (60kg) minimum figure.

British manufacturers may have decided to limit themselves to production racers (although specially prepared Norton engines were made available by the factory to selected runners in 1958), but a new Matchless single-cylinder racer known as the G50 made its TT debut in the hands of Jack Ahearn. Sharing many of the components of the AJS 7R from the same stable, it was too new to have a selling price, but the twin-cylinder Matchless G45 was available for £403, the same as the AJS 7R.

The 350cc Model 40M and 500cc Model 30M Nortons cost substantially more at £481. Anyone who bought one of those standard racers with the idea of winning at a high level would usually despatch it to one of the specialist tuners of the day, such as Francis Beart, Bill Lacey, Steve Lancefield or Ray Petty. All working with the same basic material, each of these had his own ways of lifting the performance above standard, rather like the many users of JAP engines in the 1920s. Bob McIntyre had a long-term relationship with another tuner, Joe Potts; it was on one of Joe's streamlined Manx Nortons in the 1958 Senior TT that he set the fastest lap to date by a single-cylinder machine, when he averaged 99.98mph (160.90km/h) before being forced out with mechanical trouble. Always a doughty competitor, Bob's fastest lap compared well with that of race-winner John Surtees fastest of 100.58mph (161.86km/h).

With the average British race machine outclassed in world racing, it was left to British (and Commonwealth) riders to maintain the nation's racing prestige. Two men who would go on to multi-World Championships made steady TT debuts in 1958: from Rhodesia, Jim Redman took nineteenth place in the Senior and twenty-fourth in the Junior on Nortons, while Oxford's Mike Hailwood took thirteenth in the Senior, twelfth in the Junior (Nortons), third in the Lightweight 250 (NSU) and seventh in the Lightweight 125 (Paton).

6 Japanese Takeover

In the mid-1950s Honda motorcycles were sold almost exclusively in Japan, but even so Soichiro Honda's company was the largest motorcycle producer in the world. Seeking entry to a wider market, he looked across the globe to Europe and decided to embark on a racing programme that would publicize the Honda name, gain the company engineering prestige and boost its export programme. It was a decision that changed the world of motorcycling – both road and race – forever.

Honda had achieved racing success at home, mostly on dirt roads, and after Mr Honda's visit to the TT in 1954 the company sent representatives on fact-finding trips to the Isle of Man races. Armed with cameras, notepads and many questions, their task was to discover everything they could about the TT course and how best Honda could tackle the European racing opposition that had mostly dominated the TT for its first fifty years. With that preparation, and with awareness that the TT was the best possible event in which to exhibit its products to the wider world, in 1959 Honda felt ready to make its Western debut.

After several Italian companies had withdrawn from racing in 1957, the FIM was aware of the gulf that existed in 1958 between the 4-cylinder 'works' machinery fielded by MV Agusta in the Junior and Senior classes and the mostly single-cylinder production racers that made up the rest of the entries. In an attempt to provide racing on a more even basis, they stipulated that the 1959 TT should include Formula I races for 350 and 500cc machines of the type that any rider could buy 'over the counter'. The two races ran concurrently on the Saturday before the traditional race week, with entries dominated by British singles: victories went to Bob McIntyre (Norton) and Alastair King (AJS).

Some commentators believe that Honda came to the 1959 TT expecting to compete in a 'Formula' event for 125 machines. With no such class available, however, they were pitched straight in with the 125 GP exotica from the factories of such as MV Agusta and

In early 1959 Travelling Marshal and ACU representative Angus Herbert (right) shows the men from Honda, Bill Hunt (centre) and Ichioo Nitsuma (left), over the Clypse Course.

Alastair King (left) and Bob McIntyre were two formidable riders from Scotland, and won the 350 and 500cc Formula I races in 1959.

Ducati. On their twin-cylinder 125 four-stroke RC142 models, which had the appearance of race-kitted road bikes rather than factory racers, the four Japanese and one American rider received a fierce race baptism on their little Hondas.

It was the last year that the Clypse Course was used and the twelve-strong Honda team put in many miles on roadsters outside the official practice periods, being conspicuous in their futuristic jet-style helmets. Based at the Nursery Hotel in Onchan, they were totally reliant on the machines and spares they had brought from half a world away for their five race entries. Visited by many curious westerners, including one or two perceptive riders like Bill Smith and Tommy Robb, the Honda team appeared well equipped as it worked in the hotel's garages, and the thoroughness of its preparation even extended to bringing its own doctor and cook.

Practice times showed that the Hondas were unlikely to threaten Italian machinery, and so it proved in the race as Tarquinio Provini took his MV Agusta to victory at an average speed of 74.06mph (119.18km/h). In a hint of things

Teisuke Tanaka and his Honda 125 riding through the Nursery Bends at Onchan in 1959.

to come, however, the Japanese machines did show commendable reliability. Only the American rider Bill Hunt failed to reach the finish and that was due to falling on the second lap. The four Japanese riders all brought their high-revving dohc machines the full race distance, to finish in the order:

6th Naomi Taniguchi	68.29mph (109.90km/h)
7th Giichi Suzuki	66.71mph (107.36km/h)
8th Teisuke Tanaka	65.69mph (105.71km/h)
11th Junzo Suzuki	63.81mph (102.69km/h)

Those performances were good enough to win the Manufacturers' Award for Honda, and that was something they found enormously encouraging. It also indicated to astute TT watchers that such all-round reliability offered a sound basis for development and that Honda could well become a force to be reckoned with.

In a showing that proved too good for the opposition in 1959, MV Agusta repeated its 1958 performance by taking victory in all four solo classes, with John Surtees doing the Junior/Senior double and Tarquinio Provini adding the Lightweight 250 to his 125 win. Walter Schneider led BMW's domination of the Sidecar race, so contributing to an unwelcome air of predictability about the results in all classes. Indeed, MV Agusta and BMW successes extended beyond the TT to include many of the World Championship Grand Prix.

Starting Numbers

After being discussed for several years, in 1959 the starting order for riders in the interval-start TTs held over the Mountain Course was determined by seeding the top six men and entering their names into a ballot. The idea was to give the best riders an equal chance of benefiting from racing over relatively clear roads for the first few laps, rather than, under the previously used ballot system, finding a top runner starting at number 85 and so facing the handicap of having to pass many other riders. Most riders generally appreciated clear roads to race over and were happy with the new system, but there was the occasional one who felt that he raced better in company and so preferred the old system. For spectators the new arrangement made for simpler measuring of the time intervals between the likely winners and, in those pre-Manx Radio days before all the timings were done for listeners, it made the races easier to follow.

Back to the Mountain

First used in 1954, the Clypse Course had never been particularly popular with riders or spectators and it was abandoned for 1960, with all races being run over the Mountain Course. That meant Honda riders, plus most of the other Lightweight runners and Sidecar crews, had a fresh lot of learning to do.

It was the Lightweight 125s that opened race week in 1960, with MV Agusta team-leader Carlo Ubbiali averaging 85.60mph (137.76km/h) to win the three-lap race from rising star Gary Hocking and Luigi Taveri, who were also MV-mounted. Fourth and fifth places went to John Hempleman and Hugh Anderson on MZs and in sixth came the first Honda, ridden by Naomi Taniguchi at an average speed of 80.08mph (128.87km/h), to be followed by four more Hondas. Ubbiali's race average speed of 85.60mph compared with the previous year's winning speed over the Clypse Course by Tarquinio Provini (MV Agusta) of 74.06mph (119.18km/h), showing the Mountain Course to be much faster – even for 125s – than the Clypse. In fifteenth and sixteenth places came first-time entries from Suzuki, the second Japanese manufacturer to contest the TT; its twin-cylinder Colleda two-stroke models clearly needed more pace.

Honda brought new 4-cylinder RC161 machines to contest the five-lap Lightweight 250 race. Basically a doubled-up version of the 125cc RC143 with cylinder dimensions of 44 × 41mm, 16 valves, six-speed gearbox, revving to 13,500, and with inclined engines putting out about 36bhp, they brought an exciting sound to the 250 class. Like other foreign makes before them, Honda decided to augment their home-grown riders with experienced foreigners and employed Australians Tom Phillis and Bob Brown to ride in 1960. Promising as they sounded and performed, the new four-cylinder Hondas were left in the wake of the speedy MVs of winner Gary Hocking and runner-up Carlo Ubbiali, with another Italian man and machine, Tarquinio Provini (Mondial), third. Bob Brown was the best Honda rider in fourth place, but some six minutes behind Hocking. Honda clearly had some way to go to reach a race-winning TT performance, for winner Hocking averaged 93.64mph (150.69km/h) to Brown's 89.21mph (143.56km/h). Another point that must have been apparent to Honda was that their Japanese riders could not match the speeds of the opposition. Kitano finished fifth, but his average was 81.92mph (131.83km/h), some 7mph slower than Bob Brown on similar machinery.

The return of the Lightweights and Sidecars to the Mountain Course in 1960 was judged a success in riding terms, but with only thirty-three starters in the 125 race, forty-one in the 250, thirty-one sidecars, and with all competitors being sent off in pairs at ten-second intervals, there was criticism of drawn-out races that failed to hold the interest of some spectators. It was Helmut Fath (BMW) who was first sidecar home when leader Florian Camathias (BMW) slowed on the last lap. A much-vaunted potential challenge from Eric Oliver (who had the experience of eleven races over the Mountain Course on a solo) came to nothing when a crash on his Norton outfit in practice put him out of the race.

Records

Freddie Dixon's sidecar lap record of 57.18mph (92.02km/h), set over the Mountain Course back in 1925, was broken by Helmut Fath by a margin of 28.61mph when recording his fastest lap of the race at 85.79mph (138.06km/h).

Similarly, the Lightweight 125 and 250 winners could hardly have failed to set new lap records on their returns to the Mountain Course, so long had they been away, but what could the big solos do in 1960? Of the eighty starters in the Junior and seventy-one in the Senior, all but John Surtees and John Hartle (MV Agustas) were riding British machines (predominantly Nortons). It came as no real surprise when the MVs broke both Junior and

Helmut Fath leaps Ballaugh Bridge on his way to victory in the 1960 Sidecar TT. British sidecar racers usually had their 'chairs' on the left-hand side, while European riders fitted theirs on the right. Passenger Alfred Wohlgemüth can barely be seen here.

Senior lap and race records with Hartle winning the Junior and Surtees the Senior, but what was interesting was to see privately entered single-cylinder British machines lapping faster than ever before. In the Junior class Bob McIntyre (AJS) circulated at 95.33mph (153.41km/h), while Derek Minter (Norton) became the first man to break the 100mph barrier on a single when he hustled his Steve Lancefield-tuned Norton around at 101.05mph (162.62km/h) on the second lap, to be followed at over the 'ton' shortly after by Mike Hailwood (Norton).

For all the gallant efforts of the opposition, it was MV Agusta who left the 1960 TT with yet another four wins for Italy, while a BMW-powered three-wheeler returned to Germany with the Sidecar trophy.

The high speeds recorded in 1960 were probably aided by the laying of smoother tarmac on some sections, plus the easing of bumps on places like Bray Hill and on the fast descent from Creg ny Baa to Brandish Corner. John Surtees explained that with the MV's twist-grip against the stop, major bumps could see the back wheel off the ground and allow over-revving of the engine, so threatening reliability. John obviously used his course knowledge to roll back the throttle a fraction to avoid such situations, but he welcomed the road smoothing.

Rewards

Competing in several classes at the TT required a rider to be on the Island for at least two whole weeks. When the cost of travel, accommodation, entries and running of race machinery over the exceptionally long distances involved was added to the financial equation, the commitment and expense must have been enormous, yet the prize money in 1960 was still the same as in early post-war years, with even the winner/entrant of the Senior receiving only £200, and nothing being paid as start money or towards travel expenses.

Derek Minter's fantastic performance in setting the first 100mph lap on a single earned him not a penny from the organizers, because he retired on the third lap and they paid only on results. A fortnight of early morning and evening practice honing man and machine for the big effort on race-day counted for nothing with them. Such meanness and inflexibility were later to contribute to the TT's decline in status, but at the 1960 TT one man was determined that Derek's history-making effort should not go unrewarded. Stan Hailwood, father of Derek's biggest adversary on a single, Mike Hailwood, sportingly ensured that he received a cheque for £100 at the prize presentation on the evening of the race in recognition of his efforts. Unfortunately, many other worthy runners left the TT empty-handed and badly out of pocket.

Surtees Quits

It was not uncommon in the late 1950s for top riders such as John Surtees, John Hartle and Bob McIntyre to be employed by the likes of MV Agusta and Gilera to contest just the World Championship races. Their contracts then allowed them to ride their own British machinery in non-Championship events in Britain and on the Continent. For 1960 Count Agusta would not agree to John Surtees riding his own machines, although he allowed him to dabble in car racing. John had felt a slackening of race effort by MV in 1960 and, although he had kept them on top of the world for several years with TT wins and Championship successes, he was unable to get a clear statement of their plans for 1961 and so announced his retirement from motorcycle racing at the end of 1960. With its top Lightweight runner Carlo Ubbiali also retiring, MV Agusta then announced that it would not be entering 'works' teams in the World Championships (that included the TT) in 1961.

A Year of Surprises

One thing that did not surprise riders or spectators at the outset of the 1961 TT was the mixed weather during practice, which did not give riders the opportunity to show their true form. Then, notwithstanding its earlier announcement, MV Agusta provided only a mild shock by supplying 250, 350 and 500cc machines for Gary Hocking to ride, albeit adorned with 'Privat' labels that suggested they were not 'works' machines, a ploy that fooled nobody. What did not surprise seasoned race-watchers was that, having slackened its race effort, MV paid the price with machine problems for Hocking in the 350 and 500cc races, and suffered the ignominy of withdrawing its 250 from the Lightweight race when it realized that it would be trounced.

The Senior and Junior races turned into exciting duels between riders of British machines, with Mike Hailwood taking the big one at a race average speed of 100.60mph (161.90km/h) from Bob McIntyre, with Tom Phillis on the experimental Norton twin-cylinder 'Domiracer' third, to provide the first Norton 1-2-3 in the Senior TT since 1950. All forty-five finishers in the Senior rode

How the win of Mike Hailwood (middle) in the 1961 Senior TT was celebrated with fellow Norton-mounted Bob McIntyre (right) in second place and Tom Phillis (left) in third, in the paddock after the race.

How Mike Hailwood's 1961 Senior TT 1-2-3 Victory was commemorated in later years.

British machines. In a particularly impressive Junior performance, 1960 Senior MGP winner Phil Read (Norton) outrode the ailing MV of Gary Hocking to secure first place on his TT debut. It received the headline in *Motor Cycling* of 'Private Norton Beats "Privat" MV' – point made!

Despite the prestige attached to the bigger classes they were lacking in 'works' support, but it was encouraging to see the variety of machinery entered in the Lightweight classes. Honda and Suzuki were back, and were joined in both Lightweight races by compatriots Yamaha with rotary-valve, air-cooled, two-strokes, the 125 single being called the RA41 and the 250 twin the RD48. There were Spanish 125 Bultacos, British 125 EMC (the only water-cooled machine in the 1961 TT), while Italy (after MV Agusta's late withdrawal) was represented by the names of Ducati, Bianchi and Aermacchi. The German concern of NSU no longer contested the TT with 'works' machines but its 250 single was very popular with private runners.

The Mountain Course has always been difficult territory for highly tuned two-strokes, with the changes of atmospheric pressure and temperature brought about by the variation in height from near sea level to 1,400ft causing particular difficulties for carburation. Suzukis were much troubled in practice and the East German MZ concern could not get its carburation right and was forced to withdraw its entries.

Honda Success

After only two previous years of island experience, it was Honda that seized its opportunity at the 1961 TT. With much improved machines ridden by some of the best riders of the day, the company swept to Lightweight victory taking the first five places in both 125 and 250 races, with Mike Hailwood victorious in both. Although the opposition may have been weakened by withdrawals, these were not hollow victories, for they were both achieved at record-breaking speeds. It was a stunning performance from Honda in only its third TT appearance, and after its Island successes it went on to more sweeping victories in the World Championships.

Honda's triumphs were shared by Mike Hailwood, who finished the week with a hat-trick of wins – 125, 250 and 350 – that could so easily have been four if the crank-pin of his AJS had not failed while leading the Junior on the last lap. It was not unusual for a good rider to ride more than one make of machine at the TT, but it showed tremendous versatility to ride ones with such different power characteristics, number of gears and varied control positions, particularly at such high level. Mike's successes were shared by one of Britain's biggest motorcycle dealers, King's of Oxford, for his father Stan was among the owners of the firm and it incorporated Mike's TT wins into its post-TT advertising with the slogan 'Fabulous Treble – A British Boy (Mike), A British Firm (King's of Oxford), A British Machine (Norton)'. Strangely, although there

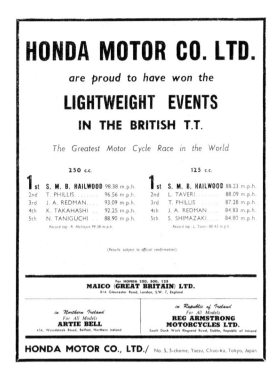

Honda proudly advertised its successes at the 1961 TT.

was reference to Mike's Lightweight and Ultra-Lightweight victories in their advertising, the name Honda did not appear. It is said that shortly after his 1961 Honda victories King's became agents for the Japanese marque.

Another Honda that achieved a first at the 1961 TT was the converted sports roadster of Fred Stevens. When the timekeeper waved his flag for Fred to go in the Lightweight 250 race, he pressed the Honda's electric-start button and departed swiftly down the Glencrutchery Road ahead of his starting companion, eventually finishing in a creditable thirteenth place.

British Turmoil

Soon after the 1962 TT the motorcycling world was shocked when AMC closed Norton's Bracebridge Street factory and transferred production to the AJS/Matchless premises at Woolwich. It was the beginning of the end for AMC's Manx, G50 and 7R production racers, with few produced in 1962 and a mere handful assembled from spares in 1963. Its products had their customary numerical supremacy in the Junior and Senior classes at the 1962 TT, but with Mike Hailwood riding with Gary Hocking on MV Agustas, the best that British makes could hope for was to occupy the lesser places. Hailwood duly won the Junior from Hocking, and Hocking then took the Senior after Hailwood had dropped out. František Stastny rewarded Jawa's efforts in coming from behind the Iron Curtain with parallel-twin four-strokes by taking a fine third place in the Junior with his Czechoslovak machine.

Changes

The 1962 TT received 344 entries from 205 riders. The timetable of races was altered slightly, and a new two-lap race for 50cc machines was introduced to run before the Senior on Friday of race week. Several small European manufacturers like Kreidler and Itom entered the 50cc TT, but it was no surprise to see Japanese machines take the three podium places. Suzuki's Ernst Degner was first home with an average speed of 75.12mph (120.89km/h), followed by Luigi Taveri and Tommy Robb on Honda RC111 models. Degner's race speed on his 50 was fractionally faster than that achieved by Cromie McCandless when he won the first 125cc race at 74.85mph (120.46km/h) eleven years earlier in 1951. A new sight in the 50cc race was that of a female solo rider competing for a Tourist Trophy: making history was Beryl Swain, who achieved a finish on her Itom in twenty-second place, and in so doing received almost as much publicity as Junior and Senior winners Mike Hailwood and Gary Hocking combined.

Unusually, it was the Sidecars that opened the race programme in 1962 and Britain's Chris Vincent surprised the previously all-conquering BMWs by bringing his low-slung

BSA parallel twin home in first place, after several of the German flat-twins retired from the race, including Max Deubel who set the first 90mph (144.8km/h) lap by a sidecar outfit. It was BSA's first ever International TT win, although they had been successful in the former Clubman's solo races.

Something that did not change in 1962 was Honda's dominance of the Lightweight 125 and 250 classes, where once again they took the first three places and, as in 1961, Bob McIntyre set the fastest 250 lap at just over 99mph but again failed to finish the race. Victory went to Derek Minter on a machine entered by British importers Hondis. It was an outstanding ride, but one that did not go

Gary Hocking holds the Senior Tourist Trophy that he won in 1962.

down too well with the Honda factory or its expensive 'works' riders, with Jim Redman particularly irked at losing the chance of a win and the associated World Championship points. Jim had to settle for second place, finishing almost two minutes behind the winner. A particularly creditable showing in the 125 race was that of Mike Hailwood on the British EMC, holding on to second place for more than two laps before being forced out near Glen Helen, leaving Luigi Taveri to win with a minute to spare from Tommy Robb.

Triumph and Tragedy

As at other TT races down the years, the excitement, spectacle, joy and glory of the 1962 series was overshadowed by the death of a fine rider. Honda had entered a couple of 285cc RC170-fours in the Junior race and Australian Tom Phillis was killed on one at Laurel Bank when lying third and trying hard to catch Hocking and Hailwood on their MVs. A popular figure who was much admired and respected, he also had an incredible desire to win. In the early 1960s there was not only intense competition between opposing teams but also fierce rivalry between riders in the same teams, since the number of

coveted 'works' rides were few while the number of riders who aspired to them were many. Tom Phillis's death had a major effect on his close friends in motorcycle racing. His Honda team-mate Jim Redman had serious thoughts of quitting but was persuaded by Bob McIntyre to keep riding. Gary Hocking felt that all the riders were being forced to press each other too hard and he persuaded Count Domenico Agusta to release him from his MV contract. The dreadful irony was that, while the reluctant Redman did continue racing, McIntyre was killed a few months later at Oulton Park and Hocking died in a car race in his native Rhodesia before the year ended.

More Changes

There has never been a year in the century of TT racing when some aspect of the event's development has not brought about change. Almost always this has resulted in progress in one or more of the many different aspects of the meeting, be it organization, rules, machines, riders, technical development or marshalling. At intervals, although it may not have been apparent at the time, the change would be such as to bring the TT into a new era, and 1963 was one such year, with three

Tom Phillis at speed on the Honda on which he lost his life in 1962.

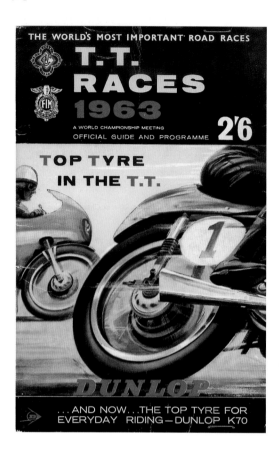

innovations that materially altered the nature of the meeting and its future: the payment of limited expenses to riders; the introduction of a rescue helicopter; and Honda contesting and winning one of the 'big' classes.

Even though the TT, owing to its location and special requirements, was the most expensive event on the race calendar, previous requests from riders to the ACU, the organizers, for financial help had proved fruitless. The ACU knew that the top men had to race at the TT because of its World Championship status, and that anyone else who could ride the event would make the necessary sacrifices to do so, simply because contesting a TT was the ultimate racing achievement.

The unsung hero in the successful move of 1963 to get a payment towards riders' travelling

expenses was top British sidecar driver Bill Boddice. As a staunch supporter of the ACU, Bill did not want to be at loggerheads with them, but he was determined to make his point, even to the extent of withholding his TT entry until he knew that money was forthcoming. In fact, it was the Isle of Man Tourist Board that came up with the money in 1963, not the ACU. The modest but welcome sum awarded to each rider who qualified to race was £10 for 50cc runners and £15 for every other solo. Sidecar entries received £25. Requests for an increase in prize money were refused and it remained the same as the immediate post-war level. But a breach had been made in the seemingly impregnable TT financial wall and, although it took many years, the contribution of riders to the success of the meeting was grudgingly accepted and eventually led to an increase in the all-important monetary rewards.

One man who fully earned his £25 in 1963 was Swiss sidecar driver Florian Camathias. Driving up through England before the practice week, his van broke down near Hinckley (that was his £25 gone on repairs!) With his prime concern being to get to the Isle of Man, he unloaded his BMW racing outfit, and he and his passenger climbed into their leathers and set off for Douglas on open pipes. There was a slight hitch at the Mersey tunnel when they could not produce money for the toll, but they were let through, made it to the boat, crossed to the Island and, for good measure, won the Sidecar TT!

Helicopter Rescue

As has been described above, a rider injured on the course in the TT's early days might have a long wait for a doctor to arrive, and then could be stuck for several hours more before being moved from the course to hospital. Even in the 1950s the organizers were understandably reluctant to allow an ambulance on the course to evacuate an injured rider, for fear of causing further accidents. By the early 1960s it was clear that the future of the races was in jeopardy unless there were improvements in medical care for fallen riders.

Already supplying fuel for the races, it was Shell Mex-BP who came to the rescue by funding a rescue helicopter for race periods. Racing had entered a period of frantic development in the Lightweight classes, with ultra-fast two-strokes being ridden to their limits by riders anxious to preserve their 'works' status and gain the generous rewards handed out by the Japanese factories in return for success. It was an activity that multiplied the dangers of racing. One of the most successful participants, Phil Read, described the compensations: 'We swept through a show-piece of classic racing competition that was boosted by an open cheque-book, the like of which we may never see again'.

Yamaha had made its TT debut in 1961, missed 1962, but returned in 1963 with much-improved 125 and 250cc models. It was Britain's Tony Godfrey, riding one of the new ultra-fast 250cc RD56 models, who provided the first mission for the rescue helicopter when he crashed at Milntown during the Lightweight 250 race. Whisked away to Ramsey Hospital within minutes of falling, his swift transfer to medical care is said to have saved his life.

Given the demanding nature of the TT course, the Tony Godfrey incident is one that has been repeated many times in the period of more than forty years since the helicopter was introduced. Such is the value of the service that today there are two helicopters on duty for every race and practice session. Without them there would be no racing.

Honda Move Up

Honda came, saw and conquered the Light-weight 125 and 250 classes at the TT in a few short years. Inevitably they then looked towards the bigger race classes just as, with their road bikes, they were progressing beyond lightweights. The Honda team had fifteen race

Even with the services of the rescue helicopter, it can be a long haul for a stretcher party to reach an acceptable landing spot with an injured rider.

Jim Redman and his 350cc Honda-four at Ballaugh Bridge on his way to Junior TT victory.

machines at the 1963 TT and it was Jim Redman who took a 'four' to an emphatic first-time victory in the Junior (350cc) TT, so making the point to race-watchers that Honda would not be satisfied until it dominated all solo classes from 50 to 500cc.

Jim Redman was a hard-headed professional who led the Honda race-team from the front. After years of trying, his first TT win came in the Lightweight 250 two days before his Junior victory in 1963. The 250 win, however, was far from straightforward for Jim. Harried, and even led for a lap, by Fumio Ito on his rapid Yamaha, Jim was glad that Ito and several other challengers dropped back or retired, for, as is so often the case in a TT, things were not going well for the race leader. On an exceptionally hot day with many corners made dangerous by molten tar, Jim's engine overheated to the extent of inflicting burns to his legs through his leathers for a period of several laps. While this was happening his Honda-4 gradually lost speed and he worried whether it would last for the full six-lap distance: it did and, to much back slapping in the paddock, Jim achieved his long-held ambition. He later told of the scene back at his hotel after he had received the coveted Tourist Trophy at the evening's prize presentation:

> Conversations were very animated and exclusively about the race. Not only mine, of course, as each rider told of his own problems and his view of the race which, for many, was the bike event of the year. I loved listening to these stories; the magnificent and incredible accounts of each one, and seeing the riders get fired up as they relived the race.

The scene Jim describes is one that has, and still is, repeated at every TT, because to each rider his race is a personal milestone of survival and achievement, whether he finishes in first or fifty-first position.

So, Honda had won the 1963 Lightweight 250 and Junior TTs, but it was a different story in the smaller classes in which it had previously put in very strong performances. Having allowed development of its 50cc four-stoke twins to be put on hold, it saw Mitsuo Itoh and Hugh Anderson take the first two places for its Japanese rivals Suzuki. Matters were worse in the Lightweight 125 race, in which Suzuki took the first three places, leaving Luigi Taveri to bring the first Honda home in fourth position. This leap-frogging of each other in both the technical and performance stakes was a common feature with Japanese manufacturers – Honda, Suzuki and Yamaha – in the 1960s.

Gileras Return

The really big talking-point before the 1963 TT was the fact that Geoff Duke had persuaded Gilera to return to racing with their 'moth-balled' 350 and 500cc 4-cylinder machines in a team named Scuderia Duke. Clearly, because he was putting his reputation on the line, Geoff believed that if Gilera took advantage of developments that had occurred in areas such as tyre technology, suspension and streamlining, they could challenge MV Agusta (and Honda) in Junior and Senior classes in 1963. Early-season races produced promising results, but a fall by team-leader Derek Minter at Brands Hatch on his own Norton resulted in a broken arm, so the Junior TT winner of 1961, Phil Read, was recruited to support John Hartle when Scuderia Duke brought 350 and 500cc Gileras to contest the TT.

The Scuderia Duke race logo.

Before the 1963 TT it was assumed that Mike Hailwood on 'Privat' MV Agustas was the man to beat in both Junior and Senior classes; Mike did his best to confirm that by ensuring, in a metaphorical throwing down of the gauntlet, that every one of his Senior practice laps was covered at more than 100mph. It was Jim Redman, Honda and fate – in the form of Mike's MV breaking down – that conspired to prevent him featuring in the results of the Junior race, and John Hartle brought the small Gilera into second place, while Phil Read retired. Come the Senior and Mike Hailwood commanded proceedings. Starting ten seconds behind John Hartle, at the end of the first lap the pair swept past the grandstand and down Bray Hill with Mike sitting comfortably on John's tail and thus leading the race on corrected time. Mike soon moved ahead on the road and, with laps that included a new absolute course record of 106.41mph (171.25km/h), ensured that he stayed ahead of the Gileras. It was no easy victory, however, for Hartle's pursuit saw him lap at 105.57mph (169.89km/h) and Read was also well over the 100mph mark. At the finish Mike was just over a minute ahead after slowing with gear-change problems, and the Gileras finished second and third. Having seen the Gileras lap the Mountain Course far faster than ever before, Geoff Duke was not disappointed with Scuderia Duke's performances but, like so many before and after, his team found Mike Hailwood to be superior on the day.

Talk of Gilera appearing at the 1964 TT with John Hartle and South American Bruno Calderella as riders came to nothing. But the company had successfully contested Continental Sidecar GPs during the 1950s and, although it had never previously brought a three-wheeler to the TT, in 1964 it loaned Florian Camathias an engine for selected meetings and he rode it in the Sidecar TT. Lying second to Max Deubel (BMW), he retired from the three-lap race, leaving Colin Seeley (FCSB) to take second place. Apart from a brief appearance by Derek Minter on a machine from Arcore at the 1966 TT, when he fell and broke an arm in practice, that was Gilera's final tilt at the Isle of Man races.

1964

In trying to cover a century of TT racing it really is not possible to do justice every year to the massive efforts of riders, manufacturers,

trade representatives and sponsors that in 1964, for example, catered for a buoyant 450 entries in the six race classes. There was a particularly impressive ninety-six in the Lightweight 250, representing twenty 'real' manufacturers (as well as a few 'specials'), among them being machines from Honda, Suzuki, Yamaha, MZ, Benelli, Aermacchi, Ducati, Paton, Greeves, Royal Enfield, Cotton, Bultaco, CZ, NSU and Moto Guzzi. Practice performances showed that, while any of the first five named companies was capable of achieving a win, there was a gulf in performance between their 250 racers and the remainder of the entries. Nowhere was this more apparent than on the flat-out 2-mile section of the course past Glenlough, through Glen Vine, Crosby Village, and on to the drop

For day-trippers, or those who could not afford a full programme, an Official Score Card was sold for each day's racing. There were twenty-nine entries in the 1964 50cc race and ninety in the Senior.

Manx Radio

Manx Radio has had a very significant impact on the enjoyment and information that spectators and rider support teams have received from the TT races since it first broadcast in 1965. Before then spectators could only hear a full race commentary if they watched from one of the popular vantage points served by the limited public address system. Before 1965 the BBC had slimmed down its 'commentaries' to brief updates, so even those who carried portable radios missed out on the real details of what was going on if they were on a remote part of the course.

Based initially in a Portakabin behind the timekeeper's hut opposite the grandstand, Manx Radio's commentator Peter Kneale could not even see the progress of the race on the main scoreboard in his first couple of years, since the BBC, despite its now scanty reports, insisted on maintaining its pole position in the grandstand commentary position. From those difficult beginnings Manx Radio progressed to its own spot in the grandstand in 1967 and added the support of commentaries from strategic positions around the course, enabling it to offer what one writer of the time described as 'wheel by wheel, gear by gear, race-length commentaries'.

An early advertisement for Manx Radio.

It was not only spectators who benefited from the greatly enhanced information that Manx Radio transmitted during the course of two-hour long TT races, because riders' support crews in the pits and at signalling points around the circuit also received the timings broadcast over the airwaves. They soon realized that the times and placings given out over the radio were up-to-date and accurate, and that the information could quickly be converted into very useful signals to riders, particularly if signalling teams were carefully positioned. Manx Radio's enhancement of support crews' ability to inform riders of their own and their rivals' positions and timings at strategic positions around the course has, without doubt, influenced the outcome of several closely fought TT and MGP races.

---

past The Highlander. It was a regular timing place for the *TT Special* and its speed trap showed the fastest passages to be by Jim Redman (Honda) at 133.33mph (214.57km/h), new Yamaha 'works' rider Phil Read 130.00mph (209.21km/h), Frank Perris (Suzuki) 127.68mph (205.48km/h), and both Tarquinio Provini (Benelli) and Alan Shepherd (MZ) at 126.80mph (204.06km/h). The best of the remainder were around the 115–120mph mark, with many others between 100 and 115mph.

Phil Read led the Lightweight 250 race with a standing-start lap of just over 100mph, the first to be achieved by a 250. Read later retired, and it was Jim Redman who brought his

Honda to victory ahead of Alan Shepherd (MZ). With a high drop-out rate among the fastest runners, third place went to Alberto Pagani (Paton), who, emphasizing the gulf in performance between the top teams and the lesser ones, was nearly eighteen minutes behind Shepherd. Redman went on to win the Junior and take second place behind Luigi Taveri (Honda) in the Lightweight 125, a race in which, unlike the previous year, when they took the first three places, Suzuki did not shine.

Mike Hailwood missed the Junior through illness, but rose from his sickbed to ride the Senior and brought his MV Agusta home at just sufficient speed to beat Derek Minter (Norton).

A New Star

Italy had sent its share of top riders to the TT in previous years – Pietro Ghersi, Omobono Tenni, Dario Ambrosini, Carlo Ubbiali and Tarquinio Provini – but in 1965 a 23-year-old who had made his name in Italian Lightweight racing made his TT debut, and he was to outshine all other Italian stars on the Mountain Course. Count Domenico Agusta hoped that the young Giacomo Agostini would be the answer to his prayers and deliver to MV Agusta not only TT wins but also 500 and 350cc World Championships. The company had already been successful in the prestigious Junior and Senior classes and at World level with John Surtees, Gary Hocking and Mike Hailwood, but what the Count really wanted was for the wins to come from an Italian rider on his Italian machine. Perhaps it was unfortunate that this dream scenario was coming about at a time when the 'Blue Riband' Senior TT was actually losing some of its glamour to the vibrant Lightweight 250 race, due, ironically, to the total domination of the big class by MV Agusta.

Mike Hailwood was still the MV team-leader and, as a 'veteran' at twenty-five years of age (and twenty-four TT races), compared to first-timer Agostini's mere twenty-three years, he was probably expected to show the Italian all he knew.

On his first visit to the TT, Giacomo Agostini rides a roadster MV Agusta past the policeman on point-duty where Broadway joins Douglas Promenade in 1965.

When the time came for Agostini's first early-morning practice, the newcomer probably wished he had remained in Italy. On a cold, wet Manx morning he piloted his MV around for two laps at a lowly average speed of 75mph. Matters improved greatly for him during the week, but it was interesting to see from the speed trap at The Highlander that Hailwood's speed on the big MV over the previous 2 miles was exactly 150mph (241.39km/h), and Agostini's 141.7mph (228.0km/h). But then a healthy degree of caution on behalf of the newcomer was no bad thing, for the TT course cannot be learnt overnight.

Crossley's Tours

Many and varied are the ways that riders go about learning how to race over the TT course, and most recognize the need for application of time and the seeking of skilled assistance. But in the 1930s and 1940s it was not uncommon for a rider to venture onto the course for his first practice lap without ever having been around it before. Such apparent recklessness might just have been acceptable in those slower days but by the 1960s it was outlawed by a race regulation that stated: 'Drivers entering the TT races who have not previously ridden on the TT circuit will not be allowed to commence practising until they have been on an officially conducted tour of the course or alternatively, have completed one lap of the course under the supervision of Travelling Marshals'. The accepted way of meeting the requirement was to go on one of the coach tours originated by former MGP winner and Travelling Marshal Don Crossley, during which an experienced former rider would give a running commentary packed with as much advice as possible.

In 1965 the MV Agustas were again beaten by a Honda in the Junior race, even though Mike Hailwood set the fastest lap on his new and speedier 3-cylinder, seven-speed model before retiring. Indeed, not only did Jim

Riders of British machines were forced to race for the lesser places in the 1965 Junior TT, dominated by Honda and MV. Here Alan Dugdale leads Dan Shorey entering Creg ny Baa with Kate's Cottage in the background. Dugdale finished in twentieth place and Shorey was sixteenth.

A tired Mike Hailwood is congratulated by his MV Agusta crew after bringing his battered machine to the finish in first place at the 1965 Senior TT.

Redman pick up his third consecutive Junior win for Honda, but Phil Read brought a Yamaha in second, leaving Agostini to come a creditable third.

MVs were still in a class of their own in the Senior, but the TT course is a great leveller, and both Mike Hailwood and Agostini were brought down to earth by treacherous road conditions that saw them fall from their 500s above Sarah's Cottage (on different laps). Indeed, the first thing Mike saw as he got to his feet was team-mate Agostini's battered MV leaning against the bank. While Ago called it a day after coming off on the second lap, the courageous and determined Hailwood picked up his fallen MV, literally kicked several pieces back into shape and got back into the race despite a broken windscreen, badly bent clutch lever, two flattened exhausts and an oil leak: he made two lengthy pit stops and still rode to victory over Joe Dunphy (Norton).

Although it did not seem to receive a mention at the time, the circumstances of Hailwood's restart might well have brought about his disqualification. Sarah's Cottage is located on an uphill right-hand bend soon after the course leaves Glen Helen for Creg

Willey's. With its steep slope, Sarah's is not the easiest place to push-start a racing bike, and eyewitnesses told of Mike rolling it downhill (against the flow of the race) to bump it into life. While he no doubt broke the rules by doing so, the reality is that Sarah's is probably wide enough to perform such a manoeuvre without getting anywhere near the racing line.

Jim Redman also won the Lightweight 250 race in 1965, so making it a further hat-trick of wins in that category in consecutive years. However, any danger of the Lightweight class becoming predictable was prevented by the no-expense-spared activities of Yamaha and Suzuki to match Honda's efforts, in this case unsuccessfully, leaving Mike Duff (Yamaha) to take second and Frank Perris (Suzuki) to come third. World Champion Phil Read – still on an air-cooled Yamaha – set the 250 pace with an opening lap of 100.01mph (160.95km/h, a first for the class) but this was later beaten by Redman (100.09mph/161.07km/h), who upon Read's retirement was able to ease his pace at the head of the field. Having his first ride on a 'works' Yamaha was Bill Ivy (contracted just for the IOM and Dutch TTs) who lapped at over 98mph before sliding off at Brandywell. Had the 'works' riders for the Japanese companies failed to deliver in the 250 class, there were other makes and riders ready to take their place, for Provini (Benelli) was fourth, Stastny (Jawa) fifth, Williams (Mondial) sixth and Milani (Aermacchi) seventh.

The 50cc 'tiddlers' still had their race on Friday before the Senior, and there were thirty-eight entries in 1965. However, there was a huge difference in performance between the 'works' entries and those of private runners. At The Highlander speed trap Ralph Bryans (Honda) recorded an incredible 109.09mph (175.56km/h), with the next fastest being Michio Ichino (Suzuki) at 100.00mph (160.93km/h). Many others were struggling to hit 80mph on this very fast stretch, leaving them with no hope of competing with the 'works' bikes, however well they rode. Race victory went to Luigi Taveri on his twin-cylinder RC115 Honda, which

50cc machines round Governor's Bridge, with Michio Ichino leading Isao Morishita. Both were riding Suzukis.

was reputed to rev to over 20,000rpm and deliver 15bhp if full use was made of its ten-speed gearbox to 'keep it on the boil'. Taveri set the fastest lap at 80.83mph (130.08km/h), with Suzukis taking second and third places about a minute behind.

It is interesting to compare the speeds of the 50s with that of the 500 sidecars, the fastest of which just managed to hit 120mph over the stretch to The Highlander. Speeds were close among the top three-wheelers with Max Deubel fastest, Fritz Scheidegger 1mph slower and Florian Camathias another 1mph in arrears. A strange introduction for the sidecars in 1965 was a 'No Overtaking' zone on the narrow and twisty approach to Ballaugh. Indicated by roadside signs, the penalty for breaking the new rule was exclusion. Max Deubel (BMW) won the race at record speed from Scheidegger. It was customary for British riders to have the sidecar mounted to the left of the machine, while Europeans had theirs on the right. Unusually, Scheidegger had his on the left, maybe because his passenger, John Robinson, was British.

After several years of trying, Phil Read gave Yamaha its first TT win when he pushed Taveri (Honda) into second place in the Lightweight 125 event riding the water-cooled RA97, with team-mate Mike Duff bringing his Yamaha into third. The Lightweight classes were still very important to the Japanese manufacturers as an aid to promotion and sales of their predominantly small-capacity products, for they were only just taking an interest in producing road bikes over 250cc.

It was Mike Duff, riding in four classes on a mixture of 'works' Yamahas and well-prepared but privately entered British machinery, who showed the differences in speeds between the classes in the figures he recorded at The Highlander:

125cc Yamaha 125mph (201.2 km/h)
250cc Yamaha 143.4mph 230.8km/h)
350cc AJS 7R 122.9mph (197.8km/h)
500cc Matchless G50 137.1mph (220.6km/h)

A man with a long history of supporting the efforts of British riders at the TT was Reg Dearden. In 1965 he brought a mere fourteen machines to the TT, whereas in earlier years he brought as many as twenty-two, plus spare engines, gearboxes and so on.

Hailwood to Honda

As ever in the 1960s, each TT race was just one part of the wider World Championship. Mike Hailwood and Giacomo Agostini left the island to compete in further Continental GPs, and Count Agusta waited impatiently for his Italian rider to match and better the pace of his British team-leader, while Mike got on with winning and clinched his fourth consecutive 500cc World Championship. Towards the end of the 1965 season the count became a little impatient and suggested to Mike that he should move over and let the young Italian taste victory, Mike did move over – to Honda, with the expectation of earning considerably more from his racing.

With his former Japanese employers promising him a new 500, a 350, a 250 and the opportunity to ride Hondas in non-championship meetings, Mike looked forward to the 1966 season. Little information was available from Japan regarding the new 500, although in February *Motor Cycle News* reported on the possibility of a V8, but by March the news was out that it would be a transverse four, code-named the RC181 model, which initially delivered about 85bhp @ 12,500rpm via a six-speed gearbox.

At MV Agusta it was announced that Giacomo Agostini, by now commonly known as 'Ago', would be the company's sole rider on 3-cylinder 350 and 500cc machines, while Honda's compatriots, Yamaha, was expected to be racing faster 4-cylinder versions of their already very quick two-strokes piloted by Phil Read, Bill Ivy and Mike Duff.

No TT?

Manx people naturally consider their island to be the 'mainland' and their principal form of transport to 'the adjoining Isles' of Britain has always been by sea. The Isle of Man was affected more than most by a seamen's strike in 1966 that extended over the TT period and prevented the races from being run on their customary dates. By juggling with the dates of the MGP, time was found for the TT to be run at the end of August, just after the Ulster GP. Revised race-days were Sunday 28 August, Wednesday 31 August and Friday 2 September. The first race-day had to be on Sunday, rather than the customary Monday, to allow many of the riders to make a quick dash by specially chartered boat to honour racing commitments at Oulton Park in Cheshire on Bank Holiday Monday. New legislation had to be passed by Tynwald, the Manx Parliament, to allow Sunday racing.

With Jim Redman out of action with arm injuries sustained at the Belgian GP in July, which eventually brought about his retirement from racing, no one was in any doubt as to who was Honda's main man at the 1966 TT – it was Mike Hailwood, who was entered in 125, 250, 350 and 500 races. The new Honda 500-4, however, had only a few races to its name when it was wheeled out to tackle the Mountain Course. Its earlier performances on the relatively smooth GP circuits had shown that it was fast enough (more than 160mph), but its handling left much to be desired and Mike was in no doubt that it would prove a handful on the island.

Other well-known names found the TT difficult in 1966, including former winners Tarquinio Provini (Benelli) and Derek Minter (Gilera), who were both sidelined during practice. An unwise temporary engine repair of the 4-cylinder Benelli 350 caused it to fail as Provini neared Ballaugh, the engine locked and he was thrown from the machine, suffering injuries that ended his racing career. In Minter's case he fell from the Gilera at Brandish and broke his arm, so putting an end to

Mike Hailwood on the 500cc Honda-four.

the company's second TT return. While 1966 saw the end of the TT careers of Provini and Minter, there were, as every year, first-time riders at the event who would achieve high finishing places. The particularly talented found themselves on the podium in the first year, while others had to graft for several years before attaining success. In 1966 Peter Williams was one of the former and Kel Carruthers one of the latter.

Although the week allowed for training was not without incident for the Honda camp, Mike Hailwood finished it at the head of the 250 and 500 practice leaderboards and Ralph Bryans was fastest 50. The 125s were headed by Hugh Anderson (Suzuki) and Sidecars by Max Deubel (BMW). Mike continued his good form into the races, winning the Lightweight 250 and setting a fastest lap of 104.29mph (167.83km/h), which that was an incredible 3.5mph faster than the previous best. Runner-up was Stuart Graham, son of Les Graham, recruited by Honda to ride one of the RC166 6-cylinder 250s after Jim Redman was injured. A convincing win in the Senior by Hailwood saw him raise the absolute course record to 107.07mph (172.31km/h),

but he was out of luck with valve trouble in the Junior, where Agostini took his MV to his first TT victory. Yamaha proved that they had the legs of the opposition in the Lightweight 125 race (even over Honda's 5-cylinder RC149), with Bill Ivy and Phil Read one and two. It was some consolation for the fact that their 4-cylinder 250s had proved troublesome throughout the TT period.

It was actually the Sidecars that had opened race week with the first Sunday TT. BMW engines were still the favoured motive force with the top men, and with chassis developments, plus the use of wider car-type wheels and tyres, speeds continued to increase. In an extremely close three-lap race Fritz Scheidegger took first place by less than a second from Max Deubel. Then came controversy when Scheidegger was disqualified for using Esso fuel instead of the Shell-BP declared on his entry form. Scheidegger maintained, and was backed by witnesses, that he had altered his brand of fuel to Esso at the weigh-in as the appropriate paperwork proved and allowed. After protracted appeals, Fritz was reinstated as winner.

Grid numbers were down in the 50cc race and, although winner Ralph Bryans (Honda

125

RC116) set an amazing new lap record of 85.66mph (137.85km/h), hitting 110.45mph (177.75km/h), the relatively small entry failed to hold spectator interest and the event's days were numbered. The last 50cc TT was run in 1968, with Ralph's record lap of 1966 standing as the fastest of all time.

The MGP practice and race weeks followed almost immediately after the 1966 TT, giving the tolerant Manx people nearly a month of road closures, noise and disturbance to their everyday affairs. It was also a month's work for many of those in the organization, marshalling, policing and reporting of the races, involving a whole army of people who give their time and enthusiasm for the TT and MGP events.

Diamond Jubilee

Returning to its normal place in the racing calendar in 1967, the TT celebrated its Diamond Jubilee. This entailed a little more pomp, a few more worthy speeches, the issue of Jubilee medals, and even the release of 2,500 racing pigeons from the grandstand to compete in the 'Pigeon TT'. All this meant little to the riders, who received the same £15

expenses as 1963 and the same prize money as 1947. However, as well as tackling races in the recognized classes, they did have the opportunity to compete in a new Production machine race of National status with three classes (750, 500 and 250cc) over three laps.

The race for Production machines opened the meeting on the Saturday before race week, and the classes were set off with Le Mans-style massed starts at three-minute intervals, the first to go being the 750s. On a works-prepared Triumph Bonneville, John Hartle led from start to finish at an average speed of 97.10mph (156.26km/h), fending off the challenges of Paul Smart (Dunstall Norton Dominator) and Tony Smith (BSA Spitfire), who finished second and third.

A Triumph had challenged for a win in the first TT of 1907 and it was another successful British make from the early days, Velocette, that took first and second places in the 500cc class with Neil Kelly and Keith Heckles. Neil thus became the second Manxman to win a TT race (after Tom Sheard), rather fitting for someone whose boyhood years had been spent living on Bray Hill.

The Production bikes drew much spectator interest, and the 250 class really had them on

John Hartle (Triumph) on his way to victory in the 750cc Production Class of the 1967 TT.

Derek Woodman on the East German MZ on which he finished third in the 1967 Junior TT.

their toes. Bill Smith and Tommy Robb started alongside each other on Bultaco Metrallas and raced that way for 113 miles (182km). At the finish it was Bill who took the win by four-tenths of a second at an average speed of 88.63mph (142.63km/h), giving the speedy Spanish machine a performance not far short of the winning 500 Velocette's 89.89mph (144.66km/h). Traditionalists were pleased to see Production machines back at the TT, for it was a move that related to the event's 'Tourist' origins. Although very different to the early Triumph, Norton and Matchless models, the Production machines of the 1960s did enough on their reappearance to gain a place in future TT meetings.

But if matters were bright on the Production machine front, they were less so in the racing classes where Honda had withdrawn support from the 50 and 125cc events, and reduced its 'works' representatives in the 250, 350 and 500 races to just Mike Hailwood

(and Ralph Bryans on a 250). The absence of more team members caused Mike to comment that Honda was getting three men's work for one man's pay. That pay was reputed to be £25–40,000 per annum, depending on who you believe, while, by comparison, Suzuki rider Stuart Graham is said to have received £4,000 per annum. Showing that he was worth the money, Mike won the Lightweight 250 race from Phil Read (Yamaha) and, in a stunning display, took his favoured 6-cylinder 297cc machine to victory over Giacomo Agostini in the Junior race. Quickly taking the lead on the road from starting companion Derek Woodman (MZ), Mike showed the opposition just what he could do with clear roads and a willing Honda beneath him. His winning margin was more than three minutes; he not only smashed the Junior lap and race records but also set a new absolute course record at 107.73mph (173.37km/h). It was all stuff for the record

A Race to Remember

With the late arrival of the Honda 500 on the GP scene in 1966, Giacomo Agostini and his MV Agusta had taken the 500cc World Championship from four-times holder Mike Hailwood and arguably held 'top-dog' status, but with his fantastic display and outright lap record in the Junior a couple of days before, had the Honda man been making the point as to who was still boss at the TT?

Whatever was going on in the battle of the minds, the two main protagonists at the 1967 Senior TT wheeled their 500cc Japanese and Italian racing machines out to do battle over six laps of the Mountain Course on Friday 19 June in ideal weather, with each knowing that they would have to give their all to gain victory. Tension was high all around, with record speeds being forecast. Although the majority of spectators wanted the British rider to win, few underestimated the strength of the Italian's challenge, even though this was only his third year of racing on the Mountain Course. They were also aware that the evil handling of the big Honda had not been cured, and that Honda banned Mike from using alternative British frames in his attempts to tame it. Known for

Giacomo Agostini punishes his rear tyre, his chain and his suspension as he takes Ballaugh Bridge in his usual forceful style.

understating difficulties and dangers, what Mike privately suffered in racing the big Honda can be gauged by an extract from Ted Macauley's *Hailwood*, in which he is quoted as saying: 'Every time I rode the 500 I used to think on the morning of the race, I wish I didn't have to ride in this event. It wasn't just the usual matter of trying to win, it was trying to stay on the thing.'

Putting such thoughts to the back of his mind, Hailwood started thirty seconds ahead of Agostini, who quickly started to claw back the starting differential and took an early lead, lapping at a record-breaking 108.38mph (174.42km/h). Wrestling with the poorly handling Honda, Hailwood upped the pace (lapping at 108.77mph/ 175.04km/h) and dragged those seconds back until he was almost level on time at his pit stop on the third lap. There he lost all that hard-earned time as he was forced to hammer a loose twist-grip back into place. For the two riders concerned, it was a typical 'against the clock' battle that is almost unique to the TT course, and they saw each other only briefly at the pit stop. Agostini left the pits with a fifteen-second lead, but Hailwood gradually reduced it and then went ahead – just – on time. Their epic high-speed battle came to an end when Agostini's chain broke on the fifth lap at Windy Corner (he was the only competitor not using Renold chain) and Hailwood went on to win at a race average of 105.62mph (169.97km/h), setting a new absolute lap record of 108.77mph (175.04km/h) and recording a hat-trick of wins for the week.

Typical of Mike was his post-race statement, 'I was lucky. If Agostini's chain had not broken I don't think I could have won', for he continued to be troubled with the loose twist-grip. It really is difficult to imagine anyone else making a self-belittling statement of that sort while in the midst of receiving all the adulation that is accorded to the winner of a Senior TT.

books and, with it being his eleventh TT win, he overtook Stanley Woods's previous all-time record.

Maybe all the build up and talk of high lap speeds prior to the Senior served as a spur to those who came behind, since for the first time for several years British riders on British machines put in 100mph laps, with Peter Williams, John Blanchard, Malcolm Uphill and Steve Spencer all hitting the ton. Not all

Bill Ivy's light weight probably contributed to the high speeds he achieved on his Yamahas. Here, he accepts a lift after damaging a foot.

On Mad Sunday riders at the Gooseneck enjoy the freedom to use all of the road.

50cc	Ralph Bryans (Honda)	108.4mph
125cc	Bill Ivy (Yamaha)	132.4mph
250cc	Bill Ivy (Yamaha)	150.6mph
350cc	Giacomo Agostini (MV Agusta)	144.6mph
500cc	Giacomo Agostini (MV Agusta)	151.9mph
	Mike Hailwood (Honda)	151.9mph
Sidecar	Max Deubel (BMW)	125.0mph
	Georg Auerbacher (BMW)	125.0mph

lasted the pace and it was Peter Williams (Arter Matchless) who finished second with Steve Spencer (Lancefield Norton) third.

In its first actual racing appearance at the TT, the Kawasaki Aircraft Company of Tokyo made promising debuts in the Lightweight classes with Dave Simmonds taking fourth place in each race. They were results that Kawasaki was proud to advertise in the British press.

Speeds

Since the first TT race there has been a keen interest in the maximum speeds achieved. With their machines lacking speedometers and rev counters, maximum velocities in the earliest years were estimated rather than calculated. The *TT Special* came into being in the late 1920s and soon started to time riders on defined stretches of the course. Sulby Straight was a favoured spot and about 1931 an average speed of 100mph over a measured mile was first achieved.

In the 1950s and 1960s the *TT Special* made more use of a virtually flat-out, but undulating, 2-mile stretch through Glen Vine and Crosby, finishing just before The Highlander. There was some debate about whether this was actually the fastest point on the course, with some giving their vote to the slightly downhill stretch between Creg ny Baa and Brandish. *Motor Cycle News* published the

results achieved in practice from a speed trap on that stretch in 1966 showing the fastest (*see the table above*).

On his 250 Yamaha, Ivy was 4mph faster than his nearest rival Stuart Graham (Honda), but the fastest Bultacos, Aermacchis, Cottons and others were under 120mph. His speed on the 125 was set with Yamaha's new water-cooled, 4-cylinder RA31 model, which was to take Bill to the 1967 World Championship title. It is interesting to see Hailwood and Agostini's 500 speeds were equal at 151.9mph (244.45km/h), although in the actual race the Honda hit 156.5mph (251.85km/h) with the MV Agusta just 1mph slower. The third fastest 500 was Jack Ahearn on a Norton at 131.4mph (211.46km/h), but a good Norton should have been able to attain just a few miles per hour faster at that spot.

Mad Sunday

Spectators keen to see what their bikes can do flock to the Mountain section of the course on the Sunday before race week, which, for good reason, is known as Mad Sunday. For a defined period of the day the 11-mile (18km) stretch of road from Ramsey to the outskirts of Douglas is made one-way and ordinary riders can indulge their racing fantasies by using all of the road, and all of their speed.

7   A Difficult Decade

The period spanning the late 1960s to the mid-1970s saw many changes to both the nature and the status of the world's premier road race meeting. The first bombshell, which affected the road-racing scene as a whole, was dropped in early 1968 when Honda announced its withdrawal from World Championship racing, due to the need to reduce costs and its opposition to FIM proposals (actually intended to reduce costs) to restrict the number of cylinders and gears in all race classes.

Suzuki quickly followed Honda's example, and after the 1968 TT Yamaha reduced its racing commitment. The closing of cheque books by the major Japanese manufacturers took away the jobs of some highly paid 'works'

This exciting 6-cylinder Honda of Stuart Graham was outlawed by the FIM's new ruling restricting 250cc race machines to two cylinders in 1969.

riders and left others with much reduced levels of support for their racing and living. It meant that such riders had to make major economies and caused them to look carefully at the meetings they contested. On the one hand they sought those that were the least costly in terms of travel and involved the minimum wear upon their expensive-to-maintain race bikes, and on the other they looked for the most generous start and prize money provisions. The TT failed them on all those counts!

What the TT did still have was high prestige in the field of racing, plus World Championship status in all its classes. Organizers of some other World Championship rounds were just as frugal in their payments to riders as those at the TT, even though some were taking the proceeds from 100,000 paying spectators. The reason why riders rode such events on derisory terms was that good showings in the World Championships earned them prestige, trade bonuses and publicity, thus giving a chance to make a name for themselves. This then offered them a strong bargaining position in negotiations for start or appearance money with promoters of non-championship events, where the crowds were lured not by the championship points at stake but by the entertainment value of the riders on view. The financial rewards for competitors in some non-championship events were very good, although the circuits used, particularly some of the round-the-houses ones in Italy, could be frighteningly dangerous, while the difficulty of extracting previously agreed start and prize money from the organizers at the end of the meeting was another well-known problem that riders had to face.

A Record TT

Seemingly ignoring the effects of Honda and Suzuki withdrawals, the 1968 TT arrived with ten races and 508 entries. While it was a record on both counts, it produced a cumbersome meeting and, given the way that the TT had grown from its traditional three races, and then from five to ten, it means that the remainder of this book will have to be selective about which events it reports in detail.

Yamaha made the most of what was supposedly its last year at the TT with full 'works' bikes, and Bill Ivy earned it a Lightweight 250 victory setting a new lap record for the class while fighting his square-four around at 105.51mph (169.80km/h). Phil Read was first home in the 125 race on his Yamaha, although it was Ivy who again broke the lap record, becoming the first rider on a 125 to pass the ton by setting 100.32mph (161.44km/h). Racing under team orders, Ivy did the agreed thing and let Read win the 125 race, although not before he made a point to Yamaha by leading the race for a while and then cheekily stopped at Creg ny Baa towards the end to check his race position. These were the sort of actions beloved by the press, who were happy to publicize the obvious growing friction between Yamaha team-mates Read and Ivy that arose from Yamaha's directive that Ivy should win both 125 and 250 World Championships. Read was a proud man who felt that he had earned the right to lead the Yamaha team and he was extremely put out. Concerning the much-publicized Ivy slowing-down incident, he later wrote in *Phil Read – The Real Story*: 'I think I'd have preferred it if he had won'.

Such was the bad feeling that, according to *Daily Mirror* columnist Ted Macauley, Read also wrote to the FIM to advise them that Yamaha was attempting to impose team orders and thus affect the outcome of races. It was an

action that did nothing for his standing with Yamaha, who saw Ivy as a younger rider of greater promise. With the company reducing its level of 'works' support for both men after the TT, it was Read who used the 44bhp output of the nine-speed RA31A and 70bhp of the RD05A models to take both 125 and 250cc World Championships in 1968 – falling even further out of favour with Yamaha and Ivy over the manner in which he did so.

Yamaha team-mates Bill Ivy (left) and Phil Read in pre-race discussion.

In the bigger classes, MV Agusta expected to win both Junior and Senior events at the 1968 TT with its 3-cylinder racers, but it was concerned about the presence of Renzo Pasolini and his 4-cylinder Benelli in the Junior, even though he was only in his second year at the TT.

Knowing the demands that the Mountain Course put on race machinery, MV brought seven bikes to the TT and recruited John Hartle to support Giacomo Agostini's efforts, having also considered Stuart Graham, John Cooper and, surprisingly, the retired Jim Redman. Unfortunately John Hartle, after really excellent performances in practice, blotted his copybook when he crashed a

Triumph at Windy Corner in the Production race and put himself out of the Junior on the MV-3. Passed fit for the Senior, he then crashed the big MV at Cronk ny Mona. When asked why he chose such out-of-the-way places to come off, John showed that professional riders' thoughts of money were never far from the surface by replying 'for only £15 start-money I'm not going to do it in front of the grandstand'. His associations with MV Agusta went back to at least 1958, and he maintained that he was the only man to have raced 1-, 2-, 3-, 4- and 6-cylinder MV Agusta machines (the last of these a one-off at Monza in 1959).

Giacomo Agostini's concern that Renzo Pasolini (Benelli) would be a threat to his MV in the Junior race turned out to be well founded, for Pasolini, with a distinctive lean-out cornering style, kept in touch with 'Ago' for most of the race, before slowing slightly and finishing second at an average speed of 102.65mph (165.19km/h).

In the Senior race of 1968 things were much more comfortable for the MV star, who finished 8½ minutes ahead of Brian Ball (Seeley) and Derek Randle (Petty-Norton) at a slower speed than his Junior win, having lost time at the pits trying to cure a sticking slide on one of his four carburettors.

With the demise of the AMC racing departments in the early 1960s, Colin Seeley had initially developed new frames for private owners of Norton, AJS and Matchless singles, and then started the manufacture of engines and a 'Seeley' machine in its own right. Colin had extensive service facilities on the Island in 1968 for those racing his products, having put his own successful sidecar racing career on hold.

Sidecar Changes

A non-championship race for 750cc Sidecars was introduced in addition to the 500cc World Championship event at the 1968 TT. The 500cc three-wheeler class was still dominated by BMWs, while the 750s were mostly powered by British twins. A few optimists thought that the 750s would outperform the 500s, but with the latter having a top speed of 125mph and most of the 750s struggling to hit 110mph, it was a forlorn hope. Race results proved the point with Siegfried Schauzu (BMW) riding the first 500 at an average speed of 91.09mph (146.59km/h) and Terry Vinicombe (BSA) first 750 at 85.85mph (138.16km/h). The fastest twin in the 750 class, however, was probably previous Sidecar TT winner Chris Vincent (BSA), who lapped at 89.11mph (143.40km/h) before dropping out.

Dashing Italian Renzo Pasolini (Benelli) on his way to second place in the 1968 Junior TT.

The withdrawal of Japanese 'works' support and a grid containing just over twenty starters spelt the end of the 50cc TT. Winner Barry Smith (Derbi) managed a 90mph top speed (20mph down on the previous year) and the next fastest was 82mph. As a spectacle it left much to be desired and did not return in 1969.

The Production races resulted in wins for: 750cc, Ray Pickrell (Dunstall Dominator); 500cc, Ray Knight (Triumph Daytona); and 250cc, Trevor Burgess (Ossa). These results, however, were accompanied by many protests over machine eligibility, particularly in the 250cc class where thirteen of the fifteen finishers had objections lodged against them. This was to become all too familiar on the Production scene over the next few years, and it led the 1968 500cc class winner and journalist Ray Knight to say, 'A Production race fails completely if everybody is not quite convinced that the machines are as you can buy'.

Post-TT

In withdrawing from the World Championships, Honda honoured commitments to Mike Hailwood by paying him not to contest the GPs, while supplying him with machines to ride in non-championship events. Mallory Park's post-TT meeting was a popular and well-paid stopover for racers returning from the island, and in 1968 one of the men waiting to prevent 500cc World Champion (and 350cc Champion-elect) Giacomo Agostini from taking home the prize money was reigning (but abdicated) 350cc World Champion Mike Hailwood, armed with his favourite 297cc Honda-6. It was a strange scenario, but Mike duly won the 350 and 1000cc races, while TT fans, many of whom were also spectating at Mallory, must have wondered what might have been if Mike had raced at the 1968 TT. That Mallory meeting was also the setting for a 'strike' by most of the riders due to contest the 250 to 1000cc final, protesting about the start money being paid to Hailwood, Agostini, Read and Ivy (who had no doubt used their

spectator-pulling power to negotiate the highest figures). It was a sign of growing militancy among riders and of the way that money was going to dominate racing in the years to come.

Restrictions

The FIM introduced new rules for 1969 whereby all World Championship classes would be limited to machines with a maximum of six gears. They also decreed a maximum of four cylinders for 350 and 500cc classes, and only two cylinders for 125 and 250cc. Introduced in a belated attempt to reduce the cost of racing, the restrictions did not go down well with manufacturers who, while they wanted to make economies, also wanted the freedom to be innovative and show off their technical and engineering expertise in the manner they chose.

Although Honda, its main opposition, was now absent from racing, MV Agusta had not been idle and was fairly advanced with a seven-speed 350 that had six cylinders in an across-the-frame layout. The FIM ruling brought an end to this project and MV switched to developing new six-speed, 4-cylinder models that would be within the rules. Yamaha had invested vast amounts of money and effort on its race programme to achieve World Championship status, but it was also hit by the new ruling, for its 125 and 250 machines both used four cylinders and more than six gears and thus were outlawed from international competition.

Trade Support

All components used in racing were subject to continual development and, as had happened since the early years, various companies sent technical representatives to the Island to support the users of their products and promote sales. Tyres, which had adopted a distinctly triangular form earlier in the 1960s, an introduction that had seen Dunlop overtake

Avon as the principal supplier of racing tyres, were now being turned out with lower profiles to give a smoother transition between vertical and lean, while also being able to handle more power. Dunlop even produced a special tyre for MV to use at the TT and the bikes from Gallarate needed wider swinging-arms fabricated to take them.

Although the range of tyres on offer was still small by today's standard, Dunlop developed different tyres for different makes of machine and came to the 1969 TT with three types and five tread styles. As usual, the company provided a tyre fitting, supply and advisory service, while performing safety pressure checks for all riders going out to practice or race, regardless of which make of tyres they were using.

Other trade concerns present were Amal carburettors, Girling suspension (with former TT winner Henry Tyrell-Smith working for them), Reynolds tubing (for whom Ken Sprayson was busy with his welding skills), Renold chains (who supplied 98 per cent of the entry and got through 67,000ft/20km of primary, secondary and magneto chain), and Shell, whose competitions manager Lew Ellis was always glad to get the two-stroke races over, as the 125 and 250 runners were notoriously fussy over the precise petrol/oil mixes they required. Although the top riders would be provided with their racing requirements from the trade free of charge, the days when everyone in an International race like the TT was supported without charge were largely gone, and private runners had to pay for such as tyres and chains.

Rider Support

While there were the usual grumbles over the cost of competing at the TT and the small financial rewards on offer, riders still flocked to take part in the 1969 event. In only its second year, the 750 Sidecar race attracted more than eighty entries (with six female passengers) and the Junior TT had 133 entries, only 100 of whom could be accepted. Support for the Production events came principally from factories and sporting dealers, with a few private runners. The organizers sought to avoid the problems of Production bikes' compliance with standard specifications by tightening the scrutineering procedures. The first of the sixty-six Proddie bikes presented for inspection in 1969 was subject to twenty minutes of detailed scrutiny. Fortunately the others did not take as long, but it was still more than four hours before the job was complete.

This 500cc Linto engine used well-tried Aermacchi heads and barrels on a specially constructed bottom end.

Among the entries were František Stastny, back with a 350 Jawa after three years' absence, Alberto Pagani on an interesting 500 Linto, Santiago Herrero with his Spanish Ossa two-stroke, and two machines powered by Crescent marine engines: the sidecar outfit of Rudi Kurth and the solo of Billy Andersson.

Benelli's Renzo Pasolini injured himself in an Italian pre-TT meeting and the company wavered over coming to the Island. Eventually arriving in the middle of practice week, it offered Lightweight 250 machines to Kel Carruthers and Phil Read. Carruthers rode his to victory over Frank Perris (Crooks Suzuki) and Santiago Herrero (Ossa) in a relatively slow race, while Read retired, claiming his Benelli to be a 'dog' of a bike that 'never looked like finishing, let alone winning'. Carruthers's TT win led to a full 'works' contract with Benelli and he finished the year as 250cc World Champion. It was interesting that there were no Yamahas in the first three in either the 125 or 250 race. But, although the company had withdrawn its full 'works' support from racing, it recognized that there was publicity to be gained by marketing production forms of racer, and its TD2 model of 1969 was earning much success elsewhere.

Kawasaki First

Dave Simmonds gave Kawasaki its first TT win in 1969 by leading home the 125 race, in which Carruthers (Aermacchi) was second. Third place was taken by popular privateer Fred Launchbury, but at the post-race engine measuring his Bultaco was found to be fractionally over the 125cc limit. The organizers did not want to take the podium position away from him, but they had to comply with the rules. They did allow a further period for the barrel to cool, even permitting it to be immersed in a bucket of cold water, but it was to no avail and Fred was excluded.

Agostini walked away with the Junior and Senior events as expected, spending much of the last lap of Friday's race responding to the waves of spectators and leaving the real racing to go on behind him. However, it was the Production races that gave close, exciting racing that really caught the interest of spectators, with Malcolm Uphill taking his Triumph Bonneville to victory in the 750 class and setting a 100.37mph (161.52km/h) lap in the process. Dunlop was so pleased with the 100mph lap by a roadster on its tyres that the K81 range of road rubber was renamed 'TT100' in celebration.

TT Costs

Having previously refused to divulge the total costs of running the TT meeting, the ACU perhaps felt it could counter the riders' continuing criticism by going public with its figures. Using those from 1967, it claimed that the meeting had incurred a loss of £1,493. Overall costs were £30,000, to which the Manx Government contributed £20,500. Income from entry fees was £4,200 (of which £4,069 went on riders' personal insurance). Riders received £12,500 in prize money and expenses. Although the TT prize money had been unchanged for many years, it was actually higher than that paid at some Grand Prix meetings, with Agostini telling *Motor Cycle News* that first prize at the French GP was a mere £70 (compared to £200 for the Senior TT).

The Isle of Man authorities had always rejected proposals for a levy on visiting race fans as a means of helping to pay for their fortnight's racing and associated activities. Thus, with no money coming in from paying spectators at the TT, income sources to the organizing ACU were limited and, unable to subsidize the meeting from its own finances, it was in a difficult position. But surely it should have realized that it could not go on paying the same meagre prize money and £15 expenses for ever. Perhaps its complacency was due to the TT's high standing in the world of racing, but increasing rumbles of financial discontent should not have been ignored by the ACU and the Isle of Man authorities in the late 1960s, for it was to cost them dear in the future.

A Bad Year

Whatever happened in the races, the 1970 TT meeting was overshadowed by the death of six riders during practice and race periods. The feelings of families and friends left behind by those luckless riders is difficult to imagine, even though all would have been aware from the experiences of others that their menfolk's racing could result in disaster. As George Turnbull later wrote in the *Daily Telegraph*:

> The TT Mountain Course plays more havoc with human emotions in one week of racing than any other circuit in the world. Joy, sorrow, exhilaration and fear – all are imposed on competitors and spectators by the unforgiving 37¾ miles of everyday road which for a short time each year become the most fearsome race arena ever devised for high speed sport.

The high death toll in 1970 made headlines both on and off the Island, with that of Santiago Herrero, the highest-profile victim, sending reverberations through the world of motorcycle racing, for he was leading the 250

World Championship when he crashed on the fifth lap while trying to better third position in the race and increase his haul of points.

The Production races were promoted from National to International status and run over five laps on the opening Saturday of race week. Meanwhile, reflecting what was happening on the general racing scene, Aermacchi and Yamaha machines matched the number of AJS and Nortons in the Junior race, while Yamaha dominated the Lightweight 250 entries with its over-the-counter racing models. Triumph Trident and Honda CB750s – the first of a new breed of superbikes – contested the Production race for road bikes, and Kawasaki made two-stroke entries for Martin Carney and Bill Smith in the Senior. Missing an Island race for the first time since the MGP Newcomers of 1958 was established star Phil Read, who was suffering from an earlier arm injury.

The organizers proposed a new starting arrangement for the solo events, whereby competitors would be despatched in groups of nine at ninety-second intervals. Tried in Thursday afternoon's practice, the scheme was not well received by riders and the organizers reverted to sending them off in pairs at ten-second intervals.

Giacomo Agostini took yet another Junior/Senior double, making the interesting

Malcolm Uphill (Triumph Trident) leads the Production race through Union Mills in 1970.

observation that, despite improvements to the course, he considered it to be bumpier than when he made his debut there five years before. Kel Carruthers and Rod Gould were first and second in the Lightweight 250 on TD Yamahas that were believed to give 45bhp with a strong element of factory support, while a new name at the TT, Dieter Braun, brought his Suzuki home first in the Lightweight 125, followed by a Maico and an MZ. BMWs maintained their customary domination of the 500 and 750cc Sidecar races, with wins going to Klaus Enders and Siegfried Schauzu.

Malcolm Uphill raced the still relatively new Triumph Trident to victory in the now five-lap Production 750 class, in which the best Triumphs reached close to 140mph through the speed trap, with Norton Commandos in the low 130s. Tommy Robb and John Cooper had the speed but not the handling with their Honda CB750, bringing them home in eighth and ninth places after exciting rides with the 4-cylinder superbikes over the island's bumpy roads.

Dunlop Tyres was particularly successful at the 1970 TT.

A New Formula

Maybe the TT organizers sensed the affinity many spectators felt for the machines used in the Production races, because, although they reduced the race distances from five laps to four, at the 1971 meeting they moved the three races from Saturday to a more popular Wednesday spot in the race programme, when Ray Pickrell (Triumph Trident), John Williams (Honda CB450) and Bill Smith (Honda CB250) were victorious on road-going machines. In addition to the Production races for bikes ostensibly taken from the showroom floor and raced, the organizers found room for a new Formula 750 race over three laps for Production-based racing machines from manufacturers like Triumph, Norton, BSA, Honda and Kawasaki, which were allowed specified performance-enhancing modifications. The regulations were similar to those administered by the American Motorcycle Association at Daytona, allowing the 750s to throw off some of the performance-restricting shackles of Production rules and howl around the Mountain Course on open pipes. Ridden by dashing young riders like Tony Jefferies, Ray Pickrell and Peter Williams, they lapped at more than 100mph, with Tony Jefferies taking victory on his Triumph 'three' at an average of 102.85mph (165.52km/h). The official report on the race said 'it is the opinion of the Stewards that racing for machines of this new type has a very exciting future', and a newspaper report added 'the formula regarded as the racing of the future is here to stay'. Perhaps they were influenced by the sight and sound of large-capacity British bikes dominating a TT, but they were correct, for Formula 750 can be seen as a forerunner of today's successful Superbike racing, and the racing of Production-based bikes eventually pushed dedicated racing bikes to the sidelines and moved into a dominant position at the TT.

Faster

Perhaps it was due to Agostini's remarks about the bumpiness of the course in 1970, but for

1971 the bumps were eased in several places and a smoother surfacing laid. Riders certainly felt the benefit of new surfacing on the long and fast stretch from before Brandish to just past Hillberry. Indeed, with competitors being used to the coarse limestone chippings of the Mountain section, the smooth surfacing caused problems for several who arrived at Hillberry travelling far faster than before, and were faced with getting through the sweeping right-hander quicker than they had previously thought possible.

The Junior race was moved from Wednesday to Monday and reduced to five laps. After his three consecutive years of Junior/Senior doubles, 'Ago' suffered the ignominy of retirement from the Junior on his MV Agusta. Some spectators were heard to cheer when the announcement of his engine failure at Milntown was broadcast, though perhaps they were cheers of relief that someone else would get a chance, rather than rank bad sportsmanship.

Agostini's retirement left Phil Read, Alan Barnett, Rod Gould and Dudley Robinson challenging for a win, but they all crashed or retired (Dudley on the last lap while leading), leaving Tony Jefferies to take victory on his Yamsel – a machine powered by a Yamaha engine in a Seeley frame.

Giacomo Agostini was forced to retire his 350 MV Agusta at Parliament Square, Ramsey, in the 1971 Junior, after hitting engine trouble at Milntown.

Phil Read (6) push-starts his Yamaha in company with Peter Williams (5) and his MZ at the 1971 Lightweight TT. Read went on to win the race.

Renowned for his Lightweight efforts, it was a surprise to many to find that Phil Read's first place on a 250 Yamaha in 1971 gave him a maiden Lightweight 250 TT win. MZ had supported the TT as and when it could afford to since Ernst Degner's first ride back in 1958, and Peter Williams held second place on one of the East German two-strokes in the early stages of the 250 race. Yamaha machines, however, had taken over the 250 class by 1971, with sixty of the seventy-six entries being Yamaha mounted and the first twenty-four places in the race going to Yamaha before a Crooks Suzuki broke the run.

The Lightweight 125 race was run in wet conditions that saw Charles Mortimer (Yamaha) victorious. But that 1971 race for 125s is probably best remembered for the presence of Barry Sheene in his only year at the TT. A late entry who managed to fit in very few laps of practice, Barry was holding second place until he slid off at Quarter Bridge on his second lap; the *TT Special* reported that 'he received no injuries and was as cheerful as ever afterwards'. But Barry's cheerfulness towards the TT did not last, and after his single experience he became one of its most vociferous critics, even after he had long retired from racing.

Although due to follow the 125cc race, the Senior was postponed until Saturday due to the poor weather. No doubt wary after the breakdown of his 350 MV, but racing in good weather, Agostini duly took a slowish win at an average of 102.59mph (165.10km/h), while Peter Williams (Arter Matchless) finished second some five minutes behind the MV and 2½ minutes ahead of Frank Perris on an air-cooled, twin-cylinder, two-stroke Suzuki.

Rider Attire

Most riders still wore plain black leathers, although a few ventured to have a coloured stripe down the arms. These stripes could be brought separately and stitched on by riders intent on being in the forefront of fashion. The pudding-basin crash-helmet was slowly being replaced by the 'Jet'-type, which Agostini had taken to wearing. There was even the occasional sighting of the full-face helmet that is obligatory wear today: in 1971 Frank Perris was one of the few to use one.

For many years the FIM ruled against the appearance of advertising on leathers and helmets. Giacomo Agostini appeared at the 1971 TT in a set of Dunlop-sponsored leathers that bore the company's name. Unchallenged by the FIM, Ago's move heralded a new era of sponsorship payments for riders carrying product advertisements on brightly coloured leathers.

Too Little Too Late?

Belatedly acting on the bad press the TT was receiving regarding prize money, the TT organizers increased the amount on offer in 1972, with the Senior winner taking a substantial £750 instead of £200. There were few serious contenders for the main prize but plenty of riders flocked to the Isle of Man for another year of racing, with a healthy sixty-five runners for the second running of the Formula 750 event and entries holding up in other classes. No doubt acting from the best of intentions, the organizers also experimented by omitting morning practice sessions and slightly extending the evening ones. As a result, the total number of laps completed in practice went down from 1,586 (in 1971) to 1,401 and riders responded with complaints that they had insufficient time to learn the course and to set up their machines properly.

After losing out on victory in the 1971 Junior when Giacomo Agostini, its sole entry, retired, MV Agusta provided support to team-leader Ago's efforts in 1972 by supplying Phil Read with a 350 and Alberto Pagani a 500. No doubt the other members of the MV team were given strict team orders but, just in case either of them harboured thoughts of outriding their team-leader, Agostini put in a practice lap at 106.28mph (171.04km/h) to show what he and the new four were capable of. It was his fastest lap since the MV's gripping contest with Mike Hailwood and his Honda in 1967. While Agostini made it clear where victory was destined to go in the Junior and Senior classes – barring mechanical problems – the situation in the other races at the end of practice-week was very open. With the second fastest overall practice lap of 104.08mph (167.50km/h), Tony Jefferies not only showed that he was a man to watch, but by achieving this on his Formula 750 Triumph Trident he snatched a measurable amount of glory from the recognized racing classes.

Formula 750 Fastest

During the Formula 750 race Jefferies could not quite match his practice pace and finished in second place to team-mate Ray Pickrell (Triumph), who averaged 104.23mph (167.74

Tony Jefferies leans his Triumph into Creg ny Baa.

km/h) for the five laps and set the fastest lap at 105.68mph (170.07km/h) – that year's fastest lap of race week. Jack Findlay finished a highly creditable third on a 3-cylinder Suzuki TR750 that fully justified its nickname of 'Flexy Flier'. It recorded the fastest speed through The Highlander speed trap at 158.60mph (255.23km/h), but Jack just could not use the bike's speed in many places. The John Player tobacco-sponsored Norton team of Peter Williams, Phil Read and John Cooper all failed to finish, although Williams reached almost 150mph through the speed trap with his 70bhp twin before the gearbox failed.

As with most years at the TT, new names appeared among the podium finishers. Tony Rutter (Yamaha) took a fine second in the Junior behind Agostini, and was followed by Mick Grant (Padgett Yamaha), who also finished third in the Senior. Charlie Williams followed 125 winner Charles Mortimer home on his 125 Johnson Yamaha, with Bill Rae (Maico) third. Powered by a König marine engine, Gerry Boret achieved his first podium finish with third place in the 500cc Sidecar race, in which Siegfried Schauzu (BMW), known to the press as 'Sideways Sid', took his seventh TT win.

TT Turning Point

One of the brightest new stars to shine at the 1972 TT was Gilberto Parlotti on his 125cc Morbidelli. Leading the 125 World Championship when he arrived on the Isle of Man for his first TT, the 32-year-old Italian was obviously keen to gain the highest possible number of points and thus extend his lead over other Championship contenders such as Angel Nieto, Kent Andersson and Dieter Braun, who declined to contest the TT. Parlotti's thorough approach to his debut TT ride attracted the comment in *Motor Cycle News*: 'It is a long time since anybody has taken such a serious attitude towards a TT race'. Arriving before the start of official practice, he put in more than fifty course-learning laps on a 750 Ducati, then turned out in every practice, did further learning laps outside official practice periods and received tuition from Giacomo Agostini.

Gilberto Parlotti treats the wet surface and white lines with caution in the early stages of the 1972 Lightweight 125cc race.

The Lightweight 125cc race was run on the Friday morning before the Senior race when the roads were wet and conditions miserable for racing. Despite the fact that he was the World Champion-elect, spectators were still surprised to see Parlotti leading at the end of the first lap, ahead of experienced TT runner Charles Mortimer (Yamaha). But three-quarters of the way around the second lap the Italian ran wide at the Verandah, collided with a line of concrete posts and was killed. The repercussions from the death of this fine rider changed the TT for ever.

Fellow Italian Giacomo Agostini felt the loss of Parlotti more than most, and he had to be persuaded to take part in that afternoon's Senior race. Eventually agreeing to do so, he delivered his customary win, with team-mate Pagani taking second place from Peter Williams, who ran out of petrol near the end. After the race, as Bob Holliday describes in *Racing Round the Island*, 'an undercurrent of anti-TT feeling that had been rippling among some of the leading riders for several seasons burst into flood'. Led by Agostini, who said that he would never race in another TT, there began a campaign to discredit and diminish the standing of the TT races. Whether it was truly the danger element or whether it was financially driven has been the subject of much discussion. Others lent their voices in support of Ago, including Phil Read, John Cooper, Rod Gould and Barry Sheene. Unfortunately, the early 1970s had seen a growing number of World Championship contenders in all classes who would not countenance racing on the Mountain Course and their absence contributed to the TT's growing isolation in the World Championship programme. It was a sad situation with so many top riders opposed to competing in the TT, and their opposition increased owing to the potential advantage that participation in the TT might give to some of the field when it came to the results of the World Championships.

The signs of opposition had been around for some while, but the time had arrived when

This is the lifestyle Phil Read had to support when racing as a privateer. Unfortunately his Cessna private aeroplane would not fit into the picture!

many top riders were no longer prepared to push themselves to the limit on the Mountain Course in return for paltry reward. Would they still have rebelled against the TT if start and prize money had been much more generous? It is probable that some would, but it is certain that some would not, for many riders were in racing purely for the money they could and had to earn from it. They may have started riding for the love of the sport, but the further they climbed the racing ladder the more serious a business it became. Some riders, however, were inconsistent in their attitudes to dangerous circuits, and despite their opposition to the TT many well-known names continued to race at non-championship meetings where safety, medical support and crowd control were sadly lacking – but where the money was good.

The whole subject of the TT received much coverage in the motorcycle press. Former riders were canvassed, with Mike Hailwood saying he could not see what all the fuss was about. Existing TT riders made noises about using a shorter course, but a poll in *Motor Cycle News* saw massive support by spectators for retention of the Mountain Course.

The top TT stars may have been moved to leave the TT, but Joan Pomfret, a frequent visitor to the island, was moved to poetry:

Why so Named?

Ago's Leap

Giacomo Agostini may have left the TT in 1972, but the fine riding performances that brought him ten TT victories are remembered, and his name remains linked to this day to the rise in the road after the bottom of Bray Hill. It was at this point that Ago showed his bravery and just how quick he was going.

Although the bump in the road has been eased in recent years, it remains a spectacular location and riders still tend to show off to spectators and photographers.

Ago's front wheel reaches for the sky as he rockets over the spot named after him.

TT Rider

May he have fine clear weather on his
    daring way,
Neither mist on the mountain
Nor a too-bright sun;
Dry roads
And a safe journey through a blue June day,
And a great burst of cheering
When the race is won.

May he have one to speed him with a
    loving heart,
Friends in the pits behind him
And the crowd's awed sigh;
Luck for a record lapping
And a faultless start,
And the deep roar of engines
As he flashes by.

May he keep fast his courage, and the will
    beneath
His sudden smile, keen judgement
And his urge to roam –
And in an Island sunset
Bear his laurel wreath
With proud and careless rapture
As he races home!

A 'Level Playing Field'

It was no surprise that vociferous anti-TT
stars like Agostini and Read were absent from
the Island in 1973, but the meeting did not
lack for entries or spectators, even though
problems at Triumph and BSA meant
no officially supported Production entries
from them. The organizers reinstated early
morning practice and upped the rewards for
first place finishers to £1,000 in the Senior,
£600 in the Junior, £500 in the Lightweight
250, £750 in the Formula 750 and £600 in
the Sidecar race.

A number of riders who had been podium
placemen in previous years were now keen to
stand on the top step. So the racing was fast
and furious in this first year that the over-
whelmingly superior performance of the MVs

in the big classes and the semi-works supported Yamahas in the smaller classes did not
put non-works riders at a disadvantage. They
saw the opportunity to gain the prestige of a
TT win snd were all prepared to fight hard for
a top spot. Tony Rutter went one place better
in the Junior than in 1972 and collected his
first win, at a faster race speed than Agostini
achieved in 1972. Charlie Williams improved
on his 1972 second place in the Lightweight
125 with a win in the Lightweight 250, and
Tommy Robb, who first rode the TT in 1958,
won the Lightweight 125. All three victories
were gained on Yamaha machines that
swamped the entries, as they did all over the
racing world.

*Jack Findlay smokes away from the starting line on his two-
stroke Suzuki.*

After Mick Grant (Yamaha) led in the early
laps, Jack Findlay, another rider who first competed at the TT in the late 1950s, brought
welcome variation to the results with a Senior
win on his twin-cylinder, water-cooled Suzuki.
Although many hoped that in Agostini's
absence Peter Williams (Arter Matchless) would
take his first Senior win (after finishing second
on three occasions), he had to be satisfied with
his customary second place, despite setting the
fastest ever lap by a single-cylinder machine
at 102.74mph (165.34km/h). But Norton
employee Peter did come home first in the
Formula 750 race, achieving an average speed of

105.47mph (169.73km/h) and an impressive fastest lap of 107.27mph (172.63km/h) on the twin-cylinder John Player Norton, which sported a new monocoque frame of his own design.

Peter Williams (JP Norton) at Parliament Square, Ramsey in 1973.

A Fast Lap

In a detailed post-race account of what it entailed to outride the Formula 750 opposition over five laps and almost 190 miles of the Mountain Course, Peter Williams used graphic phrases like:

> hard against the stop . . . flat on the tank . . . the front wheel comes off the ground . . . ride it through there on the back wheel . . . ignore the bumps . . . can usually do flat out . . . power on early . . . back wheel could suddenly go . . . the front wheel just touches the road here and there . . . properly set up with all the power coming on . . . couldn't believe I could take it flat . . . just heave on the bars . . . I sit up here but only because I don't like my head bouncing on the tank at 145mph!

It was a straight-from-the-saddle account of a racing lap from an immensely skilled and experienced TT competitor, and one that left the ordinary road-rider in envy of his

immense talent to exploit the power and handling of the Norton to the full.

Encouraging comments followed the 1973 meeting from press and public. Some maintained that the star names had not been missed, and there was no doubt that the crowds were pleased to see genuine racing for first place in the Junior and Senior classes, instead of the Agostini walk overs of recent years. The Production races were still going strong and Formula 750 was a big hit with its spectacular sights, sounds and high speeds. However, there were downsides to the 1973 TT. One was the increased domination of entries by two-stroke Yamaha machinery across several classes. The effect was to create a sameness in appearance and sound that did not go down well with spectators brought up on a variety of booming four-strokes. Another was the continued sniping at the TT by riders and some elements of the press that was clearly intended as a threat to its World Championship status.

On the GP scene Renzo Pasolini and Finland's Jaarno Saarinen had been killed in a crash at Monza in 1973 that also brought down a host of star riders. This all added to the safety concerns of competitors and they refused to race at the early-season West German GP of 1974, held at the Nürburgring, worried about track conditions in the poor weather and lack of protective straw bales. Meanwhile, seeking to safeguard what it had, the Isle of Man authorities injected more money into the TT meeting for 1974, with the races continuing to be organized and run by the ACU, which had been in charge since the first TT of 1907. Some of the extra money went on safety measures and some on extra financial rewards to competitors. It was a clear indication that, from the Island's point of view, the TT meeting was evolving from being a motorcycle racing event that received some financial input from, and yielded financial benefits to, the Isle of Man into an event that the Island was eager should maintain its International status, and in respect of which it was prepared to take the initiative, invest money and share in the promotion of the meeting, with the ACU continuing to act as organizers on its behalf.

Yamaha and Progress

Yamaha machines won all four of the recognized pure racing classes at the 1974 TT (Lightweight 125, Lightweight 250, Junior and Senior), plus the Formula 750 and 250 Production. The winners were all two-stroke machines, and the 500 Production and Sidecar 500 also went to Kawasaki and König 'strokers'. An indication of why so many riders chose the, by now disc-braked and water-cooled, production-racer Yamahas was that both the 500cc Senior (run on the Wednesday) and the 'Open Formula 750 Classic International TT Race' (given the prime Friday spot) were won by over-bored 350cc Yamahas. (The true 350 'Yams' took the first thirty-nine places in the Junior.)

Although Jack Findlay on one of Suzuki's new 4-cylinder RG500 two-strokes was a major threat to Yamaha's dominance for part of the Senior race, having to ride in damp conditions on some of the very new (for the time) 'slick' tyres put paid to his hopes. As if beating

500s in the Senior race was not a big enough feat, in the Formula 750 race the little Yamahas vanquished the mighty 750cc John Player Nortons of Peter Williams and Dave Croxford, Jack Findlay's big 'works' Suzuki, Mick Grant's Kawasaki 750 and Percy Tait's Triumph Trident. Those large-capacity machines were all ridden by top riders, but Charles Mortimer used his 'little' Yamaha to beat them all. Mortimer actually brought one of Yamaha's new 4-cylinder 700cc two-strokes to the 1974 TT, but the bike's handling and power characteristics put it into the 'point and squirt' category, and after trying it in practice Mortimer decided that it was not suited to the Mountain Course.

The Yamaha two-strokes were temperamental enough in an ordinary state of tune and required much more careful attention to carburation and jetting than four-strokes, a need accentuated by the variations in altitude and temperature found on the Mountain Course. With Yamaha turning out so many machines with near identical performance, riders who wanted to gain race advantage by having a faster bike than the opposition had to be prepared to acquire expensive 'go-faster' parts in the hope of gaining a few mph. Higher states of tune could have an adverse effect on reliability, with

Charles Mortimer on his Danfay-Yamaha in 1974.

more seizures, breakdowns and the wearing out of ever more expensive components. Again those problems were often accentuated by the nature of the TT challenge. The additional expenses of those seeking to be at the top of the performance tree did not end with costly engine-tuning components, for an earlier trend to seek improved handling from special frames grew apace and saw Seeley, Spondon and Maxton all happy to supply their expensive hand-built chassis.

There were also developments in other areas of racing motorcycles. Most riders, for example, were now using disc-brakes front and rear, while Yamaha went on to introduce cantilever rear-suspension, which gave longer travel. Tyre shape continued to adapt to cope with increased motive power and with the greater stopping power of disc-brakes, while treaded racing tyres were now available in diff-erent compounds from the two main Euro-pean suppliers, Dunlop and Michelin, that gave differing wear patterns. Experimental slick tyres were also being tried, usually fitted to cast wheels rather than to the conventional spoked types. Development in the field of the conventional twin-shock suspension units allowed for finer tuning of spring and damper rates, with a gradual move to the single 'mono-shock' suspension unit providing even more control of suspension performance, something that was increasingly required if riders were to cope with the ever bumpier nature of the Course revealed by use of the greater speed available.

TT Opinions

What was intended to be a three-man FIM fact-finding delegation to the 1975 TT turned into a brief one-man visit. The TT pro-gramme sold to racegoers had several articles explaining why the event should remain part of the World Championships, but most felt that its days of catering for what were turning into circuit-racing World Championships, as opposed to the TT's road-racing version, were

numbered. Whatever the single FIM delegate's opinions were on the event, he kept them to himself before reporting back to his masters at the headquarters in Switzerland.

Rather more open with his views was Mike Hailwood. Taking a long time to recover from a leg and foot injury received in a crash while car racing in the previous year's German GP, he was a spectator at the 1975 TT and was happy to give his opinions on various TT-related issues when approached by *Motor Cycle News*. Concerning Agostini and Read's self-imposed TT ban, he felt that they would still be racing on the Island if they had been honest enough to admit that their complaint about the TT was about lack of money, not circuit safety: 'the trouble is they made such a fuss about the safety business that they can't come back, whatever money is offered'. He claimed to know that they had been offered £8,000 to appear in 1974, but having done their best to convince the TT authorities, plus the FIM and ACU, the MV Agusta and Yamaha factories, and the race-going public that they would not return, they had driven themselves into a corner.

Mike's opinion was shared by regular World Championship and TT competitor Charles Mortimer, who also pointed out that the TT prize money was now much better than that on offer at other World Championship rounds.

As if to emphasize that the anti-TT feeling was not all about safety, Agostini, Read, Sheene and other outspoken critics were to be found racing in Belgium on the 6.55-mile public roads circuit at Chimay on the weekend between practice and race week on the Island.

Programme Changes

There were several changes to the programme of events at the 1975 TT. The Lightweight 125cc class was dropped. The capacity limit in the former Formula 750 race was increased to 1000cc and the race was renamed the Open Classic TT, with a first prize of £1,500 and riders making clutch starts in pairs. The 750 Sidecar race was opened up to 1,000cc machines. The races for Production machines of 250, 500 and 750cc, previously run over four laps, now also allowed in machines of 1000cc, reflecting the growth of this capacity among road machines, with the race distance increased to ten laps. In a first at the TT, the riding of each Production machine was shared by a two-man team, and the race continued to use a Le Mans-type start. In fact, in another first, it became a form of handicap event, for the 250s only had to cover nine laps.

Slippery Sam

Rarely does an individual motorcycle achieve celebrity status, but when owner Les Williams wheeled out the 750 Triumph Trident known as Slippery Sam to contest the 1975 Production TT, the bike already had four consecutive Production TT wins to its credit. Despite having had a hard racing life on the island in the hands of Ray Pickrell (twice), Tony Jefferies and Mick Grant, the Triumph took the 1975 partnership of Dave Croxford and Alex George to another convincing win, lapping at a record 102.82mph (165.47km/h) in the process, and taking 3 hours 47 minutes 17.2 seconds for the 378-mile (608km) race distance.

Mick Grant pilots Slippery Sam over Ballaugh Bridge.

Although Honda was pleased to announce that its machines took the first six places in the 500cc class of the Production TT, its flagship CB750 'superbikes' were noticeably absent from the biggest class.

Some interesting machines were entered among the hordes of Yamahas in the racing classes in 1975. On a British-built, 3-cylinder Barton Motors Sparton, experienced TT competitor Gordon Pantall managed his fastest ever island lap at an impressive 103.71mph (166.90km/h). This was in the Senior race, for which Harley-Davidson (Italian Division) sent a 500cc two-stroke twin for Alex George to ride. In the Sidecar race there were three British Magnum outfits powered by a 'home-made' engine built by racers Tony Wakefield and Graham Milton. Other developments in sidecar racing saw Rolf Steinhausen end twenty years of BMW domination of the 500cc class (excepting Chris Vincent's BSA win in 1962) by taking victory on his rotary-valve, two-stroke König, which was said to give 85bhp at 10,000rpm and was housed in a special Busch frame.

Although Siegfried Schauzu won the new 1000cc Sidecar race with a record lap of almost 100mph on his BMW, this was to be the last BMW Sidecar TT victory, since Yamaha was about to begin a period of three-wheel domination very similar to that previously enjoyed by the German concern.

Outright Fastest

Pre-race favourite among the eighty-five competitors for the new Open Classic race in 1975 was Mick Grant on his Kawasaki 750-3, who arrived on the island fresh from a record-breaking victory at the North West 200 meeting. Held in Northern Ireland shortly before the TT, the NW200 usually offered a reliable guide to the form of riders and machines coming on to race at the TT. Mick headed the practice leader-board on his 750 at 106.95mph (172.11km/h), but the race itself went to John Williams (Yamaha) after the Kawasaki broke

Rolf Steinhausen takes his König-powered outfit to victory in the 500cc Sidecar race of 1975.

down, but not before its rider had broken Mike Hailwood's outright lap record, set in 1967, by lapping at 109.82mph (176.73km/h). Surprisingly, Mick Grant's name did not appear among the fastest dozen in practice for the Senior, but on the day itself he took his 500cc Kawasaki to victory ahead of a swarm of Yamahas. Mick probably experienced the differing effects of the popular TT saying that can be twisted to suit the occasion: 'bad practice, good race' in the case of the 500 Kawasaki, and 'good practice, bad race' for the 750.

External Pressures

The campaign to have the TT stripped of its World Championship status continued in 1975 and the races were known to be a subject for discussion at the FIM's Berlin Congress at the end of October. There was little doubt that the Isle of Man and the world of road racing feared the worst but, surprising many, the TT retained its position in the World Championships, as *Motor Cycle* described: 'ACU delegates at the FIM Congress breathed a sigh of relief when the 1976 grand prix calendar was passed without comment, despite the Island races being such a controversial subject in recent years'.

The Isle of Man races accordingly retained their World Championship status for 1976

(although no 125cc race was held), but the event suffered ever-increasing isolation from the stars of circuit racing. A glance at the World Championship tables at the end of the 1976 season shows this clearly, for none of the top eight finishers in the 'Blue Riband' 500cc class contested the TT. The situation was not quite so bad in the 350 and 250cc classes, where TT stars Charles Mortimer and Tom Herron also rode all the Championship races and finished well up in the standings. Then, in a surprise move that probably did not endear him to the established GP riders, new Japanese star Takazumi Katyama decided to ride at the 1976 TT to gain extra points, taking second in the Lightweight race, fourth in the Senior, plus two other finishes. A similar situation to the solos prevailed among the top sidecar drivers, with half of the top ten World Championship finishers boycotting the island.

The *TT Special* took a positive approach to the 1976 meeting, saying in its first edition: 'This is the year when it must be seen that the TT is worthy of its name and high-standing in the world of motorcycle sport. We must show that it can survive in its own right and go from strength to strength.' With the Island claiming an increased number of visitors, they were entertained to plenty of close racing, with the BMW marque taking its first solo win since

Tom Herron is shown at Quarter Bridge in the 1976 TT, a year in which he also contested the World Championships.

Georg Meier in 1939, when an R90S flat-twin came home first in the Production 1000cc class, ridden by the pairing of Helmut Dahne and Otto Butenuth. John Williams was the quickest man of the week, setting a new absolute course record of 112.27mph (180.68km/h) in the Senior race before running out of petrol on the last lap and pushing his Suzuki home to finish seventh. Tom Herron came home in first place. John did take the win in the Classic race on his Suzuki TR 750, rated at more than 100bhp, and Tom took another victory in the Lightweight 250 for Yamaha.

Decision Time

The Isle of Man authorities provided the majority of finance for the TT meeting, with the ACU running the event and also having a seat at the negotiating table of the FIM, who ran world motorcycle sport. In the face of pressure from the rest of the motorcycling world, the ACU was forced to concede that the British round of the recognized World Championship racing classes would be moved from the Isle of Man Mountain Course and run on a conventional circuit in 1977. Later in 1976 it chose the former aerodrome of Silverstone for a British Grand Prix. If anyone needed reminding of the vast gulf that had opened between road racers and circuit racers, that

decision gave them all the proof needed. Silverstone was virtually flat, virtually featureless, ultra-smooth, relatively short and easily learnt. That was what the circuit racers wanted and that was what they got for 1977, for it was the sort of circuit that manufacturers developed their racing machines to tackle. In modern-day language it represented the 'dumbing down' of the art of pure road racing. There was no place for humpback bridges, pit stops and a long circuit that took time to learn and had to be ridden with skill and, in some places, restraint. Of course, a new Grand Prix meant there was a place for a new promoter, who no doubt rubbed his hands with anticipation at having acquired a prestigious event and the proceeds from the turnstiles that accompanied it.

Pessimists forecast that the TT's loss of World Championship status signified the beginning of the end for the Manx racing, while optimists regarded it as the start of a new era. The Isle of Man certainly regretted what it had lost on the World Championship front, although few concerned with racing politics would really claim to have been surprised. While the loss of conventional World Championship status was considered extremely serious at the time, however, the prospect of also losing the TT's traditional dates for its event was seen as a potential disaster for the Island's diminishing tourist trade, since TT fortnight was the busiest period of the year for visitors. Fortunately that did not happen in 1977, despite external pressures from an extremely crowded race calendar. But it is something that is still regarded as a concern, and the race dates have been threatened on several occasions down the ensuing years. The TT budget was increased to £150,000 for 1977, with £100,000 allocated for start and prize money, thus, belatedly, making it the richest race meeting in the world.

Compensation – of a Sort

In an attempt to fill the gap left by the removal of World Championship status from those TT

classes that were part of the Championship at the time (500, 350, 250 and 500cc Sidecars), the FIM sought to offer a formula for racing that reflected the TT's road-racing strength. What it eventually offered the Isle of Man in 1976 were three races for 1977 that became known as TT Formula I, II and III, catering for high-performance production machines in events that would have their own World Champions.

The FIM's proposal was not welcomed by the Island or the ACU, but after long and fruit-less negotiations it became clear that the FIM's 'Formula' racing offer was made on a 'take it or leave it' basis, for it planned to extend the number of meetings running Formula events to create a World Championship series. That meant that if Formula racing were not accepted by the Island there could be no guar-antee of protection for the TT's traditional dates. Although the ACU was forced to accept the situation, it was election-year on the island, which has its own parliament, the Tynwald, and politicians with and without racing knowledge rushed to condemn the TT's move away from pure racing machines to those of a production-based type, even though those with longer memories could recall that the Tourist Trophy meeting was originally created to cater for machines of the latter type. The politicians' actions, reported word for word in the press, did nothing for the island's relationship with the ACU, whose delegates felt that they had fought long and hard on the

island's behalf. Unfortunately, with no possi-bility of a change in the FIM's ruling, the Isle of Man's sustained denigration of the new Formula races in the latter part of 1976 and early 1977 only served as bad publicity for the TT meeting that it was anxious to promote.

Many words were written and spoken on the topic through the winter of 1976/77, including a proposal in *Motor Cycle News* that the first week of TT fortnight should be devoted to practice and racing for the new Formula events, and the second week should provide practice and race time for the other races, which they felt, with the payment of high start and prize money, would appeal to international stars who wanted to minimize their time on the island.

1977 Race Programme

Withdrawal of World Championship status from previously run events like the Senior 500 and Lightweight 250cc TTs was no bar to the ACU running non-championship races in those classes, and they were still in the programme for 1977. The traditional Junior (350cc) event, however, was dropped and the title of Junior was given to the 250 race (previously Lightweight 250). The Classic race was retained and an additional four-lap Schweppes Jubilee Classic race included. Side-cars had two races for up to 1000cc outfits, and then there were the three Formula races, with the Formula I event being run on its own and Formula II and III being run together. All the above were scattered over a race programme that began on a Saturday and finished on the following Friday.

Formula Racing

Race fans were familiar with Formula racing of big bikes, as Formula 750 had been intro-duced with great success at the TT in 1971, being 'upgraded' to become the Classic 1000cc race in 1975. They were also familiar with the Production races for 750, 500 and

250cc classes, but in 1977 the Production races were dropped and the smaller production bikes got to race in the TT Formula II and III events, in which various departures from standard specifications were allowed with the aim of maximizing performance. With conventional racing dominated by two-strokes, the capacity limits permitted for the three TT Formula races sought to encourage four-strokes by giving them a capacity advantage:

	Two-stroke		**Four-stroke**	
	over	up to	over	up to
TT Formula 1	350	500	600	1000
TT Formula 11	250	350	400	600
TT Formula 111	125	250	200	400

Honda Returns

The name of Honda was not to be seen among the winners of World Championship races in the early to mid-1970s and, apart from a couple of wins in 250 and 500cc Production classes, it was also missing from the list of TT winners. All the worldwide publicity to be gained from racing was going to Yamaha in the 250 and 350cc classes, while Suzuki had developed its 4-cylinder RG500 into a world-beater for Barry Sheene to win the 500cc class

in 1976. Although Barry's was clearly a 'works' model, in the two years after its debut in 1974 the RG500 quickly established itself as the over-the-counter racer to have in the 500 class, rather as the Manx Norton had done many years before.

Honda chose the Formula I class at the 1977 TT for its return to international racing. Exactly why it picked that moment to return is not known, but perhaps it was mindful of Soichiro Honda's maxim that 'if you are winning TT races then you are selling motorcycles'. Additionally, although few were aware, it had already made the decision to return to World Championship racing in 1979 and was working on a 500cc four-stroke machine.

Honda was a company used to success, even though its attempt to win the 500cc class with Mike Hailwood eluded it back in 1966 and 1967. So, given its return to competition, who would it choose to ride (and win) for it at the 1977 TT?

Read Returns

After his last appearance at the TT in 1972, Phil Read moved on to receive full 'works' support from MV Agusta and snatched the

Phil Read returned to ride a 'works' Honda to victory in the 1977 Formula I race.

500cc World Championships of 1973 and 1974. He then came second in 1975 to Giacomo Agostini, who had moved to Yamaha, but his championship efforts faltered in 1976 when he contested only a few rounds on a private Suzuki.

Read would have been well aware of how the TT's prize money had climbed since he last rode on the Island and, despite his voluble anti-TT stance, it is quite likely that the TT organizers made known to him what level of start money was on offer to a star of his standing. Perhaps sensing that his glory days were over, and keen to achieve a few more good pay days, he performed an amazing U-turn and announced his return to the TT for 1977. Not only was he returning, but he would have the plum ride for Honda in the Formula I race and use Suzukis in the Senior and Classic events.

Many TT fans, who liked things to be simple, straightforward and presented in two shades only – black or white – were stunned by what they saw as the arrogance of Read's action. Here was a prime mover in the post-1972 anti-faction that contributed to their beloved TT being stripped of World Championship status, and now he was brazenly returning to the event. This was the man who, as a MGP and TT winner, actually took it upon himself in 1972 to write to the Patron of the ACU, the Duke of Edinburgh, condemning the very event from which he now sought to profit. The anti-Read response of the average fan was both predictable and understandable. It even extended to race marshals, who warned that he should not expect them to pick him up if he fell off. Many ordinary Manx people who recognized the damage that his earlier actions had done to the TT were also strongly opposed to his return.

Having been racing for more than twenty years and with several World Championships and TT wins to his credit, a worldly wise Phil Read was not too troubled by the hostile reactions to his return, limiting himself merely to explaining that, as the TT was no longer part of the World Championship and thus there was no pressure to compete for Championship points, racing over the Mountain Course was once again acceptable to him.

The 1977 Races

The return of Honda and Read generated massive publicity for the 1977 TT, which, of course, was just what the organizers wanted. But although the pair of returnees looked like stealing the show, knowledgeable spectators were keen to see how some good foreign newcomers would perform, and these included men like Pat Hennen (USA), Stu Avant (New Zealand) and the sidecar team of Rolf Biland and Kenny Williams (Switzerland/UK).

It was the sidecar crew of George O'Dell and Kenny Arthur (Yamaha) who stole the show during practice, when they set the first 100mph lap of the Island on three wheels during the long Thursday afternoon session. Practice performances do not get a rider's name into the record books, but no one underestimated what the duo had achieved, and O'Dell felt justified in holding an all-night party to celebrate. At the following morning's early practice, a slightly bleary George O'Dell appeared at the start but, wisely, confined himself to the role of spectator. With a start

The Beresford Hotel served as race headquarters for George O'Dell and it joined in the celebration of his 1977 success.

number of 16 in the first Sidecar race, it was no surprise to George that the traffic ahead of him meant that Dick Greaseley, who started earlier, was the first to break the 100mph barrier in the race, but O'Dell scorched to race victory, lifting the lap record to 102.80mph (165.44km/h) in the process.

The majority of TT spectators would love to swap places with the riders, and from their race-day positions on the banks and walls around the Mountain Course they do all they can to will the stars to victory and the under-dogs to a finish. Riders are aware of such urgings from spectators, and writing later of his win in *Sidecar Championship*, George O'Dell told how in that 1977 race:

> The crowd made me do 102.80mph. As I was catching different guys, spectators would see me coming and would wave like mad at these other drivers telling them to move over . . . at the Gooseneck where you're going slowly, you're almost in contact with the crowd . . . at Governor's I could hear them shouting.

Where Does the Money Go?

George O'Dell was arguably Britain's top sidecar racer in 1977, but claimed to have received just £500 start money for the TT meeting. His win in the first race netted him £1,000, but a retirement in the second race 'with the aroma of burning clutch coupled with unwelcome engine grumblings' meant no further contribution to the heavy expenses of travel, accommodation and machine repairs. After paying his passenger £400, O'Dell reck-oned to have left the Island with less than £100 from the event.

Phil Read probably received the most start money (measured in thousands rather than hundreds) and showed in practice that five years away from the TT had not blunted his riding skills over the Mountain Course. He took the Formula I event for Honda in a race that saw deteriorating weather halt racing at the end of the fourth lap. Two days later the Senior event started in clear weather and Read set his fastest ever TT lap at 110.01mph (177.04km/h) on his Suzuki RG500, pursued by Tom Herron and Eddie Roberts. Then lowering mist on the Mountain caused the organizers to stop the race at the end of the fifth lap with Read more than a minute ahead of Herron (Yamaha), and with Roberts (Yamaha) a further one and a half minutes behind in third. Having achieved two good race pay-days, Phil was looking forward to a third in Wednesday's Classic. However, engaged in unauthorized testing of his big Suzuki on open roads the day before, he fell at Brandish, damaged his shoulder and put himself out of the race, collecting an admon-ishment from the organizers.

Another who would have received respect-able start money in 1977 based on past TT performances was Mick Grant. In a storming ride in Wednesday's Classic event, Mick hurled his 3-cylinder Kawasaki around to set a new absolute course record of 112.77mph (181.48km/h), finishing well clear of Charlie Williams (Yamaha) in a race in which the first twenty finishers all averaged over 100mph. Indeed, the leader-board at the end of the first lap of the race was a 'who's who' of current TT stars, with Grant followed by Alex George (Yamaha), Charlie Williams (Yamaha), Stan Woods (Suzuki), John Williams (Suzuki) and Tony Rutter (Yamaha), although Tom Herron was absent, having dropped out early in the race.

A New Star

One man who would have received substan-tially less start money than these established stars was Joey Dunlop. In only his second year at the TT, Joey and his support crew made the crossing from Ireland in a friend's fishing boat and settled themselves into former Irish racer Norman Dunne's premises in Hutchinson Square, Douglas. Although his entry for the 'Jubilee Classic' was not initially accepted, at the end of the week Joey was on the start line for this 'one-off' four-lapper, mounted on a strange hybrid racer fitted with a Yamaha TZ750 engine in a twin-shock frame originally built to take a Suzuki.

Although the bike was seemingly slow to get into its stride – running on only three cylinders until Ballacraine, 7½ miles (12km) into the first lap – Joey was giving it his all. But at the back of his mind he knew from practice that tyre-wear was heavy and, after checking it at his mid-race pit stop, he stopped again on the last lap in Parliament Square, Ramsey, to see that all was well for the last 14-mile (23km) blast across the rough and abrasive Mountain stretch. Joey came home for his first TT victory at an average speed of 108.86mph (175.19km/h) and a fastest lap of 110.93mph (178.52km/h). These speeds certainly put him right up with the top men in terms of performance, if not in earnings.

Joey Dunlop on his way to his first TT win in the 1977 Schweppes Jubilee Classic race.

Formula TT

Pleased to have taken victory in the Formula I race with Phil Read, Honda was also victorious in the Formula II and III races, when Alan Jackson headed a Honda 1-2-3 in Formula

II and John Kidson brought another of its machines home first in Formula III. It gave the riders instant World Champion status and was seen by Honda as a very satisfactory step back on the TT racing ladder.

Although the Formula events did not yield ultra-close racing at the front in 1977, they did hold spectator interest, and with the retention of the Junior (250), Senior (500) and Sidecar events for purpose-built racing machinery, the 1977 TT offered a much broader range of race activity than would be seen at a World Championship meeting. The 1977 TT races finished with no serious accidents to competitors, but despite everything to do with the event seemingly being shunned by the GP crowd, it is interesting to see that the first three finishers in the 350cc World Championship of 1977 (Katayama, Herron, Ekerold) had all ridden the TT, as had Pat Hennen (third in 500 GPs), Mick Grant (eighth in 250 GPs) and half of the first eight place-men in the Sidecar World Championship, where George O'Dell finished as number one.

'No Vacancies'

As well as providing organizational support to TT-related activities, the Isle of Man Tourist Board always put much traditional promotional effort into bringing more visitors to attend the entire two weeks of the TT 'happening'. But in 1978 the prospect of just one man coming to race a motorcycle around the Mountain Course put all the official crowd-pulling efforts in the shade, for it was announced in January 1978 that Mike Hailwood was coming back to race at the TT. Enthusiasts flocked to book all available accommodation and by the time of the TT every hotel, guest house, boarding establishment and camp site on the island was displaying 'No Vacancies' signs.

It is difficult to understand why Mike Hailwood, who had been away from motorcycle racing for more than ten years, during which he received a crippling ankle injury that ended a car-racing career, made a return to racing motorcycles. It is known that he rode a couple of historic races on a Manx Norton in Australia in early 1977 and perhaps that revived his interest. Further delving into the 'whys and wherefores' of his return shows that it was not driven by money, although he naturally accepted payment for his efforts.

On a visit to Britain from his New Zealand home in the summer of 1977, Mike attended the British GP at Silverstone and happened to meet Steve Wynne, the boss of Sports Motorcycles, who supplied a Ducati for Roger Nicholls to ride. Mike admired and talked about the Ducati, for he had by then signed to do an Australian six-hour race with Jim Scaysbrook on a similar machine.

A month later, during an evening practice at the 1977 MGP, the few people who noticed were surprised to see Mike appear on the start-line with a Padgetts Yamaha sporting a Travelling Marshal 'M' plate and fitted with a camera. However, as he did just a single lap with a few stops for filming and interviews, and then disappeared, no one attached much significance to that 'one-off' appearance by the twelve-times TT winner – who, incidentally, expressed himself shocked at the speed of the Yamaha! Before the end of 1977 Steve Wynne

was contacted by an intermediary about supplying a Ducati for Mike to ride at the 1978 TT. Put very simply, Steve made the necessary arrangements using his contacts with the Ducati factory and a bike was prepared for Mike's use in the Formula I race.

It had been eleven years since Mike Hailwood's last serious TT racing lap, when black leathers and pudding-basin helmets were standard wear. Of course his legion of attending fans had aged by a similar amount, even though, buoyed by his reappearance, many of them claimed to feel ten years younger. There were certainly a lot of young racers entered in the meeting on top-flight racing bikes, and they were all intent on testing themselves against this 'old' man of thirty-eight, who had ridden his first TT some twenty years before. Journalist Ted Macauley described Mike's position rather more graphically when he wrote of 'a pack of youngsters on thoroughbred race machinery, howling after his reputation'.

With a V-twin Ducati for the Formula I race, plus 250, 500 and 750 Yamahas for the Junior, Senior and Classic events, Mike was certainly due to put in some racing miles on the Island, even though the time he had for practice was much reduced due to the organizers again omitting early-morning sessions.

Mike Hailwood (Ducati) at Quarter Bridge in the 1978 Formula I race.

Although he must have known his racing return would attract publicity, he expressed concern at the intensity of pre–TT press coverage that brought a far greater level of expectation and seriousness to his efforts than originally planned. Not that he treated his comeback lightly, for at a press launch by Martini, who supported his Yamaha rides, he said, 'Nobody must expect miracles, but we're not going to the Island to swan around'.

Television crews and journalists from all over the world flocked to report on this greatest of sporting comebacks and among them, inevitably, were a few doubters, but Mike's practice performances soon put those to rest. Finishing with a fastest lap at 111.04mph (178.70km/h), he showed that he was capable of running with the best of the current TT racers, so raising race expectations to fever pitch.

Formula I Fantastic

The Formula I race was scheduled for the opening Saturday of the 1978 TT programme. Mike Hailwood came to the line with his 864cc Ducati V-twin carrying number 12 and sporting the red, green and white livery of his sponsor Castrol. Fifty seconds ahead of him in the starting order was his old adversary Phil Read, once again mounted on a 'works' Honda.

Right from the outset of the race Mike moved to the head of the field on corrected time. Riding a machine putting out just under 90bhp (his nearest rivals all had more than 100bhp on tap), he quickly got into the fast but smooth race rhythm that pays rich dividends on the Mountain Course. Mike's popularity among spectators was immense and, as he gradually closed on main rival Phil Read, they willed him to pass. This he did towards the end of the third lap, and although a quicker pit stop saw Phil start his fourth lap ahead of Mike on the road (but not on corrected time), the Honda rider had asked too much of his

4-cylinder machine in attempting to keep ahead of the booming Ducati twin. With the Honda slowing and throwing out oil, Read was forced to retire on the fifth lap.

Mike's progress through the race was untroubled and offered everything he and the crowds could have wanted. Riding consistently fast for most of the race, he set new records, overhauled those who started ahead of him and, on the last lap, was able to cruise round and savour the support he was getting from programme-waving spectators. It was an emotional race for all involved, and at the finish the coolest man around was the now thirteen times TT winner, Mike Hailwood. Despite averaging 108.51mph (174.62km/h) for six laps with his fastest being 110.62mph (178.02km/h), Mike declared, 'Truthfully, I was well within my safety limits . . . plenty left in hand had I needed it'.

A happy Mike Hailwood is besieged by autograph hunters after his win.

Ron Haslam brought his short-circuit style of riding to island racing.

Going quickly but without Mike Hailwood's smooth style, up and coming short-circuit star Ron Haslam got things wrong at Ballaugh Bridge and had a heavy tumble after losing control on landing. Ron walked away unscathed, while probably reflecting that it was the first humpback bridge he had come across in his racing career.

High Expectations

While Mike Hailwood's win in Saturday's Formula I raised expectations of success in the three other races he was to ride in 1978, the performance of American Pat Hennen in practice raised equal levels of expectation, particularly for the Senior race. In only his second year of Island racing, Hennen became the first man to lap in under twenty minutes when he rode his Suzuki around in 19 minutes 54 seconds, an average speed of 113.75mph (183.06km/h). Seemingly determined to carry his form

through to the race, Hennen set a furious pace from the outset of Monday's Senior TT. Frightening other top runners like Tom Herron with the manner in which he attacked the course and set the fastest lap at 113.83mph (183.19km/h), his ultra-rapid progress came to an end with a horrendous crash on the last lap at Bishopscourt that took him out of the race and almost claimed his life.

Tactics

Tom Herron led throughout that fateful Senior race; with the aid of five signallers, he knew his exact race position and that of his nearest rivals, saying 'I was always in control of my position on the course'. Very experienced in the ways of TT racing, Tom rode in close company with John Williams in the early stages. Although both were going hard, each had a little in hand as they tried to pace themselves and their engines to last the six-lap race.

Williams dropped out on the fourth lap with a burst water-hose and Pat Hennen (riding at number 3) moved into second place, riding closely on the road with Tom Herron, who had started at number 8 and by then had a nineteen-second lead. Hennen had actually pulled back ten seconds on Herron on lap four and seemed determined to try and reduce Tom's nineteen-second lead as they started the last lap. With his signallers telling him the position, Herron knew through lap four that Hennen was coming and the moment that he arrived on his tail, but he also knew that the young American had to pass and then draw away from him – an extremely difficult task.

No one could really blame Hennen for trying but, perhaps lacking experience in only his second year at the TT, he should have realized that even if he got back in front of Herron, the very experienced Irishman was more than fast enough to just sit on his tail and not let him get away. It was an ideal situation for the race-leader and, riding in such close proximity, Tom tried to indicate this to Pat to

hold station. But he failed, and shortly after the American went down when just a few yards from Herron's back wheel.

Various explanations were put forward for his 150mph crash, ranging from a bird strike to a seized engine. In an interview before the race Hennen had claimed 'I will only be trying 85 per cent and leaving a safety margin with road to spare', though that was not apparent during the race; but he had also expressed his worries about the possible effects of a mechanical failure.

More Expectations

Yamaha provided three 'works' bikes for Mike Hailwood to ride in 1978, but expectations of further success were unfulfilled. After experiencing difficulty in starting, a faulty steering-damper on the first lap of the Senior saw him having to ease his pace. Then, running out of petrol on the Mountain on the last lap saw him out of the race after he took fuel from a spectator to get back to the pits. Although in

Pat Hennen at speed on his Suzuki.

159

Wednesday's Junior (250) the first twenty-seven finishers were on Yamahas, Mike could do no better than twelfth place on his, with Charles (who had by then become Chas) Mortimer taking the win – his ninth TT victory. In Friday's Classic race Mike was holding second place a few seconds behind race-leader Mick Grant (Kawasaki) when his TZ750 holed a piston and brought his week to an end. Mick Grant went on to win that race, setting a new absolute lap record of 114.33mph (183.99km/h) in the process.

A strange aspect of Hailwood's return to racing was that his successful Formula I Ducati was prepared by the relatively small NCR concern, who had official links to Ducati, plus much input from Sports Motorcycles, while his Yamahas received the attention of Yamaha's far more extensive race-shop. Whereas Mike was delighted with the Ducati, he expressed himself as less than pleased with Yamaha.

Tragedy

After all the criticism received by the TT through the 1970s, the triumph of Mike Hailwood's return in 1978 did much to revive its image in the racing world, for it was a fairy-tale venture that attracted all the right sort of publicity. However, the TT's dark side had not gone away, and the reality of racing over the ultra-dangerous TT course showed itself in the first Sidecar race when the experienced Mac Hobson and passenger Kenny Birch were killed after losing control over bumps at the top of Bray Hill. In a separate incident in the same race, Ernst Trachsel crashed at the bottom of Bray after a steering-link broke and he was also killed. Although it is difficult to

write, it is a fact that those who take on the challenge of racing over the Mountain Course know that it will claim more victims and that there will be deaths among them and their racing colleagues. However many safety measures the organizers may introduce, it is the nature of the challenge and of the course that deaths will result from contesting it.

The policy of running two Sidecar races, started in 1977, was maintained for 1978. Known as Sidecar race A and Sidecar race B, an overall winner was also declared based upon aggregate performances in the two races. Dick Greaseley (Yamaha) won race A at record-breaking speed, Rolf Steinhausen won race B, and Jock Taylor (Yamaha) put up the best performance overall. To Rolf Biland and his unconventional Yamaha-powered 'Beo' went the fastest lap at 103.81mph (167.06km/h), but the previous year's winner, George O'Dell, crashed at the Bungalow, broke a leg and was airlifted to hospital by the rescue helicopter.

Advertising

A number of firms advertised the success of their products at the 1978 TT in the motor-cycle press. Dunlop expressed its pleasure at achieving almost a clean sweep in the solo and sidecar classes, while Shell had supplied at least the first five finishers in every race. Honda adverts seemed to have been written in expectation of achieving further big-bike victories, and stressed how close its road bikes were to its TT-winning machines. However, it did not achieve a big-bike victory in 1978, although it did announce a limited production run of a 'Phil Read Replica 750F2' for the road.

8 From TT Races to TT Festival

The thought of all the ordinary motorcyclists who visit the races devoting their entire time on the Island to speeding around the TT course is the sort of nightmare scenario that would attract criticism of the entire TT meeting from even the most tolerant Manx residents. Fortunately, apart from a few fanatics, most visitors look for ways of spending a lot of their time away from the course on non-race days, and there have always been a host of motorcycle-related activities for visitors to attend and participate in, as well as the normal attractions in the way of scenery and entertainment that the Island offers as a holiday resort.

The ride to the top of Snaefell on the Manx Electric Railway.

As alternatives to watching motorcycle racing, visitors may take in the Laxey Wheel.

Many biking events, such as meetings of one-make clubs, are private and loosely organized activities, but in the late 1970s the Isle of Man Tourist Board put increasing effort into providing crowd-pleasing activities of the sort that involved a more organized and costly approach, including pop concerts, bigger and better motocross and beach races, a Sprint, Enduro, the Red Arrows, vintage bike rallies, a fun-fair, and additional racing at the beginning and end of the TT period on the Billown circuit. The coordination and publicity required for these lesser happenings, which occupy many pages in the printed TT programme, have helped the event move towards what it regarded as a festival of motorcycling that, appropriately, is nowadays often known as the 'TT Festival'. The policy paid off and continues to this day, with an ever-widening range of activities bringing in many people who may not be overly enthusiastic about the racing, but who want to be part of a motorcycling event that attracts crowds from all over the world.

Manx Millennium

In 1979 the Isle of Man celebrated one thousand years of parliamentary rule by Tynwald, and the TT did its best to recognize the occasion with a little extra pomp, the issue of Millennium medals, a Lap of Honour comprising star riders and machines from the past and other events. However, the weather did not cooperate during practice and George O'Dell marked the Millennium by crashing in a cloud of spray at Ginger Hall and breaking a leg, just as he did in 1978. Mick Grant was also on the injured list, having crashed at the NW200, where Tom Herron sadly lost his life in a separate incident. A top rider, Tom was then lying fourth in the 500cc World Championships on a 'works' Suzuki.

According to the Isle of Man Tourist Board, 51,500 people came to the 'free' show that was the 1979 'TT Festival'. Maybe the Island should have imposed a small levy on visitors, for despite claims of more prize money being

paid further down the field, many of the lesser riders left the Island almost broke at the end of TT fortnight.

A new pit-lane system was brought into operation that changed the method used for the previous seventy years: refuelling was now carried out on the grandstand side of the pit-counters, rather than on the trackside as before.

Phil Read lost his 'works' Honda ride and did not contest the 1979 TT. Mick Grant was due to ride for Honda and, although he arrived to race, his NW200 injuries were a major handicap and the 'works' ride went to Alex George, after Charlie Williams was prevented from accepting Honda's offer of a ride due to a clash of oil contracts. Honda also chose the TT to launch its new Grand Prix racer. A water-cooled, 4-cylinder, four-stroke with V configuration, it was certainly not built to race at the TT, but neither did it shine in the GPs, and it left Honda still searching for the 500cc World crown.

After his superb efforts in 1978, Mike Hailwood was inundated with offers of machinery for 1979, even receiving proposals to contest the full World Championships. That went way beyond what Mike wanted to commit himself to, but he did return and contest the TT,

Spectators in the grandstand look down onto a new pit lane, with the track beyond.

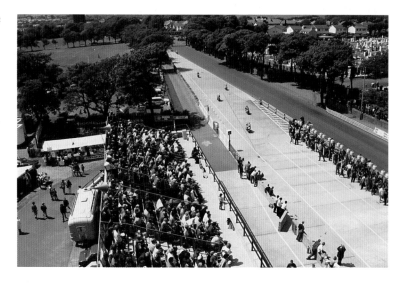

choosing Ducati again for the Formula I and a RG500 prepared by Heron Suzuki for use in both the Senior and Classic races.

Although Ducati showed a little more interest in Mike's TT efforts for 1979, the bike they produced for him was not as good as the previous year's. Problems with its handling were solved by substitution of the old 1978 frame, but a slower engine could not be cured and was made worse by the fact that the opposition was noticeably faster than in 1978. In the Formula I race Mike battled to hold on to third place, but losing first gear, being troubled by a loose exhaust, and then having to stop for a loose battery saw him cross the line in fifth place, behind winner Alex George (Honda).

With the Senior run in good conditions and his Suzuki running perfectly, Mike showed his class with a record-breaking victory over Tony Rutter (Suzuki), putting in a fastest lap of an incredible 114.02mph (183.49km/h) – faster than he had ever gone before. Mike was very happy with the level of support he received from Suzuki, but he may not have been aware that his Senior bike underwent a full engine strip and rebuild during the night before the Senior race. What was intended as a precautionary check turned into a marathon work session, when the delving Suzuki crew spotted something they were not happy with.

The 1979 Senior was Mike Hailwood's fourteenth TT victory, and with everyone aware that Friday's Classic was to be his last Island race, all hoped it would offer a fairy-tale finish to his TT career. It turned into a nail-biting race, with Mike and Alex George (Honda) disputing the lead throughout. Starting the last lap Mike was one second in the lead, but unable to increase his Senior race speed beyond 114.14mph (183.68km/h), he finally lost out to Alex by three seconds. It was a race that Mike would dearly have loved to win, but, in his words, he 'didn't want to stick my neck out any further', so he finished his TT-racing career with a second place – and fourteen wins!

New Names

While most of the attention in 1979 was focused on Mike Hailwood, there were less experienced riders putting in splendid performances to earn themselves rostrum positions and gain the attention of sponsors and the racing public. Denis Ireland, first-timer Graeme McGregor and Ron Haslam were among those who made the podium, while just off in fourth places were Graeme Crosby (Formula I), Steve Ward (Senior) and Jeff Sayle (Classic). Meanwhile, the experienced Charlie Williams broke Bill Ivy's eleven-year-old 250cc record when taking Junior victory

Charlie Williams rode Yamahas for much of his successful racing career at the TT and on short circuits.

(plus two other podiums) and Neil Tuxworth showed his enthusiasm for the TT by riding in all solo classes.

Hitting the front among the sidecars was Trevor Ireson, in his eleventh year at the TT, with Clive Pollington holding the third wheel down. The pair were comfortable winners of both three-lap races using Yamaha power, completing all their laps at more than 100mph.

Black Flag

Every rider has his own tales to tell of the races he contests, but most remain within the confines of his friends and acquaintances. One that reached the public domain concerned the black-flagging of former MGP winner Steve Ward during his race to fourth place in the Senior.

A black flag (with orange centre) is used by the organizers at a few specific locations on the course when they want to stop a rider in the middle of a race. This is usually because he has been reported as leaking oil or something is hanging loose. When he is shown the black flag he must stop, and his machine will then be inspected by a Travelling Marshal, who will either pull him out of the race or, if the problem is not severe, allow him to continue. The latter happened when Steve Ward was stopped at Ramsey during the Senior. The Travelling Marshal always records the time a rider is stopped and passes that information to the timekeepers. They then work out the additional time lost by slowing to a standstill under the black flag and restarting, add it to the time spent stationary, deduct it from his lap time and at the end of the race give him a revised overall race time and position.

Having done this to Steve Ward, they found that the revised time they gave him for the lap on which he was stopped showed that he had broken the lap record. That could have opened up a whole can of worms, so with a quick revision to their figures they produced a slightly different lap time without affecting Steve's finishing position.

Bumps

With two wins (Formula I and Classic), Alex George earned the title of top solo rider at the 1979 TT, while Trevor Ireson was top sidecar driver. Both made a post-race plea to the organizers not to smooth out any more bumps on the course, for both felt that the uneven surface served to govern speed in places and that the course was fast enough in its present state.

Bold Claims

The 1979 TT proved successful on most counts, but as the 1980 event approached the organizers put out the following statement:

> The ACU will not be satisfied to bask in the reflected glory of the 1979 Millennium TT,

This was the condition of Helmut Dahne's tyre at the end of the six-lap Formula I race in which, due to further easing of restrictions, the machines used were closer to pure racers than to road bikes. The TT Course had worn away almost the entire tread and the canvas is showing through.

Honda produced this fold-out brochure listing its 1980 TT activities.

but will plan for even better events in the 1980s. Encouraged by the world-wide public support the Isle of Man TT enjoys, we plan to make the occasion a truly international festival of motor-cycling – an occasion which will be the envy of all other countries interested in motor-cycle sport.

The 'TT Festival' theme was supported by the major motorcycle manufacturers. Kawasaki promoted a big pop concert on Mad Sunday,

Yamaha had several events aimed at riders (both present and would-be) of their machines, while Honda promoted a week of varied activities including a display of their machines and a spectacular firework display over Douglas Bay.

Pre-race publicity claimed the TT to be 'the richest motorcycle event in the world'. Prize money for all events was paid on a rider's position at the end of each lap of the race from the second lap onwards, so obviating problems experienced in the past where a rider might lead for five laps, retire on the sixth and thus gain nothing for a fortnight spent at the TT. Richest event was the Classic where a rider who led from start to finish would receive £10,000, and the second place could earn £5,000. The Senior TT winner collected a maximum of £3,500, Junior £3,000, Formula I took £5,000, Formula II and III £1,000 each, and Sidecar races were £3,000 for the first leg and £3,500 for the second.

An advertisement in the TT programme for 1980 proclaimed 'Phil Read Wins Again', but this time it had nothing to do with racing and was related to his retail bike-sales business in Surrey. On another page a smiling Mike Hailwood and Rod Gould featured in an advert for their similar business in Birmingham. They were continuing a long tradition of successful TT riders going into the motorcycle sales business on the strength of their racing reputations.

The Aggro TT

That was how the press described events at the opening race of the 1980 TT meeting, when the 'aggro', perhaps surprisingly, had nothing to do with money. Formula I was by then a strong feature of racing worldwide, and having won the 1979 World and British FI Championships, Honda came to the TT with a three-man team of Alex George, Mick Grant and Ron Haslam, determined to gain the considerable publicity arising from another TT win and World Championship. Unfortunately,

By 1980 the published TT programme had grown to magazine size, but it came with a pocket-sized race guide that included all the riders' names, numbers and other information, and was convenient to carry on race days.

George suffered a severe crash in practice at Ginger Hall, which put him out of the race and left Grant and Haslam to deal with the challenge from Suzuki, Kawasaki and Ducati-mounted riders. The man they rated most dangerous among the opposition riders was Graeme Crosby (Suzuki) in only his second year at the TT.

Crosby's allocated starting number was 16 in the Senior and Classic races, but he was given number 3 for the opening Formula I race. Not fancying the idea of the Honda team runners being able to chase him down, he asked the organizers for a lower starting position and was given number 11, which put him alongside Mick Grant on the grid. Honda was not pleased with this and twenty minutes before the start their team manager appealed against the organizers' decision. Given the

timing, it was a provocative move that earned Honda no friends, and a mere three minutes before the start Crosby was told he would have to revert to his original start number. With his mind thrown into turmoil when it should be focused on the race, he refused. It was an unsettling situation for the relative newcomer trying to face up to the dangers ahead, and was made worse by the fact that uncertain weather conditions had everyone in two minds about tyre choice: just two minutes before the start, Crosby elected to change his rear tyre.

It was Graeme McGregor who initially led the Formula I race from Ron Haslam, but then McGregor retired and Haslam lost places to Grant and Crosby, who circulated together on the road for three laps, swapping the lead. It was not until the fourth lap that Grant managed to shake off the Kiwi on the Suzuki and open up a lead of seventeen seconds. Although Crosby pulled some time back on the last lap, Grant was in control and finished the race 10.8 seconds ahead, with the fastest lap going to third-placed Sam McClements at 106.88 mph (172.00km/h).

But the aggravation with the Formula I race did not end with the waving of the chequered flag, for a protest was submitted claiming that Mick Grant's Honda was fitted with a 28-litre petrol tank instead of the maximum 24 litres permitted by the race regulations. While Honda admitted it was oversize, they were able to prove that the tank was stuffed with plastic bottles and table-tennis balls to reduce its holding capacity to 24 litres. It seemed a strange tactic, and Mick Grant's celebratory pounding of the tank at the end of the race, which created substantial dents, did not impress the Suzuki camp. After prolonged discussion by the race stewards, the protest was rejected and Grant and Honda were ratified as winners.

First for 'Croz'

It was Graeme Crosby's turn to race with an extra-large petrol tank in the Senior, but his,

This is the sort of close racing that Honda sought to avoid between their Mick Grant (12) and Suzuki's Graeme Crosby (11) in the Formula I race.

an ex-Mike Hailwood 8-gallon monster, was legal for the event. Although its bulk prevented him tucking down completely under the screen, he had a steady ride to take his first TT win in only his second year on the island. Although he described the actual race as uneventful, the first time he tried the large tank in practice was 'electrifying', for descending Bray Hill he hit a bump, was pressed down hard on the tank and received a major electric shock as the tank touched the top of his spark-plug caps.

It was actually Ian Richards (Suzuki) who rode in inspired fashion to lead the Senior for the first four laps, before retiring on the last, while Steve Cull (Suzuki) and Steve Ward (Suzuki) followed Crosby home. In the Junior race Charlie Williams led from start to finish to win from Donnie Robinson (Yamaha) and Steve Tonkin on a British-built, Rotax-engined Cotton. Much had been expected of Chas Mortimer on a 'works' Kawasaki in the Junior, but after climbing to fourth place he was forced to retire. Not content with one win, Charlie Williams (Yamaha) also took first place in the Formula II race on the same day, while Barry Smith (Yamaha) was victorious in Formula III.

In 1980 the World Formula I Championship (previously declared solely on the TT result) was extended to include the Ulster Grand Prix. Having taken second place at the TT and been victorious in Ulster, Graeme Crosby took the Championship.

Suitability?

With postponements affecting racing in 1980, questions were yet again asked about the suitability of the Mountain Course due to the adverse effect of mist and other conditions. Added to this was the sobering effect of three riders killed during the TT period and a strong statement from race veteran Bill Smith that he considered the bikes of the day had become too fast for the course. When *Motorcycle News* turned its speed gun on the runners dropping from Creg ny Baa to Brandish during the races, it showed that Graeme Crosby (Suzuki) was fastest Formula I at 163mph (262.3km/h), Jeff Sayle (Yamaha) fastest Classic at 164mph (263.9km/h) and Nigel Rollason (Barton) the fastest sidecar outfit at 144mph (231.7km/h). While the top sidecar drivers shared the concerns of the solos about speeds, some also worried about the extremely bumpy nature of

A 'Classic' Race

With Mick Grant and Ron Haslam entered for Friday's Classic race in 1980, Honda no doubt hoped to finish the week with another win. But in a surprise for the 'works' boys, it was Joey Dunlop on a two-year old TZ750 Yamaha supplied by John Rea who won the six-lap race ahead of Grant and Haslam.

Joey appeared to have a relatively smooth ride, but the spectators were not aware that on the first lap the retaining strap of his home-made eight-gallon petrol tank snapped, and that he spent the rest of the race holding it in place with his arms and knees. A rider normally considers a firmly fixed petrol tank an aid to fast riding, for he grips it with his knees when changing direction and travelling over bumps. Joey lost that aid very early on and it proved a considerable handicap.

Riding at number 3 and leading from the outset of the race, the Irishman mastered the tank problem (fitted to allow him to stop just once for refuelling) and held Grant at bay to the tune of some twenty seconds, until the end of the third lap when they both came in for petrol. Using the normal 'slow' filler, Joey was in the pits for an agonizing fifty-three seconds, but Honda had Daytona-style quick-fillers and got Grant out in twelve seconds to take the lead – that was forty-one seconds gained just on a pit-stop.

Joey then set about recovering the time he had lost. Getting faster as the race progressed, he put in a record-shattering last lap and snatched victory from Grant by a convincing twenty seconds. It was a quite stupendous ride, and on the final lap he set an absolute course record of 115.22mph (185.42km/h), taking just 19 minutes 38.8 seconds for the 37¾ miles.

Given the performance that Joey Dunlop put up against the Honda 'works' riders in the 1980 TT, there was only one course of action Honda could take – they signed him to ride for them in 1981 alongside Ron Haslam (and in preference to Mick Grant). The Honda race organization and the Joey Dunlop version of going racing were poles apart in their approach to the job, but they made things work, with credit going to Honda for bending to Joey's ways. However, he did not deliver quite the instant success Honda expected, and it was to be two years before he took another TT victory.

the course on flat-out stretches like the Sulby Straight. In such locations the bikes threatened to take control and more than one driver reported getting into a 'tank-slapper'.

The press tried to generate interest in the construction of a permanent short circuit, with the headline in *Motor Cycle Weekly* claiming 'New Island Circuit – Sadly The Only Course Left'. What it failed to realize was that race visitors did not want a sanitized short circuit substitute for the TT. They came to the island because racing over the roads was different – that was the attraction.

Mick Grant was forthright in his opposition to a short circuit, saying, 'This is probably the biggest load of nonsense I've heard for some time'. As an ardent fan of pure road racing, Mick went on, 'Why do the British have this disturbing habit of trying to destroy the traditional things in our lives. The TT is a marvellous meeting and, while it may need changes, it does not need destroying'. He felt that safety could be increased by tighter control on entries, pointing out that 'The Isle of Man is just not the place for a man who does not race regularly and it is time for the ACU to be far more restrictive in giving entries'. He also felt that the meeting could do with condensing in time – although he appreciated the requirement for the races to fit in with the growing 'Festival' attitude for a TT fortnight.

Facts and Rumours

The TT generates news throughout the year, and the winter of 1980/81 was no exception. Just seven months after he nearly died in a high-speed crash at Ginger Hall, Alex George signed to race in the big-bike classes again for Honda, including the TT. Asked if he had any concerns about riding in the event Alex, who by then lived by the side of the course at Greeba, replied, 'The circuit holds nothing but pleasure for me – I have no ghosts in the cupboard'. The speed of the medical response to Alex George's accident received some critical comment in

The rescue helicopter was able to convey an injured rider to the doorstep of the local hospital's emergency care services.

1980 and, in announcing more cash for the 1981 event, the ACU indicated that some of it would go to meet the cost of a second rescue helicopter.

Yamaha unveiled its race bikes for 1981 with the 250s and 500s incorporating their unique power-valve exhaust timing adjuster. Weights were slightly reduced, there were many minor improvements, and they came with monoshock rear suspension.

After rumours that Mick Grant would ride for Kawasaki at the TT, he actually signed for Suzuki early in the year. The Rotax concern had developed a Kawasaki-like 250 twin-cylinder two-stroke engine that had proved speedy and it attracted manufacturers like Armstrong who wanted to use it, plus people like Tony Foale and Waddon Engineering who offered frames to take the engine, which

Cotton had used to take third place in the 1980 Junior race.

The ACU announced that dump-can quick-fillers would be banned for 1981. The move followed incidents at the 1980 TT when many people in the pit lane were sprayed with petrol during their use. A few weeks after the announcement someone found a loophole in the regulations that allowed their continuing use, so the ACU was forced to confirm that they would be permitted for 1981.

In a typical example of why the rulebook gets thicker every year in trying to block loopholes, regulations for 1981 prescribed that 'Once numbers have been allocated, no rider will be permitted to change his number for any particular race'. It sounded like a well-worded rule, probably designed to avoid the bad feeling arising from the change of starting number by Graeme Crosby in the 1980 Formula I race, but it turned into one that the organizers operated at their discretion.

The traditional long Thursday afternoon practice session had been dropped in 1980 to accommodate one of the 'TT Festival' sideshows, the Grand National Scramble, but a Wednesday afternoon practice was planned to replace it in 1981.

Money Troubles

Publicizing a substantial £50,000 increase in money to be paid to riders in 1981, so taking the total to £253,000, the ACU revealed a new method of calculating start money based upon past performance, while retaining the right to pay a special supplement to riders with star appeal, and making increased payments to riders based upon their first-lap positions. The sum was made up of:

£100,000 in prize money
£16,000 in travel expenses
£6,000 for awards
£5,000 for Lap of Honour expenses
£126,000 for contracted start money

This was a very different monetary picture to the one that prevailed in the financially contentious period of the late 1960s, when the total sum on offer for the meeting was £30,000, but any thoughts that the new system would be gratefully accepted were quickly dispelled when riders such as Mick Grant, Alex George, Charlie Williams, Graeme Crosby and Chas Mortimer realized they would get less guaranteed money in 1981 than in 1980 (despite ACU claims to the contrary). Chas Mortimer was the only rider prepared to go public with actual figures and he maintained that he was paid £5,250 the previous year, but that for 1981 his guaranteed minimum was £3,000.

The situation was not helped by the fact that riders knew their expenses would be higher in 1981, for Dunlop reduced its level of support and almost all of them had to buy their own race tyres, instead of receiving them free as in the past.

More Aggro

Alex George, Charlie Williams and Mick Grant were still complaining about start money when practice opened for the 1981 TT and they threatened not to appear on the rostrum for post-race prize presentations. After it was pointed out that, in accordance with the race regulations, no rostrum appearance would result in no prize money, they quickly climbed down from their attempted show of rider-power. Unconfirmed reports suggested that what really irked them was the rumour of particularly high start money being paid to current World 350 Champion Jon Ekerold, whose only previous TT appearance was in 1976. But Ekerold soon showed that he was not present simply to cash-in on his World Championship status, for he topped the practice leader-board in the Junior class with a lap at 106.68mph (171.68km/h) on his Armstrong. Graeme Crosby (Suzuki) was fastest in the Senior and Classic classes, Ron Haslam (Honda) in Formula I and Jock Taylor (Yamaha) was the quickest man on three wheels.

With the prestigious Formula I event opening race week, the organizers hoped for a smooth running of the race without any of the controversy that occurred in 1980. Unfortunately, what happened during and after the race caused any lingering ill-feeling between the chief protagonists Honda and Suzuki to develop into something far more serious. Inadvertently in the thick of things

Jon Ekerold leaves Ramsey for the Mountain climb in 1981.

was Suzuki-mounted Graeme Crosby, who described what happened:

My bike got a puncture as we were joining the field on the road at the start. The mechanics had to take the bike out of the line-up and fit a new rear wheel, changing the sprocket at the same time. I stood at the start-line waiting for the bike to return and we were ready to roll just 10 seconds after I should have started at number 16.

Start-line officials decided that Crosby would have to start at the back of the field, without any credit for the four minutes or so that he lost. With Joey Dunlop taking an early lead and Ron Haslam second, Honda was quickly in control of the race while Crosby was left with the task of fighting his way past the sixty or so riders who started ahead of him. This he did to good effect, setting a new lap record on his final lap and seemingly finishing third. Haslam had taken over the lead from Dunlop at mid-distance after Joey had tyre troubles and had to change a wheel at his pit stop, so 'Rocket Ron' came home for what he hoped was his first TT win. Indeed, he was garlanded and feted as the winner, much to Honda's delight.

After reading the rule book, Suzuki submitted a protest to the organizers concerning the time penalty imposed on Crosby at the start of the race. The stewards of the meeting decided that Suzuki was right: Crosby's race-time should be calculated on the period that he was actually racing (excluding the time he was waiting to start) and that, as he was the rider who completed the race in the shortest time, he was the true race winner by two minutes. The luckless Ron Haslam was second, Joey Dunlop third, and newcomer John Newbold (Suzuki) dropped to fourth.

In his book *Honda – The Complete Story*, Roland Brown describes one of Honda's advertising slogans, 'Honda Enters. Honda Wins', as 'brilliant in its simplicity, outrageous in its arrogance, ruthless in its clarity'. Perhaps Honda believed the advertising, for it claimed that Haslam could have gone faster had the race team known that it was necessary, that race tactics would have been quite different, and that Honda would have beaten the Suzuki. Going on to have T-shirts printed for its race management with the wording 'Honda – Ron Did Win!', it reserved its biggest show of dissent from the organizers' decision by sending out its three men and machines for Friday's Classic race in hastily prepared black

Alex George was one of the three Honda 'works' riders in the 1981 Senior TT who were required to race in all black. He finished third – the only one of the team to complete the race.

leathers and paintwork. It was a protest no doubt supported by Honda fans, but neutral fans were bemused by Honda's actions.

Honda gained masses of publicity for its 'all-black' protest, but very little was favourable. *Motor Cycle News* proclaimed, 'The Honda racing team managed to totally disgrace themselves . . .', and ACU Chairman Vernon Cooper called the protest 'the product of a tiny mind'. Then, although Ron Haslam and Joey Dunlop turned up to receive their Silver Replicas at the customary prize-giving, they later received an order from Honda to hand them back.

Perhaps Honda spent race week in 1981 concentrating too much on protests and side issues, for when it came to the 'black' Classic race they found to their cost that Joey Dunlop did not have sufficient fuel to reach his pit stop at the end of the third lap. Joey ran out a couple of miles from the pits when, given his pace on that third lap, he might just have taken over the lead from Graeme Crosby. The time he lost pushing in to refuel put him well out of contention, and Suzuki team-men Crosby and Grant circulated together near the end with Crosby taking first place by thirty seconds. With Ron Haslam dropping out with ignition problems, Alex George, in third place, was the only black Honda to finish.

Despite the general unpopularity of Honda's stance, not everyone took Graeme Crosby's side that week, for when forced to stop early in Monday's Senior race at Braddan for a quick adjustment, Crosby recalls hearing boos from some of the crowd. Maybe they were Honda fans or, perhaps more likely, they were Ron Haslam supporters.

Before Friday's all-black Classic race protest by Honda there was almost a week of other racing to get through. There were more problems for the organizers in Monday's Senior race, when the weather deteriorated to such an extent that the race was called off after three laps and declared void. Unsurprisingly, the decision was not supported by those who had been running at the front, but found much

approval with those well down the field and the riders who had dropped out. Chris Guy was leading when the race was stopped but slid off at Braddan in the re-run and victory went to Mick Grant (Suzuki).

In Wednesday's Junior 250 race Yamaha's long-term dominance of the class came to an end when Steve Tonkin took his British Armstrong to victory at a new race record speed of 106.21mph (170.92km/h), and Kawasaki-mounted Graeme McGregor set the fastest lap at 109.22mph (175.77km/h) before retiring on lap three. Bob Jackson did bring a Yamaha home in second, but four of the first twelve finishers were not on Yamahas, something that would have been unthinkable just a couple of years before. John Ekerold challenged for the lead for the first half of the race, then a blown seal reduced his twin to a single and he lost second place.

Armstrong advertised its successful CM35 racer for £3,750 (plus VAT) after taking victory in the 1981 Lightweight 250 TT.

The Formula II and Formula III events still played a lesser role at the TT than the other classes, with some looking at them as not 'real' TT races. It was journalist and author Mick

Woollett who said of them 'they swelled the entry lists but blurred the image of the races'. Tony Rutter, however, took a good win for Ducati in Formula II and Barry Smith took his third consecutive Formula III win for Yamaha. Phil Mellor thought that he had taken second spot behind Rutter on his 350 LC Yamaha, but Phil rode with an oversize tank and, although it was stuffed with plastic bottles to reduce capacity in the same manner that Honda had used to win the 1980 Formula I race, he and sponsors Granby Motors were bitterly disappointed to find that the FIM had changed the rules and that such action was no longer permitted.

All riders fear the effect of mechanical failure on the TT course, and 1981 saw a rash of broken clip-ons, with Charlie Williams surviving a heart-stopping moment at the thirty-third when his right-hand one came off. Ray Knight suffered a similar problem, and Steve Parrish claimed to have suffered with several faulty ones.

75th Anniversary

Once the greatest international motorcycle racing meeting in the world, the Isle of Man TT had seen its programme of races much changed due to the polarization of the circuit racing and road racing factions in the sport. While many racers were happy to participate in both disciplines, increased specialization meant that some would never contest the TT. It was a far cry from even twenty-five years earlier, when competing in the Isle of Man races was seen as a major milestone in a racer's career.

By the time of its seventy-fifth anniversary in 1982, the TT meeting was regarded more and more as a major celebration of motorcycling; while the races remained the dominant feature, there were many visitors who were just as interested in the 'sideshows'. Unfortunately, there was some concern that the number of visitors was declining. Looking at all possible ways to maintain visitor numbers, the Isle of Man Government even formed a

Mick Grant, Ron Haslam and Phil Read nose-to-tail around Governor's Bridge in the 1982 Senior TT. When the correction is made for the TT's interval starting system, Haslam is actually leading Grant.

sub-committee to consider the building of a short circuit.

Phil Read made another return to race, but as he was now forty-three the stars of the day were not too concerned. Asked before the Classic race if he thought that Phil posed a threat, Mick Grant replied, 'Pose, yes. A threat, no!' Read managed to find space in a newspaper column to praise the TT and its riders: 'I don't want to knock the grand prix riders as they are a special breed on their own, but to ride and win a TT is the ultimate'. That was not going to happen again for Phil, but he did take fourth place in the Senior, where the Irish winner, Norman Brown (Suzuki), emulated Read's performance of some twenty years earlier by coming straight from a MGP victory to win a TT at his first attempt. Brown won from Jon Ekerold (Suzuki) by some twelve seconds after Mick Grant crashed at Dorans Bend. Not riding in 1982 was Graeme Crosby. Having joined a GP team run by Giacomo Agostini, Graeme found that the TT was no longer on his race agenda. He was, however, in the pit when use of a $1,000 American quick-filler saw Norman Brown in and out in an incredible four seconds at both of his refuelling stops. In a clear case of a race being won and lost in the pits, John Ekerold in second place took 29.6 seconds for his fuel stop.

What If?

Charlie Williams rode a 4-cylinder Yamaha for several years in the Senior but a win eluded him. On occasion he would have the fastest bike in the race but the GP-style four often failed him. Although he set the fastest lap in practice, the 1982 Senior looked like being another poor year for Charlie because his Yamaha was down on power from the start. By the time he reached Sulby on the second lap he felt there was no point in continuing so, assured of a friendly welcome, he pulled in at the Sulby Hotel. As he looked over the Yamaha, someone thrust a pint into his hand and told him he had been lying sixth. Suddenly he spotted a kinked fuel line that took only a few moments to straighten. Urged on by spectators, Charlie got back into the race. He knew all chance of a win had gone, but decided to find out what the Yamaha could really do, and on lap four he set a new Senior lap record of 115.08mph (185.20km/h). He did not even finish in the top twelve in the race, but Charlie got his name into the record books once more and his 115mph lap proved to be the fastest of the week.

One man who did not take long to achieve a big bike win at the TT was Ron Haslam. *Motorcycle News* summed up the 1982 Formula I race with: 'To Ron Haslam his first TT win.

Norman Brown attacks the exit from Parliament Square, Ramsey, on his Hector Neill-supported Suzuki, which gave him a Senior TT win at his first year of trying.

To his Honda team-mate Joey Dunlop a bundle of suspension problems and second place. To Suzuki's Mick Grant a new lap record and a retirement when in the lead'.

Hardly a Classic

Honda brought a new V4 (FWSV4) with them in 1982 with the thought that Joey Dunlop would ride it in the Classic TT. Although quick in practice, however, problems with a broken frame and the oil-cooler catching the road under heavy suspension travel showed that the new bike was not ready for the demands of the Mountain Course. Joey reverted to his well-tried RCB transverse four for the Classic race, which saw ten of those in the top twelve at the end of the first lap drop out before the end. The result was a first win for Denis Ireland (Suzuki) and another runner-up spot for John Ekerold (Suzuki).

The Junior race saw a similar decimation of the top runners and gave victory to Con Law (Waddon Ehrlich), while Trevor Ireson (Yamaha) won the Sidecar race A, Jock Taylor (Yamaha) took race B and, with third and fifth places, Roy Hanks (Yamaha) was the overall Sidecar winner. Both sidecar races had been led by Mick Boddice at some stage, but although Mick had been contesting the TT for many years, a win still eluded him.

With the restoration of a 350cc race in 1982, TT fans had to get used to there being Junior 250 and Junior 350 races. Tony Rutter won the new Junior 350 on a Yamaha and also came home first in the Formula II on a Ducati.

Among those celebrating the 75th anniversary of the TT were Dunlop Tyres and Shell Oils, who both claimed to have given the meeting unbroken support since 1907.

Joey Dunlop and his Honda on the cover of the 1982 TT programme.

Among the major awards to be won at the 1982 TT were trophies with names of great TT winners of the past.

Why so Named?

Hailwood's Height

One great TT winner from the past who was absent from the anniversary celebrations was winner of fourteen TTs, Mike Hailwood. In a cruel twist of fate, Mike was killed in a road traffic accident in March 1981, but although he may have gone he certainly was not forgotten by TT fans and the Isle of Man authorities. A Mike Hailwood Centre was erected behind the grandstand and a memorial plaque placed on the wall opposite the start line.

Out on the course the approach to the highest point at Brandywell was named Hailwood's Height and this simple name board identifies the place, perhaps in a manner appropriate to Mike's modest character.

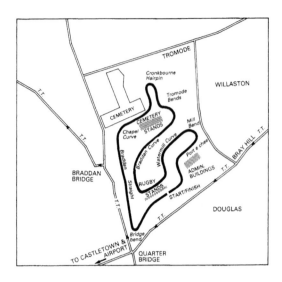

Official and unofficial plans for a short circuit appeared in 1983. This is just one of them.

Plans for 1983

It was reported in early 1983 that the Isle of Man Tourist Board had received a sub-committee's report and was considering plans for a short circuit suitable for Grand Prix racing. A figure of £5 million was mentioned and, although only at the sketch plan stage, there was confident talk of a Grand Prix (would it be the British GP or Isle of Man GP?) being

held at the end of the TT fortnight in 1985. That sounded somewhat ambitious, and there was also talk of a 24-hour endurance race being run on the new circuit before TT practice started.

Honda's plans were rather firmer in 1983 when it unveiled a new RS850R V4 to contest the British Formula I series in the hands of Wayne Gardner and Roger Marshall. Developed from the V4 roadster for American racing with no expense spared, the new bike was to be ridden by Joey Dunlop in the Tourist Trophy World Championship Formula I race, in which Roger Marshall replaced Ron Haslam, who was wanted by Honda at the Yugoslav GP. The Formula I World Championship had been extended beyond the TT and Ulster GP in 1982 to include a round at Vila Real in Portugal. Joey Dunlop secured three second places in 1982 and took his first World title. Thus he arrived on the island for 1983 as defending champion, albeit with a bike that gave away 150cc to most of its rivals and weighed 376lb (171kg). Still very much a Honda 'works' rider, Joey had nevertheless managed to negotiate a degree of autonomy in his activities, which freed him from Honda's normal strict control. It was unusual, but it was what Joey wanted.

Practice revealed several small problems with the new bike and Joey was only sixth fastest in Formula I. He was relatively untroubled with this, knowing that he always went quicker on race days and feeling that he had spent the practice time ironing out problems that were unlikely to reoccur. During the race Joey was in a class of his own. From a standing-start he broke both the Formula I and the outright course record and went on to average more than 114mph (183.5km/h) for the entire race. Despite a planned tyre change at his pit stop, he still won by fifty-three seconds from Mick Grant (Suzuki). Although many were aware that Honda ran the 850 in anticipation of Formula I being restricted to 750cc machines in the near future, what no one knew at the time was that it was the first of a six-year run of Formula I victories for the unorthodox combination of Joey Dunlop and Honda.

Described as the top privateer in the Formula I race, Trevor Nation took the opportunity to show his talent to the racing world by taking fifth place on his Suzuki, which, due to lack of money, hard-up Trevor raced on second-hand tyres. Having given up short-circuit racing for a couple of months to save for the TT, Trevor was determined to make a good showing and invested £125 in hiring a quick-filler for the race. The effect of that and his many other expenses, however, meant the £1,135 he collected in winnings was quickly spent.

Passengers Wanted

Being a sidecar passenger seems a strange occupation to outsiders. Perched on a bare platform with just a few handholds, a passenger is subject to massive acceleration, extremely heavy braking, considerable vibration, plus lots of noise and heat, all of which are accompanied by the sight and feel of the bumpy TT course flashing past at up to 145mph – a combination over which the passenger has virtually no control. While senses are being battered for three laps and 113 non-stop miles, he or she must contribute to keeping the outfit on the road by continuously moving about the sidecar platform to shift weight and thus maximize the outfit's handling, always remembering to keep at least one firm handhold.

Early practice in 1983 for previous sidecar winner Trevor Ireson was accompanied by some damp sessions and minor mechanical problems, which meant that he really did not get into his stride in setting his customary laps at well over 100mph. The Thursday afternoon session is one in which all competitors look to put in fast laps and Trevor opened with the fastest lap of the week at 104.86mph (168.75 km/h). Intending to improve on that on his second (and flying-lap), on the approach to Kirkmichael his passenger managed to convey to him that he wanted him to stop. Upon doing so, the passenger told him that he could not complete the lap at that pace. Cruising back to the grandstand, Trevor knew that he needed to find a new passenger, but one of sufficient quality was not available and he did not race. Two other drivers were faced with passenger withdrawals in 1983, one of them just grabbing a boat passage and leaving the Island without notice.

Dick Greasely and Stu Atkinson (Yamaha) raced through a mystery misfire to win Saturday's Sidecar race A, while long-time racing partnership Mick Boddice and Chas Birks won Race B after many years of trying for a Sidecar victory. Jock Taylor, who previously had been the fastest man at the TT with a sidecar, was sadly missing following his death while racing at Imatra towards the end of the 1982 season.

In less than ideal conditions dominated by strong winds, Con Law (EMC) set the first lap by a quarter-litre bike over 110mph when winning the Junior 250cc race, while Phil Mellor (Yamaha) won the Junior 350 at a slower pace. Tony Rutter (Ducati) made it a

Jock Taylor and Benga Johansson were remembered on the Island by this Manx Telecom phonecard of 1988.

10 UNITS ←

Manx Telecom

JOCK TAYLOR
BENGA JOHANSSON
1981

MANX TELECOM PHONECARD COLLECTOR SERIES 3 — 1988

hat-trick of wins in Formula II (Formula III was dropped for 1983), and in only his second year at the TT, 23-year-old short-circuit star Rob McElnea burst onto the world stage with a convincing win in the Classic at a record race average speed of 114.81mph (184.76km/h) on his big four-stroke Suzuki.

It was another young star, Norman Brown, who led the Classic for the first two laps, but his chances of winning were dashed when he could not make it to his pit stop at the end of the third lap after running out of fuel on his RG500 Suzuki at Creg ny Baa. Norman once more put his name in the record books with an absolute lap record of 116.19mph (186.98km/h) set on lap 2, but it was to be the last Island appearance of this extremely talented rider, for less than two months later an accident in the British Grand Prix at Silverstone took his life.

Looking Ahead

There was a feeling after the 1983 TT that while the racing had been close and exciting, the meeting lacked the overall 'buzz' that had accompanied the TTs of the previous few years. Although the Isle of Man Tourist Board and the ACU saw themselves as prime movers at the TT, providing finance and organization, some of the manufacturers who competed and members of the trade who supported

the event felt their words should be heard. Honda's race co-ordinator Barry Symmons emphasized the need for more activities when he said:

> The racing alone isn't sufficient to get people to the Island. The racing can be excellent, records can be smashed, but unless there are enough people on the Island, it's economic suicide for factories like ours to be there . . . Honda will continue to support the TT as long as there is a Formula I race. Dunlop, Marshall, Grant and the rest will still go to the TT whatever the start money. Much better to put more money into other events that will get bigger crowds.

Later in the year the programme of races for the 1984 TT was issued and it contained several important changes: the Junior 350cc race was dropped, maximum capacity for Formula I machines was reduced to 750cc, the Classic race became the Premier Classic, a Historic TT was introduced and Production racing returned with classes for up to 250, up to 750, and over 750cc. Sidecars also saw an addition when a 'Formula 2' class for up to 350cc two-strokes and 600cc four-strokes was introduced into the Sidecar race. The early 1980s was a time when long-wheelbase 'worm' outfits were establishing themselves in GPs, but they were not found to be at their best at the TT.

Having decided that the provision of high prize money for the top finishers had failed in its objective of luring GP stars to the TT, the amounts paid to the first three in most races was reduced quite substantially and more money was paid to the finishers from fourth downwards. The ACU felt that the top finishers' expenses were adequately covered by the individually negotiated start monies they received. It dropped the system of calculating sums for the others on the basis of several years of past performances and relied just on 1983 results, but it increased the basic travel allowance that everyone received from £100 to £125.

Qualifying

With an increase in the number of events for 1984 the organizers planned to provide increased practice time. They also tightened qualifying times for existing races by between two and three minutes, some of the new figures being:

Formula I, Junior 250 and Senior 500	26 minutes
Formula II and Sidecars	28 minutes
Classic	25 minutes

Neil Tuxworth leaves Parliament Square in Ramsey.

The Historic TT was scheduled to run on the first Saturday of race week and the Production event on the last Friday. Otherwise the race programme was much as before.

Apart from lap times, another aspect of qualifying to race is getting a bike through scrutineering, and there were pre-race warnings that inspection of bikes entered in the new MCN-Avon Production TT would be particularly rigorous. Representatives from manufacturers were on hand to assist the scrutineers and the first three bikes to finish in each class, plus three chosen at random, would be stripped for measurement. For the first time at the TT a claiming clause was contained in the regulations of the Production race, permitting a competitor to apply to purchase any other bike at the end of the race at the recommended retail price. It was seemingly aimed at maintaining equality in the competition and discouraging an entrant from lavishing too much money on preparation.

After a spate of high-speed crashes in practice, several riders found themselves under close scrutiny by the medical officer. Among these was Chris Guy, who described how 'I was flat out on the straight over Ballig Bridge when it just went out of my hands and threw

me over the top'. Chris rolled and slid for a hundred yards and managed to avoid hitting anything. Two days later he was passed fit to ride again. Not so fortunate was past winner Steve Tonkin, whose racing career was brought to an end when he crashed at Handleys with serious injuries, while Neil Tuxworth fell at Ballaugh, but recovered to race another day.

Honda v Suzuki

The only teams with a realistic chance of winning the 'big' races of Formula I, Senior and Premier Classic in 1983 were Honda and Suzuki, which meant Joey Dunlop and Roger Marshall (Hondas) versus Rob McElnea and Mick Grant (Suzukis). Joey had a different machine for each of the big races, with a 750 V4 to use in Formula I, a 500cc RS-3 3-cylinder, two-stroke GP bike for the Senior and a 920cc transverse-four with a 'works' endurance motor in the Premier Classic. The pace in practice was very fast, with Grant quickest in Formula I, and McElnea in the Senior and Premier Classic. In the new Production races Barry Woodland (Kawasaki) was fastest over 750, Trevor Nation (Honda) fastest 750 and former MGP winner and Manxman Chris Fargher top 250 on a Suzuki.

As was his custom, Joey Dunlop proved quicker in the races than in practice and took victory in the Formula I by twenty seconds from team-mate Roger Marshall, with all the Suzuki team forced to retire from the race. It was not the easiest of wins for Joey, because he was forced to stop in the early stages to wrench off the tail of an exhaust pipe that fouled the tyre when the suspension compressed. This lost him the lead and the damage it caused meant that the tyre had to be changed at a pit stop.

In a Senior race that saw the lead shared equally (and alternately) by Joey and Rob McElnea over its six laps, the Honda rider was in front on the last lap until 10 miles from the finish. Then on the NS-3, which was used to shorter GP races, the crankshaft broke and

Rob brought his Suzuki to victory at an average speed of 115.66mph (186.13km/h). To Joey went the fastest lap, when he clocked 118.47mph (190.65km/h) on lap five, a new absolute course record. Having seen Joey lose a race before through running out of petrol when running at record-breaking speed, some cynics wondered if it had happened again. This put Honda on the spot because, whereas they did not want the efficiency of their refuelling in doubt, they were also not keen to publicize the mechanical failure. In the end they settled for showing that Joey's bike did finish with fuel in the tank, but then suffered the embarrassment of his 250 running out of petrol in Wednesday's Junior race. Adding emphasis to the old adage that races can be won and lost in the pits, it was a refuelling situation that probably cost Joey victory in the Premier Classic race, for he stopped twice for petrol, while race-winner Rob McElnea stopped only once. Rob finished just fourteen seconds ahead of Joey, who would have lost much more than that in the process of slowing, taking on fuel and getting up to speed again. Mick Grant (Suzuki) finished third and regular competitor Klaus Klein (Suzuki) achieved one of his best TT results by finishing fourth. Unfortunately 1984 proved to be Rob McElnea's last TT, for he went on to concentrate on a career in GP racing.

Aussie Graeme McGregor was the star of Wednesday's racing with wins in the Junior and Formula II events on EMC and Yamaha machines, the latter win bringing to an end Tony Rutter's three-year Ducati dominance of the race. With one dream realized in winning his first TT, Graeme then raised his sights to becoming World Champion in Formula II (still run over three rounds). The new three-lap Production TT saw a wide variety of road bikes making less than steady progress over the many bumps and bends of the Mountain Course, in a manner that provided excitement to both spectators and riders. Geoff Johnson rode a Kawasaki GPZ900R to 750–1500cc victory, Trevor Nation was first 750 on a

Cranking his Suzuki over as he passes Ginger Hall is Rob McElnea on his way to winning the 1984 Senior TT.

Honda CBX750, closely followed by similarly mounted Helmut Dahne, and Phil Mellor was best 250 on a Yamaha RD250LC. As expected, protests over machine eligibility meant that the scrutineers' work continued long after racing had finished, but the 'Proddie' event was voted a success and was expected to return in 1985.

Among the new names racing on the Island in 1984 were Roger Burnett, Nick Jefferies and Robert Dunlop. Nick was the winner of

the 1983 Senior MGP and Robert won the 1983 Junior Newcomers' MGP ahead of Steve Hislop and Ian Lougher. All five names went on to prove themselves particularly talented riders, and all took at least one TT win. At the 1984 TT it was a surprise to see Ian Lougher ride in the Historic event for old bikes, taking second place on a Matchless G50 in the 500cc class behind American Dave Roper (Matchless). The 350cc class was won by Steve Cull (Aermacchi).

A little over ten years earlier, single-cylinder Aermacchis were challenging for leader-board places in the Junior TT, but in 1984 they were eligible for the Historic TT and Steve Cull rode one to victory in the 350cc class.

Changes

There were changes on several fronts for 1985. Lap speeds had continued to grow due to a combination of easing bends and smoothing surfaces, together with the considerable effect of increased machine performance. Geoff Duke was still closely connected with the TT and he was asked to look back thirty years and draw a comparison between lap speeds in 1955, when he averaged 99.98mph (160.90km/h), and the mid-1980s performances of the likes of Joey Dunlop, who lifted the absolute course record over 118mph (189.9km/h). Geoff was convinced that course changes had made a major contribution to the increase in lap speeds, saying that he thought 8 of the almost 20mph increase could be so attributed, with the remainder due to greater machine performance. The latter was not achieved with just increased engine output, but also came from major improvements to tyres, suspension and brakes.

Spectators experienced changes to their long-time travel arrangements, when the majority of the Isle of Man Steam Packet Company's shipping from England to Mona's Isle moved from Liverpool to Heysham. That change did not affect the many TT enthusiasts who travelled from Ireland, among them Joey Dunlop. But then Joey still travelled to the island by fishing boat, bringing 'himself', brother Robert, some of their racing bikes and a group of friends across the Irish Sea from Belfast to Douglas. In 1985 this resulted in what Joey describes as the most frightening experience of his life when the boat, *Tornamona*, sank just outside Belfast, taking the bikes to the bottom. Although passengers and crew were thrown into the water, they were all rescued and, eventually, so were the bikes. It was hardly the most promising start to a TT fortnight, but a mere thirty-six hours after the sinking Joey was out in practice on 'works' Hondas, setting the pace, reacquainting himself with the course and experiencing the usual changes, which included major road

improvements at Quarry Bends that saved yet another few seconds a lap.

There were changes to the race programme in 1985. Out went the Historic race after only one year, and also dropped was the big Classic race. The Senior event was given back some of its prestige by being opened up to 1000cc machines and given a Friday spot in the race programme. Although the GPs were contested almost exclusively by two-strokes across all classes (up to their 500cc maximum), the changes to the Senior reflected the growth in racing of big bikes on short circuits under the titles of Superbikes, Superstocks and such. These roadster-based over 500s were relatively cheap, easy to tune four-strokes and were increasingly used in preference to expensive to buy and run 500cc two-strokes; in 1985 they dominated the Senior entries. Although a 'works' two-stroke in the right hands probably still had the edge, the performance lines between pure racing bikes and production-derived racers was blurring at the TT. Of course, the 'works' four-strokes were inevitably the quickest of their type, but the four-strokes were attractive to riders and sponsors because they found they could upgrade stock machines at less than exorbitant cost, and be in with a chance of success.

Another move to help the privateers was that quick-fillers were at last banned and everyone used the standard gravity-fillers supplied by the organizers. There was a record 876 entries for the ten-race programme:

TT Formula I	121
TT Formula II	115
Sidecar A	93
Sidecar B	93
Junior	82
Senior	129
Production A	48
Production B	90
Production C	47
Production D	58

There were nineteen former TT winners entered and twenty-nine Manx Grand Prix winners. Riders from twenty-one countries rode machines from Yamaha (246), Suzuki (229), Honda (164) and Kawasaki (49). No other make made double figures.

V4

Honda made a big move in the early 1980s to using V-formation engines across much of its range and it was present at the TT with what its advertising referred to as 'V Force'. It proved to be a successful configuration, for at the end of race week Honda took full page advertising to proclaim the successes it had achieved. Having come back into 250cc racing for the first time since 1967 with the RS250 V2 earlier in 1985, it was delighted to take first and second in the Junior race with Joey Dunlop and Steve Cull. In the Senior Joey took first place on an RVF750 V4 putting out 135bhp and Roger Marshall was second on an RS500 V3, while Joey claimed yet another Formula I victory on an RVF750 V4, giving himself a hat-trick of wins in the week. In the Production races Mat Oxley brought an NSR250R V2 home ahead of a bunch of similar models, hitting 122mph in the process and setting new lap and race records, while in the 751–1500cc Production class Geoff Johnson was victorious on a VF1000F Bol D'Or V4.

Production 250 winner Mat Oxley was a road-tester for *Motor Cycle News* and received as big a write-up as Joey Dunlop for his TT

efforts. Honda was certainly pleased with the publicity generated by its week's work. In extensive post-TT advertising it proclaimed 'V Foremost'.

Suzuki was forced to take mostly second place to Honda in 1985, although it did gain the first four places in the 251–750cc Production race in which the still fairly new GSX-R750s showed what a force they were, while in the same race Steve Hislop, a young man with a bright TT future, took tenth place on a Yamaha. Ducati was the only non-Japanese manufacturer to achieve a TT victory in 1985 when Tony Rutter came home first in Formula II, while Sidecar race A went to Dave Hallam and race B to Mick Boddice. Sidecar racing was the only area in which Yamaha maintained what had been its previous complete dominance of the racing classes.

Trying for the Impossible

Early in 1986 the ACU announced further revisions to the basis on which it allocated the £275,000 available for payment to riders. Trying to get away from negotiating individual start-money deals, it created a four-tier system with the top riders getting £2,400, group two £1,400, group three £700 and group four £175 (£225 for sidecars). Grouping was determined by riders' performances in World Formula I, GPs, Euro rounds and endurance championships, plus recent TT form.

Honda's post-race advertisement for Geoff Johnson's Production race win in 1985.

It is difficult to believe that there were no instances of negotiations with individuals, particularly the stars who, being a naturally competitive bunch, would argue that their worth was not properly recognized if they felt an opponent was getting more. Whatever actually happened, and for all its tweaking of finances down the years, the ACU must have known that it faced an impossible task in satisfying every rider and sponsor on the issue of start and prize money.

Grandstand

New for 1986 was a brick, concrete and stainless steel grandstand replacing the timber and iron one erected in 1926. Although the new structure gave comfortable indoor facilities for race control staff, commentators and the press, paying customers in the tiered seating were still exposed to the elements. Those elements can be quite strong on the Island and they conspired to bring about the postponement of Saturday's racing, then they got together again on Monday night to blow down the scrutineers' tent and, more importantly to some, the beer tent.

To celebrate the first use of the new grandstand, the Duke of Kent paid an official visit to the races. Those who wondered about the future of the TT were no doubt impressed with the Island's investment in the new structure, but they must have recognized that the

The new Grandstand and Control Tower opened in 1986.

chance of a short circuit replacing the Mountain Course was now dead.

The 1986 Races

Despite being under a slight shadow as a move towards World Super Bike racing gained ground, the World Formula I series was extended to include more European rounds and it brought a reluctant first-time TT competitor, series leader Anders Andersson, to the Island in 1986. The Swede's appearance was clearly aimed at minimizing damage to his championship position, but realizing that he could not match the TT specialists, Anders went for a steady ride and finished twelfth in a race reduced to four laps due to worries with the weather. As the world's best pure road racer, Joey Dunlop (Honda) took his fourth successive Formula I victory and moved into the lead in the World Championship table, while another Honda ridden by Geoff Johnson finished second. The Formula I race was important to Honda and the VF motors it supplied to its 'works' runners were clearly very special, for the third Honda finisher was back in twenty-second place. The majority of competitors knew that the 750 Suzuki was by then the best privateer's bike and they filled the next ten places after the first two Hondas.

Suzuki's numerical dominance of the Formula I field was not good news for Honda, and as the week progressed the news got worse. The Production races were extended from three to four classes in 1986 to recognize the growing importance of 600cc road bikes and the trend to over 1000cc road-going models. They were also given two separate races, the first for classes B and D, and the second for classes A and C.

Class B catered for 750 four-strokes and 500 two-strokes, and Phil Mellor (GSX-R750) was first man home, followed by three other Suzukis before Dave Leach took fifth place on a Honda. Class D was for 400 four-strokes and 250 two-strokes, giving victory to

Barrie Woodland on a GSX-R400, a Suzuki model that was not available on the UK market at the time, although its TT win should have offered some good advance publicity for what was obviously a very fleet 400. Class A was for over 750cc and saw Trevor Nation (GSX-R1100) home first followed by seven other Suzuki runners before the ninth-finishing Kawasaki of Dave Leach. Geoff Johnson's 1985 winning Honda VF1000 was no match for the opposition in the early stages and did not finish the race. All the Production races saw close finishes, but that in Class C was more like a short circuit race for the two main protagonists, Gary Padgett on his RG 400 Suzuki Gamma and Malcolm Wheeler riding a Kawasaki GPZ600. Riders were started in pairs and they went off together. Padgett took an early lead but then non-stopping Steve Linsdell worked his way to the front only to ease the pace on the last lap to be sure of having enough fuel to get home. Padgett and Wheeler both stopped for fuel at the end of the first lap and had no such worries. They both got ahead of Linsdell on time and Wheeler pulled back up to Padgett on the road. Giving it their all on the last lap they caught and passed Joey Dunlop! With the lead changing twice in the last couple of miles, the grandstand crowd were on their feet to see who would be first over the line. After 113 miles of racing it was Padgett by just under a second, so completing a clean sweep of the Production classes for Suzuki.

The Production races were regarded as a success, having received support from manufacturers, dealers, riders and spectators, and they looked to have re-established the category as an important part of the TT programme.

The Sidecar races saw first-time wins for Lowry Burton and Pat Cushnahan (Yamaha) in race A, and in doing so they became the first Irish winners of a Sidecar TT. Race B went to Nigel Rollason and Donny Williams (Barton Phoenix). Both the latter were experienced racers and they used a nine-year-old engine that the previous year had powered the outfit to the fastest speed-trap time of 149mph (239.78km/h). The Formula II category was gaining popularity among the three-wheelers and the best 350cc finishers were twelfth and fourteenth in the two races.

Brian Reid (Yamaha) took an overdue first TT win in the Formula II race. Roger Burnett (Honda) took his first TT win in the Senior race from Geoff Johnson (Honda) and Barry Woodland (Suzuki). Roger was a publicity-conscious rider who had his racing career mapped out on paper from day one, and regarded his TT victory as a stepping stone to the GPs.

Bigger and Bigger

For 1987 the Senior TT was opened up to 1300cc machines and the maximum capacity for the Junior class was increased to 350cc. There were no racing 350s being built at the time but, with the intention of boosting Junior entries, the move allowed some ageing Yamaha 350s to compete. One or two riders fancied their chances on 350s that, while probably not as quick as the quickest 250s, pulled better up the Mountain. In a race that started in weather that was difficult to predict,

tyre choice was important. It was rising star Steve Hislop (350 Yamaha) who took the lead and built it to two minutes before retiring on the fifth lap, allowing Eddie Laycock (250 EMC) to move ahead and win. Second was Brian Reid on another 250 EMC and third Graeme McGregor (350 Yamaha). Just off the podium finishers was a young man who was to stand on the top step several times in future years. His name was Carl Fogarty (250 Honda) and he finished fourth. After his bad luck in the Junior, Steve Hislop confirmed that he had made the grade at the TT with a convincing win in Formula II.

It was the eightieth anniversary of the TT races and Honda put its customary effort into sponsoring the entertainment of fans outside race periods, while again supplying machines for use by the Travelling Marshals, something they had done since 1977. To most people, however, it seemed that its racing commitment was slightly less. Regular trade supporters like Shell and Dunlop were still present at the meeting, although some top runners were Michelin-shod, including Joey Dunlop: in Michelin's post-race advertising he was renamed 'Joey Michelin'. Newer names among the trade support at the event included EBC brake products, who claimed to have

An airborne Brian Reid on his Yamaha at Ballaugh Bridge.

£3,500 to be won in bonuses by users of their products.

Spectators who wanted to get a better idea of what it was like to race over the Mountain Course could sign up for a lap by coach and receive a running commentary by a top rider like Roger Marshall, Phil Mellor or Trevor Nation. Manx Radio did its bit to keep everyone better informed by separating its TT coverage from its general programmes and creating 'Radio TT', allowing it to broadcast TT-specific material for much extended hours and soon adopting the title of 'The Best Biking Station in the World'.

Mitsuo Itoh was the only Japanese rider to have won a TT (1963, 50cc) and he had the honour of starting riders in the 1987 TT Formula I race. This had come to be regarded as Joey Dunlop's event, but his usual dominance was threatened by Phil Mellor. The signs were there in the duo's respective practice times, but Joey pulled out all the stops to set race and lap records and bring his Honda home first. 'Mez' Mellor couldn't quite match the speed he had shown in practice and finished second on his Suzuki, with Geoff Johnson bringing his Yamaha into third.

There are a number of races that vie for the title of 'wettest' TT and the 1987 Senior was both a very wet and a very difficult one. On a day when the more tractable power of a four-stroke should have offered advantage, Joey Dunlop splashed to his tenth TT victory riding the peaky 500cc Honda 3-cylinder two-stroke. By now tyre development had reached the stage where riders could choose from three basic types to suit conditions: Slicks for dry roads, Intermediates for damp and patchy conditions, and Wets for continuous surface moisture. Joey was on Intermediates. That was the right choice at the start, but as conditions deteriorated from lap two it became apparent that this a serious mistake, with Joey averaging 'only' 99.85mph (160.69km/h) in a race that was shortened from six to four laps because of the weather and in which he spent his time 'correcting more slides than I've had in the rest of my racing life'.

Conditions were even worse for the Production Class A and Class C races (due to be run together), indeed so bad that the race was just abandoned and not run. It was the first time this had ever happened at the TT, because whatever the previous difficulties, the race programme was always completed.

A 'Different' Island

Apart from the TT races, the Isle of Man has always made much of the differences between itself and the United Kingdom. With its own Parliament of Tynwald, its horse-trams on Douglas Promenade, Victorian narrow-gauge steam railways and electric trams going to more distant parts, tail-less cats, kippers, multi-horned Loughtan sheep, plastic pound notes and the willingness of shops to accept almost any form of currency from the adjacent isles, it was proud of its differences and encouraged visitors to experience them – and spend!

There is also the famous three-legged emblem of Mann that many motorcyclists from afar are proud to carry as transfers on bikes and helmets.

This emblem is famous all over the world.

One very major difference between a race meeting at Brands Hatch or Donington and the Island races is the important ritual engaged in by many riders arriving to compete in the TT or MGP in which they go to say hello to the fairies! Located on the road between Douglas, the current capital of the Island, and Castletown, its former capital, is a white-washed stone 'Fairy Bridge' that is a traditional spot to pass a polite greeting to the Manx fairies and request good fortune in the forth-coming racing.

Of course, for fans of motorcycle racing 'The Island' had been different for eighty years in welcoming motorcyclists to race over its roads. Firmly lodged in biking folklore, by the late 1980s it attracted the hardened racing fan and the less committed who, nevertheless, wanted to be part of a great motorcycling event that went far beyond the racing. Previously the preserve of the race enthusiast, a week or fortnight on the Isle of Man at TT time had developed to mean different things to different people.

Another aspect in which the Isle of Man was unlike other tourist locations in the late 1980s was that it spent much money on pub-licity that encouraged people to come to the Island but then, due to reduced numbers of boarding-houses and hotels, it had great diffi-culty in finding accommodation for them all.

Instituting what it called its 'Home Stay' scheme, the tourist board encouraged private home-owners to open their doors at TT-time and take in visitors as paying guests. The policy is still in force, as is the enterprise of various companies offering inclusive package holidays covering accommodation, boat fares and other expenses. The Steam Packet's day excursions to the races were also available, and with the shift of spectators' holiday styles, many visitors now come for long weekends or split weeks, something that was not so easy when the average worker received just two weeks' holiday each year.

For those who could not get to the Island, Sky television (at that date reaching only 12 million homes in Europe) transmitted a 35-minute programme on the evening following each race, while recorded highlights were also made available to television companies world-wide. They included footage using technolog-ical advances that allowed ever smaller cameras to be machine-mounted for dramatic onboard effects.

Timetable Changes for 1988

In a year when the very running of the TT meeting was threatened by a seamen's dispute, the Formula II race was dropped and Produc-tion Class A and Class B were given individual

Metzeler was also at the TT supporting the users of its tyres.

races, while in what was a 'first' at the TT the combined Production Class C and D races took place on the Friday evening at the end of practice week. The growing profile of the Production machines at the TT saw Michelin keen to reward users of its tyres, and it offered £800 to any rider who won a Production race while using Michelins front and rear. Should no one win on its tyres, it still offered £500 for the first Michelin-shod finisher in Production Class A and B, with £300 to the first Michelin in Class C and D, together with lesser place money. Despite the omission of Formula II from the 1988 programme, the total number of entries (875) matched that of the all-time high of 1986 (876).

Although not actually part of the TT programme, there were races even earlier in practice week, when a newly introduced Classic meeting on the 4¼-mile Billown circuit in the south of the Island provided added interest for early-arriving spectators.

Joey Again

With a reduced commitment from Honda to racing in 1988, its top man at the TT, Joey Dunlop, was provided only with a bike and parts, leaving him to put together other sponsorship deals such as one with Shell Gemini oil. He also relied on his host of Irish racing contacts for the essential services that normally came with a fully supported 'works' ride. For his big-bike TT efforts he relied on his own race-kitted Honda RC30 roadster. A V4 with single-sided swinging arm, it was a far cry from the ultra-expensive Honda RVF 'works' machinery, but Joey still went out and shattered lap and race records, finishing the week with wins in the Formula I and Senior classes on the RC30 and taking a rain-hit Junior race on his 250 Honda – another hat-trick!

Joey was still the big name at the TT, but there were plenty of younger runners snapping at his heels. Steve Hislop (Honda) pressed him hard for a while in the middle of the Formula I race before dropping out, then did the same in the Senior to finish second. Steve Cull (Honda) was also a major threat for most of the Senior, setting a new absolute course record on lap two at 119.08mph (191.64km/h), before his bike caught fire on the drop to Creg ny Baa on the last lap and was badly damaged. Others who finished behind Joey in 1988 were Roger Marshall, Roger Burnett, Brian Morrison, Carl Fogarty and Nick Jefferies.

Joey Dunlop just before the start of the 1988 Formula I race.

Joey Dunlop is hidden by champagne spray on the 1988 Formula I winner's rostrum, flanked by Nick Jefferies (left), who came second, and Roger Burnett (right), who was third.

Norton

One of the big headlines at the 1988 TT was the return of a Norton team comprised of Trevor Nation and Simon Buckmaster. The company was only a shadow of the great multi-

TT winning Bracebridge Street concern of the 1930s. With its production effort now concentrated on machines powered by Wankel-style rotary engines, that was the type of bike it brought to contest the TT. With the FIM disputing the basis of calculating the rotary's

Trevor Nation rounds Windy Corner on the Norton rotary in 1988.

capacity (Norton claimed 588cc, the FIM 1176cc), the Nortons could only contest the Senior race. While their air-cooled and flame-spitting engines seemed to have plenty of power, their handling left much to be desired. In fact, evil was the word used by some onlookers to describe the way they went through the bends. Although troubled by niggling faults, both Nortons finished the race, albeit in thirty-third and forty-fourth positions.

Proddie Protests

Rumours flew thick and fast around the Island regarding the specification and performance of some of the Production bikes during practice. One of them was about a six-speed gear cluster reputedly fitted to a Yamaha FZR1000, while several GSX-R750s were claimed to have special rear shocks aimed at curing handling

problems, and the above-average speed of a few machines brought further dark whispers regarding non-conformance with the regulations.

In the actual races Dave Leach and Geoff Johnson on Yamaha FZR1000s finished just eight-tenths of a second apart after four laps and 150 miles in Production Class A, with Johnson setting the fastest lap at 116.55mph (187.56km/h), which was 3mph faster than the old record. Most Suzuki runners were on the GSX-R1100, while Kawasaki supported a three-man team of Ray Swann, Roger Hurst and Rob Haynes on its new 1000cc ZX-10 model, its best finish being Haynes in fifth place. Geoff Johnson also took the fastest lap in Class B with an average of 112.98mph (181.82km/h) while coming third on his Yamaha to winner Steve Hislop (Yamaha). It was Hislop's turn to grab the lap record in

Working as a team, Mick Boddice and Chas Birks bring their Yamaha-powered sidecar outfit into Ramsey in 1988, a year in which they won both Sidecar TT races.

Class C on a Honda CBR600 at 109.38mph (176.02km/h) when finishing third to Brian Morrison (Honda CBR600). Steve raised the record by a huge 5mph. It was a time when the growing popularity of 600cc road bikes saw manufacturers pouring much money into their development and, as always, top speed was a big factor in achieving sales. Barry Woodland (Yamaha FZR400R) won his third consecutive Class D race, knocking six seconds off his own previous lap record.

It was a double for Mick Boddice and Chas Birks (Yamaha) in the Sidecar races, with Mick's fastest lap of 107.15mph (172.444km/h) being impressively quick, if slightly shy of Jock Taylor's record of 108.12mph (173.00km/h) set back in 1981. Mick started each race with his 16-gallon petrol tank full to the brim. Designed to allow him to run the race non-stop, in the early stages it was the equivalent of carrying a second passenger.

There was no overall speed limit on Manx roads, but perhaps with racing on their minds, twenty-seven motorcyclists were fined for speeding in built-up areas during the TT period. Not only did those ordinary motorcyclists make their contributions to the Manx Exchequer, but rarely did a year go by without a real racer or two also appearing before the

High Bailiff to explain his breaking of the law in some manner or another.

Perhaps the safest place to be outside of race-times was Douglas Promenade, for it was there that the majority of the 12,000 bikes shipped to the TT could be seen lined up handlebar to handlebar in what was often called 'the greatest free motorcycle show in the world'.

'Foggy'

Although he did not shine at the 1988 TT (finishes in twelfth, fourth and seventh) 24-year-old Carl Fogarty arrived at the 1989 TT as a greater threat to the established names and as World Formula I Champion, having travelled the world to win it. Carl, whose father George was a TT competitor, first competed on the Island in 1985 when he won the MGP Newcomers' Lightweight race and took third place in the MGP Lightweight race. He continued to build his experience on short circuits and at the TT, but with a previous fastest lap of 115.8mph (186.36km/h) it seemed that he had some way to go to be on the pace of the best runners. In 1989, however, he successfully closed the gap to the opposition and took a coveted TT win. It was the fulfilment of an ambition for Carl, who said prior to the 1989

Not difficult to see in his fluorescent jacket, this Manx policeman had the task of slowing TT-time traffic.

meeting, 'Once you've done the TT, you realize there's nothing like it. And you want to win.'

Also looking to close the rather larger gap to the lead runners was Norton. The company was back with water-cooled engines ridden by the experienced Trevor Nation and Steve Cull, and the bikes were finished in John Player Norton colours. A company with a greater TT history in recent years than Norton was Honda. It came to the 1989 event celebrating thirty years of TT participation, with fifty victories to its name spread over all solo classes.

Out with the Old

With so much racing outside the GPs using heavily tuned production-based machines, new classifications and classes sprang up to cater for them on the short circuits. The TT organizers needed to have regard to such developments, for to stick to classes that had gone out of use or fashion could see major reductions in entries for the Island races. For 1989 they decided that pure Production racing was out of fashion in the smaller classes and would be replaced by Supersport 400 and Supersport 600 races. Production up to 750cc and Production 751–1300cc races were retained, and a Lightweight 125cc race was restored to the programme for the first time since 1974, giving ten races in all.

'King of the Roads' Joey Dunlop was entered for six classes at the 1989 TT. Still recovering from a thigh- and wrist-shattering accident at Brands Hatch, he came to the Island ready to race, but the TT's medical officer judged that the 37-year-old was not fit to cope with the demands of the Mountain Course. This left the field wide open for the many young aspirants to Joey's title to make their marks. Joey was on the island for the TT period and Honda kept him in the public eye for publicity purposes, receiving many indications of his fans' esteem, which was well deserved after his thirteen TT wins.

Hislop's Week

Steve Hislop, the young Scotsman who started his Isle of Man racing career with second place in the Junior Newcomers MGP of 1983, sandwiched between winner Robert Dunlop and third-place Ian Lougher, proved that he had truly come of age as a road racer in 1989 by taking a hat-trick of wins. Starting with the 600 Supersport, he went on to take Monday's Formula I at record speed, setting a new lap record at 121.34mph (195.27km/h), making him the first man to go round at more than 120mph. Strongly fancied for victory in Wednesday's Junior, he came off his 250 Honda when travelling at 135mph (217km/h) through Quarry Bends. Perhaps it was a case of the TT course issuing a warning about over-confidence, for Steve, who was very lucky to escape with no more than a bang on the ankle, went to the line for Friday's Senior just slightly subdued. But it was only slight, for he was again victorious on his Honda-supported RVF750, and he again lapped at over 120mph. Three TT wins in a week put Steve in select company and, while recognizing that racing is full of 'what ifs?', he was leading the Junior until his fall at Quarry Bends, and only missed out on a win in the Production 750 race by sixteen seconds after a terrific three-way scrap with winner Carl Fogarty (Honda) and second-place Dave Leach (Yamaha). Curiously, Hislop lost the race due to stopping twice for fuel, when winner Fogarty stopped only once, even though both rode Honda RC30s.

The high speeds achieved in 1989 extended to the three-wheelers, where Dave Molyneux and Colin Hardman achieved a first TT win in Sidecar Race A, while Mick Boddice and Chas Birks shattered race and lap records in winning Race B, in which their fastest lap was set at 108.31mph (174.30km/h) on the first (and standing-start) lap. The top twenty-one crews used Yamaha engines, with Dave Saville and Richard Crossley using their 350 to do the double in the Formula II class and just nudging the 100mph lap in the process.

The return of the 125s saw Joey Dunlop's younger brother Robert uphold the family

Steve Hislop gained a hat-trick of wins on his Silkolene-sponsored 'works' Hondas in 1989. Here he is on the way to first place in the Senior TT.

name with a win on his Honda. He was followed home by Ian Lougher (Honda), just fifteen seconds behind, after a spirited scrap with Carl Fogarty (Honda), who was a further eighteen seconds back. Robert's winning average of 102.58mph (165.08km/h) on his single-cylinder Honda was considerably faster than the last 125 winner, Clive Horton (Yamaha) in 1974 at 88.44mph (142.33km/h), although Bill Ivy had lapped at 100.32mph (161.44km/h) when winning the 1968 Lightweight 125 race on the exotic Yamaha four-cylinder 'works' model.

During a four-lap race in which they were never more than ten seconds apart on corrected time, Dave Leach got the best of Nick Jefferies to lead home eight 1000cc Yamahas in the 751–1300cc Production race. However, any feelings of triumph or desire to celebrate were dashed by the news that Phil Mellor and Steve Henshaw were killed in separate inci-

dents in the race. Their deaths contributed to a grim statistic of five rider fatalities at the 1989 TT, which caused even the staunchest supporter to stop and question the sport of TT racing and the price that had to be paid for such high-speed enjoyment. It was a curious fact that, although some years there would be no fatalities and relatively few injuries, in others there would be a heavy toll, with no one really able to say why. In 1989 the finger was pointed at the big Production bikes (lapping at over 117mph) being too much for the road tyres and suspension to which they were restricted, and there were calls for them to be banned from the TT.

The Big Four

Honda, Yamaha, Suzuki and Kawasaki were all represented at the 1989 TT and gave varying degrees of support to their 'works' efforts across the various classes. While Honda gained much pleasure, and publicity, from its five wins, Yamaha was surely pleased with the way its FZR750OW01 performed in challenging Honda, with Nick Jefferies showing his growing stature as a TT rider by bringing it into third place in Formula I and second in the Senior, whilst Dave Leach (Yamaha) lost out to winner Carl Fogarty (Honda) in the Production 750 by just 1.8 seconds.

Suzuki was not among the winners in the big-bike classes but did take first, second and third places in the Supersport 400 with its RG250s at a race-winning average speed of 105.27mph (169.41km/h), much to the delight of Mick Grant, who had retired from racing but ran the Suzuki effort at the TT. It was a race in which Kawasaki's KI two-strokes were also in contention, but rider crashes put an end to their challenge.

While half a world away in location and output from the top four manufacturers, the performances of the rotary Nortons gave cause for encouragement. In the Senior both were in the top ten for much of the race before retirement, showing that advances had been made in performance, if not reliability.

A Newcomer

Every TT brings to the event newcomers prepared to take on the awesome challenge of racing over its 37¾ miles. All know that they have to serve an apprenticeship before they can expect to achieve a high place, but they also know that tough qualifying standards mean that they quickly have to get up to race speed, for no one wants to go home and face friends with the news that he has fallen short of the required standard and failed to qualify. It is the same every year. Chris Crew, an American rider, entered for the 1989 TT and had his first ever view of the Island when he brought his GSXR Suzuki from San Francisco. He later described his experiences in the *Northern California Motorcycle Guide*. Of early practice sessions he wrote: 'you have to be willing to bet your life that you know where the next corner is going over the crest of the next hill'. Of those crests he said: 'you go over wide open in top gear, 155 or 160mph, whatever the bike will pull, with your elbows and toes tucked in, head under the fairing, just watching the white line, trying to see through the bugs'. It was a stern baptism for the American who, like all newcomers, had to temper boldness with caution. Experiencing the inevitable problems in practice, he was faced with the cost of an engine rebuild, coped with some last-minute panics before the race, but was then rewarded with a race finish and an award for the fastest newcomer.

Chris Crew wrote for a relatively small local publication, but around 200 journalists, 200 photographers and seventy television personnel were accredited by the TT press office in 1989. Their task was to spread the story of the 1989 TT across the world as had been the custom for more than eighty years, for it was still a great sporting occasion.

9   A Speedy Decade

The start of a new decade was a time for many to look ahead and attempt to predict the future for the TT meeting, which found itself operating in an ever more difficult environment in 1990. The extreme length of the TT practice and race period meant that the influence on its dates of the increasing number of Grand Prix, World Super Bike, Endurance and British Championship meetings became ever greater, and it was difficult for top riders and teams to keep two (for some it was three) weekends clear for the TT. Some riders even resorted to flying off the Island to practise and race in other meetings while competing at the TT, and with increasing use of team transporters, the logistics of getting and returning such large vehicles to and from the island often resulted in them having to come early and leave late, so further extending the big teams' TT commitments.

The Isle of Man Tourist Board spoke of the 1990s as a 'new era' for the races and one in which the event would be further internationalized. It aimed to encourage more foreign riders to compete, in the hope that this would bring more continental visitors to the Island. Increased use of foreign language road signs and the addition of race summaries in French and German during Radio TT broadcasts all helped in this direction. There were promises that even more effort would be directed at strengthening the festival nature of the fortnight.

Much of this extra effort was necessary because it was clear that the TT would soon have to stand on its own feet without links to any major World Championship events, since the World Formula I Championship had been downgraded to the FIM Coupé F1 Championship. Indeed, the rampant growth of World Super Bikes suggested the days of F1 were numbered and the TT organizers knew that many member-nations of the FIM would oppose the TT's inclusion in any other form of championship. Indeed, some federations, such as Spain, were so hostile to the TT that they would not grant licences for their members to compete in the event.

Mention was made earlier of the practical problems caused by lack of accommodation for visitors at peak times, and in 1990 the authorities experimented with the provision of a tented village on a Douglas playing field to provide 500 extra bed-spaces. Worryingly, some people claimed to detect increased opposition to the races from Manx residents, the finger being pointed, rightly or wrongly, at newcomers who had moved there for financial gain (the rich for tax purposes, and others to work in the burgeoning finance industry).

Despite its problems (and there had never been a TT without problems), the event had buoyant entry lists and was achieving ever increasing publicity via satellite transmission of the races, so it justifiably faced the 1990s with confidence. Meanwhile, on the World Championship GP front, organizers were faced with diminishing grid numbers, particularly in the 500cc class where growing specialization and expense, plus the need for riders to race up to and beyond the limit, causing frequent injuries, resulted in perhaps a dozen riders lining up to race. Things were so bad that Honda threatened to pull out of 500 GPs and proposed a complicated new championship class related to twins, triples and fours, of two-stroke, four-stroke and rotary configuration, which also incorporated minimum weight limits.

Restrictions

Among the factors that needed addressing at the 1990 TT was the old chestnut of Mr Average racer being out on the course at the same time as the top stars were lapping 10–15mph faster. Reducing the number of riders in a race meant less interest for spectators, although in theory it could have increased safety. In this instance the organizers limited themselves to talking about tightening restrictions on entries, without actually doing anything about them for a while.

Some solo riders expressed opposition to sidecars using the same course and suggested they be banned from the Mountain. Fortunately, spectator interest again won the day on that point. Sidecars had much improved their earlier image of DIY oil-leaking devices that fractured frames on every outing. The TT organizers even instigated preliminary sidecar scrutineering at UK race meetings later in the 1990s for those intending to compete on the Island, because there were many special items of preparation required if an outfit was to last for three laps of the Mountain Course.

One aspect of sidecar racing that did concern the organizers was the high speeds achieved. In truth, they had remained fairly constant through the 1980s, but Mick Boddice broke Jock Taylor's long-standing lap record in 1989, lifting it to 108.31mph (174.30km/h). With thoughts of curbing three-wheeled speeds, in 1990 riders were restricted to machines complying with the Formula II specification that from 1984 had run with the 1000cc machines as a separate class. Formula II restricted engines to 350cc two-strokes or 600cc four-strokes and Dave Saville, the man who had dominated the Formula II class since its introduction, using

The man who dominated the early years of Formula II Sidecar racing on the Island with his 350 Yamahas was Dave Saville.

Yamaha two-stroke power, continued his winning ways in 1990, lifting lap and race records above 100mph for the first time. Dave's fastest race lap of the week was 100.97mph (162.49km/h), but his was to be the last two-stroke win.

With the big-bike tragedies of the 1989 Production races still in mind, the organizers dropped the 750 and over-750cc Production classes, and reduced the maximum capacity in the Senior from 1300 to 750cc (later allowing in up to 1000cc twins). They also altered the starting system so that riders left singly at 10-second intervals rather than in pairs and, in a move aimed at curbing speeds in the pit lane, a 'stop box' was created at its entrance. Riders had to brake to a standstill under the eyes of a marshal within the white lines that delineated the 'box' on the surface of the pit-lane approach. Only then could a rider proceed to the pits.

1990 Races

Norton came to the 1990 TT buoyed by the performances of its riders, 'Big' Trevor Nation and 'Wee' Robert Dunlop, at the NW200, while Honda was present in support of the efforts of Joey Dunlop, Carl Fogarty and Steve Hislop. No doubt all teams arrived with their practice and race programmes carefully mapped out, but bad weather during practice week saw the organizers revamp the timetable.

It was Carl Fogarty who triumphed in Saturday's Formula I race and collected £6,000 in prize money. To Steve Hislop went the fastest lap at 122.63mph (197.35km/h) after overcoming early brake problems. Previous regular winner Joey Dunlop was still short of the fitness level required to ride a big bike to its limits on the TT course and came in eighth, one place ahead of the troubled Hislop. Nortons finished third and sixth, with Robert Dunlop beating team-mate Trevor Nation, while Nick Jefferies was second on his Yamaha. In an age when manufacturers increasingly looked for sponsorship of their racing efforts, Dunlop and Nation's bikes went by the title of John Player Nortons, while Jefferies was on a Loctite Yamaha.

Supersport 400s and 125s shared the same spot in the race programme, though on Saturday rather than Friday as planned. After a troubled week of practice Dave Leach was surprised to win the 400 race at record speed ahead of Carl Fogarty (Honda) and Steve Ward (Kawasaki). The 400cc four-strokes had increased their performance level over the previous few years and the first 250 two-stroke finished tenth. One place ahead of that was Jim Moodie who claimed that his 400 Honda was one of the few 'legal' machines in the race. Submitting a formal protest against seven of the machines that finished in front of his, he had it rejected on technical grounds, even though there was tacit acceptance that the other machines infringed the rules. It was a case of the manufacturers not only flexing their muscles but also resorting to blackmail by entering machines that did not comply with the regulations, so forcing the ACU to resort to expediency when they realized the field would be decimated of top runners if they enforced the rules. It was not the first – and certainly not the last – successful show of manufacturer power at the TT.

Robert Dunlop claimed the thing that impressed him the most with the speedy John Player Norton rotary was the way in which it achieved wheelspin so easily in all gears with his 9-stone (57kg) weight aboard. So it was with a demonstration of versatility totally alien to the world of GP racing that saw him climb off the Norton after third place in the Formula I race, then, just over an hour later, take out his little 8-litre Honda, ride it to the limit at record speeds and win the Lightweight 125 race.

Some riders' TT careers get off to a fast start, while others can take a few years to get into their stride. Ian Lougher had the ability to be a leader-board man at the time he moved from the MGP to the TT in 1984, but perhaps failed to match his promise. With a best

Robert Dunlop shows understandable caution as he rides his Norton over soaking wet roads at Ballacraine. His bike is finished in the colours of Norton's sponsor, John Player.

previous position of runner-up to Robert Dunlop in the 1989 Lightweight 125 race, Ian chose the 1990 Junior race to stun race favourite Steve Hislop by snatching victory and putting his name into the record book with a lap of 117.8mph (189.58km/h). It was a whole 3mph faster than the previous record and took many years to beat. Despite his high speed, Ian's victory over Steve was just under two seconds and, once again, it offered proof of the old adage about races being won and lost in the pits, for Steve's crew dropped the fuel cap inside the fairing while refuelling and the extra seconds spent fumbling for it certainly cost him the race.

Yamaha took the first five places in the rain-delayed Supersport 600 race, held on Thursday instead of Wednesday, with Brian Reid leading home fellow Ulstermen Johnny Rea, Steve Cull and Mark Farmer. In Friday's Senior the weather also played a major role.

Most riders chose to use cut-slicks on the rear to cope with unpredictable conditions that started soaking wet on lap one, were just wet for the next two, and then were wet and dry for the last two. The man most determined to cope with such nightmare surfaces was Carl Fogarty of the Honda team. Regaining the twenty-second difference in their starting times and passing a less than enthusiastic Steve Hislop 14 miles into the first lap at Kirk Michael, Carl commanded the race to win by one and a half minutes from Trevor Nation (Norton). Despite the difficult conditions he averaged over 110mph (177km/h) in a race that saw Hislop eventually retire, saying 'that's not for me'.

Anniversaries

Suzuki had a presence at the 1990 TT to commemorate 30 years of competing on the

After a courageous ride, Carl Fogarty is justified in looking proud to wear the winner's laurels at the 1990 Senior TT.

Yamaha Racing's logo to celebrate thirty years' TT racing by the marque.

Island, but the performance of its bikes gave the company little to celebrate. Yamaha had a similar anniversary in 1991, and hoped to add to its total of almost a hundred TT victories.

It was Honda that reinforced its status as top dog among the Japanese manufacturers in 1991 by taking wins in the prestigious Formula I and Senior TTs with Steve Hislop riding a hand-built 145bhp RVF750. It was Honda's tenth consecutive Formula I win, and with Steve adding the Supersport 600 race to give himself a second hat-trick of TT wins, Robert Dunlop taking the Lightweight 125, and CBR600-powered Mick Boddice doing the double on three wheels, the 1991 TT clearly belonged to Honda. Yamaha did gain consolation with victory in the Supersport 400 with Dave Leach, and Robert Dunlop also won for them in the Junior.

Honda's racing efforts in 1991 were supported by Silkolene Oils with Michelin pro-

viding tyres, and in their advertising both concerns made much of their association with the winning efforts of Steve Hislop, who was backed by the impressive line-up of Carl Fogarty, Joey Dunlop, Nick Jefferies and Phillip McCallen in the Honda team. Hislop and Fogarty both had ambitions to ride in World Championship GPs and in the early 1990s made confident utterances regarding not returning to the TT. They also both, however, found regular GP rides very hard to get and returned to the Island for the publicity and cash they could earn with good TT performances.

Too Fast

Steve Hislop was timed at an incredible claimed 192mph (309km/h) at Sulby in

During evening practice in 1991, Honda team-mates Carl Fogarty (8), Nick Jefferies (7) and Steve Hislop (11) are shown with power to spare as they crest the top of Lambfell. Just under eighty years earlier, however, when the TT was first run over the Mountain Course, some competitors had so little power that they had to jump off and run alongside their machines on this ascent.

setting his fastest lap of the week at 123.48mph (187.72km/h) in 1991, so it was no surprise to hear him say: 'That's scary – it's frightenly fast – at the speeds we're doing you just head for the gaps between the green bits'.

In a year in which the TT claimed the lives of four more riders, Steve and Carl Fogarty joined forces to ask the organizers for a 600cc limit in Island races. Not everyone agreed with them, for Joey Dunlop felt the 750 gave him the safest ride of the week. In his words, it was 'much safer than the 125s where you have to use every inch of road to avoid losing speed'. Joey was back to fitness and set his fastest ever TT lap in 1991, joining the select few who averaged above 120mph.

Speed is of little use without handling and Kawasaki was forced to withdraw its 750 entry part way through practice when, despite the best efforts of mechanics, suspension and tyre specialists, Ian Lougher declared it was not safe to ride at race-winning speed. Not for the first time, a bike that was quite satisfactory on short circuits was found wanting on the Mountain Course.

Comparisons

Although it is quite impossible to make direct comparison of the performance and handling of machines over the TT course in eras as different as the 1920s, 1950s and 1990s, there are some aspects that are worth a comparative glance. It was the experienced TT-winning Graham Walker who long ago explained how in the early 1920s the 15bhp rigid machines of the day gave a rider the toughest time at speed on the straights, and that riders prayed for a corner to get some relief. Then, in his view, the smoother roads and better-handling 45 to 50bhp machines of the 1950s offered a reasonably comfortable and easy ride on the straights, but prospective winners had to give their all on the corners to achieve race success. Perhaps Graham was guilty of simpli-fying his comparisons, for riding an unfaired 500 at 125 to 130mph in the early 1950s was never an easy ride, particularly on a windy day.

But what of the 1990s – how did Joey Dunlop cope with a 145bhp, streamlined machine fitted with the best suspension money could buy? Well, he would not have made much of a fuss about it if asked, but in reality 37¾ racing miles of a TT lap of the 1990s demanded total mental and physical effort. Mental because things changed so fast and continuously for the entire 18 minutes and 30 seconds of a lap above 120mph – so fast in fact that, although he might actually be riding through one bend, Joey's mind would be two to three bends ahead.

On the physical side, the bike would be tailored to suit Joey and his riding style in terms of seat, footrest, clip-ons, levers and other fittings to give him the best possible control, but a TT lap is one of continuous non-stop effort. Acceleration, braking, changing direction and coping with bumps would all be far removed from similar activities of forty years before, for they were relentless processes without relief that saw the bike seeking to get out of the rider's hands at every opportunity. From the trackside things may have looked fairly smooth, but in the saddle it was a very different matter. Total concentration, total effort and no mistakes, that was the only way to ride the Mountain Course at record-breaking speed for the 226 miles of a Senior TT.

A point made by Steve Hislop when he recommended a reduction in engine capacity was that a difference of 2 to 3mph in lap speeds between riders of almost equal ability meant that they were actually having quite different rides. He maintained that the marginally faster lap speeds that the fastest men were capable of were much more demanding and put them much closer to the limit.

How Many Miles?

During the 1991 TT period riders completed 4,615 laps of the Mountain Course, with racing accounting for 1,283 of them and the remainder spent practising. Several top riders rode in five solo classes and by the end of the fortnight would have put in a substantial number of miles. With probably four bikes to qualify and get correctly set up to race, those riders would aim to be out in every practice period and to take more than one bike out in each. That could easily total twenty-five laps in practice week, and completing all five races would mean another twenty-four, giving a total of forty-nine laps and 1,850 miles (2,977km). Most would also do additional miles in testing at Jurby to sort out faults or run in rebuilt engines.

As if that was not enough racing, in 1991 the Isle of Man Steam Packet Company sponsored a race meeting on the Billown circuit on the Saturday after Senior race day. Put on to entertain visitors to the 'TT Festival' who either could not or did not want to make an immediate departure from the Island, they proved attractive to riders seeking to boost their earnings, and added substantially to their tally of racing miles.

Radio TT

With the growth in race speeds and subsequent shortening of lap times, Manx Radio decided to adjust its 'around the course' commentary points that pumped out valuable race information on Radio TT. Out went Ballacraine, Ballaugh and the Bungalow. In came Glen Helen and Ramsey Hairpin, thus giving commentators Peter Kneale, Fred Clarke and Maurice Mawdsley (with Geoff Cannell on the roving microphone) a little longer to gather race times, positions and news before delivering them over the air to information-hungry spectators and race teams.

Robert Dunlop shows the effect of a hard fortnight's racing, as the man with the roving mike pounces at the end of a Steam Packet-sponsored race on the Saturday after the Senior TT.

Lap of Honour

It had become a tradition to run a Lap of Honour at the TT featuring star riders and machines of yesterday. Of course, there were a limited number of real star riders and an equally limited number of star machines still able to cope with the demands of a lap of the Mountain Course, so there was a tendency to make up the numbers with largely unknown riders on basic Gold Stars and such like. However, the lap was popular with spectators, and although it tended to be pushed about the race programme to suit the organizers it seemed destined to stay. At the back of the organizers' mind there was always the worry that some former 'star' would get carried away with the occasion and crash, but the event had a good safety record, even though it was not incident free.

On occasion a star of such standing might be considered worthy of his own personal lap of honour. That occurred in 1991 when Giacomo Agostini delighted the crowd with the sound of an MV Agusta lapping the course between Monday's races. Despite his great

An unusual 'combination' as Nick Cutmore with his Norvin hustles through Parliament Square, Ramsey, during the 1993 TT Lap of Honour. Mick Ruocco can be seen keeping the third wheel on the road.

deeds on the Mountain, Agostini could hardly have been considered to have been the best friend of the races, given his anti-TT attitude of the early 1970s. However, the Island seemed to have forgiven him, and even the Manx police were in forgiving mood when they found him about to fire up the MV on open roads at Ballaugh for a blast past the house of long-time marshal Gwen Crellin, known in TT history as 'The Lady in White'.

Contracts

Having won four races for Honda at the 1991 TT, neither Steve Hislop nor Carl Fogarty was Honda-mounted for 1992. Both would probably have chosen to be, but their riding arrangements had been in turmoil for the early part of 1992. Honda offered bikes to Hislop for the TT only but, mindful of his need for bikes for a full season, he turned them down. A deal that seemingly saw him on his way to Yamaha fell through and Steve hastily put together a package that involved the leasing of a 'works' Norton for the TT, albeit one that appeared in white.

Carl Fogarty was without a contract at the start of the season but then landed a Ducati ride that went very well in early short-circuit races. However, he had reservations about riding the Italian V-twin at the TT and made a last-minute arrangement to ride for Yamaha.

Honda's support went to Joey Dunlop and former MGP winner Phillip McCallen, the latter going to the Island in blistering form after a successful NW200, while Robert Dunlop offered a challenge to the Japanese manufacturers on a 'works' Norton in John Player colours.

Practice performance showed that all the above runners were on the pace. The Honda riders were well accustomed to their machines, but Fogarty had to get used to the transverse-four Yamaha OW01 and Hislop had a bigger problem in familiarizing himself with the Norton. Although its twin-spar alloy frame, telescopic forks, single-shock rear suspension,

all-round hydraulic brakes and radial race tyres were fairly conventional, the total lack of engine-braking from the 150bhp rotary engine was most unconventional and demanded major adjustments to riding style, braking points and so on.

An Irish Week

Many Irish racers were reared and did the majority of their racing on hedge-bound road circuits, so riding at the TT was very natural to them. In 1992 they almost monopolized the solo events. Joey Dunlop was equipped with machinery to race in five solo classes, but although all his bikes had Honda on the tank he rode a mixture of 'works' and privately sponsored machines. Still on thirteen TT wins (one behind Mike Hailwood), Joey lifted his

Phillip McCallen achieved his ambition of a TT win in the 1992 Formula I TT, bringing his Honda home ahead of Steve Hislop (Norton) and Joey Dunlop (Honda).

total to fourteen with victory in the Light-weight 125 race on his McMenemy Motors RS Honda. Raising the lap record to 108.69mph (174.91km/h) while fending off brother Robert in second place, it was Joey's only win of the week, but he described it as a satisfying one. By then forty and calling himself a publican and part-time racer, Joey's fans felt that he could retire at any time. Pleased to hear him say that he would be back for 1993, many wondered if his days of Formula I and Senior TT wins were over, probably thinking that any further victories would come in the smaller classes.

Phillip McCallen was a hard-charging young rider who, with a distinctive hunched forward and elbows-out style, never looked too far from disaster. In 1992 he achieved his ambition of a TT win and did it in style in the Formula I race, beating Steve Hislop (Norton) and Joey Dunlop (Honda) into second and third places, after early leader Carl Fogarty (Yamaha) dropped out with gearbox problems. Phillip also took victory in Supersport 600, while fellow Ulsterman Brian Reid was victorious on Yamahas in Supersport 400 and Junior races.

On the last day of race week in 1992 the Irish were looking to take the Senior race and make it a clean sweep. There were, however, some eighty other riders prepared to contest the issue. Among these were Scotsman Steve Hislop and Englishman Carl Fogarty, two talented and highly motivated young men with reputations to uphold, and with strong ambitions to succeed in the wider world of racing.

'Works' Support

As Steve Hislop and Carl Fogarty found out when trying to make their racing plans in 1992, the level of 'works' support for racing fluctuates from season to season. Although Honda gave continued support to the TT after returning to the event in 1977, the level of that support varied from year to year. No doubt like all business activities the Honda race shop

was affected by budgetary restraints, availability and competitiveness of its bikes, involvement of financially supportive sponsors and other factors. Yet even when the top Japanese companies appeared to be giving the TT 100 per cent support, the autobiographies of top riders of the 1990s are littered with complaints that they came to the Island without the latest forks, brakes or engine modifications. It is in the nature of such riders to expect the best to maximize their competitiveness, but the true level of support that the manufacturers provide is sometimes difficult to judge.

Even the big manufacturers had come to rely on a major sponsor contributing towards the cost of their race efforts. In addition, the growth in advertising on machines and riders' clothing created competition for the most prominent positions, and so provided manufacturers and riders with opportunities for increased income from the payments that

Michelin was among the successful suppliers of tyres to the race winners at the 1992 TT.

A Race to Remember

The Senior TT had recovered much of its former prestige and with it the top Friday spot in the race programme. The day of the 1992 Senior race dawned fine and saw Hislop, Fogarty, McCallen, Joey and Robert Dunlop all in with the chance of a win after impressive practice times, and fans around the course felt certain they were in for a treat. They were not disappointed, for it turned into a race that would be talked about for years to come. Just four seconds covered the first three – Fogarty (Yamaha), Hislop (Norton) and Robert Dunlop (Norton) – on corrected time as they hurtled past the grandstand at more than 160mph to complete the first lap. Robert dropped back slightly and four seconds then covered the first two for the remaining five laps of extreme racing effort. There was a little ebb and flow in the gap at pit stops, but so small was it that the lead changed five times between Fogarty (Yamaha) and Hislop (Norton). This was TT racing at its best and, although spectators only saw the two contestants once every 18½ minutes, Manx Radio's commentators conveyed the excitement of the race for the whole of each lap and listeners around the course strained to hear every word as they were caught in the tension of the 226-mile battle. Unlike on short circuits, it was a race in which the top two did not see each other, for the interval start kept them 2½ minutes apart (Fogarty rode at number 4, Hislop at 19). Informed only by signals from their support crews, it was pure TT racing where each man rode his own race in a typical against the clock TT contest, while his opponent did the same elsewhere on the course.

Everyone knew that there was little in the way of tactics involved, for these young men were pushing to the limit, and some worried they were pushing too hard. It was not just the substantial prize money they were racing for: both wanted to prove a point to Honda, both were without a TT win in 1992, both were desperate to gain the worldwide publicity that accompanied a Senior win, and both wanted to be victorious in the personal battle between Fogarty and Hislop that dominated the pre-race headlines. There was a lot at stake and, unlike some races where the crowd detects that the rider at the front is in control and riding within himself, no one was in any doubt that these two were giving their all. It added spice and tension to their confrontation and, in a wonderful result for

Steve Hislop powers his Norton out of Ballaugh towards Quarry Bends and Senior victory in 1992.

Taken from the same position but at a slightly different angle to the previous photograph, Carl Fogarty (Yamaha) shows the determination he put into his ride to second place.

British fans, it was Steve Hislop who eventually triumphed over Carl Fogarty and his Yamaha, so giving Norton its first Senior TT win since 1961. The evenly matched duo both entered the record books, with Steve setting a new race record average speed of 121.28mph (195.18km/h), while Carl grabbed the outright lap record in an all-or-nothing last lap attempt to catch Steve, leaving it at 123.61mph (198.93km/h).

While Steve Hislop and Carl Fogarty were well matched in terms of racing talent, the competition between the small Norton concern and the huge Yamaha empire was seen as the motorcycling equivalent of the battle between David and Goliath, with the successful performance of the 'White Charger' (as Steve's bike became known) quickly assuming legendary status in TT history.

resulted. It is natural for the average race-goer to assume that if a bike or rider sports a logo of a component manufacturer or supplier, then he is using that product – but is that always the case? In 1992 Ferodo claimed to have supplied brake components to TT winners who actually sported stickers of competing suppliers. Presumably the latter paid more to advertise!

'Works' support was virtually non-existent for sidecar competitors and in 1992 Geoff Bell and passenger Keith Cornbill took their privately entered Yamaha to a double victory at record-breaking speed. In an amazing display of consistency, the pair won Sidecar Race A at an average speed of 101.50mph (163.34km/h) and Race B at 101.49mph (163.33km/h). That represented a difference of six-tenths of a second in the time they took to cover the 113 miles of each race.

The rights to course-side advertising were held by the race organizers and they used income from letting prime spaces to help defray the cost of the races. Traditional spots like Quarter Bridge, Braddan Bridge and Ballaugh Bridge fetched premium rentals, for advertisers knew that the banner proclaiming their company or product name would be seen worldwide in press photographs and televised transmissions. They would also appear in the photos and videos taken by race fans that would be looked at for years to come.

Kiwi Challenge

The way that the small Norton concern successfully challenged the might of the Japanese manufacturers in 1992 was most impressive, but its motorcycles were at least the product of a reasonably conventional motorcycle factory. In 1993 the unorthodox racing brainchild of New Zealand architect and property developer John Britten appeared on the Island in tones of pink and purple in an attempt to do the same. If TT watchers were shocked by the unconventional Kevlar and carbon-fibred

Advertising tends to be concentrated at popular spectator spots and those that offer photo opportunities. Ballacraine was such a location when this shot was taken back in 1931, but the spot lost its popularity after sensible restrictions that no longer allowed spectators to stand in the road, and the hotel's conversion to a private dwelling.

The unconventional Britten's first appearance in the Isle of Man was in 1993 with Shaun Harris riding.

150bhp V-twin's garish colour scheme, they were absolutely stunned when it proved to be the fastest machine through the grandstand speed trap at 165mph (265.5km/h).

While optimists looked to the Britten for yet another David and Goliath performance, pessimists forecast that the demands of the TT course would reveal its inadequacies. In the hands of TT newcomer Shaun Harris both took a degree of satisfaction, for after troubled practice the bike performed well in the Senior, holding eleventh place and lapping at more than 116mph (186km/h), until robbed of a finish by an oil-line failure.

New Zealand was a long way to have come from and then miss out on a finish. The Britten stable seemed well funded, but TT prize money was fairly static with the Senior being the richest race of the week, offering £6,250 to a start to finish winner. One extra payment for 1993 was that every race starter was guaranteed a sum of £250 'subject to the competitor making a bonafide attempt to compete in the race'.

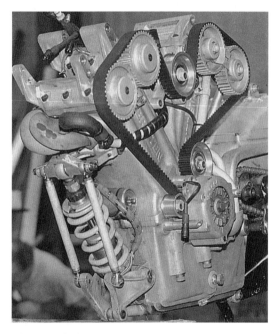

The twin-cylinder Britten engine.

The Greatest?

Joey Dunlop did return to contest the TT in 1993 and in winning the Lightweight 125 race he went to the top of the table of the greatest

number of TT wins. The inevitable comparisons were made between him and those below him in the table – Mike Hailwood, Giacomo Agostini and Stanley Woods – but no firm conclusions could be drawn from such an exercise. Like every top rider Joey's TT career had been littered with ifs, buts and if onlys. He felt that with a little more luck his total of wins could already have been close to twenty, but, as it was, fifteen was the actual figure. Regrettably his performances in the big bike races of 1993 showed him starting well but then fading away as the race progressed, adding weight to the speculation that his Senior and Formula I rides might be coming to an end. There was unlikely to be a middle-weight solution, for although he raced them, Joey was not an enthusiastic rider of 600s.

With him having won so many races, it is easy to pass off number fifteen as just another race. But, apart from the obvious record-breaking achievement, his ride came after a troubled practice week with machine problems and the last-minute borrowing of an engine from James Courtney's sponsor for the race. Joey had previously gone on record as saying that riding a 750 at the TT was easier than riding a 125. It is a little difficult to believe that was not said tongue-in-cheek to suit an occasion, but his description of the 125 race gives a hint of the effort involved in the four laps and 151 miles of racing: 'In the entire race, apart from the pit stop, I only lifted my head above the screen once – to get a signal from Johnny Rea at Windy Corner on the last lap'.

While Joey was an established star at the TT, among the top six finishers in the solo classes in 1993 were up and coming riders who would go on to wins or podium places,

including Jason Griffiths, Iain Duffus, Dave Morris, Mark Baldwin, Bob Jackson, Simon Beck, Ian Simpson and Colin Gable. Rob Fisher looked a threat for the future in the sidecars.

Noticeably absent were Steve Hislop and Carl Fogarty, who were trying to advance their careers in other fields of racing, although 33-year-old Trevor Nation returned on Fogarty's 1992 Yamaha, having previously announced his retirement from racing.

At Last

Former winner of the Senior MGP (and the Manx Two Day Trial), all-rounder Nick Jefferies was in his tenth year at the TT. Having previously recorded four second places and taken four fourth places in 1992, he came to the 1993 TT as a member of the Honda 'works' team. By then forty years old, he fully justified Honda's faith in him by winning the Formula I race, ahead of team-mate Phillip McCallen. Positions were reversed in the Senior, delayed by a day, when Phillip was first home, followed by Nick and Honda privateer Steve Ward.

Robert Dunlop and rising star Mark Farmer rode 888 Ducatis in the Senior (where twin-cylinder machines up to 1000cc were allowed to compete against 750-fours). Indications were that the big twins were faster than

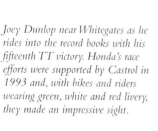

Joey Dunlop near Whitegates as he rides into the record books with his fifteenth TT victory. Honda's race efforts were supported by Castrol in 1993 and, with bikes and riders wearing green, white and red livery, they made an impressive sight.

in 1992, and Mark held second place until running out of fuel towards the end of the second lap.

Jim Moodie won both Supersport 400 and 600 classes at record speeds, riding a Yamaha in the 400 and Honda in the 600. Although the organizers had dropped the up to 1300cc Production class after 1989, just four years later Moodie lapped as fast on his 600 as the fastest 1300 of a few years before. Brian Reid took the Junior on a Yamaha for the second year. His race average speed in 1992 had been 115.13mph (185.28km/h) and in 1993 it was 115.14mph (185.29km/h). Brian was a good and consistent rider, but with the times being a year apart, he would have put their closeness down to coincidence rather than strategy.

The man who looked set to win the Junior was Phillip McCallen (Honda) but, due to a stop for fuel at the end of the second lap, he was concentrating so hard on overtaking a slower rider after Governor's Bridge that he steamed past the pits at full-bore. His pit attendants packed their gear away, for they knew that he would not complete another lap. On the run down to Quarry Bends some 18 miles into his third lap, the Honda spluttered, Phillip pulled in the clutch and coasted to a halt, right at the spot where a film crew was standing. The first thing they did was ask him what the problem was. What could he say?

An innovation for 1993 was the provision of a practice lap for Friday's Senior runners on the Wednesday of race week. It was aimed at refreshing the memories of those who had not ridden since the end of practice week, and to allow others to try final machine adjustments. They were despatched after the Supersport 600 race.

Sidecars

The Formula II specification was introduced for all sidecars in 1990 with the aim of curbing speeds. However, with rapid development in the 600cc four-stroke class for road bikes, solo and sidecar race machinery using the same

By 1993 the majority of sidecar teams used 4-cylinder 600cc engines, although a few still fitted 350cc Yamaha two-stroke twins. The outfit of Neil Smith and Terrie Salone pictured here was unusual in using twin-cylinder Ducati power.

engines also increased their speeds. In 1993 Manxman Dave Molyneux with Karl Ellison in the chair took a double sidecar victory and lifted the lap record to 104.27mph (167.80km/h) using 4-cylinder, four-stroke Yamaha power. The four-strokes had ousted the previously successful two-strokes from the top positions in sidecar racing and the 'strokers' gradually faded out of the class.

Although they were powered by engines from recognized manufacturers like Yamaha and Honda, most drivers used the products of specialists such as Windle, Ireson, Shelbourne, Baker and the 1993 winner Molyneux for the chassis that housed those engines. Using conventionally welded steel tubes, rather than the monocoque carbon-fibre devices on modern GP chairs, steering was by either leading or trailing link, while suspension had to be set up specially to suit the TT course, and a large fuel tank fitted to allow completion of three laps and 113 miles non-stop. Each Sidecar race offered a Manufacturers Team Award; Ireson and Windle were frequent winners.

New to the Sidecar TT in 1993 was Rob Fisher (Honda 600), but he was quickly identified as a potential future winner. Many newcomers to TT racing try to acquaint themselves with the twists and turns of the Mountain Course by watching videos taken by cameras mounted on the bikes of quick men like Joey Dunlop or Steve Hislop. Rob Fisher watched a video every day on the approach to his TT debut, but his was of the specially staged 100mph lap by rally driver Tony Pond in a Rover Vitesse a few years earlier. Presumably the line taken by a car was more akin to that of a sidecar outfit than the one taken by a solo.

Headlines

There was plenty to make the headlines during the approach to the 1994 TT. The official UK Yamaha team run under the Loctite banner was unable to reach terms with the TT organizers and announced in March that it would not be on the Island. However, its team members Jim Moodie and Mark Farmer were left free to make their own TT arrangements.

Nine-times TT winner Steve Hislop earned the biggest headlines by announcing that he would be on the Island as part of the Castrol Honda team, riding the new RC45 models developed from the RC30. Steve had been quoted as saying after 1992 that he would not return to the TT, but in 1994 he was quite open that he was returning for the money. Explaining things a little more fully, 32-year-old Steve told how his basic contract with Honda paid for his participation in only the European rounds of the World Super Bike Championship, and that he needed some £18,000 to meet the costs of competing in the other rounds. There were rumours that he was being paid vast sums for his TT return, which in turn generated animosity and envy, but Steve maintained that his start money was £7,000 and claimed it was what other top stars were receiving in 1994. It was a good headline-making story, but Steve then created publicity of the wrong sort when he openly criticized the handling of the Honda RC45 on the approach to the TT. Unfortunately, as he had shown before and would show in later years, if ever there was a star rider who would have benefited from assistance in the management of his public relations (and finances), it was Steve.

Rather less dramatic news was that the organizers introduced a race for single-cylinder machines in 1994 and received forty-four entries. They were to run in the race for 125s on Monday morning, and with the 125s being the fastest single-cylinder machines around the Mountain Course (with Joey Dunlop's record lap of 108.69mph in 1992), people were interested to see how the big four-stroke singles would go in speed terms (there were forecasts of 110mph laps). There was also a question mark over whether their roadster-derived engines would last the four laps and 151-mile race distance.

Qualifying times were reduced for 1994:

Formula I and Senior	22 minutes
Junior and Supersport 600	24 minutes
Lightweight 125, Supersport 400 and Singles	25 minutes
Sidecars	27 minutes

The Britten racer was back seeking more headlines, and accompanying it from New Zealand came a total of sixteen riders, fourteen of them newcomers and ten forming part of a John Shand-organized ride on identical FZR600R Yamahas.

The Kiwi newcomers were probably well briefed on what to expect from Island racing, but the reality of what they had to tackle would still have come as a shock to this spirited bunch of young men, the majority of whose racing experience was of short circuits. Apart from the difficulties of gaining international licences, organizing entries and accommodation, and funding their visits from across the other side of the world, when they arrived they had to acquaint themselves with the course, attend rider briefings, do the compulsory conducted lap in a coach, and then uncrate and prepare their stock Yamahas to race.

Entered in the Supersport 600 event they would have scanned the practice schedule to find that they had just six sessions in which to learn how to race over the famous TT Mountain Course. If they were lucky and did not suffer any problems, that would probably allow for twelve learning laps.

During the race all the Kiwis performed creditably on what were virtually standard road bikes, without even the tuning allowed by Supersport regulations, and with Robert Holden their highest finisher in ninth place. So good was the overall performance of the team that it was later awarded the prestigious ACU Maudes Trophy. This trophy has a long history and had previously been awarded for a wide range of exceptional motorcycling achievements, mostly by road-going machines. To receive it for a racing performance was a major achievement.

Sadly, the Britten effort was hit by the tragedy of rider Mark Farmer's death during Thursday afternoon's practice after a crash at the Black Dub. Robert Holden had already decided to forego his Britten ride and only Nick Jefferies was left from the three-man team. Unfortunately, his Formula I and Senior races lasted for just over one lap each. It was a bitter blow to John Britten, who had put so much effort into his TT challenge, and it also served to reveal the dark side of the TT to the other Kiwis.

Yamahas of the 1994 Kiwi team lined up just behind the pit road.

PRACTICE PERIODS

❏ Monday May 30
05.15 – 06.00 hrs.	Newcomers · 125/Single Cylinder
06.05 – 06.55 hrs.	Sidecars
18.15 – 19.00 hrs.	Newcomers · 125/Single Cylinder
19.00 – 20.50 hrs.	Senior/TT F1 · Supersport 600 Junior/Supersport 400

❏ Tuesday May 31
18.15 – 19.55 hrs.	Senior/TT F1 · Supersport 600 Junior/Supersport 400
20.00 – 20.50 hrs.	Sidecars

❏ Wednesday June 1
05.15 – 06.00 hrs.	Senior/TT F1 · Supersport 600 Junior/Supersport 400
06.05 – 06.55 hrs.	Sidecars
18.15 – 19.00 hrs.	Newcomers · 125/Single Cylinder
19.00 – 19.55 hrs.	Senior/TT F1 · Supersport 600 Junior/Supersport 400
20.00 – 20.50 hrs.	Sidecars

❏ Thursday June 2
14.00 – 15.25 hrs.	Senior/TT F1 · Supersport 600 Junior/Supersport 400
15.25 – 16.10 hrs.	125/Single Cylinder
16.15 – 17.05 hrs.	Sidecars

❏ Friday June 3
05.15 – 06.55 hrs.	Senior/TT F1 · Supersport 600 Junior/Supersport 400

(A Sidecar practice may be arranged if previous practice periods have been seriously disrupted)

18.15 – 20.50 hrs.	Classes to be announced during Practice Week

❏ Saturday June 4
EMERGENCY ONLY

The practice timetable for 1994, with Seniors getting an extra lap on Wednesday 8 June.

The 1994 Races

Honda no longer made use of its advertising slogan 'Honda Enters. Honda Wins', but it would have been appropriate to describe its 1994 TT performance in the major classes. In the Formula I race, rescheduled to Sunday, Steve Hislop showed that he had lost none of his TT skills by leading home team-mates Phillip McCallen and Joey Dunlop to capture all the podium places for Honda, the trio repeating the process in Friday's Senior race. Whatever qualms Steve may have had about the new RC45 model, and he worked hard in practice to iron out the handling problems he had earlier complained of, he certainly did not let them get in his way during the racing.

In the smaller classes Joey Dunlop was victorious in the Lightweight 125 and the Junior. In the former he did not have his usual tussle with brother Robert, for the younger Dunlop was lying badly injured in hospital after the back wheel of his Honda collapsed in the Formula I race. In the Junior Phillip McCallen looked set for victory until he ran out of fuel for the second year running. Just as important to Honda as the individual race wins was the fact that they also took the Manufacturers Award in five races. After delaying Saturday's Formula I, bad weather also caused the postponement of Monday's racing to Tuesday, and allowed Honda to catch the mood of the 1994 meeting in its post-TT advertising.

HONDA SHINES THROUGH

Yamaha could also look back on several victories by their products in 1994, even if they were not in the premier events. Jim Moodie won the Supersport 400 and Iain Duffus the Supersport 600 after ten years of trying for a TT victory, while Rob Fisher was a double-winner of the Sidecar races at record speeds in only his second year of racing at the TT. All used FZR-derived engines. In the newly introduced Singles race Jim Moodie took another Yamaha-powered victory on a 660 Harris-framed model, setting the fastest lap at an impressive 112.66mph (181.30km/h). Robert Holden was second on a Ducati, and former MGP winner Jason Griffiths took his first TT podium finish with third place on a 660 Spondon Yamaha.

The organizers expressed themselves as pleased with the new Singles race even though not all the forty-two entrants could lay their hands on suitable machinery. Of the twenty-nine competitors that came to the line there were eighteen finishers, a figure considered to be satisfactory.

More Changes

For 1995 the race for 250s lost the title of Junior TT and adopted the name Lightweight TT. It was open to 201–250cc twin-cylinder two-strokes and 371–400cc 4-cylinder four-strokes, the latter having previously raced in the Supersport 400 race, which was dropped from the 1995 programme.

The Junior TT name was given to machines to FIM/ACU Supersport 600 regulations, previously covered by the Supersport 600 race, which was also dropped from the 1995 programme. Although not specifically a change for 1995, the Lightweight 125 race had gradually become more commonly called the Ultra-Lightweight TT.

On the financial side the ACU juggled with start money arrangements yet again, and riders protested at the result – yet again!

On the world stage Carl Fogarty won the 1994 World Super Bike title on a Ducati and, as is the way of these things, it was no surprise to see more Ducatis than usual entered in the 1995 TT. Ridden by good runners such as Robert Holden, Michael Rutter, Iain Duffus and Simon Beck, they showed much promise but most did not have the reliability to achieve good race finishes.

Honda's team comprised the experienced Joey Dunlop, Nick Jefferies, Steve Ward and Phillip McCallen, although Phillip was trying to establish his name away from the TT and commitments to a round of the European Thundersport series meant he had to give the Senior a miss. With their RC45s

Michael Rutter was among those riding Ducatis in 1995.

again finished in Castrol Honda colours, it was McCallen who took victory in the Formula I race, riding the last two laps with a slightly loose wheel. Joey Dunlop was second and Simon Beck kept his Ducati together to take a splendid third place. Lacking the support of a 'works' team, Simon said a public thank you to his parents for their support of his racing efforts, which included remortgaging their house so that he could compete.

Honda had won every Formula I race since 1982 and made much of the fact in its post-race advertising. The win was the start of another good week for the Japanese concern as Joey Dunlop went on to take the Light-weight and Senior races, Iain Duffus the Junior and Mark Baldwin the Ultra-Lightweight. It was Mark, on a 125 Honda he had rented for the race, who, after concealing his true speed in practice, provided the story of the week by coming from behind in a record-breaking last lap to snatch victory by just six-tenths of a second from Mick Lofthouse (Honda). The two had been rivals from MGP days and Mick, who finished two minutes ahead of Mark on the road, was already being acclaimed the winner when the news came through of his close defeat on corrected time. He was left to rue a slow-speed slide to earth at Parliament Square in Ramsey during the race, for it almost certainly cost him victory.

Ducati did claim a TT win with Rob Holden in the Singles race, and Rob Fisher did a double for Yamaha-power in the Sidecar races A and B.

The 1995 TT had arrived with a changed programme of events, but its star riders departed requesting even more changes for 1996 covering such topics as revised race classes, free ferry crossings, a graded start-money system, improved prize money and tougher qualifying standards. There was nothing particularly new in their demands, except that they also sought a five-year plan for the TT meeting, so that arrangements were not altered every year!

Even the Travelling Marshals' bikes were finished in Castrol Honda colours in 1995. They were on duty for every practice session and race, during which competitors were recorded as doing a total of 3,936 laps and 139,505 miles. Ned Bowers is shown here approaching Creg ny Baa.

Joey's Future?

The perennial topic of whether Joey Dunlop would, or would not, be back at the TT the following year occupied space in the motorcycle press after the 1995 event. Honda had previously made clear that they would provide him with race machinery for as long as he wanted to race. Joey's reported comments, however, suggested retirement was on his mind. *Motor Cycle News* claimed that he could retire in September 1995, quoting him with the words, 'I am definitely thinking long and hard about retiring . . . I will see how I feel at the end of the season'. Joey's manager, Davy Wood, seemed to be thinking along the same lines: 'Joey has realized that he's no dynamo any more and can't go on forever. This may well be the beginning of the end of Joey's great career'. The 43-year-old publican from Bally-money was not racing just at the TT, for he was still doing a full season of Irish racing, and perhaps it was becoming too much.

TT fans had read similar, though not quite so serious sounding, reports before, but Joey (no need for a surname) had become a TT institution, and no one wanted him to go. While the majority saw just the racer, what they did not know was that at heart he was a family man. He had also taken to making one-man mercy missions to eastern Europe in a van loaded with essentials for those who would otherwise have to do without. Perhaps wider issues in life than racing were occupying his mind. It certainly surprised his close friends when he gave up smoking later in 1995 and started fitness training, and maybe that encouraged them to think that he would continue racing.

Watching the Races

With almost 37¾ miles of track available to spectate from without payment (the only exceptions being the grandstand and a couple of enclosed areas like Braddan Bridge), there is somewhere on the Mountain Course to suit every race viewer's taste. Most treat a race day as an outing and take a radio for the commentary, extra clothes to cope with changes in the weather and, if new to the TT, a map. If leaving Douglas, the experienced set off in good time, for traffic is usually heavy and there is nothing worse than being turned off the course because roads have closed before getting to a pre-planned viewing spot.

For the gregarious a course-side pub can offer the ideal – somewhere like Ginger Hall or Creg ny Baa – but the end of Cronk y Voddy Straight or the Bungalow will also meet demands for a bit of company and offer faster racing. All of the locations offer the opportunity to move between races if required, even if from the Bungalow watchers are still trapped inside the course while the roads are closed.

Virtually every type of race location is available. Spectators can choose between fast, sweeping bends like those at the 11th Milestone or, with the opportunity to see riders approaching and departing over a long distance, somewhere fast like the Graham Memorial or Windy Corner. Then there are medium-speed locations like Ballacraine or the Gooseneck, although the latter can seem rather faster when you are as close to the bikes as is permitted there.

Spectators get a spectacular view of the 'S' bend at Braddan Bridge.

For spectators who want to be close to the action, the Gooseneck allows a close-up view of riders and machines.

Slow corners offer a good view of the riders without too many heart-stopping moments: Governor's Bridge and Ramsey Hairpin are obvious choices. For those who want to experience potentially heart-stopping moments, the bottom of Bray Hill, bottom of Barregarroo and, to a lesser degree, Hillberry, all fit the bill.

For those prepared to pay and be at the hub of affairs there is always the grandstand. The sight of riders flashing past at more than 160mph is impressive, but it can get a little boring after a while, although pit stops can enliven things.

A representative survey of those who came to the Island at TT time in the mid-1990s yielded some interesting results. Asked why they came to the TT, 46 per cent said that it was just for the racing, 41 per cent said they came for the festival and atmosphere, while the remainder claimed to be interested in both. Asked if they watched every race, 74 per cent said yes and 24 per cent no. Food for thought for the tourist board and its 'Festival' organizers was that only 5 per cent thought their organized events justified the tag of excellent. Asked if they would be returning, 79 per cent said yes, but a worrying 19 per cent said no.

There could be little doubt when looking at a group of TT spectators that they represented a cross-section of almost all the sub-specializtions that exist within the motorcycle movement. Barbour-clad 'vintagents' could be seen alongside those in the latest expensive multi-coloured leathers (complete with obligatory knee-sliders and back protectors), while riders of cruisers, middle-of-the-road tourers and those who looked as though they had just ridden an enduro could also be seen in their varied motorcycling attire. But not everyone visits the TT by bike. Total visitor numbers are usually in excess of 40,000 for the fortnight, but figures from the Steam Packet Company show that they ship some 12,000 bikes and 3,500 cars and vans over that period. While many vans may carry two or three bikes, there are still plenty of people present without two-wheeled transport.

Many of the machines lined up on Douglas Promenade are the latest in sports bikes, but there is plenty of exotica from other eras, much of it only coming out for special occasions such as a visit to the TT. Admiring such bikes during a walk along the Promenade before going off to other forms of entertainment is an enjoyable ritual for many visitors.

More Money

Some of the riders' string of requests left for the organizers after the 1995 TT were met for 1996, including the injection of more money that brought the island's basic budget for the event to more than £500,000. Substantial increases in prize money meant that a start-to-finish leader of the richest event of the week, the Formula I TT, would earn £13,000, with the Senior TT paying £10,000. Part of the thinking here was that although earlier efforts to tempt GP stars to the TT with big purses failed, such outstanding prize money might bring in top short-circuit riders.

The reintroduction of a Production TT for four-strokes of 701–1010cc also met riders' wishes and encouraged the return of Suzuki with 'works' entries for Jim Moodie and Shaun Harris. The inclusion of a Production event allowed many dealers to enter machines on a smallish budget and, attracting the support of tyre and oil companies, gave riders the opportunity to gain more bonus monies. Given their experiences during the late 1980s, it was only after very careful consideration that the organizers brought the Proddie bikes back; informed opinion at the time was that the handling of the mid-1990s' bikes and the road tyres available for their use made them much better suited to racing than those that competed in the last Production TT in 1989.

The prospect of almost standard Honda Fireblades, Yamaha Thunderaces, Kawasaki ZX-7Rs, Ducati 916s and Suzuki GSX-R750s in competition around the TT course was bound to generate interest from spectators as they watched top riders push them to the limit, for many rode the same models.

TT Time Again

On the Isle of Man there is always an unofficial countdown to the TT among the many enthusiasts for the event. Informal greetings from Easter onwards usually begin with 'Only X weeks to TT' and are often countered with 'Can't come soon enough!'

Individuals and race teams usually endeavour to get their TT plans in place in good time, but there could be many a slip before they arrived, either in respect of the arrangements made for bikes to ride or, as was often the case, riders suffering injury in other events. The 1996 TT experienced its share of withdrawals, losing Simon Beck, previous TT winner Dave Leach, former British 600 champion and TT newcomer Mike Edwards, former 250 GP rider Bruno Bonhuil and double MGP winner James Courtney through injury. Nick Jefferies was doubtful and Robert Dunlop was still fighting back to fitness after his TT accident in 1994. Worst news of all was that veteran Steve Ward had been killed in a race accident in Sweden just a few weeks before.

Seen by some as biting the hand that used to feed him, World Super Bike Champion Carl Fogarty made disparaging remarks about the TT in the *News of the World*, and then accepted an invitation to appear at the event in 1996 as an all-expenses-paid celebrity guest. Steve Hislop, a Manx resident for some years, announced that he would be riding at the TT, but photographs showed that it would not be for the Honda Britain race team, but for the Purple Helmets, a zany bunch of Manx-based riders with a crazy riding display on much-modified Honda 90s. They were usually joined by Manxman Steve Colley, who took a break from competing in the World Trials Championship to entertain TT crowds with his trick-riding.

Actually achieving far more pre-race publicity on the run-up to the 1996 TT than celebrities Fogarty and Hislop, or even the competing Dunlop, McCallen and all the other riders combined, was 35-year-old Francesca Giordano. The glamorous Italian rider featured in several national papers as well as the motorcycling and Manx press. When it came to the Lightweight race Francesca lapped at a healthy rate in excess of 90mph on a virtually standard Yamaha 400, while the fastest woman around the TT course at the time,

As light relief from the serious business of racing, Steve Hislop was known to don purple helmet, dark glasses and old riding coat, and join the zany Purple Helmets in some of their crowd-pleasing activities at TT time.

Sandra Barnett, put in laps above 110mph on her Honda RC30, but with very little publicity.

Two newcomers who made quiet and relatively unpublicized TT debuts in 1996 were former British 250cc Champion John McGuinness and, with a TT pedigree running from his grandfather Allan, father Tony and uncle Nick, a young David Jefferies.

Sponsorship

Everyone was used to sponsorship of riders and race teams, so during the early 1990s the TT organizers encouraged firms to sponsor a race. Alfred McAlpine Construction started the ball rolling by sponsoring the Senior TT and so the meeting's premier race became the Alfred McAlpine (IOM) Senior TT. By 1996 Total Oils was sponsoring the Formula I,

Zak Facta the Lightweight, FFO the Junior, Performance Bikes the Production, and McAlpine the Senior.

A rider with a particularly unusual sponsor was Manxman Decca Kelly, whose Honda for the Junior was finished in the blue and yellow colours of Aeromega, who provided the rescue helicopters at the event. Taking twenty-seventh place, Decca was glad to have made his way to the finish unaided.

McCallen's TT

TT greats like Mike Hailwood, Joey Dunlop and Steve Hislop had all achieved three wins in a week, but in 1996 Phillip McCallen went one better and entered the record books by making his 1996 tally four, all on Hondas. Phillip started with a win in the Formula I race on his RC45 and used the same bike to take the Senior at the end of the week. In between he was successful on a CBR600 in the Junior and on a Fireblade in the Production. He was even on course for a fifth win in the Lightweight, before he holed an exhaust as his suspension went down on full travel through the dip at the bottom of Barregarroo.

While it was clear to spectators that the 'standard' Production bikes did not handle quite as well as the 'racers', it was not sufficient to worry the organizers in that area. McCallen's fastest lap was 118.93mph (191.39km/h) on his Fireblade, and he was of the opinion that he could have got round at 120mph if he had been pushed. Reliability was very good, with only six retirements from fifty-three starters.

Joey Dunlop won the Lightweight and Ultra-Lightweight races on his Hondas and the only other make to get a look in among the solo winners was Yamaha, when Jim Moodie gained victory for it in the Singles race.

It was Dave Molyneux and Peter Hill who won both sidecar races on their DMR outfit and left the lap record at 111.02mph (178.66km/h), a huge increase of 3.5mph on the previous best. 'Moly's' practice times were so fast that there were whispers of illegal fuels and/or oversize engines. Seriously offended by the rumours and determined to scotch them, he had his fuel tested in practice – result, all in order – and his engine was stripped and measured after the first race – result, well within the limit at 598cc.

Light and Dark

The TT has always been strong on nostalgia, and showing the light side of a fortnight's activities it welcomed sixteen historic Moto Guzzi racers to participate in the Lap of Honour, as part of the company's seventy-fifth anniversary celebrations. The man who led them off was former TT winner Bill Lomas riding a priceless original V8, followed by a replica V8 ridden by its builder Giuseppe Todero. Veteran Bill rode the whole lap, while

'young' Giuseppe lost control and fell from his £500,000 machine at Braddan Bridge less than 2 miles into the lap. Fortunately, the only damage was to the bike's fairing and Giuseppe's pride.

Once again, however, the dark side of the TT showed itself when four riders were killed in practice and racing, among them potential race winners Mick Lofthouse and Robert Holden. Only a couple of weeks before the event 28-year-old Mick described how his mission was to win a TT in 1996, in either the Lightweight or Ultra-Lightweight class. Just as determined was Robert Holden, who already had a Singles TT win to his credit from 1995 but wanted more. It was not to be. Both were good enough riders to try to ride on the fine line that allowed them to race hard enough to achieve victory, while still showing respect for the demands of the course. Regrettably, both must have strayed over it.

Rider deaths invariably brought a bad press from certain quarters; after the 1996 TT the President of the FIM, who had never been to the event, expressed his concern at the negative effect such bad press reports could have on motorcycle racing as a whole. However, there were plenty prepared to leap to the defence of the TT, despite the sometimes callous attitude to death that it sometimes portrayed to outsiders. Riders, organizers, marshals and most spectators knew that the TT was a dangerous event that could, and did, bring death and injury to riders. No one tried to hide that aspect of racing over the formidable Mountain Course, but they knew that amongst the headline-making tragedies they were part of an event that tested men and machines in a way that no other in the world could do. For almost ninety years riders had taken on the challenge presented by the TT and – the crux of the matter – as long as riders wanted to meet that challenge, those with the enthusiasm for the races would continue to organize them on the riders' behalf. Riders of lesser standing would point to the TT being too dangerous . . . too difficult to learn . . . too expensive . . .

too long . . . too far to travel, and would settle for a scratch around the likes of Brands Hatch short circuit to fulfil their racing ambitions. Other riders and, it should be said, organizers – for it would be easy for them to walk away from the event in the face of criticism – look for the ultimate challenge presented by the TT, just as so many have done before them.

Anniversary Year

The TT celebrated the ninetieth anniversary of its first running in 1997. Celebrations were limited, but Geoff Duke did unveil a celebratory plaque opposite the original 1907 starting line at St John's and the Manx Treasury issued commemorative coins.

The plaque unveiling was during race week, but practice week commenced with the usual 'early light of dawn' proceedings, with riders lined up ready to depart at 5.15am for a fortnight of high-speed activity. Phillip McCallen was the fastest man in practice and finished the fortnight as 'Man of the Year', collecting a hat-trick of wins for Honda in Formula I, Production and Senior.

Phillip McCallen lost the chance to make it four wins in 1997 when he came off his 250 Honda at high speed going through Quarry Bends. After a long slide in which he was fortunate not to hit anything, he escaped with minor cuts, friction burns and bruises. Just two days later he was back in the saddle and taking victory in the Junior, although, declaring that

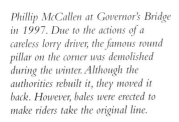

This plaque was unveiled at St John's to commemorate the ninetieth anniversary of the running of the first TT in 1907.

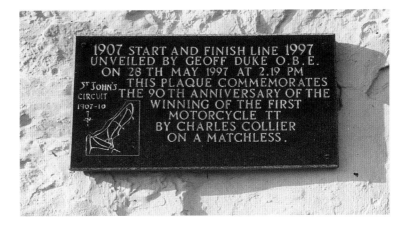

Phillip McCallen at Governor's Bridge in 1997. Due to the actions of a careless lorry driver, the famous round pillar on the corner was demolished during the winter. Although the authorities rebuilt it, they moved it back. However, bales were erected to make riders take the original line.

Roy Hanks and Phillip Biggs on their Ireson outfit rode at number 1 in the 1997 Sidecar races, winning Race A.

he could still see the marks in the road from his 250 spill, he was understandably cautious through Quarry Bends!

Joey Dunlop had been tying for the lead in the Lightweight with McCallen before the latter lost time changing a wheel at his pit stop. Joey had opted for a harder tyre that would last the whole race, and he went on to win conclusively from Ian Lougher (Honda), who was only 1.4 seconds ahead of John McGuinness (Aprilia); in just his second year at the TT, McGuinness set the fastest lap at 116.83mph (188.01km/h). Ian Lougher took victory in the Ultra-Lightweight from Denis McCullough, with Robert Dunlop coming third in what was his first TT since his major crash in 1994. All were on Hondas. Ian Simpson (Honda) rode to his first TT win in the Junior, emulating his father Bill who won the 1976 two-man Production race with Chas Mortimer.

Sidecar wins went to Roy Hanks (Race A) and Rob Fisher (Race B), with Wendy Davis finishing both races and making TT history by becoming the first woman driver of a sidecar at the TT.

The 1997 Senior race broke with tradition:

instead of riders entering in advance, entry came by invitation of the organizers. In addition, it was opened to Production bikes of 701–1010cc and to 500cc GP specification two-strokes. The organizers extended their invitation to the fastest eighty runners in the week's earlier races. Among them were Joey Dunlop and Jim Moodie mounted on Honda NSR500 production two-stroke racers that were said to cost £90,000, give 135bhp and, at 115kg, weigh only slightly more than a 250. Moodie did bring his 500 home in third place, but 750cc RC45s in the hands of McCallen and Rutter took the first two places. Once again it had been a good year for Honda at the TT, but with Castrol having put its money into Honda's World Super Bike team, Honda Britain was unable to attract the support of another major sponsor, and so the TT machines raced in its black and red livery.

Qualifying

Qualifying times were tightened yet again for 1998, but although an occasional rider might not be up to speed, most of the entry had no trouble in meeting the required standard. With

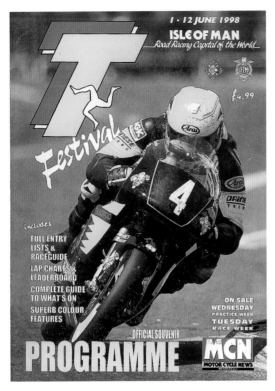

The official programme carried the words 'TT Festival' on the cover to indicate that much of its contents dealt with more than just the racing. This one from 1998 depicts Ian Lougher in full flight on his 125 Honda as he rode to victory in the Ultra-Lightweight TT of 1997.

Formula I and Senior
21 mins 30 secs = *c.* 105mph
Junior/Production
22 mins 30 secs = *c.* 100mph
Lightweight
23 mins = *c.* 98mph
Ultra-Lightweight/Singles
24 mins = *c.* 94mph
Sidecars
25 mins 30 secs = *c.* 90mph

The Clerk of the Course always had the right to waive absolute compliance with qualifying times if he judged fit. In the case of a top runner who had qualified in two or three classes but missed out in one due to machine problems, he had a fairly simple decision to make. But often it was a newcomer wearing his required orange jacket during practice who failed to reach the qualifying time and appealed to be allowed to race. To ease things in that particular area the rules were amended to read 'Newcomers will be granted 90 seconds extra over the stated qualification time providing that any Newcomer using this extra 90 seconds to qualify will be required to wear their orange jacket throughout the race'. A newcomer who achieved the general qualifying standard did not have to wear his orange jacket during the race.

McCallen Out

Phillip McCallen had been Honda's top performer in the previous few years, but a back injury sustained at Thruxton not only put him out of the 1998 races but threatened his future racing career. It was very unfortunate, for he was down to ride a rather special RC45. The NSR500s that appeared at the 1997 TT may have sounded expensive at £90,000, but nobody was able to put a value on the RC45 prepared for McCallen to ride in 1998, for it was far removed from the standard racer. The engine was to full 1998 World Super Bike specification and the chassis much modified. That all meant only the very best and most expensive

the organizers keen to have European riders competing to help attract foreign spectators, there was always a smattering of foreign names unknown to TT followers at the foot of the entry list, and occasionally one did not make the qualifying standard, while others circulated at the very back of the field. All entries were vetted for experience, but there was still a big speed differential between the fastest and slowest entries that could translate into three minutes a lap (or five seconds a mile). Total entries numbered 706 and, although there was a slight decrease in Formula I and Production races, the overall figure was higher than in 1997 and the Junior was heavily oversubscribed. The revised qualifying times riders had to meet were:

components were used, giving McCallen's mount the edge in performance, handling and reliability. It was also sufficient justification for Honda having Japanese technicians on hand.

To add to Honda's rider problems, Joey Dunlop was far from fit after a crash at Tandragee that left him with a broken collar bone amd cracked pelvis, and missing part of a finger. Top sidecar man Dave Molyneux was also Honda-powered but his return to the TT after a year away was threatened by a hand infection, so its top men on two and three wheels were in trouble. However, although it was not good news at the top for Honda, there was strength in depth in its solo attack, with Iain Duffus, Ian Simpson, Michael Rutter, Jason Griffiths, Nick Jefferies and Jim Moodie either receiving direct or partial support from Honda Britain. Moodie was slightly doubtful for the TT having cracked a bone in his wrist at the NW200, where Robert Dunlop also broke his leg. The Japanese company was determined to do well in 1998 to commemorate its fifty years as a motorcycle manufacturer and, away from the racing, it brought a hugely impressive 'History of Honda' exhibition to the Island, showing that its successes went far beyond motorcycle racing. The Honda name seemed to be everywhere at the TT, except on the wrapping to the six thousand straw bales that lined the course and prominently carried the name of Suzuki!

Despite its massive presence, Honda could not guard against the freak accident that befell Iain Duffus when, not riding a bike, he fell in the paddock and broke his leg. It was bad luck for Iain who had worked hard down the years to achieve 'works' support from Honda in the Junior and Production races of 1997, then had support extended to include the Formula I and Senior races in 1998.

The results of practice week suggested that Honda victories might be scarce, for Yamaha machines topped the times in the Lightweight and Production (with the new R1 model), while Simon Beck made people sit up and take notice by heading the Formula I and Senior

classes on his Kawasaki. That was a performance that would certainly not have been in the script drafted by Honda's public relations men before the event.

Bad Practice, Good Race

Honda had sufficient experience of the TT to be aware of the old saying of 'Bad Practice, Good Race' and, after a relatively troubled practice week, it really hoped for better things in race week. With the saying once again proving its worth, Honda went on to win every event in 1998 except the Singles race, where Dave Morris again brought his BMW home first.

While winning eight out of nine races is a basic statement of Honda's achievement in 1998, it gives no hint of the intense fortnight of activities shared by those closely involved with the racing – riders, mechanics, sponsors, trade, organizers, marshals and press – each individual with his or her own tales to tell of the 1998 TT.

Among those who showed good form at the NW200 races that preceded the TT were Ian Simpson and Michael Rutter, both riding for Honda Britain. Moving from racing in Northern Ireland to racing in the Isle of Man, Michael Rutter, son of multi-TT winner Tony, looked favourite to win both the Formula I and Senior TTs with Simpson probably second. In the Formula I race, however, postponed from Saturday to Sunday, Michael was leading when he lost a contact lens and slowed to let fellow contact lens wearer Ian through for a win. Then in the Senior he was forced to retire from the lead after getting a puncture, which again gave Simpson the win. Rutter gained some consolation when he beat Simpson to first place in the Junior, with Manxman Paul Dedman finishing third.

The Senior race yielded an example of the truth of another TT saying, this time the one about races being won and lost in the pits. It was Bob Jackson who came home second in

The win by Dave Morris in the 1998 Singles race gave BMW victory for the second year.

Ian Simpson took two TT victories in Honda's black and red colours in 1998.

225

the Senior on a Kawasaki just 3.7 seconds behind Simpson, but had he not lost time with a fuel cap that was reluctant to go back into place after refuelling, Bob would have won the race. His Kawasaki could not quite match the pace of the 'works' Hondas, so he had an enlarged fuel tank made that meant he would have to stop only once in the Senior to the Hondas twice. It was a strategy that almost worked.

It was Joey Dunlop's turn to play the strategist in the Lightweight race, and his did work. Pre-TT race injuries meant that he could not cope with a 750 on the island and so had to forego his big-bike rides in 1998. Indeed, so troublesome were his injuries that he thought of scratching from the meeting. However, on a wet and misty Lightweight race day, when the organizers reduced the laps from four to three, Joey out-thought the opposition and the organizers to take an against-the-odds victory. Scheduled to stop at the end of lap one for fuel like most of the other riders, Joey used his long TT experience and judged that, as the weather deteriorated soon after the start, the organizers would be forced to stop the race early. This happened at the end of lap two, by when he had gained time over his main opponents by not having stopped. His canny

reading of the situation gave him TT win number twenty-three, which made it his fifth Lightweight victory in a row. Joey's win was not all about strategy, for he actually put in the fastest lap of the race and, given the injuries the 47-year-old was carrying, the biggest factor in his success was probably his bravery, for many younger riders found conditions too hard to take and pulled in to retire.

So Honda had a good year in 1998 and attained their 100th TT victory. It happened in the Production race with Jim Moodie riding a Fireblade. It was an event in which Yamaha hoped for success with its R1 model, which was a 'big' bike designed on small bike principles. The pre-TT magazine assessments rated the R1 as a giant leap forward for road use, several describing it as 'the ultimate sports bike', and Allan Benallick seemingly confirmed their words by putting his on top of the practice leader-board, although there were concerns about whether it could complete two laps at race speed on its standard 18-litre fuel tank. Designed from scratch by a team led by Kunihiko Miwa, the R1 had the appearance and weight of a small 600 allied to an output of 140bhp. But how would it rate at the TT? Race fans on other sports bikes like Honda Fireblades and Suzuki GSX-Rs were as

The YZF-R1 Yamaha in roadster form.

keen to find out as the manufacturers, for a good Production TT result could influence their buying and thus future sales. In the event the new R1 did not quite match the Fireblades, so Yamaha had to settle for fourth to sixth places with its new model in 1998.

Honda v Yamaha

The two Japanese giants had fought many a battle for TT honours over almost forty years of racing and both had experienced periods of supremacy. In the early 1960s their struggle had been to have the best Lightweight 250, but in 1999 both wanted victory in the Formula I and Senior TTs, to boost sales of their large-capacity road bikes. With the Formula I race opened up to any four-strokes from 700cc up to 1010cc (including Production bikes) and also to 500cc GP two-strokes manufactured after 1994, the result was effectively to create a second Senior race. It was the organizers' response to requests from riders and sponsors for changes that would allow them more rides with just one machine.

In the months running up to the 1999 TT there was a feeling that Honda's long reign in the big bike classes was under threat. The young David Jefferies was in stunning form at the NW200 and, riding 1000cc V&M Yamahas with Iain Duffus, many thought that he was the man to bring Honda's seventeen-year reign as winners of the Formula I race to an end. Honda decided to stick to 750s and 500s for the Formula I race, but it lost Ian Simpson to a pre-TT injury, and so Simon Beck was given a 'works' RC45 to ride alongside Joey Dunlop and Jim Moodie (RC45s) and John McGuinness (NSR500). Michael Rutter also received Honda support, although commitments to 500cc GP racing meant that he flew from the Island in the middle of practice week to race in Germany, so missing the Formula I race. Crankshaft problems in practice with the full 'works' World Super Bikes specification RC45 had Joey wondering whether to take over a standard model. Then,

just as Simon Beck was about to reap the rewards of a 'works' ride after many hard years as a privateer, he was killed in a tragic accident at the 33rd Milestone. At the end of practice Jim Moodie (Honda) was just ten seconds faster than Iain Duffus (Yamaha), with both men expected to go faster during racing. Despite his NW200 form and third place in TT practice, many felt that David Jefferies (Yamaha) needed more Mountain Course experience before being good enough to take a TT win.

Red Flag

Normally used only to signify the end of a practice session, the red flag made two other appearances at the TT in 1999. In a quirk of the Manx weather, thick sea mist rolled in during Tuesday evening practice to reduce visibility between Governor's Bridge and the top of Bray Hill. Although only affecting a short length of the course, riders could not race through it and so they were red-flagged well before Governor's Bridge, brought to a standstill and then travelled in convoy behind a Travelling Marshal to complete the lap.

At the start of Saturday's Formula I race riders were being despatched at ten-second intervals when the news was flashed to Race Control that number 34, Paul Orrit, had crashed while descending Bray Hill. Except for one previous occasion back in 1914 (coincidentally on Bray Hill) all accidents on the TT course had been dealt with by marshals under warning flags, but in this instance the decision was taken to stop the race. Riders already racing were red-flagged at Sulby Bridge and when all were there they rode back via Ramsey and the Mountain to the grandstand behind Travelling Marshals.

It was quite an exceptional occurrence for a race to be stopped in that manner, because in the 1912 incident riders despatched ahead of the fallen one were allowed to continue racing, while those still waiting to start were just held until the road was clear, before the starting procedure recommenced. H. Vaughan

Knight, the 1914 rider, escaped serious injury and, although Paul Orrit badly damaged his hand and wrist, it could have been much worse.

The 1999 Formula I race was eventually restarted over a shortened four-lap distance. It was TT master Joey Dunlop and his Honda that led for the first two laps, but at the end of the race it was young pretender David Jefferies who took his first TT win to give Yamaha its first Formula I victory in what was the twenty-third running of the event, twenty-one of which had been won by Honda. The winning margin was just fifteen seconds from Joey, and in third place was Iain Duffus (Yamaha) with James Courtney (Ducati) in fourth. Jim Moodie (Honda), John McGuinness (Honda) and Phillip McCallen (Yamaha) all retired with mechanical problems, but the newly allowed 1000cc machines proved their worth, while Ian Lougher was the first to finish on a 500cc two-stroke, coming in fifth.

David Jefferies finished the week as he started, winning both the Production and Senior TTs on the Friday of race week. Both victories were on Yamahas and he also achieved second place in Wednesday's Junior.

But with Jim Moodie winning the Junior for Honda and John McGuinness (Lightweight 250), Paul Williams (Lightweight 400), Ian Lougher (Ultra-Lightweight), Dave Molyneux (Sidecar A) and Rob Fisher (Sidecar B) adding to the marque's victories, the score at the end of the week was 'Honda 6, Yamaha 3' (with BMW taking the Singles race). On paper that looked a convincing victory for Honda, but, having taken wins in the big classes that really counted in publicity and sales terms, overall victory at the 1999 TT really went to Yamaha. Everyone knew that Honda poured money into its ultra-special 'works' RC45s, and they were also aware that the winning Yamaha R1 was still a comparatively new road-based model. It had already made a big impact in the sales charts and now it had done so on the track. *Motor Cycle News* pulled no punches with the post-TT headline, 'A £20,000 proddie Bike Shouldn't Humble £500,000 Honda RC45s. Someone Forgot to Tell David Jefferies'.

'DJ', as young Jefferies was frequently known, averaged 119.50mph (192.31km/h) for the four-lap production race on his standard R1 and 121.27mph (195.16km/h) on his

David Jefferies passes Ginger Hall on his V&M Yamaha. Note the way he has been grounding the belly-pan of the fairing.

Senior TT bike, which was tuned for the six-lap race by V&M Racing. In what was perhaps a tactical move by Honda in the Senior aimed at breaking the Yamaha of Jefferies, Jim Moodie set a new overall lap record of 124.45mph (200.28km/h) from a standing-start to lead at the end of the first lap. But Honda's tactics failed when, just 8 miles into his second lap, Moodie was forced to pull out of the race at Ballig Bridge with a shredded rear tyre that could not stand the pace.

It was an unusual year insomuch as Joey Dunlop (who rode most of his races at number 12 instead of his customary number 3) and Phillip McCallen left the 1999 TT without a win. Joey no doubt went off to ponder whether he would return in 2000, but Phillip declared that it had been his last TT. An all-or-nothing rider, he had moderated his style a little, but fears of further injury, the development of outside business interests and other factors brought his exciting Isle of Man racing career to an end. The TT itself finished the 1990s receiving the support of road-racing specialists and a good number of short-circuit stars who were happy to combine the two racing disciplines. David Jefferies sought to enhance his short-circuit career, and as a reward for his TT successes, later in 1999 Yamaha announced that they were providing him with 'works' R7s to race in the British Superbike Championship in 2000 in a V&M Racing team. The promise of top-quality machinery with support from Japan was a move that not only strengthened the rider's racing chances but also made him and his team a more attractive package for sponsors, who tended to give their support to those with the best chance of success.

Pirelli featured David Jefferies's 1999 TT victories in this advertisement for their tyres.

10 Racing into the New Millennium

With the arrival of the year 2000, the word millennium was much heard. In a world full of pundits looking at what life would bring in the years ahead, the TT received its share of consideration and predictions. Those whose interest lay solely in the racing turned their thoughts to who would be the TT's Millennium Man over the Mountain Course, while those taking a broader look wondered for how many years into the next millennium the TT would continue to be run. On the latter point there was optimism that it would survive to celebrate its centenary in 2007, but those of a pessimistic nature saw the date as a potential cut-off point. When quizzed, many were unclear why they felt that way, but then throughout its life the TT has been faced with people trying to write it off. The strange thing is that it was often enthusiasts for the meeting who showed the most pessimism.

What was good to see was that the Isle of Man authorities were full of enthusiasm for the future, and the Minister for Tourism, former MGP competitor David Cretney, flung his weight behind making the TT Festival ever more successful. Rider and spectator interest ran at high level for 2000, for the races paid excellent prize money and the ancillary entertainment was extended to include several nights of street parties. The result was that 721 entries were received from twenty countries for the ten races, and newspaper headlines reflected increased interest and growth in televised transmissions of races, saying: '500 million will tune in to watch the TT'. Top road-race specialists like Joey and Robert Dunlop, Jason Griffiths, Ian Lougher, James Courtney, Adrian Archibald, Gary Dynes and Richard Britton were joined by riders who also spent much time racing on the short circuits, including David Jefferies, John McGuinness, Michael Rutter and Iain Duffus. There were also young racers coming through like Richard 'Milky' Quayle and Ryan Farquhar, while quality Commonwealth riders Blair Degerholm, Shaun Harris, Bruce Anstey, Paul Williams and Brett Richmond promised to help make a bright start to the millennium. Even with such a wealth of racing talent in contention, however, no one was prepared to bet against 'King of the Roads' Joey Dunlop celebrating the millennium with another TT win.

Practice

First practice of 2000 was on the opening Saturday evening of the fortnight. It was a departure from the normal timetable that usually saw newcomers making their racing acquaintance with the course in the cold light of Monday's dawn, when damp roads and visibility problems were most likely to occur. This change enabled the organizers to reduce morning practice sessions to just two. Most welcomed the move, although others saw it as a step towards removing a unique aspect of the TT (and MGP) meetings for both riders and spectators. Among the newcomers in 2000 were the Argentinian riders Walter Cordoba and Eduardo 'David' Paredes, who had both followed the races for many years in press

Riders queue on the Glencrutchery Road, ready to start a practice session.

reports, satellite TV broadcasts and videos. They were now the first from their country to have the opportunity to fulfil their Island dreams and race over the Mountain Course.

Joey Dunlop was once again riding for Honda, but this year on an SP1 V-twin (and Fireblade transverse-four, if required), with John McGuinness also receiving full 'works' support and Iain Duffus, Jim Moodie and Adrian Archibald giving Honda strength in depth on new race versions of the Fireblade. These had received very little testing, but were built to show that Honda's top road bike could go head to head with Yamaha's R1. In response, Yamaha advertised that its highly successful YZF-R1 model was 'sharper, quicker and lighter' in its new form, and it had David Jefferies and Michael Rutter riding examples prepared by V&M Racing.

125mph Lap

Talk of a 125mph (201.17km/h) lap in 2000 almost became reality in practice week when David Jefferies (Yamaha) twice went over 124mph, and spice was added to the proceedings when Adrian Archibald (Honda) became the first to lap at over 120mph (193.12km/h)

Suzuki celebrated the fortieth anniversary of its first appearance at the TT with a tented display in Nobles Park, but gave little direct support to the racing.

231

on a 600. Practice times are of importance to riders and teams but they mean little to the organizers, who only recognize as official times set in a race and therefore worthy of entry in the record books. Joey Dunlop had a rather more troubled practice than Jefferies, having to cope with a stuttery power delivery and finding that the new SP1 did not handle well over the Mountain Course and that, as he described, 'it won't stop shaking its head'. Making a multitude of changes to fork and rear suspension settings, Joey and the other riders lost valuable practice time to bad weather in the latter part of the week, and the 48-year-old must have approached race day with reservations about fighting his Honda over 226 racing miles.

By the time of the last practice scheduled for Friday evening, many riders were desperately short of track-time to get their bikes set up properly, and some still needed to complete more laps in order to qualify to race. Travelling Marshals' reports of low cloud and generally wet conditions had the organizers in a quandary on that Friday evening, for while they wanted to run the session, the safety of competitors and the problems associated with using the rescue helicopter in poor visibility had them in two minds. Travelling Marshals were in almost constant motion on the course seeking information for Race Control. Eventually it was decided to allow the solos to run in an untimed session, with the sidecars to follow, but when it came to the sidecars' turn even lower cloud from the Gooseneck to Kate's Cottage put their session in jeopardy. In a compromise move, since the first Sidecar race was due to run the following day and competitors wanted to bed-in new tyres, chains, brake-pads and the like, the chairs were allowed to run at racing speed on the 23 miles from the start to Ramsey, where they were red-flagged. The forty or so outfits that had taken advantage of the restricted session were then escorted in convoy by Travelling Marshals across the misty Mountain and down to the finish at Douglas.

With Dave Molyneux away competing in the World Sidecar Cup, Rob Fisher started as favourite and duly won both Sidecar races with his Honda-powered outfit that had Rick Long in the chair. Although they averaged just

Joey Dunlop was extremely versatile, riding and winning on everything from 125s like the one shown here to Honda's biggest racers.

under 110mph in both races, Molyneux's race and lap records remained intact.

For all the talk of rising stars for a new millennium, it was a multi-TT winner of the old one, Joey Dunlop, who collected win number twenty-four in Saturday's opening race of 2000, the prestigious Formula I event. The next solo race, the Lightweight 250, was on Monday, and the winner was Joey Dunlop. Wednesday morning brought another solo race, and the winner was Joey Dunlop. Race week was only half over and Joey already had a hat-trick of wins, bringing his total to twenty-six. What a man!

On the Wednesday afternoon it was David Jefferies's turn to win a race for Yamaha by taking the Junior at a record race average speed of 119.13mph (191.72km/h), while Adrian Archibald (Honda) set the fastest lap at 121.15mph (194.97km/h). In abysmal weather on Friday morning, Jefferies rode to a second victory in a Production race shortened to two laps at 99.34mph (159.87km/h), with Manxman Richard 'Milky' Quayle second.

That poor weather caused postponement of the Senior to Saturday, when perfect racing conditions allowed the young Yorkshireman to also make it a hat-trick of wins for the week. It was a race in which he averaged 121.95mph (196.25km/h) and became the first to break the 125mph barrier with a record lap of 125.69mph (202.27km/h). His speed equated to a lap time of 18 minutes 0.6 seconds and was a pace that fellow hat-trick man and third-placed finisher Joey could not match even though he tried. Indeed, so hard did Joey try that he set his fastest ever lap of the TT course at 123.87mph (199.34km/h).

2001

Everyone knew that without Joey Dunlop's presence the TT of 2001 was going to be very different from those of the previous twenty-five years in which he rode and won, but it was not until the spring that people realized just how different a year it was going to be. Large

No More Joey

Joey Dunlop was an enigma to many throughout his career of twenty-six TT wins, five Formula I World Championships, and countless victories at the Ulster GP and NW200. An unassuming star who was the peoples' hero back home in Ireland, on both sides of the border, he was protective of his family. Throughout the 1990s he showed his concern for others by making many unpublicized trips to eastern Europe taking essential supplies to the needy. Honoured with an MBE and an OBE for his services to motorcycling and charities, he was a respected star on the world motorcycling scene who just loved to race motorcycles. A month after the TT he packed a couple of bikes in a van and set off to Estonia to take part in a small race meeting. There, on a rain-soaked track wending its way through a forest, he left the road on his 125, hit a tree and was killed.

It is doubtful if the world of motorcycling had ever been so united in sorrow as it was after Joey's death, and an estimated 50,000 people turned out for his funeral in Ballymoney. The MGP took place on the island some six weeks after his death and, in an unforgettable tribute, five thousand motorcycle-mounted fans did a lap of the closed roads of the Mountain Course in his honour. Bikes of every size and description travelled at ordinary speeds over the same roads that he had covered so many times while racing to twenty-six wins – and with only one small spill.

This memorial to Joey Dunlop is located adjacent to the former Murray's Motorcycle Museum near the Bungalow. Astride a Honda, Joey looks over the Mountain Course and up to Hailwood's Height, named after another multi-TT winner who met an early death away from the Island, Mike Hailwood.

parts of Britain were ravaged by a foot and mouth epidemic and the Isle of Man, with its large farming community, was desperate to prevent the disease spreading to its shores. After much consultation, the decision was taken to cancel the TT meeting. It was a hard one to make, but the prospect of 40,000 visitors being dispersed for a fortnight of racing and practice around the fields that bounded the course was a risk that was too great to take.

Ordinary visits were allowed and some 12,000 race fans came for a non-racing holiday, but the absence of a proper fortnight of racing brought home to local businesses just what it meant to miss out on their busiest two weeks of the year. The Manx Government felt it necessary to introduce compensation schemes for those who had suffered loss, and it was noticeable that among those in the queue for a handout were the island's biggest hotels.

But not all Isle of Man businesses seek just to take from the TT. Several sponsor individual races and some sponsor riders, either directly with cash and machinery, or indirectly through giving free accommodation in hotels or private houses. A joint sponsorship deal that caught the eye with bikes and riders turned out in corporate colours was that between Lloyds TSB Bank (Isle of Man) and the enthusiastic Alan and Mike Kelly of Mannin Collections. It is not every bank that sponsors a TT rider, but as Andy Webb, Island Director for Lloyds TSB, explained: 'To outsiders, it may seem strange to see a bank sponsoring motorcycle racing. The reality is that racing is at the heart of the Manx community. The TT is the most famous road race in the world, drawing in thousands of visitors and creating many spin-offs for local business.' Lloyds TSB was a relative newcomer to racing, but Mannin Collections had been active sponsors since 1988.

Norman Kneen, one of the riders sponsored by Lloyds TSB and Mannin Collections, shows his sponsors' names and colours to good effect as he rounds Governor's Bridge.

Duke's
The series of bends at the 32nd Milestone are now called Duke's after the legendary Geoff Duke, who particularly relished riding them. His TT heyday was in the 1950s, when he was even known by the man in the street for his exploits on the Island and at World Championship level. He then moved to live on the Island, developed many business interests there and was always prepared to help promote the TT if asked.

Almost fifty years after his TT successes over the Mountain Course, Geoff Duke was finally honoured for these and his many other efforts to publicize the Isle of Man's name worldwide.

A great ambassador for the TT, Geoff Duke speaks at another function to promote the event.

TT Return

Two years is a very long time in racing: riders and teams change each season, as do their plans and the targets for their efforts. Rumours were rife on the approach to the 2002 TT about who would ride what, although the organizers were pleased to have an early indication that Honda and Yamaha would have 'works' entries. Indeed, Mark Davies, boss of Honda UK, said: 'The TT is part of our heritage. As long as the event is here, we'll be here too.'

One of the strongest rumours was that eleven-times TT winner Phillip McCallen was planning a return, perhaps on an RC45 bored to 1000cc. That rumour came to nothing, as did talk of Jim Moodie riding a Suzuki; instead he signed to ride for Yamaha via V&M Racing. It was V&M who featured in the really big pre-TT news when David Jefferies decided to switch from their Yamahas and join Ian Lougher in riding Suzukis for Temple Auto Salvage (TAS), which was receiving strong support from Suzuki. The previously dominant Yamaha R1 had set new design and performance standards, but Honda and Suzuki had not sat back, for with the R1's race successes they had seen the sale of Yamaha's road

bikes soar at the expense of their own sales. Honda came to the 2002 TT with lightened and more powerful CBR900RR Fireblades for John McGuinness and Adrian Archibald, while Suzuki's GSX-R1000 had also been much improved and was known to be a flier. As riders changed their allegiance (in Jefferies's case less than three months before), a few toes were inevitably trodden upon, and tensions were created that added to the strong spirit of competition that accompanies every TT.

Many technical developments in the world of motorcycling are pushed along by the efforts of manufacturers seeking to steal a march on the opposition in the field of racing. The 180bhp 'works' Formula I bikes that came to the 2002 TT were capable of giving their output at up to 12,500rpm for much of the race. There had been moves towards fuel-injection, re-mappable ignition systems, slipper clutches, electronic gearshift, quickly detachable wheels (to aid mid-race tyre changes), ever more refined suspension front and rear, much enlarged radiators and a general striving for lightness. The bike manufacturers' efforts were supported by increasingly specialized tyres, as the

David Jefferies reminds spectators just how close they can get to the action as he uses almost all of the road on his TAS Suzuki at the Gooseneck in 2002.

tyre companies tried to build stability, consistency and durability into their products.

The greater the scope for tuning and adjustment in almost every aspect of the bike, including ignition, suspension, brakes and tyres, the harder it became for riders to set the bikes up to optimum levels in the limited practice time available. They needed time on the course to do so and that was often in short supply, particularly if riders were running in several classes. The variations in Manx weather did not help with fine tuning, because changes in wind direction, wet and dry roads, and even temperature variations (particularly for two-strokes) could affect the settings required.

Welcome Back

Island businesses were pleased to see the races back and visitor levels matched those of earlier

years. No one in the world of motorcycling had sought the cancellation of the 2001 TT, but there is no doubt that the break in the long tradition of racing over the Mountain Course brought home to many people just how important the TT Festival was to them. The organizers gave a substantial boost to the prize money for each race and then added a one-off, welcome-back bonus of £5,000 to each winner, which meant that a start-to-finish leader of the Formula I race would collect a huge £25,000, as would the winner of the Senior. With a newly created Joey Dunlop Trophy and £10,000 going to the man with the fastest combined times in the Formula I and Senior races, there was a lot of money for the fast men to ride for. Promising to be one of the best TTs ever, the rewards available at the 2002 event must have caught the attention of top riders and sponsors who did not normally

The cover of the TT programme for 2002 announced the return of the world's greatest road race.

contest the event, and the organizers hoped it would attract more of them to race on the Island in the future.

The racing of production-based machines was now a dominant aspect of the TT races. Pure racing machinery could only be found with 125 and 250cc machines and the number of 250 entries had been falling. Adjusting the race programme to suit, the Lightweight 250s lost their separate race status and ran at the same time as the Junior race. Perhaps as a response to that treatment the entry of 250s dropped from more than forty in 2000 to just twenty. The gap created in the programme was filled with a Production race for 600s run over three laps on Friday morning before the Senior. Another change saw the Singles race dropped and the Lightweight 400 race run with the Ultra-Lightweight 125s.

While racing in a TT normally served to bar a competitor from riding in the MGP, an exception to this rule was made in respect of the Production races, where they could ride without losing MGP eligibility. The 2002 TT already had entries from twenty-two former MGP winners, including 2000 Senior victor Ryan Farquhar, and they were joined by a string of aspirants to an MGP win who felt that a Proddie ride in the TT would help with their course-learning for the September races.

New for 2002 was the introduction of random breathalyser tests for riders. It was perhaps fortunate that they did not have breathalysers at the first TT, for after his win in 1907 Rem Fowler told how 'twenty minutes before the start a friend of mine fetched me a glassful of neat brandy tempered with a little milk. This had the desired effect and I set off full of hope.' There were also trials of machine-mounted transponders for timing purposes in several classes and, in a move aimed at improving safety, new types of 'Air-fence' barriers were in position at selected locations. As a tribute to Joey Dunlop, riding number 3 was not used in the solo races except in the Senior, where numbers were allocated on the basis of times and not by seeding. Aside from the professional racing, track days were introduced at Jurby airfield for those who wanted to emulate the stars, several of whom were expected to visit and give advice. Among race sponsors in 2002 were Duke, the Hilton Hotel and Casino, Scottish International, IOM Steam Packet and Standard Bank Offshore.

An Early Start

Mindful of the time they lost from the 2000 practice period due to bad weather, and the need for newcomers to be allowed adequate time on the course (plus the fact that everyone had been away for two years), the organizers brought forward the start of practice to an early session on Saturday morning. The weather greeted this move with strong rain and wind, causing a delayed start and convincing the star names to stay in bed. Although good weather allowed fast times on Monday evening, the weather was poor for much of practice week and in two of the poor-weather sessions the fastest sidecar clocked a better time than the fastest solo, albeit at 97mph. That was another first at the TT.

Bad weather usually involved more activity

for the eight-man Travelling Marshal team mounted on their yellow and black Fireblades, supplied by courtesy of Honda and looked after by the local Honda agent, Tommy Leonard Motorcycles. Customary pre-practice and pre-race checks of conditions increase in poor weather and radio messages fly between the team and Race Control as the Clerk of the Course tries to get a course-wide view of road and weather conditions.

Why so Named?

Joey's
Although it made no actual difference to the course as ridden, riders and spectators had to get used to a new name for the 26th Milestone, when it was renamed Joey's in 2002.

In memory of a great rider and, fittingly, in recognition of his twenty-six TT victories, this nameboard carries no surname, but the whole of the motorcycle racing world knows that it acknowledges the achievements over the Mountain Course of William Joseph Dunlop, known to one and all as Joey.

Adrian Archibald was on a Honda 954 Fireblade in 2002, but could not match his earlier performances.

Man or Machine?

David Jefferies came to the 2002 TT having collected a hat-trick of wins in 2000 on a Yamaha and then proceeded to do the same thing again on the TAS Suzuki. In circumstances where a rider changes machines and continues to win races, there is a tendency to give most of the credit to the rider, but team-mate Ian Lougher backed Jefferies' performances with a win, three second places and a fourth on similar Suzuki machinery (and a 125 win on a Honda), so perhaps this was an instance where the credit was shared by man and machine.

Jefferies's wins came in the Formula I, Production 1000 and Senior races, and all were achieved in relatively comfortable and con-

trolled fashion. In the Senior he dipped well below the eighteen-minute lap barrier, setting a fastest time of 17 minutes 47 seconds, a record speed of 127.29mph (204.85km/h). His rapid progress seemed to spur second place Ian Lougher (TAS Suzuki) and third place John McGuinness (Honda) to set their own fastest ever times in the Senior.

Yamaha achieved victory in the Junior with Jim Moodie and in the Lightweight 250 with New Zealander Bruce Anstey. As Bruce's mother was Manx, his performance received plenty of coverage in the Isle of Man's newspapers.

A performance that received even more local coverage was that of true Manxman

Bruce Anstey was a busy man at the 2002 TT, riding bikes from 125 to 1000cc and winning the Lightweight 250 race.

Richard 'Milky' Quayle in winning the Light-weight 400 race. A popular and engaging racer who made his way up through the ranks of MGP winners, his words when interviewed on the top step of the rostrum were: 'I never wanted to be a brain surgeon. All I wanted to do was win a TT'. After nearly nine years of racing and with more than his share of misfortune, 'Milky' achieved what many strive for but relatively few achieve. Leading from start to finish on his Honda, he won by twenty-two seconds.

The Blue Riband?

For more than fifty years the Senior TT was the most important race of the meeting. It was given the prime Friday spot on the race programme, and race week customarily moved towards its climax with the running of what was known as the Blue Riband. But the growth in importance of Formula I racing through the 1970s and 1980s, allied to the loss of specialist Grand Prix-type machines from the Senior, saw a reduction in its importance and it lost its prime position, being pushed about to suit the organizers' convenience. Through the 1990s it recovered some of its prestige and its end of week position, but, with many riders wanting to get away to busy race programmes at the weekend, there was a tendency for some to leave early and miss the Senior, making the number of riders in the Friday race often less than that shown in the spectators' programmes.

With the switch to Senior entry being determined by the fastest eighty qualifiers rather than by the normal pre-race method of entry, the situation regarding non-starters grew noticeably worse. It was understandable that at the end of a fortnight's racing there would be riders missing through injury or major machine failure. In addition, however, now that fast MGP-type runners were allowed to compete in the Production TTs, it was inevitable that about a dozen of them appeared among the fastest eighty qualifiers for the 2002

Senior: but, of course, none turned up to race in the Senior because it would have ruled them out of the MGP. While the organizers tried to counter the loss by hastily extending invitations to a few of the less speedy qualifiers, it created a chaotic and embarrassing situation for commentators like Geoff Cannell who had to announce a long list of non-starters and alterations to entries. In 2002 only fifty-one started and, with twenty-one retiring, a field of thirty riders was not enough to hold spectators' attention or command the title of Blue Riband, notwithstanding the record-breaking speeds achieved by the men at the head of the field. It was a problem needing a speedy solution, for quantity as well as quality is needed for a TT race to be successful in the eyes of those watching.

While most people knew that competing at the TT (Production classes excepted) made a rider ineligible to take part in the MGP, there was another twist to the ruling. For twenty years the MGP meeting had included hugely popular Classic races for the machines of yesteryear. The regulations for those Classic races did allow TT competitors to take part: Bob Heath did so with particular success in the 1980s and early 1990s, Phil Read and Nick Jefferies were slightly less successful. Even Joey Dunlop had a go on an Aermacchi. At the 2002 MGP, 'Milky' Quayle, winner of that year's Lightweight 400 TT, contested the Senior Classic MGP and came home victorious on Andy Molnar's Manx Norton. In doing so he achieved a unique 'double'.

A Balancing Act

Putting aside the problems over entries in the previous year's Senior race, in 2003 the TT meeting was in a reasonable state of balance. Its excellent prize money ensured that all the top road racers competed, along with good men from circuit racing who could adapt to the roads. Manufacturer support was particularly good for 2003 and promising young riders continued to enter. The problems associated with getting to and from the Island (involving the cost and choice of dates) and the availability of accommodation had not gone away. They remained as problems, but nothing is perfect! Overall the organizers had a successful meeting that justified the money invested in it, bringing the Isle of Man massive publicity for its name via satellite TV transmissions of race highlights, as well as the income the racing brought to the Island.

The festival aspect of the fortnight continued to grow with new events. The commercially run track days were augmented by Honda offering off-road experience on a fleet of twenty-five machines. Then the growing sport of Super Moto featured in a meeting at Jurby, while the established Moto Cross, Beach Cross, sprints, grass track and trials events continued to be run, along with an occasional hill climb. One-make clubs all had their special meets, a vintage rally had a week of events, while bungee-jumping and special 'rides' went on round-the-clock on Douglas Promenade, adding to the regular evening wheelie and burn-out sessions. Rather more organized were the appearance of bands and groups, although there were mixed receptions to the artists who were booked. Putting on a race meeting to suit all tastes created difficulties, but they paled into insignificance compared to the difficulty (impossibility?) of choosing groups that would suit everyone, for it was most certainly an area where one man's meat was another's poison.

Something that occurred every year and was not welcomed by the Manx authorities and public was the considerable increase in road accidents that occurred over the TT period. No one wanted to see visitors damaging themselves, particularly as their 'accidents' so often involved innocent members of the Manx public trying to go about their normal lives. Road safety was a message that the authorities tried to get across, but it was a difficult task to convey during a period of high-octane excitement for 12,000 motorcyclists riding roads that an hour before might

No one could accuse the Island's road safety authority of not trying to catch the attention of TT visitors!

have been a race track, and over which there was no overall speed limit.

Timekeeping

Since the very first TT the progress of riders in a race had been timed with hand-operated watches. The team of timekeepers occupied a position overlooking the start and finish line and, assisted by spotters whose job was to identify and warn them of riders approaching along the Glencrutchery Road, they recorded every rider at the start and finish of each lap of practising and racing. Times were noted on official timekeeping sheets and speeds were derived from substantial reference books in which figures for speed against time were all pre-calculated. The figures recorded were

Timekeeping boxes opposite the grandstand.

passed to time auditors who double-checked that all was correct.

By a system that involved the use of slips of paper, clothes pegs, drainpipes and Scout messengers, the times were passed to the men who maintained the scoreboard opposite the grandstand. They then painted each rider's lap times against their numbers, for spectators and pit attendants to see. In the early days of public address and broadcasting, times were also passed by telephone for onward broadcast.

After the experiments of 2002 involving the use of machine-mounted transponders, the organizers decided that for 2003 the use of transponders would be mandatory and would be used to determine the race results, although manual timekeeping was retained for the year – just in case! Timing points at Glen Helen, Ballaugh, Ramsey Hairpin, the Bungalow and Cronk ny Mona allowed for a major improvement in the information that was automatically (and immediately) fed back to computer screens in the timekeepers' and commentary boxes, thus permitting the progress of a race to be more closely monitored and the information quickly made public via the commentaries from Radio TT. Whatever the new system did for the technicalities of timekeeping, there was no doubt that it created added

excitement for spectators to receive up-to-the-moment time gaps between riders contesting the lead. There were many benefits from the new system. For example, in a six-lap race commentators could see from the early laps if an individual rider vying for the lead made or lost ground over rivals over different sections of the course, and this allowed them to make more informed comment about what was likely to happen in the closing stages of a race. For rider support crews the greater frequency of timing information also allowed for more accurate signals to be passed to their riders although, inevitably, the lesser lights got rather fewer radio mentions than the stars.

Entries

When entries closed for 2003 all classes were oversubscribed and 319 individual competitors (169 solo and 75 sidecar crews) were accepted to race. For some reason the TT had gained popularity with French competitors and there were ten solo and six sidecar outfits from France, plus entries from nineteen other countries.

Formerly classed as Lightweight 250s with their own race (even if latterly run alongside the Juniors), the 250s lost their separate race

A member of Mark Parrett's support crew holds out the signal board with his race position for Mark to read as he slows for Sulby Bridge.

To help pay for their racing efforts, French sidecar crew François and Sylvie LeBlond sold wine with a label that featured them leaping Ballaugh Bridge.

Sharing a paddock campsite wih the LeBlonds was the Voxan équipe, whose booming French-made V-twin offered spectators a welcome change in exhaust note from the dominant transverse fours.

status in 2003. They were allowed to enter the Junior (600) race and there was an award for the best 250, but it was one more step towards the axing of this once so popular class.

Manufacturer Support

Mention was made earlier of how manufacturer support for the TT fluctuated down the years, but 2003 looked like being a good one with five concerns involved. Since its return to Island racing in 1977 Honda had been present every year and achieved considerable success, although in the last few years it had lost its number one spot to Yamaha and Suzuki in the all-important big classes. In 2003 it concentrated its TT effort on the second-fastest man around the Mountain Course, Ian Lougher, providing him with the 2002 World Super Bike-winning SP2 of Colin Edwards. There were considerable advances over the SP1 that Joey Dunlop rode in 2000, with revised fuel-injection, a slightly less rigid frame giving better traction and handling, plus the major engine changes introduced in the middle of the 2001 World Super Bike season. Not that the SP2 worked straight from the crate on the Island. No one really expected it to, but after tracing initial problems with stability at high speed to the tyres, Ian soon felt confident that he had a good set-up for the Formula I and Senior races on the 180bhp V-twin, which appeared in red and black Honda Britain livery.

Honda also provided limited support to Dave Molyneux with engines for his self-built DMR outfit. Dave came to the 2003 TT not having ridden since the previous October, for he had been too busy building outfits for his closest rivals.

Yamaha entered Jason Griffiths on an R1 built initially to British Superbike specification, but with slightly lower compression, 24-litre fuel tank, stronger fairing and strengthened bracketry to take the pounding it was to receive on the roads. The starter motor was retained to save precious seconds on getting away after pit stops.

Suzuki support went to David Jefferies and Adrian Archibald under the TAS banner. Although David was a favourite for TT wins in 2003, based upon past performances, he was slightly off the pace at the NW200 a couple of weeks before and admitted his concern that Adrian would press him hard. The GSX-R1000s were said to have about 8bhp more than in 2002 and came with an improved chassis.

Ducati representatives were John McGuinness and Michael Rutter, but pre-TT problems in British Superbike rounds saw Michael's entry withdrawn by Team Renegade, losing him the chance of what might have been a couple of good pay-days. Apart from a Singles win at the TT on a BMW, victory in the big classes had eluded John McGuinness although, as third fastest lapper on the Island, he had six podium places to his name. Relatively inexperienced at riding the Ducati, John was nevertheless confident of doing well at the TT, saying of his 185bhp V-twin: 'Compared to the Fireblade I rode last year [second in Formula I, third in Senior] the Ducati stops, turns and holds a line much better'. With three factory engines and a 999R for the Production race, John was entered under Paul Bird's MonsterMob banner. The Ducati came with a reputation as being difficult to start, and the team had permission to use a portable roller starter after pit stops, but it was a process estimated to add 5 seconds to each restart.

Nearly three decades after it last made a full 'works' effort at the TT, Triumph entered three of its 140bhp Daytona models in the Junior and Production 600 races, to be ridden by Jim Moodie, Bruce Anstey and John McGuinness.

The production heritage of all these machines was plain to see, but the days when lightly modifying production machines allowed manufacturers to go racing at far lower cost than with special GP models was now past. Wheels, forks, rear-suspension, brakes, tyre, radiators, fairings, exhausts and engine

John McGuinness takes a careful line through a glistening Ballacraine during an evening practice for the 2003 TT. The setting sun in his eyes also makes John cautious with his Triumph Daytona.

internals (where permitted) were all special racing components, meaning that the best bikes were now very expensive to build and maintain.

Black Thursday

David Jefferies was relatively slow in early practice before quickening his pace, while team-mate Adrian Archibald was fast from the outset. Was 'DJ' beatable? That question was on quite a few people's lips, but it was one that was not to be answered. The long Thursday afternoon practice session is broadcast on Radio TT and the expectations of listeners were raised when the commentator described TAS Suzuki team-mates Archibald and Jefferies as streaking past the grandstand at 170mph almost nose to tail. Those watching at Quarter Bridge, Braddan Bridge and Union Mills thrilled to see the two aces pushing each other hard, while those further on at Greeba, Ballacraine and Glen Helen waited in anticipation.

But it was just Adrian Archibald who passed those spots – there was no David Jefferies. Had he encountered a mechanical problem and stopped? The sense of worry for spectators increased as the flow of passing riders slowed to a trickle and then ceased. Clearly there had been a major incident that brought riders to a halt. Although nobody wanted it to be so, most felt that it involved David Jefferies. Riders did eventually start to come past again, but no one could concentrate on what was happening on the course. Radio TT's commentators were still broadcasting, but were telling spectators everything except the one fact they wanted to know – what had happened to 'DJ'? The answer was that he had fallen with his machine at the ultra-fast left-hand kink in the centre of Crosby. Man and machine struck a wall and the finest TT rider of his generation was killed.

Other competitors, many of whom were close friends of the fallen rider, were halted by the incident and were witness to the aftermath. All were deeply shocked, as were the thousands of race followers who eventually came to hear what had happened. In a pre-race interview in *Motor Cycle News*, David Jefferies was quoted as saying, 'At the TT I ride well within my limits. If you get it wrong you either hit a stone wall. . .'. These were the words of a man who knew the dangers and was prepared to take them on. With nine TT victories to his name, made up of three hat-tricks in 1999, 2000 and 2002, he was the outstanding talent from the three generations of the Jefferies family that had contested the TT and MGP from the early 1930s and been ever-present as competitors or on the organizational side through the efforts of grandfather Alan (second place in 1947 Clubman's TT), father Tony (three times a TT winner) and uncle Nick (one TT win and many podium finishes).

Suzuki Victory

It was a chastened TAS Suzuki team that decided it would continue to race and so went about its preparations for the opening Formula I race. Boss Phillip Neill and his father Hector's involvement with racing went back a long way (to include 1983 TT winner for Suzuki, Norman Brown). The team had experienced tragedy before and knew that it was inseparable from the racing game.

When the riders came to the line for Satur-day's Formula I race there must have been thoughts of David Jefferies in the minds of top runners such as Archibald, Lougher, McGuinness and Griffiths, all of whom had counted him as a friend. A delay of one hour in the start-time may have allowed some low-lying fog to clear, but it did nothing to help clear the minds of riders who were trying to get into the mood to race. Showing the remarkable resilience required of all front-line road racers who have to overcome personal tragedy, injury and machine troubles that would halt lesser men, Adrian Archibald (TAS Suzuki) rode to Formula I victory, finishing more than one minute ahead of Ian Lougher (Honda), John McGuinness (Ducati) and Jason Griffiths (Yamaha). It was Adrian's first TT win, but one that was achieved in sad circumstances. It came as no surprise that he dedicated his victory to David Jefferies, and that the victor's champagne stayed corked after the post-race garlanding ceremony.

Often late in putting his TT arrangements together from distant New Zealand, experienced runner Shaun Harris took his first TT victory when he rode a Suzuki home in the Production 1000 race, a feat he repeated for Suzuki in the Production 600

In a first at the TT, Adrian Archibald contested the Senior TT under number 0.

event that was curtailed due to poor weather on the Friday.

For the Senior, which was delayed until Saturday, then further delayed during the day and reduced to four laps, Adrian Archibald was allocated riding number 1. However, as numbers were allocated on the basis of times set in practice, and as he had not quite matched the late David Jefferies's time, Adrian obtained approval to ride as number 0.

It was the top 'works' runners who headed the Senior field when the race eventually got under way: at the end of the first lap Archibald led by just 3.15 seconds from McGuinness, with Lougher close behind in third. Things remained close on the second lap when Archibald set the fastest lap of the race at 126.82mph (204.09km/h), even though it was one that involved slowing down to enter the pits for refuelling. He left 15 seconds ahead of McGuinness (might that have been 10 seconds if John had not needed to use the roller to

restart his Ducati?) and built on his lead to win by 20.8 seconds from McGuinness, with Lougher third on his Honda and Griffiths fourth on the Yamaha. As usual, there was a prize of £1,500 for the best 750cc finisher in the Senior race, and it went to Mark Parrett (Kawasaki).

In what had been an emotional rollercoaster of a fortnight for all at the 2003 TT, Bruce Anstey produced the surprise of the week by racing a Triumph Daytona to victory in the Junior race, so giving British fans something to cheer. Patriotically finished with the Union flag on the nose of its fairing, the Triumph came home ten seconds in front of Ian Lougher (Honda), Adrian Archibald (Suzuki) and Ryan Farquhar (Kawasaki), so beating the best that Japan had to offer. Anstey's bike must have been a real flier, for fellow Triumph runners Jim Moodie and John McGuinness (no mean runners) came home in ninth and tenth places.

In the Lap of Honour at the 2003 TT the letter 'H' stood for Hailwood, for Mike Hailwood's son David did a lap on a Triumph Trident.

Richard 'Milky' Quayle rode this Suzuki with support from Padgetts, whose name has been associated with the TT for more than thirty years.

At a time when manufacturers acknowledged that race successes sold motorcycles, Honda had to be content with wins by Chris Palmer in the Lightweight 125 and Dave Molyneux in Sidecar Race B. It was not what they were used to at the Isle of Man races.

A Price to be Paid

In a very macabre outlook that Island racing induces, some riders believe that the TT course demands payment in tribute of riders' lives each year, and when that happens they breathe more easily. The death of a star like David Jefferies was bound to make front-page news, but the death of Peter Jarmann at the 2003 TT attracted far less publicity. However, Peter was well known to real fans of the TT as one of the regular stalwarts who made up the numbers in the races, and so kept them interesting after all the stars had flashed past at the head of the field. He came from Switzerland to race in the TT each year (and often in the Southern 100 and Classic MGP events) and on the Monday of race week he rode to ninth place in the Lightweight 400 race. Such was his enthusiasm for all things connected with the TT that, a few hours later, he wheeled out a Classic Bultaco to ride in the Lap of Honour that took place after the Production 1000 race. Less than half a mile from the start the Bultaco seized; Peter was thrown against an unyielding wall on Bray Hill and was killed. Once again motorcycle racing and the Mountain Course had conspired to show its cruel side.

One man who managed to cheat death in 2003 was 'Milky' Quayle. Coming over the rise at Ballaspur on his big Suzuki, he touched his left shoulder against the rock-face. Man and machine were projected diagonally across the road to hit the opposite bank and he was sent cart-wheeling down the road. Seriously injured, 'Milky' decided that he had been one of the lucky ones and, putting his family first, he retired from racing. He remains committed to the sport that allowed him to achieve his life's ambition and win a TT, and today he fulfils a role in promoting the event and attracting new riders.

Tragedy struck away from the TT later in 2003 when Steve Hislop, eleven-times winner on the island, was killed in a helicopter crash shortly after winning the British Superbike title.

Promotion

One of the many ways in which the TT is promoted is via the power of the press. Although it could sometimes, with justification, be critical of the event, Britain's mass-circulation *Motor Cycle News* always gave the races good coverage. During the run-up to the 2004 event former editor Adam Duckworth explained how, 'The TT is brilliant, frightening, fun, dangerous, anachronistic and, for that reason alone, a jewel that we must never lose sight of', while current editor Marc Potter visited after an absence of seven years and felt things were better than ever. There was little doubt that the unique character of the event served as a magnet to attract people from all over the world, for all realized that nowhere else could they see such a 'festival' of motorcycling, dominated by racing over the famous Mountain Course. It was a high-speed fortnight for many visitors, but one event in 2004 that actually ran at controlled speed was an organized Lap of Honour in memory of David Jefferies by 3,500 bikers riding the 37¾ miles in front of thousands of spectators on Mad Sunday. It was an impressive tribute and many of those riding and watching sported 'DJ' tribute T-shirts, bought in aid of the David Jefferies Memorial Fund.

Organization

Since 1907 the TT meeting had been organized by the ACU. Every year its senior officials and selected voluntary helpers packed their bags for a fortnight away, made passage to the Isle of Man, checked in at the best hotels and enjoyed an all-expenses-paid holiday. Well, that was how it was seen by the countless number of Manx enthusiasts who also put in a fortnight's effort (three weeks in the very early days) in support of the racing, with many also fitting in their normal day's work.

While many genuine friendships formed between ACU and Manx helpers, there were also frequent tensions between the two tiers of organization. In the 1920s the ACU threat-

ened to take the races away from the Isle of Man if it did not contribute towards the direct running costs of the event. The Island has always met the many indirect costs of the TT, such as course improvements, and eventually did start to make direct contributions, initially to meet the expenses of riders coming from overseas. This grew until it reached the present-day position where it meets almost the whole cost of the event. As its financial contribution increased, so the Island demanded a greater say in the running of the races.

By the new millennium the ACU had transferred almost complete control of the running of short-circuit meetings in the UK to promoters, leaving just the TT to be run

A significant moment in TT history: Jim Parker of the ACU (seated left), David Cretney, representing the Isle of Man Government (seated right), David Mylchreest of the Manx Motor Cycle Club (standing left) and Ted Bartlett of the ACU (standing right) sign documentation that transferred the running of the TT to the Island.

from its Rugby headquarters and by the staff it moved to the Island for TT fortnight. Down the years there had always been low-key agitation for the Island to take over the running of the event, for the Manx Motor Cycle Club was experienced in running the Manx Grand Prix over the same Mountain Course and had a suitable organization in place. It was a change that could not be achieved without the agreement of the ACU, but after much discussion the major controlling body of UK motorcycle sport eventually granted a licence to the Isle of Man Government to run the TT for twenty years, and the Government appointed the Manx MCC to organize and run the event on its behalf from 2004.

No one knows exactly how many people are required to run the TT. The programme sold to spectators lists some 150 officials, ranging from the race management team, through the Clerk of the Course, scrutineering team, start/finishing line team (numbering seventeen people), Travelling Marshals, timekeepers and scoreboard staff, to the Press Officer, Incident Officers, Medical Officer,

Welfare Officer and Chief Environmental Officer. They are the tip of the iceberg, for on race days the aim is to have 1,200 marshals dispersed around the course, plus doctors, paramedics, rescue helicopters, recovery vehicles and Civil Defence radio-communications staff, all on active duty; other support services, such as hospital staff, road-sweepers and highway workers, are on standby should they be needed. Every race has a scheduled 180-minute count-down to the start. Taking a round figure of 1,500 support personnel on duty it means that, before a race with an entry of seventy-five, an average of twenty people move into place to support each rider.

'New' Organization

The average spectator was little affected by the appointment of the Manx MCC as new organizers for the 2004 TT, although, in a couple of controversial moves, morning practice was abandoned and the Formula I and Senior races reduced to four laps distance. As with many changes at the TT it was surprisingly difficult

Jason Griffiths came to the TT from the MGP and has achieved many podium places, latterly for Yamaha.

to discover the real reason for them. In respect of dropping the long tradition of morning practice, there were mutterings about not being able to get enough marshals on the course so early in the day (marshals have been used as a scapegoat for a number of the TT's ills), while from close to the organization came the guarded revelation that riders were not happy with modern-day tyres in the sometimes patchy damp conditions that could be found at an early hour. In reducing the meeting's two premier events from six to four laps the organization justified its action by claiming statistics showed that more accidents happened towards the end of a long race. It was a change opposed by many riders and spectators.

Racegoers noticed an ever-growing attitude of caution exercised by the organizers in respect of the conditions in which riders were allowed to race. This was shown in more frequent delays to the start of races, as they waited for roads to dry and mist to lift, while for 2004 they introduced an additional warning signal comprising a white flag with a red diagonal cross to indicate 'lack of adhesion other than by oil'. Allied to the organizers' caution came increased influence from the Health and Safety Executive on aspects such as refuelling and spectator locations around the course. The latter caused much concern, particularly to experienced fans who had watched from a particular spot for perhaps twenty years, only to be told that it was no longer safe to do so. The TT was changing and some riders and spectators did not like what was happening.

The Entries

With a total of 731 race entries, including thirty-seven foreign and fourteen female riders, the 2004 TT welcomed back ten former winners and many regular leaderboard names who were still looking for a win, among them being Jason Griffiths, Ryan Farquhar, Richard Britton, Nigel Davies, Gordon Blackley, Steve Linsdell, Jun Maeda from Japan, and from the Isle of Man Gary Carswell and Paul Hunt on solos, plus sidecar duo Nick Crowe and Darren Hope. A surprise late entry among the sidecars was 2002 World Champion Klaus Klaffenbock, with Christian Parzer in the chair.

John McGuinness said all the right things about his R1 to please Yamaha's public relations people, including 'it's the only bike I've ever hit jumps on nailed, and it lands dead straight'. Vic Bates was at the top of Crosby Hill to capture John and the Yamaha 'nailed' at over 160mph – but far from straight!

Honda had lost its previous dominance in the larger categories of the road-bike market as Suzuki, Yamaha and Ducati wooed the buying public with impressive performances at the TT and in World and British Superbike racing. In a move that probably would not have impressed Soichiro Honda, the response of the company's British arm was again to provide support for just Ian Lougher, doing it via Mark Johns Motors. It claimed it was too busy to support the TT fully, although some watchers felt that it was an attempted snub to the meeting as changes it had asked for had not been implemented. Cynics contented themselves by pointing out that Honda had not done much winning on the Island of late. Kawasaki had a presence with Ryan Farquhar riding under the Winston McAdoo banner, and there were many who thought that Ryan was overdue a TT win.

Yamaha supported Jason Griffiths and John McGuinness and, showing that the Japanese manufacturers still rated the TT highly, UK Sales and Marketing Director Andy Smith said how Yamaha Japan first presented the R1 to him with the words 'Think of it as an Isle of Man bike'. The R1 certainly proved itself as a TT winner, although a little more thought from Japan in the design stages as to its fuel consumption while racing in the Production classes might have seen it fitted with something larger than its standard 18-litre fuel tank. Riders knew that getting two laps from a tankful was touch and go, and the way the fuel warning light always blinked ominously on the descent of the Mountain on the second lap was a psychological barrier to keeping the throttle to the stop.

Having read about the TT in Argentina in their younger days, Walter Cordoba and David Paredes were now TT regulars and were themselves making headlines in the sports pages of their home newspapers. Back on the Island for another year of racing, neither expected to win a TT but both were close to achieving 110mph laps with their 600 Hondas in the Junior.

Judging that the experiment with the Senior TT of the past few years of inviting the fastest eighty qualifiers in practice to contest the Friday race was a failure, the organizers reverted to the traditional method of taking pre-race entries, and eighty-two were received.

The Racing

Without a regular ride on the short circuits in early 2004, John McGuinness came to the TT supported by Yamaha with R1 machinery. In what was to prove a very successful visit, John had a secret weapon in his race team in the shape of non-riding Jim Moodie. Admitting to being 'a bit laid-back, a bit lazy, a bit last minute', John found the well-organized and vastly experienced TT-winning Scot to be just the person to do a bit of thinking, pushing and organizing for him. Perhaps Moodie lifted a little pressure from the rider and gave him confidence, and although the effect of rider confidence cannot be measured in lap times, for a family man like John who did not intend to push himself over the limit, a settled state of mind must have been a big plus. Indeed, many riders have said that a relaxed approach to

During the 2004 Formula I race, the eventual winner John McGuinness (Yamaha, 3) has his main rival Adrian Archibald (TAS Suzuki, 1) just where he wants him. Having caught and passed Archibald on the road, McGuinness knows that he has a 20-second lead as the two of them heel through the sweeping bends of the 11th Milestone at 140mph.

riding the TT course yields faster laps than pushing hard. With a slowish start but an overall good practice week, John rode the Formula I race with plenty of confidence, racing to victory by eighteen seconds over Adrian Archibald (TAS Suzuki) and setting a new lap record on the first lap of 127.68mph (205.47km/h). Bruce Anstey (TAS Suzuki) was third and Jason Griffiths brought the other 'works' Yamaha into fourth, with Ian Lougher (Honda) fifth.

Switching to a private Honda for Monday's Lightweight 400 race, the thirty-year-old McGuinness took a comfortable victory for the second year on the trot. The Ultra-Lightweight race for 125s was run as a separate race at the same time as the 400s, but everyone knew that, just as with the racing 250s allowed to run in the Junior, the year of 2004 was to be the final TT appearance for both of these pure racing machines. Once again the reasons put forward by the organizers did not quite ring true, as race fans looked at British and World Championships still catering for good fields in both of these capacities. Was it manufacturer interest and pressure seeking to clear the programme for other classes that caused the organizers to run down and then drop the 125s and 250s? Who knows – but it certainly had the effect of reducing the number of individual riders contesting the TT thereafter.

Chris Palmer won Monday's Ultra-Lightweight race, setting the fastest lap at 110.52mph (177.86km/h) in a field comprised entirely of Hondas. Second place went to five-times TT winner Robert Dunlop, who announced that the axing of the 125 class meant that it was his last TT. Joint sponsors of three riders in the race, Lloyds-TSB and Mannin Collections were another concern unhappy with the organizers' decision to drop the 125s. They had plenty of opportunity to race the 125s elsewhere but, as Manx organizations, they did wonder why they could not do so at the TT. Monday's second race, the Production 1000, was unusual as it was stopped at Sulby Bridge on the first lap as sea mist crept in to affect the relatively low-lying

With the brakes of his Honda applied and front forks on full depression, Chris Palmer prepares to take Sulby Bridge on his way to victory in the 2004 Ultra-Lightweight race.

Riders are red-flagged at Sulby Bridge on the first lap of the Production 1000 race after visibility problems affected part of the course.

Dave Molyneux and Daniel Sayle made up undoubtedly the top sidecar crew at the 2004 TT.

In 2004 Nick Crowe and Darren Hope were on a rapid rise to TT stardom.

Cronk y Voddy area. Rerun on Tuesday, Bruce Anstey seized the chance to break the McGuinness grip on the 2004 races and bring his Suzuki home ahead of John's Yamaha by eighteen seconds for his third TT win.

In a double Manx-double, local sidecar crews Dave Molyneux/Daniel Sayle and Nick Crowe/Darren Hope took first and second places in both Sidecar races with their DMR Honda outfits, 'Moly' lapping at over 113mph and equalling Rob Fisher's total of ten TT wins. Former World Champion Klaus Klaffenbock made a steady debut, building up to a 104mph lap, and promised to return to race again.

With track conditions less than ideal due to oil spillages in several places, John McGuinness exercised a degree of caution in the Junior race and still came up with a win for Yamaha on his R6, ahead of Bruce Anstey's Suzuki. The usually steady Ian Lougher was lucky to get away unharmed from a first-lap crash on his Honda on the approach to Union Mills.

With just Friday's two races, the Production 600 and Senior, left to run, fans wondered if John McGuinness, the star of the meeting to date, could achieve a new TT milestone and win them both, so lifting his victories for the week to a record-breaking five. As ever there were other riders with eyes on the top places in those races and it was Ryan Farquhar who broke his TT duck by winning the Production 600, so giving a rare victory to Kawasaki and its ZX6. In a close and exciting race, Ryan had just 2.3 seconds in hand over runner-up Bruce Anstey (Suzuki) at the finish. John McGuinness was in contention for the lead until a steering damper bolt snapped on the third lap, causing him to ease the throttle as his R6 became a bit wayward on the bumpy stretches. Showing his form in the afternoon's Senior, McGuinness led the race until the third lap when clutch failure forced him out at Glen Helen. With Yamaha's other rider Jason Griffiths out on the first lap, plus Ryan Farquhar and Shaun Harris as other early retirements, Adrian Archibald (Suzuki) moved into the lead and held it to the end of the four-lap race. To McGuinness went the fastest lap at 127.19mph (204.69km/h), Bruce Anstey (Suzuki) earned another second spot and Manxman Gary Carswell (Suzuki) took advantage of the retirement of several top runners to snatch third from another local, Paul Hunt, after he dropped out on the last lap. It was Archibald's second Senior TT win on the trot and with it went the Joey Dunlop Trophy and £10,000 for the best combined finish in the Formula I and Senior. Coming from Joey's home town of Ballymoney, the trophy meant much to Adrian, as did the almost £20,000 he earned from Senior victory.

Among those to catch the eye at the 2004 TT was Martin Finnegan for his sometimes hectic riding style and his increase in speed over the previous year, plus newcomer Guy Martin, whose first ever lap of the Mountain Course was completed at 112mph and who finished the fortnight with a lap of over 122mph and seventh place in the Senior race.

Major Changes for 2005

It was customary for the programme for the next TT to be announced either at or soon after the current year's event and TT followers soon heard that, for 2005, gone were two-strokes, gone were the names Formula I, Lightweight and Production, and in came Superbike, Superstock and Supersport racing, leaving only the Senior and Sidecar A and B titles remaining from the 2004 event. The organizers explained that the programme had been changed to suit the views of riders and teams, and that 'the key features of the new programme are a reduction in the number of classes and a harmonization of those classes with what happens elsewhere in motorcycle racing'.

The TT had allowed itself to become slightly out of step with the categories of machines raced on the UK short circuits, causing extra expense to riders who had to modify their bikes to meet the TT regulations, so harmonization of specifications made sense. Reducing the number of classes also meant fewer individual machines to prepare, but the result was that there were just three solo classes in 2005. TT Superbike replaced Formula I as the major class, with machines complying with World Super Bike or British Superbike

specification. Production racing was replaced by TT Superstock for machines of over 600cc meeting the specifications of FIM Superstock and MCRCB Stocksport. The third class was for Supersport Junior TT bikes complying with FIM Supersport or MCRCB Supersport rules. All three of the new categories were eligible to contest the Senior TT.

The reversion to an all four-stroke TT mirrored the situation at the first TT races of 1907, although 100 years ago this was by accident rather than by design. Similarly the wholesale use of production-based machines in 2005 was another echo from 1907. But in seeking to justify the exclusion of pure racing bikes (125 and 250 two-strokes), partly on the grounds of cost, everyone conveniently overlooked the fact that the Superbikes prepared for 2005 were out-and-out racers sharing few components with their production origins, and prepared on a no-expense-spared basis by the factories to win on the world stage and sell their road-going products.

The outcome was a programme of just seven races with the Supersport Junior TT runners given two races classed, like the sidecars, as Race A on Monday afternoon and Race B on Wednesday morning. Other changes for 2005 saw the opening Saturday Superbike and closing Friday Senior TT revert to six laps, while the option for MGP competitors to compete in Superstock (formerly Production) without ruling themselves out of competing in the 'amateur' races was withdrawn. The result was an entry of just 244 individual competitors, although it was pleasing to see Honda, Suzuki, Yamaha and Kawasaki giving 'works' support.

An innovation was that the first practice lap by those falling into the Newcomers category was made under the control of Travelling Marshals riding at the head, middle and tail of the orange-jacketed group of first-timers. Due to the extremely windy conditions of the opening session, the organizers sought to take pressure off riders, and discourage them from taking risks, by telling them that no

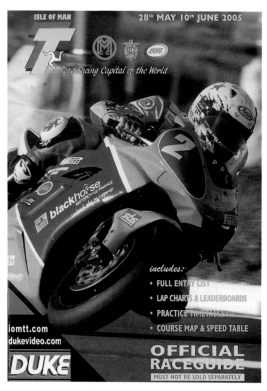

The cover of the Official Race Guide for 2005. The Isle of Man has long called itself the 'Road Racing Capital of the World'.

times would be recorded. John McGuinness (Yamaha) was the fastest man at the end of practice week, with Adrian Archibald (Suzuki), Richard Britton (Honda) and Martin Finnegan (Honda) also showing well, while Ian Lougher (Honda) and Bruce Anstey (Suzuki) were a little slower. Time was lost with several wet practice sessions, and previous caution by the organizers manifested itself into a statement from the Clerk of the Course, Neil Hanson, that the organizers would no longer start a race in wet conditions, though he did explain that: 'If it rains during a race riders must make the best of it . . . but if I felt conditions were dangerous I would stop the race'. It was the increased power outputs of modern superbikes and the increased specialization of racing tyres (solo and sidecar) that brought about this move in the interests of safety, but it

was one that suggested riders and spectators could look forward to even more delayed starts and postponements as the fickle Manx weather exercised its options to interfere with racing in years to come.

With extra effort being put into the 'Festival' aspect of the TT, there would certainly be things for fans to do if racing was to be postponed, and official word was that '2005 will see the greatest collection of entertainments and shows ever seen at a TT Festival'. New events included TT chat shows with star riders as part of the evening entertainments, and paddock walkabouts on race days. There were also plans for a grandstand to be erected on Douglas Promenade for spectators to view organized stunt-riding displays and other entertainments.

Although much improved, the TT paddock drew complaints from riders every year, sometimes arising from unrealistic expectations, and the organizers promised more tarmac and a better layout for 2005. There were also going to be several small screens where transponder timing information on riders would be displayed during a race in the paddock/grandstand area. The same area provided a base for such concerns as K-Tech Suspension and Arai helmets to provide a service to riders using their products, while other commercial outlets sold race-style clothing, helmets and so on to the general public.

2005 Racing

The first postponement came on the opening day of 2005 race week. Wet roads and poor visibility meant the races were transferred to Sunday, when road conditions were good for the inaugural Superbike event. John McGuinness used the policy that yielded success in 2004 and went hard from the start, revving his Yamaha to 13,500 and leaving the competition to play catch-up. That was something that they could not do and, after early challenger Richard Britton retired, John was able to limit his revs to 12,000 in the closing stages and come home thirty-six seconds ahead of

Adrian Archibald after 226 racing miles, leaving rising star Martin Finnegan to take third place. It was former Moto-crosser Finnegan who featured in lurid press photos showing him grinding the belly-pan as his Honda went on to maximum suspension depression at the bottom of Barregarroo, and of him leaping high and long at Ballaugh.

Top sidecar man Dave Molyneux had Daniel Sayle in the chair again, but the pair were sidelined by an ignition fault in Sidecar Race A and victory went to Nick Crowe and Darren Hope (Honda). In Race B Molyneux and Sayle smashed lap and race records when taking their Honda to victory over Crowe and Hope. Recording the first official sub-20-minute sidecar lap, the winners left the record at a staggering 116.04mph (186.74km/h). A scare in the last half-mile of the race when a wheel-bearing started to fail was accompanied by post-race revelations of one or two other faults not previously experienced, suggesting that venturing into the uncharted territory of 116mph on three wheels was going to call for a rethink on design.

Monday's racing started with TT Superstock (formerly Production) over three laps, which was open to 4-cylinder machines over 600 and up to 1000cc, 3-cylinder machines over 750cc and up to 1000cc, plus twin-cylinder models over 850cc and up to 1200cc. It was monopolized by the Japanese manufacturers, with just an Aprilia of Mike Hose and MV Agusta of Thomas Montano to give a touch of variation and provide a change in exhaust notes. After leading the race until the closing stages, Adrian Archibald ran out of petrol on his TAS Suzuki, leaving team-mate Bruce Anstey to take the win from Ian Lougher (Honda), Ryan Farquhar (Kawasaki) and Jason Griffiths (Yamaha). To Archibald went the fastest lap at 126.64mph (203.80 km/h). Suffering two inexplicable high-speed slides early in the race, a de-tuned John McGuinness retired his Yamaha. But McGuinness could not afford to stay de-tuned for long because less than two hours after pulling in he

The TT is always a busy time for mechanics and helpers.

was due to ride in the Supersport Junior TT Race A, where 4-cylinder machines over 400 and up to 600cc, plus twin-cylinder over 600 and up to 750cc were permitted. After a close struggle against the clock in which they were separated by less than one second (although fifty seconds apart on the road), Ryan Farquhar retired his over-heating Kawasaki, leaving Ian Lougher to take the win at an average speed of 120.93mph (194.61km/h), from back-on-the-pace John McGuinness (Yamaha).

Ryan Farquhar made up for his Race A disappointment when he rode to victory in Wednesday's Race B of the Supersport Junior TT. What looked like being a closely contested race, as Farquhar, McGuinness and Lougher all contested the lead in the early stages, turned into a comfortable win for Ryan, with Jason Griffiths (Yamaha) second and Raymond Porter (Yamaha) third, following the retirement of McGuinness and Lougher. The retirement rate was higher than expected in Race B, in which there were fifty-eight finishers compared with seventy in Race A, and it was widely felt

Two riders who finished the 2005 event with their highest-ever TT positions were Jun Maeda (11) and Guy Martin (15). Here they heel over at 140mph to pass the 11th Milestone, with Guy 30 seconds ahead on corrected time.

that the increasingly super-tuned nature of the 600cc Supersport fours was such that they could not be guaranteed to last for practice and two races. Notwithstanding the excellent mobile workshop facilities (and temporary garages) enjoyed by the top teams, an engine rebuild now entailed the use of more specialized facilities, something that was not possible between races. Perhaps even after nearly a century of racing the demands of the Mountain Course had once again been underestimated. Rumbles of discontent on the issue suggested that it might be an area for change.

Unreliability was also evident in Friday's Senior TT, in which there were thirty non-finishers from seventy-nine starters and rostrum places were affected. There seemed little doubt that John McGuinness was heading for a win as he made his usual fast start and set the fastest lap of the race on his opener at 127.33mph (204.91km/h), and it was a position he held to the finish. Adrian Archibald held second until forced out with a puncture, while team-mate Bruce Anstey

wisely retired when his Suzuki 'did not feel right'. Potential rostrums were lost by Richard Britton and Martin Finnegan with slow pit stops, and Ryan Farquhar lost third place with a broken engine. Although Ian Lougher gladly took advantage of the situation to finish in second place, he was troubled with tyres that went off after just one lap. Renewing them at each refuelling stop (at the end of laps two and four) restored the grip, but it did not last. Taking third step on the rostrum was Guy Martin (Yamaha), in only his second year at the TT, who beat Martin Finnegan by just over one second to snatch the honour.

As there was only one race on Friday in 2005, a little more ceremony was attached to the Lap of Honour for Classic race bikes and riders. Former TT riders were sent off in the first grouping of about eighty riders, followed by a second group of fifty riders on Classic racing machinery controlled at the front by Travelling Marshals. The organized presence of Classic machinery was also extended to cover the weekend after the Senior, during which they were displayed in several locations and did laps of honour at the post-TT race meeting on the Southern 100 circuit.

Comparisons

Manufacturers, riders and sponsors had seemingly achieved what they wanted in 2005: a TT meeting spread over just seven races comprising three solo classes and sidecars, two groups from which (Sidecars and Supersport Junior) each had two races. But what of the TT's 40,000 spectators – was there enough variety to keep them coming?

As the MGP approached, two months after the TT, a Manx newspaper chose to make the sort of comparisons that must have gone through the minds of many fans of Island racing, describing the TT races of production-based bikes as: 'little more than three 1000cc and two 600cc solo events of similar design and outward appearances to the over-the-

Take your pick! TAS Suzuki was entered in all solo classes.

counter machines ridden on the open roads by the majority of road riders worldwide'. Although omitting mention of the Sidecar TT, it went on to point out that the MGP hosted some 400 individual competitors. It then indicated the variety of the MGP programme, with separate races for Newcomers on modern machinery in three different classes, races for modern machines in Lightweight and Ultra-Lightweights (open to the two-strokes dropped by the TT), plus Junior and Senior races for 600 and 1000cc machines in which riders were clocking laps above 120mph. In addition there were events for Lightweight, Junior and Senior Classic machines (using Classic capacity ratings), offering considerable variation of machinery by sight and sound.

Strangely, the newspaper posed the question as to whether the increased specialization at the TT might be a good thing, wondering if narrowing the spectator appeal in June might prevent their numbers growing and, with the easier availability of boat crossings and accommodation during the MGP period, perhaps encourage some TT fans to visit the MGP instead.

While there are some who have swapped attendance from the TT to the MGP (for a host of reasons), it was difficult to believe that

with the amount of money that the Island pumps into the TT it would want to see any decrease in numbers attending the premier event. However, it was still early days with the new arrangements of organizers and race classes, and there was bound to be speculation as to where the TT was heading.

What Races?

By the early months of 2006 there had been no announcement of the programme of races for the coming TT. Rumours flew in the press and on websites as to why there should be such an unprecedented delay. When the programme was eventually announced it was accompanied by much 'PR speak' about the lengthy discussions that had been held with all interested parties, but by then most people knew that one of the problems that had delayed matters was internal disagreement between those who paid for the races and those who organized them. The few who still believed that the delay was due to extensive consultation were no doubt surprised to see that all the talk had yielded little more than the fully expected omission of the second Supersport Junior Race and a hint of something extra for 2007.

The manufacturers had clearly got their way again about the dropping of the second 600 race, but that left the 2006 TT meeting with just six races. While it was natural to want to retain the support of the manufacturers and the associated status it conferred on the event, perhaps the TT organizers had got into the habit of leaning too far one way and not giving sufficient thought to spectators. From the earliest days through to the late 1960s the TT barely needed to worry about its status, for it was indisputably fixed at the top of the racing tree. When its position was threatened in the early 1970s, worries about maintaining status were paramount to the organizers. But, as was shown when it lost its World Championship 'GP' standing (followed by the loss of its World Championship Formula I title), the TT could stand alone. The same scenario prevailed with regard to protecting its dates against challenges from World and British Championship rounds, something the organizers became obsessed with. Yet during the opening weekend of the 2005 TT meeting there was a British Super-

bike round held at Croft, and over the middle weekend there was a Moto GP meeting at Mugello, with barely a mention of them affecting the TT.

Having laid those bogies from the past, it now seems to be the manufacturers who have captured the organizers' minds. Many are aware that commercial forces want the TT condensed into a much shorter period than the current two weeks. Will they get their way? On current form, yes. But it is to be hoped that the organizers will listen to more than just the manufacturers' views, for whatever their current demands, it should be remembered that they also need the TT as a showcase for their products.

Entries

Much of the considerable effort that goes into attracting new riders to race on the Isle of Man now falls to former winner 'Milky' Quayle and to Paul Phillips. Established riders receive personal approaches, offers of financial terms, and encouragement to come and look at the course, while up-and-coming riders are often brought to the Island in groups during the off-season and shown what the TT has to offer. Some of the funding for such group visits is paid for by the Mike Hailwood Foundation.

Wade Boyd tips into the right-hander of Quarter Bridge in 2002. The extrovert Wade has also ridden in Motocross and served as a sidecar passenger while on the Island. With his hair dyed in various colours, he has brightened the TT scene for many years.

An American newcomer to the TT, Jeremy Toye, is shown here on the Suzuki that he rode for regular TT sponsor Martin Bullock.

The TT still captures the imagination of riders from near and far. Coming in the near category, the entry list for 2006 contained the name of a twenty-year-old from Ramsey, Conor Cummins. Growing up with the TT on his doorstep, Conor's early racing was on the UK short circuits, where he showed much promise. Confident enough to go straight into the TT (rather than via the MGP), he gave local racing fans much to look forward to.

America has provided individual riders in the TT since the earliest years and such names as Jake de Rosier, Putt Mossman, Pat Hennen, Chris Crew, Thomas Montano and Wade Boyd, a colourful regular entrant, have left their names in TT history.

In 2006 Thomas Montano was back, and he was joined by two other Americans, Mark

Miller and Jeremy Toye, billed as 'two of the leading riders in American Superbike racing'.

Free Entries!

For almost 100 years riders had complained that they were required to pay an entry fee for each event to entertain spectators who viewed the racing for free. In 2006 entry fees were abolished, although riders still had to convince the organizers that they were good enough to race on the TT course and, after entries were accepted, they then had to meet the qualifying times. Indeed, the ACU showed they still had influence on the event by introducing a 'TT Licence' for riders, which tightened the qualifying requirements.

Other pre-event news in 2006 was that top runner Ryan Farquhar would miss the meeting through injury and that the recipients of 'works' machinery would be: Bruce Anstey and Adrian Archibald (TAS Suzuki); Guy Martin for AIM Racing, Jason Griffiths for Yamaha UK and Paul Hunt, the fastest Manxman, for Team Racing (Yamaha); John McGuinness for HM Plant, Martin Finnegan for Klaffi Honda, and Ian Lougher riding for Paul Bird's Stobart Honda BSB team (Honda). Top man on a Kawasaki was Ian Hutchinson. While they represented the very experienced top runners, making his TT debut with just a MGP Newcomers victory to his name was William Dunlop, son of Robert, while Conor Cummins described himself as 'shell-shocked' to be given last-minute support by Team Racing Yamaha. The organizers were clearly pleased with the level of 'works' support received, and came out with the contestable claim that 'Without doubt the overall entry for the 2006 TT races will be the strongest ever to have been assembled. . .'. The Sidecar races were also well supported, and received a boost with the news that past podium man (and Roy Hanks's nephew) Tom Hanks was returning, with Phil Biggs in the chair.

One of the Best Ever?

This was the organizers' claim at the finish of the 2006 TT and few would challenge their opinion. Despite a cold and windy start to the first two practice sessions, riders were soon up to speed and showing promise of an exciting meeting. Determined to keep his crown as 'King of the Mountain Course', John McGuinness showed he was prepared to work to do so by completing five laps of practice on Tuesday evening – a rare occurrence for any rider. Then, as temperatures increased throughout the remainder of an almost totally dry fortnight, so did the pace on the track. It was McGuinness who unofficially broke the outright solo lap record on Wednesday evening by averaging 127.81mph (205.68km/h), and Dave Molyneux did the same to the sidecar record by averaging 116.22mph (187.03km/h).

While there were plenty of solo runners snapping at McGuinness's heels with fast laps, Molyneux and passenger Craig Hallam were in a class of their own on three wheels, for their nearest challengers were slower by several mph a lap. But then disaster struck the super-fast pair during Thursday afternoon's practice. Moly always made a big effort to take the right-hand sweep of Douglas Road Corner, Kirk Michael, as fast as possible, because it determined the speed he would achieve with the throttle against the stop over the next 3 miles to Ballaugh Bridge. On Thursday he made a good passage through the Corner and Kirk Michael village, so setting his Honda-powered machine to take Rhencullen flat-out. Travelling at 145mph, the front of the outfit lifted slightly over the rise as usual, but then it continued to lift, rose vertically on the rear wheel and turned over onto its back. As it slid down the road it burst into flames and was destroyed. Hallam was thrown clear, and despite being trapped underneath when it inverted, Molyneux also got out before it caught fire. Although it was a major disaster in one sense, both men realized how incredibly lucky they were to

Cameron Donald (Honda) had a superb 2006 TT and is seen here attacking the Glen Helen section of the course.

escape with minor injuries, but they were out of the 2006 TT.

By the end of practice John McGuinness (Honda) had shown that he was the man to beat in the solo classes, but Guy Martin (Yamaha), Bruce Anstey (TAS Suzuki), Ian Lougher (Honda) and former MGP-winner Ian Hutchinson (Kawasaki) were not far behind, although other favourites, such as former winner Adrian Archibald (TAS Suzuki) and Martin Finnegan (Honda), who had gone so well in 2005, were a little off the pace.

McGuinness carried his practice form into the opening race of TT 2006, Saturday's Superbike event. With a pace that suited the hot weather, John scorched into the lead on his Honda, breaking the outright lap record on his first standing–start lap and raising it again on the second lap to 127.93mph (205.88km/h), by which time a man whom some fancied for a race win, Guy Martin

(Yamaha), was already out of the race with machine problems, something with which he was to be afflicted throughout race week. Kawasaki's Ian Hutchinson and Honda-mounted Ian Lougher were just twelve seconds in arrears at the end of the first lap, but McGuinness passed the grandstand at over 170mph and widened the gap on the second lap. Thereafter he controlled the race from the front, and with Lougher moving ahead of Hutchinson at the first pit stop after the Kawasaki rider lost time wiping spilt fuel from his controls, the race pattern was set. After six laps McGuinness came home forty seconds ahead of Lougher to give Honda a welcome double and their first big-bike TT win since Joey Dunlop in 2000. With Martin Finnegan and Cameron Donald bringing their Hondas into fourth and fifth places, it was Ian Hutchinson, third on his Kawasaki, who was the best of the opposition.

Ian Lougher on the 2006 Stobart Honda wears the sides of his huge rear tyre.

Next race on the programme was Monday's Superstock for 1000cc machines. Formerly called the Production race, this brought victory for Bruce Anstey (Suzuki), with Ian Hutchinson (Kawasaki) in second place and Jason Griffiths (Yamaha) third. Best placed Honda was John McGuinness in fifth, which suggested that while Honda might be the top machine in the big racing class, they had to give way to others in Superstock/ Production at the TT. McGuinness took his second win of the week in Wednesday's Supersport race on his 600cc Honda, but the big news was that after another fine second-place finish Ian Hutchinson was disqualified on a technical infringement. During post-race scrutineering his Kawasaki was found to have fractionally more cam-lift than allowed by the race regulations. Although everyone agreed this offered no power advantage, he was stripped of second place, allowing Bruce Anstey (Suzuki) to move into second position and Jason Griffiths (Yamaha) into third.

In the absence of Dave Molyneux from the Sidecar races, Nick Crowe and Darren Hope (Honda) won both without threatening the lap record. Their main opposition came from Steve Norbury and Scott Parnell (Yamaha) in a field of some sixty outfits. Plagued by mechanical problems, former World Sidecar Champion Klaus Klaffenbock (Honda) failed to shine in a year in which people thought he might show his true class after serving a two-year 'apprenticeship' over the Mountain Course.

The Fastest

In what was the fastest race in TT history, victor John McGuinness (Honda) took just 1 hour 47 minutes 38.5 seconds to cover the 226 miles of Friday's six-lap Senior TT. Setting a new race record average speed of 126.18mph (203.06km/h), he also lifted the outright lap record to an incredible 129.45mph (208.32km/h) in what were perfect race conditions. John's win (his eleventh) was not unexpected, but the performance of second-placed Cameron Donald (Honda) astounded everyone, for he was in only his second year at the TT and finished just twenty-six seconds behind McGuinness.

Spectators looked in awe at the continuous black line that these record-breaking machines left on the road for the entire 37¾ miles of a TT lap, and it was now customary for riders to change their rear tyres during fuel stops at the end of the second and fourth laps of the race.

Few were surprised to hear of speeds above 200mph being achieved on the Sulby Straight. With a 130mph lap in sight, even talented newcomers like Manxman Conor Cummins and American Jeremy Toye recorded laps of over 120mph in their first year at the TT. Where would it all end?

Almost a Century

Much of the talk during the spare time between races at the 2006 TT was about the forthcoming centenary of the event in 2007. Current worries about the direction the races were taking were put to one side as people looked forward to celebrating 100 years of racing. Indeed, and perhaps worryingly, there seems a chance that the actual racing in 2007 might take second place to nostalgia, for a large proportion of those who had already booked accommodation and passage (some as far back as 2004) for 2007 were not sitting watching the racing in 2006, because they were former enthusiasts who were not particularly interested in the current race scene. Such people were booked to return in 2007, often after many years' absence from the island, because the centenary would allow them to look back and relive personal TT memories.

For a few of the 'greybeards' coming to the centenary celebrations it would be the 1950s they wanted to revisit – would Geoff Duke, Bill Lomas and John Surtees be there in 2007? Others were brought up on the 1960s deeds of Phil Read and Giacomo Agostini, and there was a good chance that Ago would attend and let them hear once more the sound of an open-piped MV Agusta. Mick Grant, Chas Mortimer and Charlie Williams might be just some of the stars of the 1970s in attendance, having earned their places with multiple TT wins in the years when 'strokers' ruled the Island. Those visitors who still liked to think of themselves as youthful probably hoped that top men from the 1980s like Graeme Crosby, Alex George, Ron Haslam, Nick Jefferies and Mick Boddice would put up spirited performances in what would, surely, be multiple Laps of Honour by former riders, while 1990s TT fans hoped to see the likes of Carl Fogarty, Phillip McCallen, Robert Dunlop and Jim Moodie on parade. The centenary of the races was eagerly awaited by TT fans world-wide.

Those with a liking for motorcycle history knew they would be able to look back down a tunnel of 100 years not only of motorcycle racing, but, equally important, of motorcycle development, because the TT races have been the ultimate practical proving ground for many advances in design. For a century successful designers returned home with gains in performance that spanned engine, transmission, ignition, braking, handling, carburation and other components. However, those whose designs were faulty would be found out by the uniquely demanding nature of the Mountain Course, and for them it was a case of back to the drawing board – or, in today's world, to the CAD machine.

11 TT Centenary and Beyond

It seemed that the 2006 races had barely finished before promotion of the 2007 event was in full flow. Enthusiasts needed little convincing that the centenary of the first running of the TT would offer great racing, and even the attention of those with fringe interests in road racing was captured by the high level of media exposure. The result was a greater than usual number of visitors booking to attend what was clearly going to be a special event.

So once again the TT was news, as it had been for the past 100 years, and expectations built ever higher as race time approached – and none more so than for the owner of UK vehicle registration plate TT 100, who offered it for sale for £50,000.

In late spring of 2007 the 37¾-mile (60¾km) Mountain Course began to receive its customary preparation to ready it for racing. Minor road repairs were carried out, hedges and grass banks were cut back, kerbs repainted black and white on bends, roads swept, warning signs erected, advertising banners put in place, and along with thousands

With hedges trimmed and kerbs painted, this 'between the hedges' stretch of the Mountain Course is on the approach to Handley's Corner.

of protective bales, more lengths of air-fencing were positioned to aid rider safety on dangerous corners.

With John McGuinness having set a new outright lap record speed of 129.45mph (208.28km/h) in 2006, there was much talk of the milestone 130mph (209km/h) barrier being broken in 2007, particularly as John claimed he had not been riding to the limit when he broke the record. It was only seven years since David Jefferies rode the first 125mph (201km/h) lap, but lapping at that speed in 2007 might not be good enough even for tenth place on a 1000cc Superbike, while it was also expected that 600cc Supersport machines would very soon achieve *their* first 125mph average lap speed.

Course Improvements

Over the preceding century there had been many improvements to the roads of the TT Mountain Course, which had contributed much to the reduction of lap times. Between the 2006 and 2007 races, the Highway Authority carried out major works to ease the line of Brandish Corner, and top riders estimated that the realignment would save them four to five seconds a lap, so helping to bring the magic 130mph (209km/h) figure ever closer. Some TT fans imagine that such road improvements are made for the benefit of the racers, whereas their prime purpose is to improve safety for ordinary users – although their effect on the TT is never far from the minds of the engineers who design them.

Re-enactment

There was plenty of activity outside actual racing during the fortnight of the 2007 TT Festival, much of it of a celebratory nature. One event which captured the imagination of visitors and residents was a re-enactment of the first TT of 28 May 1907, which ran over the original St John's Course, starting at Tynwald Hill.

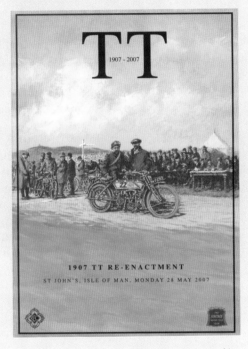

1907 TT RE-ENACTMENT
ST JOHN'S, ISLE OF MAN, MONDAY 28 MAY 2007

With the organization of the 're-enactment' in the hands of the Isle of Man Section of the Vintage Motor Cycle Club, some 100 riders on early machines did a lap of the old course over closed roads, generating a wonderful atmosphere and delighting thousands of onlookers. Many dressed in period riding gear, and TT stars such as Guy Martin, Mick Grant and Nick Jefferies participated on borrowed machines, while 'Milky' Quayle rode his 'Shuttleworth Snap' replica, based on the bike that George Formby rode in the 1935 TT-related film *No Limit*.

The lap was not without its problems for some, just as the original event had been for pioneer riders in 1907. A few bikes were reluctant to start, others stopped for repairs en route, and some riders had to help along their low-powered mounts on the ascent of Creg Wyllies, either by pedalling or by jumping off and running alongside them.

The start of the 2007 Re-enactment Run at Tynwald Hill. Some riders have already been despatched, and these are awaiting the signal to go.

To recognize the centenary of the Tourist Trophy meeting, five-times TT winner of the 1950s, Geoff Duke, unveiled a commemorative plaque opposite the original start line.

The Racing

Despite the many other attractions, in 2007 it was the modern racers that most people travelled to the island to see, for those riders following in the wheel-tracks of legendary names of the past were the very best road racers of the day – established TT winners such as Ian Lougher, Adrian Archibald, John McGuinness, Bruce Anstey and Ryan Farquhar, along with the names of rising stars Ian Hutchinson, Martin Finnegan, Guy Martin, Conor Cummins, and first-timer from the British Supersport scene, Steve Plater. As ever, some riders were missing through injury, amongst them fast Aussie Cameron Donald, who fell at the North West 200 a couple of weeks before. On three wheels Dave Molyneux, Nick

Paddock workshop scene.

Crowe and Klaus Klaffenbock were among top 'chairmen' preparing for battle.

There were six races to be contested, with solos running in the Superbike, Superstock, Supersport and Senior TTs, while sidecars had two races. All events received sponsorship and thus attracted titles such as the Bennett's TT Superbike Race, the Pokerstars Supersport Race and the Bavaria Sidecar TT 'A' Race and 'B' Race. Interspersed amongst the racing and helping to fuel the air of nostalgia at the 2007 event were parade laps featuring former riders, many on race machines from their particular era.

As usual there was a week of practice before racing proper. For riders it was a busy time as most were entered in several classes, while for teams such as HM Plant Honda and TAS Suzuki, who handled 'works' machines on behalf of the Japanese factories, it meant particularly long hours.

The pace in practice was hot, with John McGuinness heading the leaderboard on a Honda in the Superbike and Senior classes, while Suzuki-mounted Bruce Anstey was fastest in the Superstock and Supersport categories. Top sidecar man Dave Molyneux was beset with problems, and fastest in the class was double winner from 2006, Nick Crowe (Honda), passengered by Dan Sayle.

Tyre Troubles?

Come race week, and after the long build-up and huge sense of expectation, Saturday's opening races were postponed until Sunday. The public were told that this was due to poor visibility on the Mountain, but there was a strong suspicion that a tyre-related factor contributed to the postponement, for no suitable tyres were produced for either the super-powerful 1000cc Superbikes or the sidecars to enable them to race safely in Saturday's mixed wet and dry conditions. The absence of such tyres had been known about for some time and it was a major cause of concern, and while there was no easy solution, it was a problem that would not go away.

Sunday's racing saw John McGuinness (Honda) ride to victory in the opening Superbike race under still less-than-perfect course conditions, with Guy Martin (Honda) taking second place, some forty seconds in arrears. It was John's third consecutive victory in the class, and he had also won the last Formula 1 race in 2004 (the title by which the Superbike TT was previously known).

Earlier mention has been made of the old saying amongst TT competitors of 'bad practice, good race', and although usually left unsaid, the reverse was also known to apply. Dave Molyneux (Honda) seemed to confirm its truth in 2007, because after a troubled week's practice he rode to victory in both sidecar races, while the man who had set the pace in practice, Nick Crowe, was forced to retire on each occasion. Nick's only consolation came from setting the fastest sidecar lap of the week at a new record lap speed of 116.67mph (187.72km/h), before his Honda expired on the demanding full-bore climb of the Ballahutchin, which leads away from Union Mills. Modern data logging shows that the 600cc sidecar engines spend far more of a Mountain Course lap on full throttle than solos, so giving them a shorter racing life.

Few were surprised when Bruce Anstey (Suzuki) went to the front at the outset of the

Superstock race, for he had won it in 2005 and 2006. Never headed, he led home John McGuinness (Honda), with Ian Hutchinson (Honda) third and Martin Finnegan bringing an MV Agusta into fourth. It was a fairly rare appearance and a high placing for the Italian marque with a proud TT history.

Wednesday's Supersport TT had everything that race fans could want. Top riders were on machines from all the major Japanese manufacturers and on British Triumphs, so almost everybody had someone to support. Throw in a record-breaking pace, pit-stop drama for the early leader Bruce Anstey, stunning performances from up-and-coming riders in the form of winner Ian Hutchinson and lap record setter Guy Martin, and it all made for a memorable race. As was becoming the custom with the Supersport event, the time margins between the top men were small, and this made for a particularly nail-biting final lap, as riders wrung every ounce of power from their engines while trying to hold on to hard-earned places. It was 'Hutchie's' first TT win, and was achieved despite his carrying a restricting shoulder injury.

Could Friday's 'Blue Riband' Senior event offer a spectacle to match the Supersport race at this Centenary TT? Well, conditions were good, and John McGuinness stormed into the race lead, completing the opening standing-start lap at 129.88mph (208.98km/h). Bettering this on his flying second circuit, John smashed the 130mph (209km/h) lap speed barrier, taking just 17min 21.99sec to cover the 37¾ miles (60¾km) at an average speed of 130.35mph (209.73km/h). Holding the opposition at bay, he reeled off the six laps to win from Guy Martin by 32sec. It took 1hr 48min 11.1sec of unrelenting concentration and physical effort for John to achieve his win, because to relax for a moment could have seen his 200bhp Honda take control and bring disaster.

John McGuinness was the only man to do a 130mph (209km/h) lap, and his record-breaking win set the seal on a memorable TT. But as departing visitors bought their

John McGuinness celebrates another Senior TT victory.

centenary souvenirs, enjoyed a last pint of Manx ale and packed for the journey home, the meeting was coming to terms with a last lap accident at Joey's (twenty-sixth milestone) in the Senior race, in which rider Marc Ramsbotham and two spectators were killed and two marshals severely injured.

Repercussions

In the aftermath of this serious incident numerous official departments and insurance companies were involved, reports were prepared, some race officials resigned, and a platform was provided for the airing of views by those who opposed the TT.

Motorcycle racing can be dangerous, and whilst the accident at Joey's was of a freak nature and the first at the TT to cause spectator fatalities, it brought greater attention to the issue of spectator safety. A subsequent course-long review resulted in many places previously used for race viewing being put out of bounds on the grounds of potential risk. Ironically, the review even caused some safe areas to be lost to use, as landowners adjoining the course were fed stories about their potential liabilities and the need to take out expensive insurance.

While the effects of the new spectating restrictions in 2008 were certainly not welcomed, in some cases they were overdue, and although it meant that the TT course could no longer be considered as an almost 37¾ mile (60¾km) long grandstand, many miles of roadside viewing still remained available. Nevertheless, that did not prevent long-time race fans regretting the loss of their favourite viewing points, now occupied at race-times by an army of 'Prohibited' signs.

A New Century of Racing

TT fans visit the Isle of Man primarily for the racing, and are mostly unaware of the extensive 'politicking' that goes on behind the scenes, as individuals and groups pursue personal agendas, sometimes leaving the racing to take second place. In what was a shock move, after just four years in the hands of the Manx Motor Cycle Club, organization of the 2008 races reverted to the ACU under the banner of their ACU (Events) Ltd, bringing a new clerk of the course, Eddie Nelson.

Race fans barely noticed the difference in organizers, although the meeting itself saw some changes. Back came the second Supersport race, and surprisingly, back came 125 and 250 Lightweight TTs. They were to run on the day after the Senior TT on the 4¼-mile (6.84km) Billown Circuit in the south of the island, home to the Southern 100 race meeting. Not everyone agreed on the alloca-tion of TT status to the Lightweights at Billown, and despite the good prize money available, it turned into a short-lived venture for the two-strokes.

One thing that was noticed by returning fans in 2008 was the absence of commentator Geoff Cannell on Manx Radio's TT broadcasting. Sadly he had died late in 2007, and the distinctive voice that was first heard over the airwaves in 1968, was lost to listeners.

Most of the star riders were back, but Honda's decision to concentrate its 'factory' efforts elsewhere meant that John McGuinness competed on Padgett-prepared Hondas, and Ian Hutchinson moved to an AIM Yamaha, while in an unrelated change Ryan Farquhar reverted to Kawasakis supplied by McAdoo Racing. The phenomenally fast Steve Plater – he had achieved a 125.61mph (202.1km/h) lap in his 2007 debut year – returned on an AIM Yamaha, while much pre-event publicity concentrated on promoting competitors Conor Cummins, Martin Finnegan, James Hillier, Ollie Linsdell and Gary Johnson, plus brothers William and Michael Dunlop, as the 'Young Guns'.

All the top sidecar runners returned, and there was a sense of anticipation concerning the TT debut of triple world sidecar champion Tim Reeves, with Patrick Farrance in the chair. Tim knew that piloting a 600cc Formula 2 outfit on the Mountain Course was a very different challenge to sliding a 1000cc Formula 1 version around short circuits, but

Tim Reeves in action at the 2008 TT, with passenger Patrick Farrance.

he had done his homework and was quietly confident of making a respectable showing.

Manx Weather!

At the start of practice week in 2008 the Manx weather was not in a co-operative mood and competitors were challenged with a combination of strong winds, rain and mist. This put extra pressure on them, for it reduced the time available to get up to race pace and to achieve the right machine set-up. By the end of the week, fastest runners amongst the solos were John McGuinness, Cameron Donald and Guy Martin, with Nick Crowe heading the chairs.

The larger-than-life Guy Martin seemed to attract more than his share of pre-race publicity, and following his two second places in the big bike classes, and fastest lap in the Supersport race in 2007, his good showing in practice for 2008 brought what was becoming a customary prediction – that this was going to be Guy's year for a TT win. He made no secret of the fact that it was something he desperately wanted.

With the customary Superbike TT opening 2008 race week, the early laps looked as though Guy's dream might come true, as he reeled them off at 129mph (207.56km/h) and

Guy Martin looking for a TT win in 2008.

led the field. But on the fourth lap he encountered mechanical problems that caused his retirement – as had happened to his nearest rivals John McGuinness and Ian Hutchinson earlier in the race. This allowed Cameron Donald (Suzuki) to move to the front, and although challenged by similarly mounted Bruce Anstey, Cameron eased away to take his first TT win, following it two days later with a victorious ride in the Superstock TT.

Three laps and 113 miles (182km) was the task faced by the sidecars as they came to the grid for their first race, but favourite Dave Molyneux completed less than one of those miles before mechanical issues forced his retirement. Closest challenger Nick Crowe raced away to win, after fighting off John Holden in the early stages, while debutant Tim Reeves showed his class with a superb third place.

With the two Supersport races in 2008 appearing in the Monday and Wednesday race programmes, victory in the first went to Bruce Anstey. But as Bruce was celebrating his 'win' and Steve Plater his second place, there came a post-race announcement that Bruce and his TAS Suzuki had been disqualified due to a technical infringement relating to the exhaust cam lift. This promoted Plater to first in only his second appearance at the TT.

Putting aside his first-race disappointment, Bruce went out in the second Supersport event and rode to a convincing 34sec victory over Ian Hutchinson at record-breaking speed, his fastest lap being 125.36mph (201.7km/h).

The second sidecar race provided a strong home showing, with victory going to Manxman Nick Crowe, passengered by Englishman Mark Cox, and second place to Manxies Dave Molyneux and Dan Sayle. Among the sidecar runners was former world champion, Klaus Klaffenbock. By now he had been contesting the TT for several years and had increased his race pace year on year. In that second race in 2008 he finished in fifth place, just ahead of Tim Reeves.

Thirteen times a TT winner, John McGuinness came to the start of Friday's 2008

A typical start-line scene – Gary Johnson awaits the signal to go.

Senior TT with two second places and two retirements from his week's work, but no victory. Taking up position behind the familiar start line on the Glencrutchery Road, he found a pack of on-form challengers there, all keen to rob him of what had become his customary place on the top step of the Senior podium. If he was worried he didn't show it – though if he had known how the opening laps would go, he might have felt some concern.

It had become John's TT race style to set a blistering pace from the outset, gain an early lead, and then control the race from the front – but as that 2008 Senior event got under way, it seemed that several other riders were adopting the same tactic!

John did hold the lead on the first lap as far as Ramsey, but lost it to Bruce Anstey on the Mountain climb, and the New Zealander led by half a second at the end of the lap, with Cameron Donald and Guy Martin only a couple of seconds behind. In a six-lap race such as the Senior, riders come into their pits at the end of the second and fourth laps to refuel and

have a new rear tyre fitted. Anstey still led when he made his first pit stop, but stepped off the bike and retired with mechanical problems.

At the second pit stop it was Anstey's team-mate Cameron Donald who led McGuinness by a couple of seconds, but it was not to last. As a result of what his TAS Suzuki team described as 'oil leaking from a crankcase damaged by the repeated pounding at the bottom of Barregarrow', Donald was forced to ease the pace on what had become a slippery Suzuki, allowing McGuinness to take victory by 50sec, with Ian Hutchinson in third. This being his fourteenth TT win, John McGuinness moved into a tied second place with Mike Hailwood for the greatest number of individual TT victories.

Ease the Throttle?

The potential for suspension-compressing spots such as the bottom of Barregarrow to cause machine damage if ridden at the limit was well known, and certainly Phillip McCallen lost a Lightweight 250 TT victory here back in 1996, when he holed both the exhausts on his two-stroke Honda. Others have collapsed their suspension and broken fairing and seat fixings at this point.

It was probably fearless former moto-crosser Martin Finnegan who introduced other top riders to what has become the current extreme way of riding it, as he grounded and scraped his belly-pan on the road here back in 2005. The superb handling of modern machines allowed Martin to get away with this style of riding, and others have followed his example. However, perhaps riders would be better off actually easing the throttle here to save their machines – although with today's races often being won by small time margins, few will do so.

Ducati

To recognize the fiftieth anniversary of Ducati's TT debut, spectators were entertained by a parade lap of Ducati machinery on

Senior day, ridden by exponents of the marque such as Carl Fogarty, Trevor Nation, Tony Rutter, Paul Smart, Shane Byrne and Ian Simpson. Also in the field were David Hailwood on what was announced as the machine that his father Mike took to victory in his TT comeback ride of 1978, and evergreen Sammy Miller, who rode a Ducati at the TT in the marque's debut year, way back in 1958.

Lightweight TTs

The races run on the Billown circuit received respectable entries of about forty each and delivered close racing. Chris Palmer (Honda) was successful in the Isle of Man Steam Packet 125 Ultra-Lightweight TT, and Ian Lougher (Honda) was first home in the similarly named 250 Lightweight TT.

Close action at Billown, as Chris Palmer heads Ian Lougher in the 250 Lightweight TT of 2008.

Forwards

The TT had a period early in the new millennium when it seemed to outsiders that it was stagnating. While stars of the road-racing scene still provided good race action and were backed by a sizeable field of riders, most of the latter were never going to challenge for a win and their speeds were often well down on those of the top riders. Some came under the heading of occasional racers.

That scenario has changed with the requirement for competitors to hold a Mountain Course Licence from 2006, which is only available to those who can prove that they have competed in a specified number of races at different circuits in the preceding year. In addition, the substantial prize money on offer at the TT, combined with an active recruitment campaign, has brought in 'new blood' in the form of good riders from the British short circuits and from abroad, who think that they can adapt to the roads. At the 2009 event there were riders from twenty-one countries, in races that now have a slightly smaller number of entries than in the past, but where the overall quality of riding is higher.

Riding the TT used to be a natural progression for many who competed at the MGP. But this is no longer so commonly the case, because the high standard of riding now required for TT entry means that fewer MGP riders meet the grade. One who certainly did and who made his TT debut in 2009 was Dan Kneen. He was a Manxman from a racing family, and had ridden to a record-breaking three wins in the 2008 MGP.

It's a Business

The TT continues to run over the roads of the Isle of Man due to the tolerance of the Manx people and business community, and, ultimately, thanks to the authority of the Manx government, which controls the all-important issue of road closures and invests much money in an event aimed at boosting the Manx economy. Difficult as it may be for sporting race fans to accept, the TT is a business operation and has to show a return to those who put money into it in many different ways. That motive has become ever more apparent in recent years, causing many fans to talk of the 'corporate TT', where commercial interests threaten to take precedence over sporting ones. A single day's VIP hospitality ticket is £800, and platinum packages are available for £1,200 to 'enhance the TT experience' – or, quoting from the advertising: 'Why not book a table for eight?'

Essential as the 'corporate' side of the TT may have become, its accompanying lavish spending does not go down well with the ordinary TT fan, who may have saved all year for his visit. However, he is the one who is free to choose his spot to watch the racing, and it may be on the Mountain, perched on a Manx sod bank, with just the wide open spaces for company. Then, as the racers appear as distant dots in the landscape, get gradually larger, before cranking over and sweeping past just a few feet from where he sits, he is the one getting a TT experience that money cannot buy.

Honda Prominent

For the healthy number of fans who came to the 2009 TT Festival, there was again more than just the racing to look forward to. One topic which could not be missed was the celebration of the fiftieth anniversary of Honda's first appearance in Island racing. Back in 1959 it had used the former Nursery Hotel in Onchan as its base, and had tackled the 125cc Ultra Lightweight TT over the Clypse Course with a team of Japanese riders, plus American rider Bill Hunt. Those first little Hondas lacked speed compared to the winning Italian machines of the day, but they showed reliability, taking the team prize in the process.

By 2009 Honda motorcycles had recorded some 146 TT wins, and an exhibition of Honda racing machines and photographs showed present-day followers just how racing motorcycles had developed over the past half-century. In addition, many of the company's exotic race machines of the 1960s – when, for most of the decade, there were no restrictions on the number of cylinders and gears – were paraded around the Mountain Course, delighting the eyes and ears of those present.

Even more important for the 2009 TT was the fact that Honda was once again providing 'factory' support to the meeting under the HM Plant banner, for John McGuinness, Steve Plater and sidecar man Nick Crowe. All the regular TT stars were also present, including eight times winner Ian Lougher, who recorded his 100th TT start when he left the line in the opening Superbike race.

Who is That?

Mention has already been made of the increased commercialism of the TT. This extends to racing in general and is very apparent when comparing the appearance of the 'works' Hondas of 1959 and 2009, along with their riders. In 1959 the bikes came with the Honda name on the basically silver tank and fairing, whilst riders wore plain black leathers and boots, with white crash helmet carrying the logo 'HM' for Honda Motors.

Today, bike and fairing will usually have a bright background colour and be covered in

John McGuinness and his Honda show off his many sponsors.

Naomi Taniguchi and his 125cc Honda at the 1959 TT.

sponsors' names, whilst riders' leathers, boots, gloves and helmet will comprise what can often seem to be an uncoordinated mix of bright colours, with yet another batch of sponsor's names fighting for space. Should a top competitor be riding for more than one major sponsor, then he is likely to change the whole colourful ensemble from race to race.

Back to the Racing

It was two-times winner from 2008, Cameron Donald, who carried his form through to practice for the 2009 event and recorded the fastest ever lap of the course at 131.46mph (211.52km/h), to keep John McGuinness off the top spot of the practice leaderboard. But Cameron's superb efforts on the 'Relentless Suzuki by TAS Racing' 1000cc machine were to be in vain, for late in practice he fell at Keppel Gate and suffered shoulder injuries that prevented him from racing. Other familiar names occupied high placings on the leaderboard, with young Michael Dunlop surprising fellow Supersports competitors with the fastest lap at 125.09mph (201.27km/h), and Nick Crowe heading the sidecars.

Michael Dunlop's practice sessions on his Yamaha R6 were rather more successful than the ones he did on a Norton. New owner of the Norton name, Stuart Garner, brought a bike to the Island for him to ride, but it proved a troublesome return.

Valentino Rossi at the TT!

To add to the general buzz of expectation as race week approached, multi-Moto GP champion Valentino Rossi came to the Island to ride a parade lap of the Course, in the company of fellow Italian and former TT great, Giacomo Agostini.

Most stars from other disciplines of motorcycle racing recognize the unique nature of the TT and its long history, and while they will never contest an Island race, many of them are curious about the event. Aided by the

Valentino Rossi parades a Yamaha at the 2009 TT.

efforts of sponsors such as Yamaha and Dainese Leathers, Valentino rode a lap on what had been a delayed opening race day. He then watched the Superbike race, presented several awards, shook many hands, and left with his motorcycling education enhanced.

Racing in 2009

Honda showed its fifty years of TT experience and John McGuinness demonstrated all his class in winning the first race of 2009, the Superbike TT, from team-mate Steve Plater. In control at the front throughout the race, John watched his signalling boards and, when told that Plater was pushing on the fifth lap, he was able to up his pace and win by 18sec. Hondas were also third, fourth and fifth with Guy Martin, Ian Hutchinson and Gary Johnson, followed by Adrian Archibald (Suzuki) and Ian Lougher (Yamaha).

Conor Cummins rides through his home town of Ramsey.

In the first sidecar race Manx protagonists Nick Crowe and Dave Molyneux battled it out at the front, until Crowe retired on the second lap. Thereafter, Molyneux (Suzuki) was relatively unchallenged, finishing almost one minute clear of Phil Dongworth.

As in the Superbike event, Hondas filled the top five places in the first Supersport race. Rider order was different, however, with Ian Hutchinson first, followed home by Martin, Amor, Plater and McGuinness. Bruce Anstey set a new lap record of 126.55mph (203.62km/h), but as in the Superbike race, his Suzuki let him down.

It was Ian Hutchinson who yet again led Honda into the first five places of the Superstock TT. In doing so, he showed how close the Superstocks were to the Superbikes, by putting in a fastest lap of 129.75mph (208.77km/h).

It was to be the second Supersport race before a manufacturer other than Honda got a win in 2009, with Michael Dunlop (Yamaha), Bruce Anstey (Suzuki) and Conor Cummins (Kawasaki) filling the first three places. Steve Plater was Honda's best finisher, in fourth place. For Michael Dunlop, son of Robert and nephew of Joey, it was his first TT victory and one that was achieved in damp conditions.

The second Sidecar TT was a disastrous event, with a first lap accident that ended the racing careers of Nick Crowe and passenger Mark Cox: they collided with a hare on the approach to Ballaugh Bridge, and losing control, crashed heavily. Most TT race incidents are managed with yellow warning flags and riders are able to continue racing once past the point of the incident. In this instance, the spread of debris and the scale of emergency support required for the severely injured competitors was so great that the race was stopped, and then abandoned.

Two days later, few were surprised when John McGuinness went to the front of Friday's Senior TT and stayed there. With Steve Plater holding a strong second place, Honda looked like finishing the week as they had started it, in this, their fiftieth year at the TT. But as they

had discovered over the previous half century, not everything goes to plan over the Mountain Course, and here, in the prestigious Senior race which means so much to manufacturers, John's drive chain snapped as he left Ramsey on the fourth lap.

It was a failed drive chain that cost Agostini a probable Senior race win in 1967, but even though the bikes of 2009 were putting out three times the bhp of those from 1967, chain failure was something which just did not happen in the twenty-first century – except at the TT. Honda's expectations now transferred to the other HM Plant rider, Steve Plater, who rode a controlled last two laps to win from Manxman Conor Cummins (Kawasaki). It was Steve's second win in his short TT career, while locals were very happy with Conor's continuing climb up the TT ladder.

TTXGP – Electric Bikes

The customary pre-event build-up to the 2009 TT, and the subsequent excitement of the racing, was accompanied by mixed reactions to an earlier announcement that on Senior race day there would also be a one-lap race over the Mountain Course for clean-emission motorcycles – come the day, this translated into battery-equipped machines using electrical power.

Those who enquired found that the 'TT' in 'TTXGP' had nothing to do with the century-old Tourist Trophy title: rather, it was an abbreviation of 'Time Trials Xtreme Grand Prix'. A claimed pre-event entry of twenty-

A Moto Cyzsz entry in the TTXGP race.

eight machines was much reduced by the time race day arrived: they whirred around to complete their 37¾ miles (60¾km), and it was Rob Barber (Agni XO1) who set the fastest lap at 87.43mph (140.67km/h) and thus claimed first place in what was termed the 'Best Buy Pro Class'; Chris Heath (Electric Motorsport) was first home in the Open class.

Just as competitors in the first TT of 1907 were rationed as to the amount of petrol they could use and sometimes had to ease the throttle to ensure they completed the race distance, so in 2009, TTXGP runners had to manage their battery power. Some may well have been able to travel faster than they actually did on the run to Ramsey, but that was no good if they then did not have enough left to make the Mountain climb.

A Final Farewell

As in 2008, Lightweight and Ultra-Lightweight TT races were run on the final Saturday of race week on the Billown circuit. Entries were again in the order of forty for each event, and overall victory went to Ian Lougher in both classes.

It was to be the last TT fling for the two-strokes, which made up the entire entry in both races. 'Strokers' contested the TT from its early days, but it was in the 1960s that they began to dominate entries at the expense of four-strokes, attracting complaints that they all looked and sounded boringly the same. With their passing and replacement with four-strokes – which nowadays also look and sound mostly the same – came a wave of nostalgia for the sight, sound and smell of racing two-strokes. But it was too late at the TT, which had been running just production-based four-stroke machines on the Mountain Course since 2005.

TT Tales

Every TT meeting generates its share of stories, and in one of those 'can you believe it?' incidents, Eric Wilson pulled into his pit to refuel at the end of the second lap of the 2009 Superbike race to find it deserted. Seemingly, officials had informed Eric's pit crew that he had retired out on the course, so they had packed up and left. Race over!

When Ian Hutchinson slipped off at Quarter Bridge while holding third place on the last lap of the 2009 Senior race, it must have been one of the most expensive spills in TT history. Twice a winner earlier in the week, he was favourite to take the Joey Dunlop TT Championship trophy for the best overall performance of the week, which came accompanied by a cheque for £10,000. When that was added to the £9,000 he would have received for third place in the Senior, plus unknown amounts of 'bonus' money from his trade sponsors, it amounted to an extremely expensive fall.

Times Change

Fifty years ago, the few magazines of the day would barely mention the TT in their columns, until after they had got the busy Easter sporting weekend out of the way. There would then be a modest build-up, followed by comprehensive reports on practice and racing, before they wound down over the following few weeks with features on the year's top riders and some technical analysis of the machines used. Then all would go quiet for TT fans, because it was an era when magazines were virtually the only source of news.

Today the TT is year-round news for those who use the different information sources available. Much is generated on the official TT website www.iomtt.com and by the organizers' publicity machine, which issues regular news items and has an annual media launch of each year's events. In addition there are specialist magazines and newspapers such as *Island Racer* and *TT News*, plus Manx Radio's transmissions which can be accessed by fans, both local and those scattered world-wide who use the internet. A fairly recent development is that during the actual TT period, people can sign up and receive text messages advising them of mid-race positions and race results.

News for 2010

There was plenty of TT-associated news available on the run-up to the 2010 event. Well known competitors from the British short circuits such as David Johnson, Dan Hegarty, Hudson Kennaugh, Dan Cooper and Stephen Thompson, plus Irish Superbike champion Brian McCormack, were all said to be going to make their TT debut, and whilst they were unlikely to trouble the established stars, past winner Cameron Donald was fit again and was certainly expected to do so. A not-so-good item of late news was that Steve Plater would not ride due to injuries received at the NW200: though not life-threatening, they did lead to his retirement from racing. Keith Amor took Steve's ride in the top HM Plant Honda team.

Fastest American rider, Mark Miller, was returning to try and improve on his 125mph (201km/h) lap and break into the top ten placings, whilst leading Moto GP star Jorge Lorenzo, and thirteen times a World Champion Angel Nieto, were to do a parade lap. Looking forward to his ride, Jorge said: 'It will be a great honour for me because this is one of the most famous and epic races – it still keeps all the meaning of real motorcycling, and pilots who ride here deserve the greatest respect.'

There was an entry in the Superbike and Senior TTs from BMW with Rico Penzker riding. The marque had a successful TT history with some thirty wins to its name in both solo and sidecar classes, but had been missing from the TT for some years. Another German manufacturer with a presence on the island was Porsche, not on two wheels but four, because the company provided the official cars for the high-profile jobs of post-race course opening, plus inspection laps.

Fifty years ago Suzuki followed Honda to the TT, with entries for the 1960 event. Like Honda, it found a major performance gap between its 125cc Colleda two-strokes and the highly developed Italian four-strokes, but it learnt from its early TT experiences, returned with ever more advanced models, and took many victories in the ensuing half century. In 2010 it celebrated that first appearance with a display of Suzuki race machinery and a parade lap on Senior day. It was one in which multi World Champion Loris Capirossi was down to ride.

The Manx government had taken control of the 'zero emissions' event and it was no longer 'TTXGP' but newly named 'TT Zero'. A £10,000 prize was on offer to the first such machine to lap at 100mph (160km/h).

One-Man Show

In 2010 the TT was a seven-race meeting again, with five solo and two sidecar events, excluding TT Zero. Practice speeds were high, with all the customary names appearing on the leaderboards: Ian Hutchinson finished practice week as fastest solo, leaving the great John McGuinness in second, while the outfit of Klaus Klaffenbock and Dan Sayle was quickest amongst the chairs, ahead of sidecar legend Dave Molyneux, passengered this year by Patrick Farrance.

Come race week, and practice form was translated into race-winning performances. Put simply, Ian Hutchinson destroyed the opposition and won all five races for solos.

Ian Hutchinson in spectacular action at Rhencullen on his Supersport Honda in 2010.

Klaus Klaffenbock and Dan Sayle at Governor's Bridge, en route to victory in 2010.

With the incident-hit Senior TT reduced to four laps, that amounted to a total of twenty-two racing laps of the Mountain Course and well over 800 racing miles (1,287km). His incredible five race wins in a week had never been achieved before, and few imagine it is ever likely to be done again. Already a three-times TT winner when he came to the 2010 meeting, the quiet thirty-year-old from Bingley was in the form of his life, as he piloted his Padgetts-supplied Hondas to TT glory and his name into TT history.

Klaus Klaffenbock brought his LCR Honda home first in both sidecar races. His winning margins were three seconds from Dave Molyneux in the first race, and just over one second from John Holden in the second. So in his seventh year of TT racing, it seemed that 'Klaffie' had found a secret weapon that enabled him to jump from a previous best of fifth, to a double first. Many felt that his passenger choice of Dan Sayle had something to do with it: a four-times previous winning passenger over the TT Course and a double MGP winner on a solo, not only did Dan know every inch of the course, but he was probably the best passenger of the day.

With the TT Zero race eventually fielding nine runners and just five finishers, the electric bikes had a long way to go before they would generate real enthusiasm among TT followers. But even though they did not offer much of a spectacle to the majority, those closer to the action recognized that it was an area of rapid technical development. Winner Mark Miller (Moto Czysz EIPC) provided one indication of progress, with a winning speed of 96.82mph (155.78km/h), which was almost 10mph (16km/h) faster than the previous year's winning speed of 87.43mph (140.67km/h).

Not All Glory

For all the celebrations that followed a TT victory and the lasting glory that accompanied it, there was often a more sober side to island racing. In 2010 Martin Loicht was killed when he fell at Quarry Bends, and Paul Dobbs lost his life in a crash at Ballagarey. Both were family men, and their accidents happened during the second Supersport race, held on Thursday after a Wednesday postponement. The consequences of such crashes are usually invisible to race fans, but are devastating to the families involved.

In the following day's Senior TT, Guy Martin also fell at high speed Ballagarey's right-hand sweep. After the previous day's incident there, everyone feared the worst, but he survived with relatively minor injuries, despite his machine bursting into a spectacular fireball and causing the race to be red flagged. It was restarted over a shortened four laps distance, during which Conor Cummins joined those who had lapped at 130mph (209km/h)– but then he fell at high speed on the Verandah, sustaining serious injuries.

Such incidents show the dangerous side of TT racing – but three months later, away from the perilous Mountain Course, on the wide open spaces of Silverstone, five-times a TT winner in 2010 Ian Hutchinson was involved in a first lap crash, coming together with other bikes and then hit by another machine as he lay on the track. The compound fractures to his left leg which he sustained in the incident were to prove a major set-back to his racing career.

Celebrating Another Centenary

It was told in Chapter 1 how the original Tourist Trophy meeting was created to encourage development of the primitive motorcycles of the early 1900s, but by the end of the first decade of that century, many manufacturers were lagging behind regarding the introduction of desirable features such as variable gears, chain drive, and so on. So for 1911 the TT organizers decided to push them into making such improvements, and they did this by moving the TT races to the far more demanding Mountain Course.

Five laps over almost 190 miles (306km) of unsurfaced roads, with a mountain to climb on each lap, was a tremendous challenge for men and machines in 1911. However, the organizers' decision was vindicated, and British manufacturers were left to count the cost of their complacency when two-speed, chain-driven Indian machines from the USA took the top three places in the first Senior TT run over the Mountain Course.

Despite the vision shown by those early TT organizers, they could hardly have imagined that motorcycles would still be racing over their course 100 years later, and that speeds would have risen from the race average of 47.63mph (76.64km/h) set by Oliver Godfrey in winning the 1911 Senior, to almost 130mph (209km/h) in 2011.

As the centenary of that first Mountain Course TT approached, followers of the event took in the news that BSB star Simon Andrews and Bol d'Or winner Guillame Dietrich were to make their island racing debuts, as were eight new sidecar crews. Also, current World Champion sidecar crew the Birchall brothers were back, although fourteen times winner Dave Molyneux was absent.

Publicity was also given to the fact that the organizers had spent another £65,000 on 'Reticel' air-fencing, bringing their recent spending up to £350,000 on this modern aid to rider safety. Recognizing that some spectating spots had been lost after recent safety purges, 'Fan-zone' temporary grandstands were to be provided at several good spectating locations on the course, together with associated facilities such as catering, toilets and wi-fi – though spectators would, of course, have to pay to use them.

Dunlop was named the TT's 'Official Tyre Partner' for 2011 – their advertising banners were present back in 1907, and have been most years since.

'Musical Saddles'

There were always year-to-year changes of riders between top teams, sometimes for financial reasons, sometimes through fall-outs, and at others because a rider sought a perceived performance advantage from a change of machinery. For 2011 John McGuinness split his services between the new Honda TT Legends team for 1,000cc bikes and the long-established Padgetts concern, who provided his Supersport 600 Hondas. Another move for John was that he would be first away in all races at number 1. For many years he had been number 3, or lower.

Ian Hutchinson had switched to top-flight Yamahas provided by Shawn Muir of SMR Racing. It was a move that promised much but yielded little, due to Ian's lingering leg injuries, which actually prevented him from riding the 2011 TT.

Bruce Anstey was now riding for Padgetts Honda and Guy Martin took his place at TAS Suzuki. As ever, Guy was in the public eye, and in this particular year he was seen in a six-part television series called *The Boat that Guy Built*. More conventional publicity for the TT came from ever-increasing world-wide television coverage of the racing, often with same-day transmissions, plus documentaries and films such as *Closer to the Edge*, and a regular supply of DVDs showing on-bike laps, historic races and suchlike.

There was limited pre-race publicity for the TT Zero event in 2011, but it was back and attracted quality riders such as Michael Rutter, Dan Kneen, James Hillier and John Burrows among its seventeen entries.

On the Start-line

The current start-line opposite the grandstand is the fourth one used for TT races on the Mountain Course and has been employed since 1926.

Setting off singly at 10sec intervals, riders rocket away from the start and almost immediately plunge down Bray Hill, not knowing what the next 225 miles (362km) of racing will bring them, but with each having a personal target, which might relate to achieving a certain finishing position or setting a specific lap time. Early victories in 2011 went to experienced riders, with John McGuinness first in the Superbike race, Klaus Klaffenbock and Dan Sayle making it three sidecar wins in a row by taking Sidecar Race 'A', and Bruce Anstey recording his eighth TT win, when bringing his Honda home at the head of the field of some eighty starters in the first Supersport race.

Just as it began to look as if the meeting was going to be dominated by the established stars, young Michael Dunlop pipped John McGuinness for first place in the Superstock race to record his second TT win, then Gary Johnson achieved his maiden TT victory in the second Supersport race, as did the pairing of John Holden and Andy Winkle in Sidecar Race 'B'.

Come the last race of the week, the Senior TT, and it was the experienced John McGuinness who started at the front as number 1 and finished at the front to collect yet another TT win. Bruce Anstey was second and Guy Martin third. Podium places were the story of Guy's week, and while others might have been satisfied with such high finishing positions, he was disappointed that he had still not secured a TT win.

Regrettably the TT Zero race failed to 'electrify' the crowd, with only nine starters. However, although Michael Rutter (Segway Moto Czysz) just failed to record a 100mph (160.9km/h) lap on his winning ride at 99.64mph (160.3km/h), he did hit an impressive 149.5mph (240.5km/h) through the Sulby speed trap. By comparison, the fastest

Michael Rutter leaves Ramsey during his winning ride in the 2011 TT Zero race.

sidecars recorded 145mph (233km/h), and fastest solo was Michael Dunlop at 195.6mph (314.7km/h).

In amongst all the 2011 TT activity, Yamaha celebrated the fiftieth anniversary of the marque's Isle of Man racing debut with a parade lap and display of race machines.

Attendance

Official attendance figures at the TT are usually published after the event and customarily show a total figure of over 30,000. Those are for the whole fortnight and they peak in race week, with well over 20,000 present. Figures were higher than average for 2011, but although the Manx authorities work hard to increase the number of visitors, the TT is not the easiest event to attend, particularly for those who make last-minute decisions to visit, because transport and accommodation is limited at peak times and is booked well in advance. Indeed, for many regulars, their last job before leaving the island after a fortnight's high-speed action is to book for the following year.

Other Races

The Isle of Man describes itself as 'The Road Racing Capital of the World', and it is not only the TT which runs over its roads. In July there is a week of racing at the Southern 100 meeting, which is held on the public roads of the Billown Circuit. A pre-TT meeting for Classics, followed by a post-TT meeting for modern bikes, is held on the same circuit. Then in late August there is a fortnight of racing at the MGP, run over the Mountain Course by the Manx Motor Cycle Club since 1923. For many years the MGP included races for Classic bikes, but for 2013 the Isle of Man government took control of that aspect of the event, pumping money into what it is now calling the Classic TT, attracting established TT stars to compete on bikes from earlier eras and hoping to boost spectator attendance.

Until recently there were also the Jurby Roads meetings – to distinguish them from the season-long Jurby Airfield short-circuit meetings – but they have not been run for several years, due to deteriorating road surfaces.

The TT Festival is Buoyant

The Mountain Course centenary meeting of 2011 gave a further boost to the TT's ever-increasing popularity across many fronts: riders, sponsors, visiting spectators, worldwide television viewers, on-line listeners, DVD buyers and downloaders, even though that activity took place against a background of general economic downturn. Most of those involved in the TT were not free from economic constraints, but perhaps they took the view that the healthy dose of excitement and escapism offered by the TT Festival deserved priority in their spending.

As commercial rights holders for the TT races, the Isle of Man government was always on the lookout for ways of what it described as 'creating additional revenue streams from the event', and using it to promote the Isle of Man in general. With that aim, it announced that it was exploring the possibility of building on the event's current high profile and creating a 'TT Races World Championship Series', to be held internationally, over what it ambitiously envisaged as new road-racing courses.

Return of the Lightweight TT

The approach to the 2012 TT saw the usual pronouncements, comprised of facts, hopes and fantasies. Among the facts was that a new Lightweight TT race would be run over three laps and 113 miles (182km). This had nothing to do with the former racing of two-strokes under the same title, because it was now for bikes of 'Super Twin' specification, which meant 650cc twin-cylinder four-strokes, consisting primarily of Kawasaki and Suzuki machinery. It was a class already established at

A marshal displays a 'Sun' flag at Union Mills, to warn riders coming out from under over-hanging trees that it will be directly in their eyes.

other venues, and a healthy prize fund ensured entries from top riders.

Although triple sidecar TT winner Klaus Klaffenbock had retired from racing, he intended to enter the Birchall brothers for the 2012 event, while five times a sidecar winner Nick Crowe, who was still fighting TT injuries sustained in 2009, had also taken up the role of entrant. In his case he was running Tim Reeves for his NCR team. To add spice to the sidecar race, Dave Molyneux was back after a year's absence, confident that Kawasaki power and Patrick Farrance in the chair would yield more victories.

Also came the news that rider hopefuls such as Jamie Hamilton, Jimmie Storrar, Lee Johnston, Karl Harris and others from the short circuits intended to make their TT debuts, if all their plans materialized. And there were rumours that hard-charging Michael Dunlop intended contesting the Sidecar TT. Most reactions were of surprise tinged with worry, although in the event Michael confined himself to two wheels at the TT. However, there must have been a hint of fact amongst the fantasy, for he did race an outfit later in the year, earning creditable finishes at Scarborough.

Cynics probably felt that eighteen entries for the TT Zero race might be considered fantasy, for on past form, perhaps half that number would start. However, one TT Zero entry which did catch the attention was from the renowned Mugen concern, with a bike to be ridden by John McGuinness.

Among the principal entrants/sponsors of riders, Padgetts were fielding Bruce Anstey in all solo classes except the new Lightweight TT, along with John McGuinness in the Superstock and Supersport events, plus Gary Johnson in the Superbike and Senior races. TAS Racing gave Conor Cummins a big boost on his comeback from injury, with rides on Tyco Suzukis alongside Guy Martin, while Ian Hutchinson was on Swan Yamahas. KMR Kawasaki supported Ryan Farquhar in all solo classes, including the new Lightweight TT, where Ryan, who had done much to promote the class, was fancied for the win.

Before any winning could take place, there was a week of practice to allow bikes and riders to get up to race pace. Sunny weather for the opening sessions resulted in good times achieved, but the fine weather also brought problems: as explained by John McGuinness, 'The biggest problem was the sun, and at places like Appledene and Greeba Bridge, as well as a couple of spots over the Mountain, it was really treacherous, so I had to be really cautious.' With practice being held in the evenings, the sun was blindingly low in the sky as riders headed west from Douglas to Ballacraine, before they turned away from the sunset and headed north towards Kirk Michael.

Grid Positions and Racing

Prior to 2012, riders started each race in number order. However, for 2012 the organizers introduced a change of procedure. Numbers 1 to 20 were despatched in numerical order as before, but the 'grid' positions of the remainder were determined by their practice times, and the fastest went first. There was no change to their riding numbers. In the sidecar class, numbers 1 to 10 went in order, and thereafter riders went in relation to their practice times.

John McGuinness and Dave Molyneux were each listed in the programme as carrying race number 1 in the solo and sidecar races.

Both proved worthy of the number by topping their classes in practice and winning their opening day races, namely Superbike and Sidecar 'A'. John was pressed in the early stages, but efficient pit-stops saw him gain 6sec on his nearest rival at his first stop and a further 3sec at his second stop. He always had a slick pit-team, and the importance of those 9sec gained while stationary was apparent at the finish, for he was only 14sec clear of second-placed Cameron Donald.

In the first Supersport race Cameron Donald was again the chaser, but it was a battle royal, resulting in the second-closest finish ever recorded at the TT, in which in his runner-up position he was just 0.77sec behind Bruce Anstey. The same day's Superstock race resulted in another win for John McGuinness, his nineteenth TT victory.

The start of Wednesday's racing was delayed, eventually getting underway with the SES TT Zero event and ten starters. Victory went to Michael Rutter on his Segway Moto Cyzsz at a speed of 104.06mph (167.43km/h), with John McGuinness second and Mark Miller third. The only other finisher was Rob Barber.

Michael Rutter's 'ton-plus' lap cost the Isle of Man government the £10,000 prize it had offered for such an achievement. While the overall spectacle offered by the electric bikes left much to be desired, the government saw it as money well spent, for there were representatives from the 'clean tech' industries of many countries present, and it was an area of island business activity that it was trying to promote.

Despite such behind-the-scenes activity, the reason that the majority of visitors were on the island was for the racing: they saw Michael Dunlop take victory in the second Supersport event, while Cameron Donald recorded his third runner-up spot of the week. In Sidecar Race 'B', Dave Molyneux managed to keep Tim Reeves and Dan Sayle at bay to take his sixteenth win on three wheels.

Friday was scheduled as Senior race day, but the early weather was poor and the forecast for

Spectators applaud Ryan Farquhar as he rounds Governor's Bridge on the last lap of his winning ride in the 2012 Lightweight TT.

the rest of the day was no better, so racing was postponed until Saturday. That decision brought a degree of chaos, and the rearrangement of plans for organizers, riders, thousands of visitors and local residents. Unfortunately Saturday's weather was initially poor, although a much delayed Lightweight TT finally got under way at 6.30pm, yielding victory to Ryan Farquhar with lap speeds of 115mph (185km/h) – which surprisingly, given the conditions, were as fast as had been set in practice.

Despite the fact that the Lightweight TT was run, a late afternoon inspection lap by new Clerk of the Course Gary Thompson, accompanied by John McGuinness, Ian Lougher and Conor Cummins, brought the momentous decision to cancel the Senior TT. There had been previous postponements, but this was the first time the event had been cancelled in its long history.

Feedback from the riders to Gary was that 200 bhp of Superbike on slick tyres was a dangerous combination at race speeds over the wet and dry Mountain Course that Saturday. With no other tyres available that would last the distance, he had no option but to abandon the Senior race. It was not a matter of a further postponement, because the 2012 TT meeting had run out of time.

The disappointment is plain to see, as Guy Martin's Senior TT bike is wheeled away by mechanics, after the 2012 race was cancelled.

It was the misfortune of the new Clerk of the Course to have inherited a problem that many had seen coming in recent years, but where everyone had gone on accepting ever-increasing amounts of power until, suddenly, more than half of the races at a TT meeting could be at risk of not running, because the sort of conditions that are too bad for Superbikes will almost certainly prove dangerous for sidecars, given their limited choice of tyres.

With the decision made in 2012 not to run the big bikes on the grounds of safety, a worrying precedent has been set for future events.

The Future

The TT races maintain their long-running importance to motorcycle buyers and manufacturers, because as well as the spectacle they offer, everyone is aware that if a bike performs successfully under the stresses imposed by six laps of the Mountain Course, then it is the best possible demonstration of its performance and reliability. TT successes have always influenced buying decisions, and getting customers to buy their model, rather than a competitor's, is one of the primary reasons that manufacturers go racing. TT success, along with associated advertising, puts a motorcycle firmly in the buyer's eye.

The TT is a complex event and because there are so many facets to running it, there is always something to engage those with a bent to criticise. That has been the case for over 100 years, but it has weathered many a controversy and remains a unique event that captures the imagination like no other.

Its multi-faceted aspect is reflected in the range of organizations that have a say in the running of the races and the TT Festival as a whole. These include the Manx government with its various departments, the FIM, ACU, major motorcycle manufacturers, sponsors, riders, marshals, spectators, the media and, not to be under-estimated, whoever provides the insurance that allows the meeting to be run, for no insurance might mean no TT.

Not every resident of the Isle of Man supports the event, for it makes a massive impact on, and causes huge disruption to, their everyday living. That is made worse by unpredicted road closures brought about by the inevitable surge in road traffic accidents, race postponements and suchlike.

There remains a strong sense of supportive tradition that links most island people to the TT, but sometimes tradition is not enough to sustain an event, and so the TT must ensure that it continues to go forward, bringing varied and quality racing to spectators, showing consideration for the Manx people in its organization, and offering the island a financial return on the money it pumps into the entire TT Festival.

Then, if the Isle of Man continues to welcome the races, if riders still want to ride them, if organizers want to run them and spectators to watch them, there is every prospect that the TT meeting will continue. The result should see new generations of machines and riders take to the Mountain Course to thrill watchers with their speed and prowess, just as previous generations have done with great adventure, for over 100 years.

Index